W9-BDL-467

ALSO BY JEFFREY TOOBIN

True Crimes and Misdemeanors: The Investigation of Donald Trump

American Heiress: The Wild Saga of the Kidnapping, Crimes and Trial of Patty Hearst

The Oath: The Obama White House and the Supreme Court

The Nine: Inside the Secret World of the Supreme Court

Too Close to Call: The Thirty-Six-Day Battle to Decide the 2000 Election

A Vast Conspiracy: The Real Story of the Sex Scandal That Nearly Brought Down a President

The Run of His Life: The People v. O. J. Simpson

Opening Arguments: A Young Lawyer's First Case—United States v. Oliver North

Homegrown

TIMOTHY McVEIGH
and the Rise of
RIGHT-WING EXTREMISM

JEFFREY TOOBIN

Simon & Schuster
NEW YORK LONDON TORONTO
SYDNEY NEW DELHI

Simon & Schuster
1230 Avenue of the Americas
New York, NY 10020

First Simon & Schuster hardcover edition May 2023

SIMON & SCHUSTER and colophon are registered trademarks of Simon & Schuster, Inc.

For information about special discounts for bulk purchases, please contact Simon & Schuster Special Sales at 1-866-506-1949 or business@simonandschuster.com.

The Simon & Schuster Speakers Bureau can bring authors to your live event. For more information, or to book an event, contact the Simon & Schuster Speakers Bureau at 1-866-248-3049 or visit our website at www.simonspeakers.com.

Interior design by Paul Dippolito

Manufactured in the United States of America

1 3 5 7 9 10 8 6 4 2

Library of Congress Cataloging-in-Publication Data is available.

ISBN 978-1-6680-1357-1
ISBN 978-1-6680-1359-5 (ebook)

Library of Congress Control Number: 2023932965

To Rory

Contents

Homegrown

PROLOGUE

1776

The spirit of rebellion was in the air on January 6, 2021. Vice President Mike Pence was due to certify Joseph Biden's victory in the 2020 presidential election in a ceremony at the Capitol. But supporters of President Donald Trump, and Trump himself, were mobilizing for a confrontation that they hoped would change the outcome. The Proud Boys, a right-wing extremist group, had crafted a nine-page plan for storming the Capitol and other buildings in Washington; it was called "1776 Returns." Two days earlier, Stewart Rhodes, the leader of the Oath Keepers, another extremist outfit, said, "We're walking down the same exact path as the Founding Fathers." Quoting George Washington addressing his troops in 1776, he went on, "The fate of unborn millions will now depend, under God, on the courage and conduct of this army." On the eve of congressional certification, Alex Jones, the *InfoWars* host and conspiracy theorist, held a boisterous rally a few blocks from the White House and said, "We declare 1776 against the New World Order. We need to understand we're under attack, and we need to understand this is 21st-century warfare and get on a war-footing." He then went on an *InfoWars* broadcast to say, "This is the most important call to action on domestic soil since Paul Revere and his ride in 1776." (The ride was actually in 1775.) On the morning of January 6, Lauren Boebert, the Republican congresswoman from Colorado, tweeted: "Today is 1776."

By that time, crowds were already gathering at the Ellipse to hear Trump rally the troops. Rudy Giuliani, the president's lawyer and warm-up act, told the crowd, "Let's have trial by combat!" When it was his turn onstage, Trump sent the same message. "You'll never take back our country with weakness. You have to show strength, and you have to be strong," he told the throng. "We're going to walk down Pennsylvania Avenue. I love Pennsylvania Avenue. And we're going to the Capitol. And we fight. We fight like hell. And if you don't fight like hell, you're not going to have a country anymore." Thus roused, thousands of his supporters marched that way.

At the Capitol, the swarming crowd chanted, "1776! 1776!" Many flew the Gadsden flag, the yellow banner of the revolutionary era, which bears the words DON'T TREAD ON ME. When the first group breached the doors of the west front, they snarled at the outnumbered and helpless Capitol Police officers, "1776, motherfuckers!" Chris Hill, a Marine veteran who led an extremist group from Georgia, called the attack on the Capitol a "shot heard round the world," echoing the words used to describe the Battle of Lexington on April 19, 1775. He added, "The second revolution begins today."

When the Capitol rioters spoke of the Constitution, it was almost always of only one provision—the Second Amendment. They regarded the right to "bear arms" as a license for citizens to fight back against the government. As Rhodes, of the Oath Keepers, put it, the purpose of the Second Amendment was to "preserve the ability of the people, who are the militia, to provide for their own security" and "to preserve the military capacity of the American people to resist tyranny and violations of their rights by oath breakers within government."

Later, many of the January 6 rioters explained their actions as analogous to those of the colonists during the American Revolution. "When we talk about 1776, we see that there was a lot of violence. We had to go against the government, and people died. And something good came out of that," D. J. Rodriquez, one of those arrested inside the Capitol told his FBI interviewer. "I, personally, felt that this is something that the Founding Fathers of the country understood was going to happen again one day and that we would be needed to do something righteous." Defending the insurrection, Congresswoman Marjorie Taylor Greene, who operates as the id of the modern Republican Party, said, "And if you think about what our Declaration of Independence says, it says to overthrow tyrants."

Nineteen days after the Oklahoma City bombing in 1995, Timothy McVeigh was summoned from his cell for his first meeting with his attorney, Stephen Jones. In that initial conversation, McVeigh was only too pleased to take credit for the attack on the Alfred P. Murrah Federal Building. From the start, Jones knew that the case of the Oklahoma City bombing was no whodunit.

So, in his first conversations with McVeigh, Jones wanted to explore a simple question: Why? Why had this twenty-seven-year-old man, who appeared ordinary in so many ways, committed this horrific act?

As he entered the prison conference room, McVeigh had his hands manacled behind him. In a small concession, he was allowed to be cuffed in front when he sat at the metal table bolted to the floor. "Call me Tim," McVeigh told Jones. They made small talk about the inmate's mail. He had already received a marriage proposal and ten dollars in cash.

When Jones moved on to the bombing, McVeigh continued in the same relaxed, almost serene way. He talked about mass murder just as he did about his beloved Buffalo Bills. For McVeigh, the destruction of the Murrah building, and of the lives of those inside it, was more than just permissible. It was mandatory, his duty as a patriotic American. He had no regrets, no second thoughts.

How could McVeigh see murder as justified, much less required?

Read the Declaration of Independence, he instructed his lawyer—and not just the famous part. To McVeigh, the more important section of the Declaration came later, and he recited it from memory: "Whenever any Form of Government becomes destructive of these ends, it is the Right of the People to alter or to abolish it. . . . When a long train of abuses and usurpations . . . evinces a design to reduce them under absolute Despotism, it is their right, it is their duty, to throw off such Government." McVeigh took the same message from Patrick Henry's famous speech from 1775, the one which concluded "Give me liberty or give me death." He recited what else Henry had said: "If we wish to be free—if we mean to preserve inviolate those inestimable privileges for which we have been so long contending . . . we must fight! I repeat it, sir, we must fight!"

At the Murrah building, McVeigh fought.

His actions, he explained, were a direct response to the "abuses and usurpations" of the federal government, especially those at Ruby Ridge and Waco. In the months that followed, McVeigh would return obsessively to these two events, just as he had fixated on them in the period leading up to the bombing.

The Ruby Ridge saga began in August 1992, in rural Idaho, when U.S. marshals attempted to serve an arrest warrant for weapons charges on a right-wing activist named Randy Weaver. When Weaver refused to surrender, the marshals and FBI began a siege on his property. In one skirmish, a deputy marshal and Weaver's fourteen-year-old son (as well as the family dog) were killed. A few days later, an FBI sniper killed Weaver's wife as she stood in a doorway holding their baby daughter. After an eleven-day standoff, Randy Weaver surrendered.

Six months later, in February 1993, the Waco siege in Texas followed a similar pattern, with even more disastrous results. Agents from the Bureau of Alcohol, Tobacco and Firearms attempted to serve arrest and search warrants for weapons charges at a compound run by a religious sect called the Branch Davidians. During that original operation, four federal agents and five Branch Davidians were killed in a firefight. The FBI took over the scene and conducted a siege of the buildings, which were controlled by David Koresh, the Davidians' leader. After fifty-one days, on April 19, the FBI launched a tear gas assault on the compound, which caught fire. Seventy-six Branch Davidians, including Koresh, died in the conflagration.

McVeigh chose to bomb the Murrah building on April 19 because it was both the second anniversary of the Waco raid and also the date of the "shot heard round the world" in 1775, the beginning of the American rebellion against the British. In his own mind, McVeigh was the heir to the heroes of the Revolution. As McVeigh told his lawyer, "the government laid down the ground rules for warfare" in Ruby Ridge and Waco. Citing his favorite Sylvester Stallone movie, McVeigh said the government had drawn "first blood. It's like the song from *The Lion King*—'The Circle of Life.'" What goes around comes around.

But it wasn't just Ruby Ridge and Waco. There was President Bill Clinton's support of a bill banning assault weapons. McVeigh received a BB gun from his grandfather when he was nine years old, and he remained obsessed with firearms for the rest of his life. He loved to shoot, and he was a skilled marksman in both civilian and military life. The issue of guns represented the core of his political worldview as well, a lesson which he also said came from the Founding Fathers. While McVeigh had not read many books about American history, he had steeped himself in right-wing magazines. McVeigh endorsed the view of the Framers' intentions that was published in *Soldier of Fortune*, and *The Spotlight*, published by Liberty Lobby. He told Jones that his hero Patrick Henry called guns the "teeth of liberty," and McVeigh loathed any attempt to regulate their possession. He had joined the National Rifle Association as a teenager and faithfully read *American Hunter*, the NRA's official magazine. Clinton's signing of the assault weapons ban on September 13, 1994, sealed McVeigh's decision to proceed with the bombing the following spring.

"How are patriots supposed to defend themselves when their right to bear arms is infringed?" he asked Jones. "The best defense is a good offense. They're coming for the gun owners next. Enough is enough."

There were, then, three powerful ideological motivations for McVeigh's decision to bomb the Murrah building: the obsession with gun rights; the perceived approval of the Founding Fathers; and the belief in the value and power of violence. These feelings were replicated, with extraordinary precision, in the rioters on January 6 as well as many of the other right-wing extremists who have flourished in the quarter century since the bombing.

There was a paradox in McVeigh's patriotism, just as there is among his ideological successors. They profess to love their country, but detest nearly everything about the contemporary United States. For McVeigh, Ruby Ridge, Waco, Clinton, and guns were just the start. He called himself a white separatist, not a white supremacist (as if there were meaningful difference between the two); he abhorred immigration, both legal and illegal; he wanted women to return to their traditional roles in the home; and he resented the industrial decline that had ravaged the Buffalo region. For Jones, McVeigh's invocations of the American past raised a question: To what era did McVeigh want to return? When was America great?

"I want a country that operates like it did 150 years ago—no income taxes, no property taxes, no oppressive police, free land in the West," he said. In his recitation, McVeigh didn't mention the existence of slavery.

How can we know with certainty what McVeigh believed and why?

He was probably the most thoroughly scrutinized criminal in American history. While the federal investigation of the Oklahoma

City bombing was led by the FBI, it also included dozens of other federal, state, and local law enforcement agencies. In all, the investigation produced 30,000 witness interviews and accumulated 150,000 photographs, 500 hours of videotape, and 400 hours of audiotape. Dozens of witnesses were questioned in secret grand jury proceedings. The inquiry probed every part of McVeigh's brief life—his upbringing in western New York, his service in the military, and his activities leading up to the bombing in Oklahoma.

McVeigh's defense did a comparably extensive examination. Stephen Jones assembled a massive team, which included sixteen other lawyers as well as private investigators, paralegals, and support staff. (The tab to the government for McVeigh's defense ultimately ran to about $20 million.) Jones and the other lawyers interviewed McVeigh for dozens of hours, always taking careful notes of what their client said and then sharing the reports with the rest of the team. Jones also hired a court reporter and conducted a transcribed, eight-hour examination of McVeigh in which he described, in precise detail, how he planned and executed the bombing. Jones retained a forensic psychologist to examine McVeigh and evaluate his state of mind; he hired a polygraph examiner to test the veracity of McVeigh's account of the bombing. In addition, the defense team conducted dozens of interviews with McVeigh's family and friends, to understand the roots of his character and conduct.

In ordinary circumstances, the vast majority of the investigative material from both the government and defense would remain secret. The public record would for the most part be limited to what was disclosed during McVeigh's criminal trial. However, in 1999, Stephen Jones donated his entire file on the case to the Briscoe Center at the University of Texas library in Austin. The collection runs to 650 linear feet, which amounts to 635 boxes, with approximately 1 million pages of documents. It includes the memos describing the defense team's interviews with McVeigh as well as extensive correspondence between

McVeigh and his lawyers. The entire record of the defense team's factual investigation—hundreds of witness interviews, including those with McVeigh's family—is in the collection. There are also hundreds more pages of internal memos detailing the team's legal strategy. (Because of an attorney's obligation to keep client confidences, as well as the attorney-client privilege, much of this material would customarily be forever off-limits to outsiders, even after McVeigh's death. Jones took the view, which is strongly contested by others, that McVeigh had implicitly consented to Jones's disclosure of the material.) The defense file in the Briscoe Center also includes everything that prosecutors disclosed to the defense as part of discovery before the trial. As a result, the archive includes the fruits of the government investigation as well—hundreds of FBI interviews of witnesses (known as 302s) as well as dozens of summaries of grand jury testimony. For such a complete record of a major criminal investigation to be available for examination is unprecedented in American history.

From the moment the Oklahoma City bombing took place, it was portrayed as the work of outsiders, of individuals who were sinister anomalies from American norms. In the first hours after the attack, this became an effort to blame the attack on foreigners, especially Islamic radicals from the Middle East. (It had been just two years since Ramzi Yousef orchestrated the first attack on the World Trade Center.) Within hours of the assault on the Murrah building, Steven Emerson, a noted authority on terrorism, said on a live CBS News broadcast that the attack "was done with the intent to inflict as many casualties as possible. That is a Middle Eastern trait." He added that Oklahoma City was "probably considered one of the largest centers of Islamic radical activity outside the Middle East," which it was not. Dave McCurdy, an Oklahoma congressman who had recently stepped down as chair of the House Intelligence Committee, said there was "very clear evidence" that "fundamentalist Islamic terrorist groups" were behind the attack. (There wasn't.) On the radio, Rush Limbaugh said "his gut" told him that "Middle Eastern terrorists" were responsible. "You dogs, you cannot hide!" Limbaugh said. "And when you are found, it will be the worst day you can possibly imagine! . . . And if we trace it to a particular nation, what about hitting the nation anyway, even if we don't know who exactly did it?"

After McVeigh was arrested and the evidence against him became overwhelming, a different kind of distancing took place. To this day, McVeigh is often described as a "survivalist," an isolated and eccentric figure like Ted Kaczynski, the Unabomber, who carried out his terrorist attacks by mail from a remote cabin in Montana. In a similar vein, McVeigh has been called "antigovernment," as if he were a kind of anarchist opposed to all forms of authority. Both descriptions are inaccurate. Rather, McVeigh had a different ideological profile, one with deep roots in American history and a modern legacy that extends to the present day.

McVeigh was not "antigovernment"; he was a right-wing extremist who defined his politics in opposition to the federal government of President Bill Clinton. In January 1993, as Clinton was inaugurated, McVeigh sold most of his possessions, left Buffalo, and took off on the road. Up until the bombing, a little more than two years later, McVeigh lived as an itinerant, never staying in any one place for more than a few months. But he was not a survivalist, or even a loner. He belonged to a community—the one he found on the gun show circuit. The gun shows were often major events, some with thousands of attendees. McVeigh never made much money, selling books, bumper stickers, and even guns and ammunition when he could find them. But he mingled, talked, listened, and proselytized. He was with like-minded people who were committed to a rising political movement.

In the early 1990s, while McVeigh was on the road, Newt Gingrich, then a Georgia congressman, was turning the Republican

Party into an incendiary force of opposition to the new president. Gingrich's unofficial partner in this enterprise was Rush Limbaugh, whose radio voice accompanied McVeigh on his long drives across the country. (The first book McVeigh sought out after he was arrested was Limbaugh's best-seller, *The Way Things Ought to Be*.) Both Gingrich and Limbaugh and their followers engaged in rhetorical violence at a pitch the country had rarely heard before on national broadcasts. Gingrich instructed Republican candidates to use these words about Democrats: sick, pathetic, lie, anti-flag, traitors, radical, corrupt. In 1994, Gingrich claimed, "People like me are what stand between us and Auschwitz. I see evil all around me every day." At around the same time, Limbaugh said, "The second violent American revolution is just about—I got my fingers about a quarter of an inch apart—is just about that far away." When the Republicans, led by Gingrich, won a midterm landslide that year, gaining fifty-four seats and control of the House of Representatives, the new members elected Limbaugh as an honorary member of their freshman class.

Gingrich and Limbaugh were the voices of an ascendant right-wing authoritarianism, the movement that McVeigh embraced. In particular, McVeigh took Limbaugh both seriously and literally. McVeigh spoke so calmly and openly about the need to fight back against Clinton's federal government because he knew that many other people agreed with him. His goal, McVeigh told his lawyers, was to push the Republican revolution one step further: the bombing would be the fuse that led to a nationwide rebellion against Clinton and other defilers of the Framers' Constitution.

That didn't happen, of course, not exactly. Still, to an extent that is rarely appreciated, McVeigh's bombing had a lasting and sinister legacy. Right-wing terror spiked immediately after Oklahoma City—with an abundance of conspiracies (some thwarted) to attack government targets. They were acts of right-wing political rage, and in later years they followed a pattern based on the occupant of the White House.

They increased under Bill Clinton, then dropped under George W. Bush, and then spiked—dramatically—under Barack Obama. Indeed, the amount of right-wing political violence—especially bombing conspiracies and mass shootings—amounts to one of the lesser told stories of the first Black president's tenure in office. As with the Oklahoma City bombing, these acts of terror were not random lightning strikes by demented individuals; they were targeted political acts of right against left.

The political response to right-wing terror followed a pattern as well. Conservatives have long minimized the threat of right-wing violence and, as in Oklahoma City, sought to blame terrorism on foreigners or left-wing groups. This was especially true after the terrorist attacks of September 11, 2001. Because those attacks were genuinely the work of radical Muslim extremists, the right created almost a presumption that all terrorism originates with Muslims. (This has included an enduring, if futile, effort to tie the Oklahoma City bombing to Muslim operatives.) McVeigh understood the potential of his right-wing compatriots for joining him in violent action. "I believe there is an army out there, ready to rise up, even though I never found it," McVeigh told his attorney Jones. But that doesn't mean his army wasn't there. McVeigh failed to find his army because he had no efficient way to locate and mobilize potential allies; in other words, McVeigh didn't have the internet, in particular social media. As it turned out, there *was* an army of McVeigh's heirs out there, but it took the invention of cyberspace for the soldiers to find one another.

Donald Trump broke the pattern of right-wing terror rising under Democratic administrations and falling during Republican ones for a simple reason. He encouraged it. Trump won election as president, served in office, and sought to remain there after he lost in 2020 by embracing political violence. From his earliest campaigning to the final moments of his presidency, Trump employed the language of not-so-veiled physical threat. He encouraged attendees at his rallies to "knock the hell" out of protesters, told police officers to slam their prisoners' heads into car roofs, and praised a congressional candidate who body-slammed a journalist. Then the insurrection of January 6 represented the apotheosis of Trump's presidency—when the implicit menace in Trump's language, amplified over social media, was translated into unprecedented violence.

After the storming of the Capitol, the language of violence became standard within the modern Republican Party. In a speech in Texas in July 2022, Trump said, "Despite great outside dangers, our biggest threat remains the sick, sinister, evil people within our own country." After Dr. Anthony Fauci, the government official who led the response to the Covid pandemic, announced he would be retiring, Florida governor Ron DeSantis said, "Someone needs to grab that little elf and chuck him across the Potomac." After the FBI obtained a warrant and searched Trump's Mar-a-Lago home in August 2022, Senator Rick Scott, the leader of the Republican Senate campaign committee, compared the federal government to "the Gestapo." This is the kind of language that inspired McVeigh to destroy the Murrah building, just as it incited the January 6 rioters. And these words were just those of mainstream figures. The language of their rank-and-file supporters on social media and talk radio was even more incendiary. This kind of rhetoric led to political violence in the past and will do so again in the future.

The insurrection on January 6, and much else in the contemporary conservative movement, show how McVeigh's values, views, and tactics have endured and even flourished in the decades since his death. That makes the story of Timothy McVeigh and the Oklahoma City bombing not just a glimpse of the past but also a warning about the future.

CHAPTER 1

The Blueprint

As the twentieth century began, the infant automobile industry faced an existential challenge. Internal combustion engines quickly overheated, rendering them nearly useless. Then, in 1907, a self-described "electrochemist" named Herbert Champion Harrison immigrated to the United States from England and came up with a solution. He designed a radiator with what became known as the Harrison hexagon core. It was vastly more efficient and cheaper to manufacture than previous models. Harrison built a small factory on the banks of the Erie Canal in Lockport, New York, about thirty miles north of Buffalo. In 1911, he assembled and sold 131 radiators and 2,245 the next year. In 1925, after the business moved to bigger quarters in Lockport, sales increased to 1,189,294 radiators. Harrison Radiator, which later became part of General Motors, propelled one of the great industrial booms of the twentieth century.

For a time, fate and circumstance favored the Buffalo area with multiple gifts. As the terminus of the Erie Canal, the link between the Great Lakes and the Atlantic Ocean, the city became a port of great consequence, first for grain and then for the raw materials for steel. This led to the creation of giant steel mills on the banks of the Niagara River, and a host of related factories and businesses sprang up nearby. Entrepreneurs like Harrison and John Oishei, who invented the windshield wiper, flocked to the region.

Throughout the middle years of the century, the problem at the Harrison complex was a shortage of employees. The factories in and around Buffalo expanded so quickly that they were desperate for people to hire, and a pipeline of workers from Appalachia helped fill the need. Caravans of families from the struggling hill towns of West Virginia and Pennsylvania made the trek to western New York. But that wasn't enough, especially as Harrison Radiator began to meet a new demand from General Motors—for air conditioners. In 1963, Harrison built 994,000 air-conditioning units, which were installed in 35 percent of GM cars that year. The Harrison Radiator complex comprised more than a score of buildings on 495 acres, with 6,800 employees. Three shifts kept the factory busy twenty-four hours a day. One of the new hires that year was Bill McVeigh, Timothy McVeigh's father.

The McVeighs came to western New York from Ireland during the Great Famine, and they were farmers for generations, until Bill's own father, Ed McVeigh, abandoned the wheat fields for work at Harrison Radiator, where he toiled for thirty years. Bill never really considered doing anything except following his dad there. Bill signed up for the night shift—midnight to 8 a.m.—and he continued working those hours for the next three decades. For families of their generations, back-to-back tenures of thirty years were not unusual.

In 1963, the same year that Bill McVeigh started work at Harrison, he met Mildred "Mickey" Hill at a DeSales Catholic High School alumni bowling event. They married two years later, when Bill was twenty-three and Mickey was twenty. They were mismatched from the start and built a conventionally unhappy life together.

Mickey was bubbly and outgoing, and her dreams, unlike Bill's, extended well beyond Buffalo. She had wanted to be an airline stewardess, as the job was then known, and enrolled in a training program in Hartford. But after a few months, she came back to Lockport to marry Bill and quickly had children. Their daughter Patty was born nine months after their wedding; Timothy James followed on April 23, 1968, and Jennifer came along six years later. Mickey sublimated her early ambitions with a part-time job as a travel agent. When Bill wasn't at the factory, he was a homebody, who longed only to play softball on his days off from work. Both parents drank—Bill, beer, and Mickey, whiskey sours. (Perhaps as a result, Tim hardly ever drank alcohol.) Tim's earliest memory of his father was of Bill hitting golf balls in his backyard and accidentally shattering a window in a neighbor's house. Bill was so distraught that he broke into the house and repaired the window before the neighbors returned home. Tim always thought of his father as dutiful in the extreme.

Both the prosecution and defense scoured Tim's early life for clues to what he would become, and they found a troubled, but hardly extraordinary upbringing. Tim liked *Sesame Street* and then comic books, which he organized fastidiously. He was an adequate student, rarely created problems, and won awards for perfect attendance. His parents bought him a Commodore 64, a first-generation personal computer, and he did some modest hacking, under the code name "Wanderer." Tim was neither part of the in-group at school nor a social outcast; he had a small group of friends who nicknamed him "Chicken"—his tall, gangly frame reminded them of the noodles in chicken noodle soup. Like many teenagers, McVeigh had little interest in the world outside his everyday existence. Later, passing the time in prison, he made lists of his favorites in popular culture, and his taste was conventional. McVeigh liked war movies, especially those with Clint Eastwood. His favorite was *Unforgiven*, Eastwood's modern, morally ambiguous take on the Western. His other favorite movies: *First Blood*, with Sylvester Stallone as John Rambo; *Heartbreak Ridge*, with Eastwood as a Marine instructor; *Kelly's Heroes*, another Eastwood action film about World War II; and *All Quiet on the Western Front*, the World War I classic about disillusion in the military.

His top songs were "(Don't Fear) the Reaper," by Blue Öyster Cult; "Renegade," by Styx; and "Bad Company," by Bad Company.

Tim watched his parents' marriage unravel. Mickey used her travel agent status to visit Las Vegas, London, and other tourist destinations; Bill never went with her. In an interview with a defense psychologist, "Tim recalled that he would hear discussions in which his mother would ask his dad to have sex, but his dad would say he was too tired. Tim's bedroom was right next to his parents. He recalled that these discussions about sex between his parents embarrassed him." Mickey moved out of the family home with both girls for the first time in December 1979, when Tim was eleven, and they stayed away for about two months. About a year later, she left with just Jenny for about the same amount of time. When Mickey was home in Lockport, she frequented the bars downtown. Bill and Mickey split for good in 1984, when Tim was sixteen. Mickey took custody of Patty and Jenny and moved to Florida. As Tim saw it, his mother kept moving away with her daughters and leaving her son behind—making Tim the victim of a kind of "Sophie's Choice." His rage at his mother was intense. Later, Tim told a coworker that his mother was "a slut, whore, and drunk, and that he hated her." Mother and son reestablished a measure of contact a few years later, mostly by letter, but the pain of Tim's abandonment by her never fully healed. In Florida, Patty went to nursing school and married young. Jenny, on the other hand, stayed in touch and grew closer to Tim as they both grew up.

In the mid-1980s, when Tim was living alone with his father, their lives were becoming more precarious—economically as well as personally. The Buffalo area was reeling from the forces of economic realignment. High-wage union jobs were disappearing as the auto companies and others moved operations first to the South and then outside the United States altogether. Bill McVeigh felt the effects at Harrison Radiator. He was making about $18 an hour (a good union salary when the minimum wage was $3.35 an hour), but he was laid off several times. Even though he had always been put back on the payroll, the trajectory was clear. Tim never showed any interest in Harrison, and Bill never encouraged him. There would be no third-generation McVeigh at the plant, much less another thirty-year tenure. It was inconceivable for Tim or anyone else of his generation. (The Harrison plant now employs about 1,500 people.)

Living alone with his dad in his final years of high school, Tim developed what would become the consuming interest in his life—guns. Tim had owned a BB gun since he was a boy, and his father allowed him as a young teen to shoot his .22 caliber rifle at tin cans in their backyard. (Their home was technically in the hamlet of Pendleton, a semi-rural suburb of the suburb of Lockport, where the houses were far apart and there were still plenty of farms.) Tim spent a lot of time at his grandfather's and with his friend Steve Hodge. Both his grandfather and the Hodge family were avid hunters, like many people in the area. When Tim was fifteen, he applied for a hunting license, which required him first to take a National Rifle Association class as an after-school activity. Tim wasn't much interested in hunting, but he loved owning and shooting guns. He took a part-time job at Burger King and plowed most of his earnings into weapons. McVeigh became an expert marksman, which he remained for the rest of his life.

Tim graduated from Starpoint High School on June 29, 1986. For the quote next to his yearbook photo, he wrote, "take it as it comes, buy a Lamborghini, california girls." McVeigh had no contact with women in California (a place he had never been) and little experience with them anywhere else. He told defense investigators that he lost his virginity to a coworker at Burger King, who was married and older. McVeigh never had what would conventionally qualify as a girlfriend, someone he saw for more than a month or so. He had occasional sex (often with the wives of friends), but never a genuine relationship. Likewise, Tim could never afford a Lamborghini or any other kind of sports car; instead, after graduation, he sold his comic book collection and his computer to buy a used junker.

Tim's gun-collecting became an obsession. "To get away from the tension in my house," he told his lawyers, he would take long walks in the woods with whatever weapons were around. Tim added a .410 shotgun and borrowed weapons belonging to his grandfather and the Hodges. The degree of McVeigh's interest came through in a letter to Lou Michel and Dan Herbeck, two Buffalo-based journalists who later wrote a book about McVeigh called *American Terrorist.* In this letter, he wrote:

> Here's why some people may view gun collections to be "excessive," but why survivalists don't. Do you have any tools at home? Let's look at your screwdrivers. A big one? A really big one? A standard size? A small one? A micro-small one? And these are just flat-tip, right? What about Phillips head? Wrenches—just one? What I'm getting at here is that you need the right tool for the job, right? So it is with guns, and survivalists—preparing for many possible scenarios—need to have the right "tool" for each potential "job."

McVeigh then elaborated on what he regarded as the "Minimum 'tools' needed":

> 1) Semi-auto, mag-fed rifle—for home self-defense. (Ask those storekeepers in the L.A. riots if this is reasonable!)
> 2) Hunting/sniper rifle (usually bolt-action)—for sustenance, large game. Also defense against entrenched "marauder."
> 3) Shotgun—for fowl hunting and specialty apps. Like flares, etc.
> 4) .22 cal. Rifle—for honing shooting skills (cheap ammo) and small game (rabbit, squirrel).
> 5) Pistol—for close-in self-defense.

Most of the references to McVeigh as a "survivalist" relate to this brief period. In fact, McVeigh never tried to live as a survivalist; that is, to prepare for an off-the-grid life following a nuclear war or natural disaster. Rather, McVeigh's idea of survivalism related mostly to his gun collection, not the other tools of survival.

McVeigh's political interests took hold after he graduated from high school, when he quit his job at Burger King and spent several aimless months hanging around his father's house in Pendleton. The effect of economic decline, an obsession with guns, and a search for scapegoats defined McVeigh's existence. Neither the business world, the government, nor his family provided a stable base for McVeigh to contemplate his future. As the sociologist (and MacArthur fellow) Jennifer Carlson has observed, "Gun-carrying men are not just motivated by crime and insecurity but also by a loss of American values, a loss of masculine dignity, and a loss of confidence in the state." Moreover, as the psychiatrist and scholar James Gilligan has written, "One of the special characteristics that predispose men to commit murder, or other serious physical violence, is an unusually strong wish to be loved and taken care of, and unusually strong feelings of being inadequate and unlovable." To that point, the story of McVeigh's life was one of loss—of both family cohesion (and of his mother in particular) as well as economic security. Guns gave him a measure of power and control. When Tim turned eighteen, he registered to vote as a Republican. This was a shift in family loyalty because his father was a lifelong union man and Democrat. But McVeigh's life amounted to an early prototype for what would become known as the aggrieved Trump voter. (In 2016, Pendleton cast 67 percent of its votes for Trump.)

McVeigh joined the National Rifle Association at a transformative moment in the politics of guns. For more than a hundred years after its founding in 1861, the NRA was a largely apolitical organization devoted to shooting skills and gun safety. But starting in the late

1970s, the NRA became ferociously partisan, dedicated to stifling any attempts to limit gun ownership. In this period, too, the NRA embarked on a project, in both the courts of law and of public opinion, to rewrite the meaning of the Second Amendment; for generations, the courts had held that the amendment related only to state militias and not to private gun ownership. In the 1980s, the NRA, and the conservative movement, embraced the idea that the Second Amendment endowed individuals with a right to bear arms. So, when it came to guns, McVeigh did more than simply advocate for his own right to own and use firearms; he joined an ascendant political crusade, which grew more extreme over the course of his lifetime and beyond.

McVeigh also came of age when the splintering of the news media began in earnest. His father belonged to a generation where people of all political persuasions read the local newspaper (*The Buffalo News*) and watched the evening news (usually with Walter Cronkite). These media customs produced a measure of shared consensus, if not about political controversy, then at least about underlying facts. Anticipating the trends of a later day, Tim tailored his media consumption to his ideological predilections, starting with *American Hunter*, the NRA magazine. McVeigh even studied the small advertisements in the back pages. He responded to one for a novel called *The Turner Diaries*. The book arrived by mail, and he read it for the first of many times. It changed his life, as it did numerous others.

The cover of *The Turner Diaries* lists the author as Andrew Macdonald, which was a pseudonym for William Luther Pierce, who led a white supremacist, neo-Nazi organization called the National Alliance. The novel, first published in 1978 and circulated mostly by direct mail through advertisements in conservative magazines and mailing lists, tells a gruesome tale of a right-wing revolution in the United States. At the beginning of the story, which is set in the then-present day, the federal government and economy are controlled by a sinister Jewish cabal known as the System. Under a law called the "Cohen Act," all privately owned firearms are subject to confiscation by the government. (In *The Turner Diaries*, gun control is the essence of tyranny.) The System is racially biased in favor of Black people. Under its rules, Black people are allowed to attack whites with impunity; whites are punished for defending themselves.

Earl Turner, the hero of the book and its narrator, leads a secret resistance group called the Organization. Turner's opening salvo is an act of terrorism—bombing the FBI building in Washington. "We drive a truck into the main freight entrance of the F.B.I. building and blow it up in the freight-receiving area." The book describes the making of the bomb in detail: Turner and his allies assemble about five thousand pounds of ammonium nitrate fertilizer, cases of blasting gelatin, and sticks of dynamite stolen from a construction shed. When the day comes, Turner sets off the bomb without warning, killing about seven hundred people. He allows that most of his victims were innocent bystanders "no more committed to the sick philosophy or the racially destructive goals of the System than we are." Still, for Turner, the ends justify the means. "There is no way we can destroy the System without hurting many thousands of innocent people—no way. It is a cancer too deeply rooted in our flesh. And if we don't destroy the System before it destroys us—if we don't cut this cancer out of our living flesh—our whole race will die."

McVeigh embraced the ideology underlying *The Turner Diaries* including the paranoia about immigration and race-mixing, which has been a preoccupation of white supremacists throughout American history. In later years, as demographic change increased the nonwhite portion of the population—"demographic war," Turner calls it—this movement would come to be called, during the Trump era, the replacement theory or the Great Replacement. Its leading expositor was Tucker Carlson, of Fox News, who said that Democrats had designed an immigration policy that intended to "change the racial mix of the country. . . . In political terms this policy is called the 'great replacement,' the replacement of legacy Americans with more obedient people from faraway countries." Carlson's concerns were echoed across the conservative political universe, with many adopting the term "white genocide" to describe the threat they faced. For example, the most notorious chant at the white supremacist rally in Charlottesville, Virginia, in 2017 was "Jews will not replace us!" (President Trump famously described the confrontations at that rally as having "very fine people on both sides.") Earl Turner's mission was to protect "legacy Americans" from the depredations of Blacks, Jews, and the foreign born. That became McVeigh's mission, too—and that of his political heirs.

Crucially, for McVeigh, the bombing of the FBI building in *The Turner Diaries* sparks a broad rebellion against the dreaded System. Turner instructs a confederate on the "unique historical role of the Jews as the ferment of decomposition of races and civilization" and leads a grotesque carnival of violence against Blacks and Jews. The attacks reach their climax on what Turner calls "the Day of the Rope," when the Organization tortures and murders its enemies: "One famous actress, a notorious race-mixer who had starred in several large-budget interracial 'love' epics, had lost most of her hair, an eye, and several teeth—not to mention all her clothes—before the rope was put around her neck." In later years, "the Day of the Rope" became a kind of extremist code for the moment when white people take their revenge against their enemies.

Toward the end of *The Turner Diaries*, the United States is convulsed by a nuclear Civil War. Sixty million Americans are dead. The epilogue points to a happy ending. By 1999, the Organization had won a global war, and "the dream of a White world became a certainty."

The violence in *The Turner Diaries* is so lurid, almost cartoonish, that it's tempting to dismiss the book as political pornography. In fact, the *Diaries* reflects an ideology with deep roots in American history. Turner portrayed his quest as one for individual freedom, and as the historian Jefferson Cowie has observed, "Those defending racism, land appropriation, and enslavement portrayed themselves, and even understood their own actions, as part of a long history of freedom." Over time, Cowie wrote, "freedom" served as the ideological scaffolding for many kinds of oppression and white supremacy, including "Indian land dispossession and removal, mob political violence, lynching, convict labor, Jim Crow, resistance to school integration, and the fight against voting rights." As with many right-wing extremists, especially in recent history, McVeigh's concept of "freedom," like Earl Turner's, centered on guns—their belief that they should have the right to buy any kind of firearm at any time. Moreover, as Cowie notes, the white supremacist conception of freedom has long been especially threatened by *federal* power. George Wallace, for example, "spent his career repeating an enduring and widespread American promise to keep federal power at bay." The key to Wallace's appeal, in the North as well as the South, was that he "tapped into generations of concerns that local white people's freedom was yet again under siege by federal powers." Earl Turner acted on that same obsession with federal overreach when he parked the explosive-laden truck in front of the FBI building—and so, ultimately, did McVeigh when he lit the fuse in his truck at the Murrah federal building in Oklahoma City.

It is difficult to overstate the influence of *The Turner Diaries* on McVeigh. In a letter to his childhood friend Steve Hodge, which was written four years before the Oklahoma City bombing, McVeigh enclosed a copy of the book and wrote, "Read the book when you have time to sit down and think. When I read it, I would have to stop at the end of every paragraph and examine the deeper meaning of what I had just read. . . . I am not giving you this book to convert you. I do, however, want you to understand the 'other side' and view the pure literal genious [*sic*] of this piece." (Notwithstanding some imperfect spelling, McVeigh turned out to be a skilled and forceful writer.)

McVeigh's gun obsession, as well as his fixation with *The Turner Diaries*, fed an interest in self-dramatization, which was striking in someone who had led such a circumscribed life. Hodge told McVeigh's lawyers that Tim "wanted to go out with his finger on the trigger and empty casings all around him. Tim seemed to feel destined for a violent death." Inspired by Earl Turner, Tim began building primitive explosives, which he stored in the basement of the house in Pendleton. His father indulged Tim's new hobby, which also became a nervous family joke. "If we have a fire, are we going to blow up?" Bill would ask his son. Tim said yes, adding, "So if the fire department ever comes, we are just going to stand back and watch it go, right?"

McVeigh's purchase of *The Turner Diaries* put him on mailing lists for other like-minded literature. From the catalog of William Pierce's National Alliance, he furthered his interest in homemade explosives with *The Anarchist Cookbook*, which was published in 1971 for use by anti–Vietnam War radicals. Then came *The Poor Man's James Bond*, a macabre how-to manual, with dozens of recipes for bombs and poisons, as well as instructions for how to turn ordinary guns into automatic firing machines and how to kill with bare hands. McVeigh became a fan of a monthly NRA feature called "The Armed Citizen," which showed ordinary citizens using their guns to protect themselves from criminals. None of this, however, gave him the means or inclination to make a living.

Impatient with Tim's idleness, Bill urged him to continue his schooling, and Tim enrolled at Bryant & Stratton, a two-year business college near their home. He had shown some aptitude for computer programming, and B&S offered courses. Tim lasted a little more than a semester. The courses were stupid and juvenile, he told his father (and later his lawyers), and he knew more about computers than the teachers did. Tim would never take responsibility for his failures, always blaming someone or something for his disappointments. But what to do, especially since he wanted to buy more guns? Even when he was living at home, the wages at Burger King didn't pay enough to support his gun habit. So, he hit upon the idea of channeling his interest in guns: he passed a background check and became an armed guard for Burke Security, an armored car service.

This was a turning point for Tim, his first job with real responsibility, a regular salary, and a chance to see the world beyond his hometown. It was also an important part of his political coming of age. Before taking this job, McVeigh had had almost no exposure to Black people. His high school graduating class was all white, and he had rarely left Lockport and Pendleton, which were classic white-flight suburbs. Like virtually everyone else McVeigh had encountered, the workforce at Burke was nearly all white as well.

The job with Burke mostly involved making 150-mile runs from Buffalo to Syracuse. (McVeigh loved to drive fast, and he received several speeding tickets on this route.) Burke also required Tim to make deliveries to check-cashing facilities in Buffalo's inner city. As McVeigh later recounted in an interview with his lawyer Stephen Jones, "The first thing I remember would be the derogatory terms everyone would use that I wasn't used to—your Mark Fuhrman 'N' word, you know, 'nigger,' and 'porch monkey.'"(A detective in the O. J. Simpson case, Fuhrman had been discredited when it was revealed that he used the n-word to describe Black people.)

McVeigh later told his lawyers that he, personally, had no negative views of Black people, but he came to learn why his white colleagues were antagonistic. "I started seeing, as I worked there, why they would come to those opinions. We would have a special delivery the last of every month to these check-cashing places. We would have to run them emergency shipments of money, and as we would drive up there, there would be a line of welfare recipients three blocks long, waiting for money. We had to push our way in over their shoulders with our guns drawn, with nothing but Black people looking for their welfare checks. And you would see as you drove by their houses during the rest of the month that all they would be doing is sitting on their porches. Hence, 'porch monkeys,' waiting for their check." It's impossible to know now whether McVeigh was lying or exaggerating, or if there was any connection between these deliveries and welfare. Still, these ideas stayed with McVeigh and reinforced the racial attitudes he'd absorbed from *The Turner Diaries*. He was, by his later teenage years, a thoroughgoing racist.

With no social life to speak of, and some savings from gifts from his grandparents, McVeigh plowed his salary into more guns. According to his father, the collection included some pieces that were worth as much as $1,000 as well as an AR-15 assault weapon. Sometimes, McVeigh would show up at work with bandoliers and several weapons. (His colleagues regarded these appearances as more childish than scary.) He stopped shooting in Bill McVeigh's backyard after neighbors complained and joined the Tonawandas Sportsmen's Club, a local gun range. He and a high school friend named Dave Darlak bought a ten-acre farm for about $6,000 in an especially rural and isolated part of New York State, about eighty miles south of Lockport. McVeigh had no interest in growing anything there; he just wanted a place to test out his weapons. Sometimes Tim would bring along Jenny, his little sister, to watch. The neighbors complained there, too, but there was nothing they could do.

Still, in the spring of 1988, when McVeigh had just turned twenty, he was restless, uncertain of what he wanted to do with his life. He was living at home, stuck in a dead-end job, and he loved no one and nothing as much as shooting guns. His political views were a cauldron of resentments—against politicians who wanted to take away his guns and people (especially Blacks) who, he believed, had jumped ahead of his kind in the American hierarchy. None of this was especially unusual. What made McVeigh different, and what led to the horror that followed, was his messianic streak, his sense that he was destined for great things and a dramatic end. By this time, too, *The Turner Diaries* had planted the thought of a truck bomb demolishing a government building and leading to a political revolution. Tim wasn't going to find that kind of drama in his father's house in Pendleton.

One afternoon in May of 1988, Tim told his father how he was going to shake up his life. Bill was flabbergasted. He shouldn't have been.

CHAPTER 2

Kindred Spirits

Obsessed with weaponry and destined (in his own mind) for glory, McVeigh did the obvious thing. He enlisted in the Army. He told his dad that he was due the following day at Fort Benning, in Georgia. It was a measure of Bill's obliviousness, and the absence of communication between the two of them, that Bill was so surprised. Tim had taken advantage of his father's employee discount and bought a new car, a Chevy Geo Spectrum, with a turbo-charged engine, which he nicknamed "the Road Warrior." Driving through the night, McVeigh made it in time to start basic training on May 24, 1988. On that first day, Tim McVeigh met Terry Nichols.

Their friendship, which curdled into a conspiracy, was born in the military. The two men were among the earliest, and certainly the most prominent, examples of the link between modern right-wing extremism and the armed forces. This connection carried forward to the January 6, 2021, riot at the Capitol. About 7 percent of the adult population are either veterans or active-duty service members, but approximately 15 percent of those arrested belonged to those groups. Those charged with more serious crimes, like sedition, consisted overwhelmingly of veterans. The Proud Boys and Oath Keepers, two extremist groups whose members were leaders of the insurrection, were dominated by veterans. The prevalence of veterans among the extremists raised the question of whether the military attracted those predisposed to violent political action or whether service in the armed forces radicalized those who might not otherwise turn to terror.

As for McVeigh, he was inclined toward extremism when he enlisted. He joined the military principally because it would allow him to indulge his passion for weaponry—not an unusual reason—but he already had a distinct right-wing political profile as well. He was angry at Blacks, whom he regarded as parasites, and a government which he thought was going to take away his guns. (In a letter to a friend, McVeigh said, referring to Black people, "I have seen real evil.") These sentiments meshed well with the rage that coursed through his favorite book, *The Turner Diaries.* But McVeigh, at age twenty, had no historical or legal context for his views. He always thought of himself as a patriot—he had enlisted to serve his country, after all—but he didn't know much American history or how his ideas meshed with the founding concepts of the United States. McVeigh had the anger and the energy, but he didn't have any real justification for how he felt. That's what Terry Nichols provided. Nichols's fraudulent erudition fused with McVeigh's feral energy to build the road to Oklahoma City.

Nichols also came of age in a period and place of decline—amid the farm crisis in Michigan. Like others of their own and subsequent generations, both Nichols and McVeigh lost what they regarded as their birthright—opportunity, economic security, and cultural status. Like McVeigh, Nichols was never poor, never desperate for a meal. But the story of his life was of a middle-class existence inching ever further out of reach.

Terry Nichols was born on April 1, 1955, and grew up in rural Lapeer County, north and east of Flint, in Michigan's thumb. He was the third of four children of Joyce and Robert Nichols. Despite being thirteen years older, Terry's background resembled McVeigh's in many respects, starting with their parents. Robert Nichols was stoic and hardworking; Joyce was volatile. Joyce and Robert farmed, growing corn, wheat, and oats. But their farm never produced enough money to support four children, so Robert, like Bill McVeigh, worked nights at a Buick factory in Flint. James, the second oldest, took to farming early, but Terry had other dreams. He was quiet, even withdrawn, and an above-average student in high school. After graduating in 1974, he went to Central Michigan University, with hopes of becoming a doctor or dentist. But like McVeigh, Terry dropped out of college after about a semester and told his parents that the work was unchallenging and uninteresting. It's more likely he simply couldn't keep up and came home in defeat, the first of what would be many.

Family disasters multiplied. Les Nichols, the oldest son, nearly died in a welding accident, and he was terribly disfigured, losing his ears and nose. After twenty-four years of marriage, Joyce and Robert went through a rancorous divorce. Terry was a little older than McVeigh was when his parents split. Like McVeigh, Terry largely blamed his mother for the rupture, and in particular took issue with her drinking. According to Robert, his ex-wife once drove her car into a field and slammed into his tractor, destroying both vehicles. On another occasion, when police stopped Joyce following a hit-and-run accident, they saw her throwing beer bottles out the window. She then threatened the officers with a chainsaw. After the divorce, Joyce used her settlement to purchase a 160-acre farm outside the small town of Decker, about an hour from Lapeer, and she summoned Terry to help James and her make it work.

Michigan's rugged winters always made farming more precarious than in the lower Midwest, and Joyce bought land just as the farm crisis of the 1980s hit. The region, and the Nichols family in particular, were buffeted by high interest rates, inflation, and the 1980 grain embargo against the Soviet Union. There was also a series of floods.

The demands of life on the farm didn't suit Terry, and he disliked his brother's domineering personality. Terry fled to Colorado, where he tried to make it as a real estate salesman. But after a few months, when his mother and brother asked for more help at the farm, Terry returned.

Lana Walsh was a neighbor who saw Terry driving a tractor, and she struck up a conversation. In less than a year, in 1980, when Terry was twenty-five, they were married. She was five years older, already twice divorced, with two children. She was as impulsive as Terry was taciturn, but she at least had a real job as a real estate broker. She and Terry had a son, Josh, in 1982. Terry did carpentry, made a few life insurance sales, and helped with the farm. Mostly, though, he was at home raising his son as well as Lana's other two children. One day, Lana's sister Kelli came to babysit, and she met James, who was also living there. One thing led to another, and Kelli and James wound up getting married. The two brothers were now married to two sisters. As Lana liked to tell friends, "It was a small town, and there wasn't much to choose from." The house in Decker was good-sized, with five bedrooms, but it was still crowded with the two blended families—Terry and Lana with their three children, and James and Kelli and their newborn son, Chase.

James was the dominant figure in the house, and as the family farm floundered, he found explanations in the kind of right-wing conspiracy theories that had long circulated in the region. In the popular imagination, Michigan calls to mind the urban grit of Detroit, but this is misleading: Michigan is Detroit—attached to Idaho. The great mass of the state is rural, agricultural, and a hotbed of right-wing extremism. This has been true for decades, going back to the rise of the Ku Klux Klan in the 1920s and the success of Father Charles Coughlin, the anti-Semitic radio priest, in the 1930s. The farm crisis would foster another great reactionary movement in the 1980s and '90s. The Michigan Militia would not be christened for another few years, but the people who would become part of the movement, including the Nichols brothers, were developing an agenda. They blamed their financial problems on international organizations like the United Nations, and big-city bankers and, closer to home, the federal government. James became an avid reader of *The Spotlight*, published by the Liberty Lobby, a venerable right-wing group. Typical headlines ran along the lines of: "Citizens Fight Forced Fluoridation," "US Sovereignty Passed to UN," "Beware Global Police." The consuming obsession was the threat of gun control, with articles headlined "Take Gun Grabbers Seriously" and "New Attempts to Grab Your Gun." *The Spotlight*'s readers called themselves populists and constitutionalists, with their views aligned with those of the Founding Fathers. For the Nichols brothers, the Second Amendment was sacrosanct. "No one has the right to tell me that I can't have a gun," James often said. "That is protected in our Constitution."

Terry listened to his more outspoken brother, and the messages got through. Terry's political views, which had been a relatively minor part of his life, became more important. In the meantime, the farm wasn't doing any better, and perhaps not surprisingly, neither were the two marriages. Lana was spending more time in Detroit, looking after her mother, who was dying of cancer. Terry had no real job, no prospects, no apparent future. "Terry got real down on life," his father later told *The Washington Post*. "He didn't care what he had done or if he had done. He lost his vitality."

Lana decided to try a last-ditch effort to bring her husband back to life. She brought him recruiting material from a local Army outpost. Perhaps, she suggested, Terry should enlist. (This may also have been an attempt to get Terry out of town and out of her life.) The military was an unlikely notion. Terry was thirty-three years old, far older than most new recruits. He had a home and a young son to support. But Terry had already made several failed attempts to leave the gravitational pull of Michigan farm life, and he decided to make one more. Like Timothy McVeigh, in May 1988, Terry Nichols found his way to Fort Benning for basic training.

At first, the Army was all that McVeigh hoped. Soon after he arrived in basic training, his skill as a marksman earned him a commendation as a sharpshooter. He wrote to his old friend Steve Hodge, back in Lockport, "Two weeks of basic, then I get a two-day leave! I'm still thinking like Tim. While everyone else is getting laid, I'll be searching pawn shops for ammo and explosives! . . . Girls are the least of my concerns now. (No, I didn't turn faggot.)"

All through the summer, McVeigh sent a series of nearly joyful letters to Hodge, his father, grandfather, and sister Jenny. He even wrote to his mother, from whom he was largely estranged. He had some complaints—the heat, the lack of sleep, the demands of the sergeants—but he was loving the Army, even the haircuts. ("We got our second hair cut today," he wrote Jenny. "Today I got a 'high & tight.' It's the 'in' look for buzz cuts. The hair is thick on top & low on the sides—sorry, no camera, no pictures.") He delighted in recounting the drills, especially those that involved shooting. He was amused that in the Army, you must call it a "weapon." "If you say 'gun,' you have to do push-ups," he wrote. McVeigh was thriving. "The army and me (I) are getting along well," he wrote Hodge. "I barely ever get yelled at and they (everyone) likes me, mainly because I do my job AND that little extra. I always have my shit together (locker straight, etc.)." He ended a letter to his mother this way: "I asked if I could have my picture taken w/ an M-16, and the photographer said 'Mommy's didn't like that!' They could not face the fact that their sons were being trained to kill. Every time we are called to attention, we must yell—

"'Wild Deuce!' (2nd platoon)

"'Blood makes the grass grow! Kill! Kill! Kill!'"

McVeigh made another good friend at Fort Benning. Michael

Fortier was the same age, and he came from the rough town of Kingman, Arizona, which sits near the point where Nevada, California, and Arizona meet. Kingman was once a railroad crossroads, and the famous Route 66 passed through town, but by the late 1980s, it was shabby and depressed. Fortier had been a chess champion in high school, and a good student, but Kingman had little to offer him, so he drifted into the Army, albeit without McVeigh's obsession with guns. And unlike McVeigh, Fortier's chief interest in life was getting high, mostly with pot, but also with whatever else he could find, including acid and crystal meth. He was devoted to his high school girlfriend, Lori Hart. On the surface, McVeigh, Nichols, and Fortier appeared to have little in common, but they bonded over politics.

Nichols became the tutor and McVeigh and Fortier his students. Terry Nichols was never as demonstrative as his older brother James, but both had absorbed what became known as the militia agenda. Nichols put a constitutional gloss on the views McVeigh had already embraced. "One thing I came to understand while in the service was not that some people say 'pop' instead of 'soda,'" McVeigh wrote to journalists Michel and Herbeck, "but I began to understand the principle of states' rights vs. an (intended) weak central govt. I began to understand the intentions of the Founding Fathers." Publications like *The Spotlight* often cloaked their reactionary ideas with the sanction of history. Nichols introduced McVeigh to the full text of the Declaration of Independence, the speeches of Patrick Henry, and even excerpts from the work of the seventeenth-century political philosopher John Locke. The agenda was quasi-libertarian, but it was aggressive and militaristic, too. On the right to bear arms, these publications served as a sort of advance guard for where the conservative movement was heading. When the NRA began advocating for an individual's right to bear arms under the Second Amendment, the rationale was for self-defense. But Nichols took the argument a step further: the Second Amendment existed not just to be free of government regulation of firearms but for citizens to exert control over the government, to fight back against the overreach of bureaucrats. At the time, in the 1980s, this was an extreme view—that the Second Amendment existed to provide individuals with a violent check on the federal government. But as the Republican Party moved rightward, many more adopted it, including the leaders of the January 6, 2021, insurrection. As Stewart Rhodes, the leader of the Oath Keepers, put it, the Second Amendment exists "to preserve the military capacity of the American people to resist tyranny and violations of their rights by oath breakers within government." Likewise, according to Nichols's ersatz patriotism and garbled history, government, especially the federal government, was the enemy.

As a soldier, Terry Nichols struggled from the start. Immediately nicknamed "the old man" and "pops," he barely survived basic training. At least a decade older than his fellow recruits, he struggled to get through the physical tests, the long morning runs, the clambering over obstacles. Nichols's superiors liked him, appreciating his maturity compared to the near juveniles around him. In October 1988, five months after he enlisted, Nichols received word by mail that Lana had filed for divorce. McVeigh's friendship was a comfort. And there was one area in which he excelled. Nichols was also a skilled marksman, and he and McVeigh enjoyed spending time together at the rifle range.

At around the same time that Nichols found out that his wife wanted a divorce, the three friends learned that they were all going to Fort Riley, near Junction City, Kansas, for their first real assignment in the military. Riley has been an Army base since before the Civil War, when General George A. Custer was in charge. By the twentieth century, Riley was known as the home of the 1st Infantry Division—or the "Big Red One," for the red numeral on its insignia. That division had played a storied role in major combat operations, and when McVeigh, Nichols, and Fortier arrived, it was a leading training center for mechanized warfare. Soldiers roamed its 100,000 acres and learned how to operate tanks.

Fort Riley sits in the Flint Hills of Kansas. The forbidding landscape of rolling mounds and rocky soil, largely devoid of trees and carpeted with native grasses, has resisted many attempts to cultivate and settle it over the decades. Even more than the rest of Kansas, it's lightly populated. (Its population peaked in 1900.) As one local historian noted, "Jobs have largely migrated to a handful of nearby cities—Manhattan and Topeka to the north, Emporia to the east, El Dorado and Wichita to the south and west—leaving behind a smattering of shrinking towns with gap-toothed Main Streets and abandoned farm machines rusting in fallow fields." This is the region that became the base of operations for Nichols and McVeigh over the next several years. In every meaningful sense, the Oklahoma City bombing plot was hatched, and the bomb itself was built, in these quiet hills.

Nichols only lasted a few months at Fort Riley. Lana had moved out of Decker with her two sons from her earlier marriages; she sent Josh, who was just seven, to live with Terry at the base. But Terry was working as a driver for a top general, which entailed frequent overnight deployments. Caring for his son became impossible, and Nichols received a "hardship discharge" after just a year in the service. In May 1989, he again returned home to Michigan in defeat, just as he did after college and Colorado. Now a single parent, he soon made yet another attempt to restart his life, this time in Las Vegas, where he enrolled in a training program for slot machine repair. But that didn't work out, and before long he was back at the Decker farm once again.

James had also split with his wife, so the two brothers were now the lone adults in the house. They became ever more alienated from conventional life. Terry turned against modern methods of agriculture and food preparation. As James would write, Terry had an "obvious love and appreciation for organically grown foods, free from chemicals and pesticides. He grinds his own organically grown wheat for flour to bake bread and breakfast cereals. He had his own equipment for making distilled water for drinking." Distrust of fluoridated water was a hallmark of right-wing conspiratorial thinking.

Publications like *The Spotlight* and *Soldier of Fortune* came to the farm, and like McVeigh, Terry developed the habit of perusing the small advertisements in the back pages. Within a few months of his return, he saw an ad from a father-and-son travel agency called Paradise Shelton Tours. It didn't take much decoding to see what was really being advertised—a mail-order-bride operation in Cebu City, in the Philippines. Shelton also ran ads in Cebu City, looking for women who might want to escape poverty by marrying an American. A woman named Flordaliza "Lisa" Torres replied, and later introduced her sister Marife (pronounced Mary-Fay) to the Sheltons. In August 1990, Nichols made the long trip to Asia, and he and Marife were introduced. He returned to Cebu City two months later, and they were married. Terry was thirty-five; Marife was sixteen. He told friends that Marife was just what he was looking for, a tiny (less than five feet tall and a hundred pounds) and deferential girl.

Terry came home without his bride: it took him about seven months to complete the paperwork to bring her to Michigan. "That one episode soured Terry on government," his father told *The Washington Post*. "He originally told me it would take six weeks for her to come here, but it was red tape, red tape, red tape." When Terry finally returned to the Philippines, to bring Marife home at last, he found her pregnant with another man's child. The news might have prompted another man to cut off the engagement and return to the States, but Terry accepted the disappointment and adopted the child, whom they named Jason Nichols.

But as Nichols was once again frustrated, McVeigh found the opportunity he wanted. He was going to go to war.

CHAPTER 3

Mr. Spotless

The United States Army had both professional requirements, which were clearly defined, and social norms, which were more open to interpretation. On the job, McVeigh did his duty by being skilled and disciplined. He didn't make trouble; he followed orders; he rose in rank quickly. As for the customs at Fort Riley, a lot of soldiers were racist, sexist, and obsessed with guns—and so was McVeigh. McVeigh came to the military with an inclination toward white supremacy, right-wing fanaticism, and vigilante violence. His extremism grew and festered as a soldier.

Shortly after McVeigh arrived in Kansas, he attended a recruiting presentation for the Army's most elite units—Special Forces (also known as the Green Berets), and the Delta Force. The Green Berets originated during the Korean War, with the mandate to engage in unconventional warfare, including guerrilla operations, often in enemy-occupied territory. They frequently serve long deployments in miserable conditions. Delta Force is smaller, more elite, and much newer, having been created in the 1970s. The operatives specialize in single high-risk actions, such as counterterrorist raids and hostage rescues. McVeigh knew that service in either of these units would be the culmination of everything he worked for and valued as a soldier.

Not incidentally, their exploits were frequently chronicled in *Soldier of Fortune*.

"I was reasonable enough to realize that I could not meet the expectations they laid out for Delta Force," McVeigh informed his attorney Stephen Jones, "but I knew I could meet the expectations they laid out for Special Forces. I knew my test scores, my physical test scores, my road march times, et cetera, fell within those parameters." So, this became his focus: to join the Green Berets.

McVeigh made a name for himself at Fort Riley. Unlike his friends Nichols and Fortier, McVeigh stood out from the beginning. He was fastidious about his appearance, always wearing creased trousers, shined shoes, and polished brass, which earned him the nickname Mr. Spotless. He trained incessantly, even on his own time. He marched around the base carrying a heavy pack; he studied training manuals; he taught himself to disassemble and assemble weapons—blindfolded. Several of his former commanding officers would later tell the FBI the same thing: "I wish I had a platoon full of Tim McVeighs." Soon after he was promoted to corporal, McVeigh flourished during a two-week training program in Germany, where he won an award for marksmanship. (He also enjoyed the opportunity to drive 125 miles per hour on the autobahn.) After McVeigh reveled in a month of combat training in Fort Irwin, in California's Mojave Desert, he spent Thanksgiving 1989 with Mike Fortier's family in Arizona.

McVeigh chose to save money and live in the barracks, rather than rent an apartment in Junction City. Many of his fellow soldiers chose to blow their salaries at strip clubs and bars near the base. McVeigh agreed to be the designated driver for these outings, and his colleagues would cover his Cokes. McVeigh soon saw a business opportunity in his teetotaling, and he started hiring himself out as a taxi service. Drunken soldiers would call his room in the middle of the night, and he'd show up in his car—for a price. McVeigh soon expanded his services: he'd do laundry, substitute for guard duty.

Eventually he started lending money at loan shark rates and earned another nickname: the Jew.

On weekends, McVeigh spent his earnings at gun shows and pawn shops in Kansas. Privately owned weapons were not allowed in the barracks, so McVeigh hid his in the trunk of his car until he convinced a friend named Jesus Rodriguez to store them in his house. The collection would eventually include revolvers, shotguns, rifles, a 9mm handgun, and an AK-15 assault weapon. Back in his room, McVeigh continued to avidly read *Soldier of Fortune* as well as military and gun manuals, and reread *The Turner Diaries.* Fellow white soldiers who were interviewed later by the FBI said they never agreed with McVeigh's views on race, but McVeigh himself claimed he found a receptive audience among them. Black soldiers who were interviewed said McVeigh kept a careful distance from them. He bought copies of *The Turner Diaries* for Michael Fortier and several other friends at the base.

Fort Riley was polarized along racial lines. Anti-white and anti-Black graffiti marred many walls. The racism that McVeigh began to express during his security guard days in Buffalo deepened in the Army. Among his complaints about Black people were "the loud rough music, the low riders together with bass music, the loudness in the barracks and everywhere else, the staying up and keeping others up all night, the playing of dominoes loud all night. . . . It seemed like a form of psychological warfare, in which Black soldiers were purposely bothering other people." McVeigh wrote Hodge from Fort Riley, "I used to call black people 'black,' because I only saw one side of the story. Now you can guess what I call them." Fellow soldiers later reported to the FBI that McVeigh was fond of the n-word and referred to Black children as "nig-lets." In the Army, McVeigh thought he was a victim of affirmative action; when two African Americans were chosen over him to attend sniper school, McVeigh was outraged because he thought he was better qualified. Later, with his lawyers,

McVeigh tried to downplay his bigotry, explaining that he was "thrust into a new culture" in the military, a culture of Black people who were "loud, sort of arrogant, touchy." But he also said, "Nothing of great value has ever been accomplished or contributed by a Black person." And if Blacks could wear a shirt that said Black Power, he could wear one that said White Power—and he did.

Newer to McVeigh's political worldview was hostility to women's rights. Women remained essentially a foreign species to him, baffling and sometimes angering him. At Fort Riley, he came across women recruits for the first time, and he was appalled. "This was the first time that a female was assigned to our class," McVeigh told Jones, "and a little bit of politics came into this. This is where I get my opinions about women in combat. . . . And it was just a joke. We had to post extra guards so she could go to the bathroom, she couldn't pull her weight digging, she couldn't carry the M-60 when it was her turn to be assigned to it. You started seeing that the infantry was no place for a woman. . . . And it was immediately after this course that I started paying heightened attention to the political atmosphere created by Patricia Schroeder [a congresswoman from Colorado at the time] that women should be allowed in combat, it was their right, equal rights. I started taking exception, and this might have opened my political eyes also. Well, what other opinions do they have that are wrong? You know? Well, of course, they just don't understand guns."

McVeigh appeared to be a quietly competent soldier, with a sideline as an industrious freelance assistant to his colleagues. But as he made clear in his letters to Hodge, there was anger simmering beneath the surface. "The influence of the Army and the people around me have changed/are changing me in many ways," he wrote. "I now see a much larger portion of the whole picture including gang warfare, cocaine use, and the insignificance of law enforcement. I will never be the same." McVeigh regarded the police as extensions of the overweening hand of government—a departure from conventional right-wing views. He came to regard law enforcement in a hierarchy of disdain, with his greatest tolerance for local authorities and most hostility for the FBI. (His hostility to the federal government placed him in a long political tradition.) In the military, these views didn't yet prompt McVeigh to act out, but the rage was there, building.

The Army did not create McVeigh's extremism from scratch, just as the military did not take average recruits two decades later and turn them into Oath Keepers and Proud Boys. McVeigh and his successors were predisposed for violent political action. But their experiences in the Army enhanced and accelerated the process of radicalization and made these men, McVeigh in particular, more enduringly dangerous.

The Bradley Fighting Vehicle was designed both to attack targets on the battlefield and to transport troops. A Bradley moves on tracks and has a turret like a tank; it also has room to carry as many as nine soldiers and a commander, a driver, and a gunner. The gunner has to be able to aim and fire a precision missile from the main antitank weapon from the turret as well as a 25mm cannon and a high-caliber (7.62mm) machine gun. The gunner will deploy these weapons while the Bradley is moving, often over rough terrain, in any kind of weather, day or night. "I've gotta tell you," McVeigh wrote to Hodge, "I've got a real hard-on for being the Gunner." At the age of twenty-two, he was the top-rated gunner out of 120 at Fort Riley.

Suddenly, in the second half of 1990, it looked like McVeigh might see combat. In August, Saddam Hussein invaded Kuwait, and President George H. W. Bush vowed, "This will not stand." Bush created a multinational alliance to counter the Iraqi aggression, and throughout the fall, as Hussein resisted the pressure to withdraw, the chances for war grew.

Bush began sending troops to Saudi Arabia in late summer, as a staging area for a possible raid to liberate Kuwait. The mission was known as Operation Desert Shield, and the soldiers at Fort Riley awaited their orders. At that same moment, McVeigh received the news he had long wanted to hear. He had passed the preliminary tests and received orders to travel to Fort Bragg, in North Carolina, for the twenty-one-day tryout for Special Forces, starting on November 11, 1990. But at the same time, his unit was ordered to Saudi Arabia. So where would McVeigh go? "Special Forces usually overrides everything in the military. They are the elite," he told Jones. "Or would I go to the call-up? They had three or four days to try to straighten it out, and they determined that I was going with my unit over to Saudi. That was all right. I didn't know what would happen with Special Forces training. I figure I could just reapply when I got back."

McVeigh and a hundred or so fellow soldiers (in what was called Charlie Company of the 2nd Battalion of the 16th Infantry Regiment of the 1st Infantry Division) shipped out to a National Guard airfield in Topeka. They were part of a massive wave of 700,000 American troops headed to the Gulf region. Each soldier was issued an M-16 rifle, a fifteen-day supply of ammunition, and a five-day supply of food. Because Saddam Hussein had a history of using chemical weapons, the soldiers also received an unnerving addition—a nerve gas survival suit, including an injection kit designed to counter the effects of poison gas. McVeigh jotted a mordant note to his hometown friend Hodge as he prepared to leave the country. "If there isn't a war, we stay one year," he wrote. "If there is, I'll probably be back a lot sooner—in a box."

Charlie Company took a circuitous route to the Gulf, finally arriving in early January 1991. The Saudis had no place to billet thousands of American troops, so they improvised housing near the Kuwaiti border. McVeigh's unit stayed first in apartment blocks that were meant for immigrants and then in tents in the desert. Charlie Company readied for action and then . . . nothing happened. Weeks passed, diplomatic efforts continued. McVeigh had little to do except wait.

Most of the unit's heavy equipment, like the Bradleys, was arriving by ship, and eventually the 244 combat vehicles arrived, all painted with Chemical Agent Resistant Coating. Passing the time, McVeigh wrote a lot of letters. To his grandfather: "I heard the Bills lost the Superbowl—Ruined my whole week." McVeigh went on, "Now it's just a waiting game. Only fate knows if I'll be ok. The U.S. is going to kick some serious ass, no doubt, but there will be a cost." To his sister Jenny, on the same day: "I'm catching hell trying to write back to everyone. We've been practicing for the attack day and night. I'm really not nervous; kind of indifferent. If it's my time, it's my time. There's nothing you can do about that. I'm not nervous about doing my job; it's instinct now. . . . I'm right on top of the Iraqi positions. (300 meters). If the artillery and air prep don't do their job, I'm pretty much S.O.L."—shit out of luck.

With Hodge, McVeigh did some macho posturing. "We're going to bust through so fuckin' quick, the Iraqis will think it's a bad dream and when they blink to wake up, they'll be dead!" He went on, "I've made up my mind—no prisoners. It may be on my conscience for years, and I may be accused of killing defenseless people, but when push comes to shove and my life (along with the lives of everyone in my vehicle) is on the line, you've got to do what you've got to do."

The Bradleys arrived, and the soldiers began final preparations for the invasion of Kuwait. McVeigh was assigned to be gunner in the tank commanded by the leader of his platoon, Second Lieutenant Jesus Rodriguez (who had allowed McVeigh to stash his guns in his home in Kansas). Their Bradley was formally designated C-11, but McVeigh came up with a better name and scrawled it in block letters across the turret: BAD COMPANY. It was one of his favorite songs, whose lyrics seemed to fit the moment: "Behind a gun . . . I'll make my final stand."

Hussein had a deadline of January 15, 1991, to withdraw from Iraq. When he didn't, the Americans and their allies began a bombing campaign, turning Operation Desert Shield into Operation Desert Storm. The ground invasion of Kuwait took on a new urgency, and McVeigh's Bradley was given an especially dangerous assignment. "Bad Company" would lead three other Bradleys behind a group of minesweepers to commence the battle. Eight M1 Abrams tanks, twice as heavy and more armored than the Bradleys, would come next. "The Bradley . . . is more susceptible to fire than the tank," McVeigh told Michel and Herbeck. "The tank commander reasoned that . . . if the Bradley goes first and blows up, the Abrams can come up behind and push it through, with its horsepower, and ignite any other mines that might not have been taken out by the mine vehicle. . . . In other words, he sent us in first as a sacrificial lamb. It happened to be my vehicle." McVeigh wrote Hodge, days before the battle was to begin, "I key the entire task force! Of course the glory has a price—'Shot down in a Blaze of Glory' couldn't be more dramatic/melodramatic!" As they waited in the desert for the signal to attack, McVeigh was promoted to sergeant. He also reenlisted for another two-year hitch.

At 5:02 a.m. on February 24, 1991, McVeigh and his comrades launched their assault. At first, they encountered no Iraqi troops, then three hours later, they fired their first shots at what appeared to be an infantry unit. The Americans had trained for a pitched battle, but it would turn out that the Iraqis had neither the resources nor the will to put up much of a fight. As the official military history of McVeigh's unit put it, "Soon, Iraqi troops were surrendering in droves."

On the second day of the ground war, McVeigh's Bradley, commanded by Rodriguez, continued its rapid advance. At one point, Rodriguez spied what looked like a machine-gun nest dug into the desert about a mile away. Despite the distance, and with the Bradley in motion, Rodriguez ordered McVeigh to fire. McVeigh stared into his viewfinder, which had twelve-times magnification, and squeezed the trigger on the 25mm cannon to launch a high-explosive shell. At the last minute, an Iraqi soldier stood up. "His head just disappeared. . . . I saw everything above his shoulder disappear, like in a red mist," McVeigh told Michel and Herbeck. The explosion also killed a soldier who was standing next to the one who took the direct hit. McVeigh received the Army Commendation Medal. According to the citation, he had inspired his fellow soldiers by "destroying an enemy machine-gun emplacement, killing two Iraqi soldiers and forcing the surrender of 30 others from dug-in positions." McVeigh was awarded four other medals, including a Bronze Star, for his service in Desert Storm. Even though commendations and promotions came quickly in wartime, McVeigh's achievements stood out. A promotion to sergeant in less than three years and then a Bronze Star marked him as an enlisted man with a bright future.

The war turned into such a rout that the allied forces, under the command of General H. Norman Schwarzkopf, declared a unilateral cease-fire just one hundred hours after the ground attack began. A few days later, McVeigh's company was directed to an airstrip near the town of Safwan, where Schwarzkopf was presiding over a peace conference of sorts. He was in fact dictating the terms of surrender to his Iraqi counterparts. As a reward for its excellent performance during the brief war, Charlie Company was invited to provide security. The Bradley vehicles and Abrams tanks were lined up in a massive show of force for the Iraqis and the television cameras. Still riding an adrenaline surge from his war heroics, McVeigh wrote a breathless letter to his mother on March 5. "If you didn't see me on the news yesterday, you never will," he wrote. "We were guarding the peace talks, and our Bradley was parked 50 yards from the main tent. Everyone got us on film—CNN, ABC, NBC, CBS, UPI, etc. I talked with Tom Brokaw (cool guy), and had my picture taken shaking Gen. Schwarzkopf's hand. . . . We're lucky most of the Iraqis didn't fight. They had some serious shit stashed in their holes."

Better news for McVeigh quickly followed. On March 26, an officer informed him that his orders had come through for Special Forces tryouts. He had thirty minutes to gather his gear in the desert and figure out a way to report to Fort Bragg in North Carolina on April 1. "At that point everyone was trying to get back from the Gulf. I had to find any way I could," McVeigh told Jones. "I jumped on the back of a Chinook [helicopter] that was already overcrowded, got to the Kuwaiti airfield. This is where my charismatic skills came in. There was a female Air Force sergeant there that was not going to let me on, and I just kind of sweet talked her into letting me on this flight to get back to the States."

This moment, as McVeigh's plane left the Persian Gulf, ranked as the precise high point of his life. He had found a welcoming home in the Army, and he had tested himself in war and emerged as a decorated hero. His dream was tantalizingly within reach.

CHAPTER 4

The Ties Fray

The Green Berets were founded in the 1950s, but they became famous in October 1961, when President John F. Kennedy visited the Army's Special Warfare Center at Fort Bragg and declared that they would be the nation's main counterinsurgency force. He also decreed that Special Forces soldiers—and they alone—would be allowed to wear the coveted green headwear. Thanks in part to the John Wayne movie from 1968, the unit came through the Vietnam War with its reputation intact. When McVeigh arrived for his tryout in 1991, the glow endured.

McVeigh was in ragged shape when he reached Fort Bragg. The months in the desert had been exhilarating but exhausting. Cooped up inside the Bradley, eating only field rations, he knew that his fitness and strength had suffered. His route home had taken him on a mix of military and civilian flights from Kuwait to Saudi Arabia to Spain to Newfoundland to Connecticut to Kansas to North Carolina. He was jet-lagged to boot.

Still, the first few days after the war were heady. As one of the first Desert Storm soldiers to return, McVeigh was saluted and admired wherever he went. Airline pilots introduced him, and passengers applauded. He had a one-night stand with a woman he met in a bar on his route home. Still, McVeigh had his work cut out for him. He was one of five soldiers just back from Desert Storm for the tryouts. Given the swift turnaround, the Special Forces brass asked if they were ready for the twenty-one days of tests. "At that point we were so excited to be back and weren't thinking," McVeigh told Jones. "We said, 'yes.' We kind of knew in our hearts we weren't. But we were going to try it." In the previous year, before the war, just 43 percent of the applicants earned the right to be Green Berets.

At 250 square miles, or 160,000 acres, Fort Bragg is considered the biggest military base in the world. (It is named for Braxton Bragg, a commander in the Confederate Army.) The post itself, with all the housing and facilities, occupies just nineteen square miles. The rest is a rugged mix of North Carolina terrain—forests, mountains, rivers, and lakes. The Green Beret course sprawls across that landscape in a famously brutal test. By tradition, soldiers don't flunk out of the tryout: applicants simply give up when they know they can't endure more punishment. "Part of the way special forces works is that you are never told. You judge yourself," McVeigh told his lawyer Jones.

The first day began in a classroom, and then McVeigh had a one-on-one assessment with a psychologist. The physical tests started the next day. McVeigh did well on the morning obstacle course. After lunch, the soldiers were instructed to put on their packs for a long march of unknown duration. McVeigh had been issued a new pair of combat boots, which he hadn't had the chance to break in. "I knew something was wrong," McVeigh told Jones. "My knees were aching, blisters started breaking out on my feet, and that was just the first road march." As he pushed himself through sandy terrain, his pain turned to agony. He made it through the full five miles of this march, but he knew he couldn't continue. Back at the barracks, he told an officer he was dropping out. He had lasted two days.

It was a shattering defeat. The Green Berets were everything for McVeigh; he had no plan B. As was his pattern, McVeigh would later insist that he never wanted to be in Special Forces all that much anyway—just like he dropped out of college because he knew more than his teachers. (In the same spirit, years later, he said he knew more about criminal defense than his lawyers in the bombing case.) McVeigh rationalized his failure in Fort Bragg by saying in a letter to Jenny that he knew the Green Berets were involved in illegal activities, including drug running, and he wanted no part of it. He said the Green Berets were too oriented toward book smarts and strategy, while he was looking for a more action-oriented mission. This was nonsense; rather, McVeigh had failed the most important test of his life, and his future was suddenly void. Some of his defense lawyers would later darkly joke that the officers who kept McVeigh out of the Green Berets caused the Oklahoma City bombing. That wasn't true, of course, not least because McVeigh himself abandoned the tryout, but McVeigh's failure at Fort Bragg began a spiral that ended four years later at the Murrah building.

Most of McVeigh's unit had not yet returned from the Gulf, so he was given a thirty-day leave. He drove from Kansas to New York to see his father and then to Florida, to visit his older sister, who had married a wealthy electrical contractor in Pensacola. He swam in his sister and brother-in-law's pool, and they took him out to expensive restaurants. Later, he would say that he was turned off by their "snob" lifestyle—the same word he used to dismiss the suburbanites who were buying houses in Lockport. It's not clear whether he was offended, or just disparaging what he knew he could never have.

McVeigh became even more alienated when he returned to Fort Riley. He was following a familiar pattern among generations of warriors: they come home from battle and suffer a catastrophic letdown. McVeigh was aware of this. "There are ups and downs, especially after a war. It's an extreme upper, so you are going to have an extreme downer after war," he told Jones, wondering if he had post-traumatic stress disorder. (If he did, it was never diagnosed.)

So, like many veterans, McVeigh became cynical about what had happened overseas and what awaited him in the States. Many get through this transitory stage and resume ordinary lives; McVeigh did not. "My unit was back, everything was changing, the old guys were getting out—the old guard, the men I went through basic with," he told Jones. "We were getting in these new guys who were going through what they call 'no stress basic,' where they can't tell you to do 20 push-ups because you say your name wrong, which is how we did it in the old Army. These kids, they were like brats." At twenty-three, McVeigh was portraying himself as a grizzled protector of the Army's traditions. His disquiet, however, was rooted in his own restlessness.

McVeigh moved off base. He didn't rent an apartment where most of his fellow soldiers lived, in Junction City, a relatively bustling place, adjacent to the military complex. Instead, he and a group of friends rented a house in Herington, a bedraggled former railroad crossroads of about two thousand people, located thirty-five miles south of Fort Riley. (Given the speed at which McVeigh usually drove, he could make it to work in under thirty minutes.) Unlike in the barracks, McVeigh could keep his gun collection with him. He soon fell out with his first group of roommates—they were slobs and he was fastidious—and he found another place to live in town. But his roommate there wanted McVeigh's bedroom to install both his waterbed and his fiancée. McVeigh soon wanted out of there, too.

McVeigh's disaffection pushed him to leave Fort Riley emotionally as well as geographically. Just as the political glow from Desert Storm wore off quickly for President Bush in 1991, the same happened with many veterans of the war. McVeigh wondered what really had been accomplished. Iraq was out of Kuwait, but was the world any better? McVeigh heard a rumor that Bush's family had personally profited from the invasion. He recalled to Jones, "It all boiled down to just economics and money. That was the big thing that crushed me." (It's not clear what McVeigh was referring to regarding the Bush family, but it seems to be a conspiracy theory.)

McVeigh came to believe that the United States should simply stay out of other countries' business. "Our Constitution says we have a right to keep and bear arms, and yet we are determining it's our right to go over to someone else's country and take away their guns from them, and leave them helpless," he said. "You have no right to judge other countries from overseas when you don't live there. Didn't the British try to do exactly that to us when we founded America? We threw over that yoke, and now 200 years later we are doing the same to other countries." McVeigh's political judgments were not sophisticated or even fully coherent—nor were they particularly unusual. As usual, gun rights were at the center of his worldview.

McVeigh didn't let his disaffection undermine his job performance, and his skills as a Bradley gunner remained intact. In September, he earned a place in the official history of his regiment by achieving a perfect score in a shooting exercise. "The winning crew, consisting of 2nd Lieutenant Mike Pound and gunner Sergeant Tim McVeigh, took top honors by not only hitting all targets presented, but by doing it in less time than [the other] one-thousand-point crew." For McVeigh, this became a kind of capstone to his military career. Without a future in the Green Berets, there was nothing else he wanted to do in the military. So, after three and a half years in the service, he resigned, with an honorable discharge, effective in December 1991. He had served only six months after returning from the war.

With nothing else to do, and nowhere else to go, McVeigh returned to his father's house in Pendleton. His sister Jenny, who had just turned eighteen, was living in Tim's old bedroom, so he slept on the couch in the living room. The arrangement was difficult: Jenny was doing a lot of partying in those days, coming and going at all hours. Worse yet,

Bill McVeigh—who had settled into an irritable bachelorhood—was in a precarious situation at Harrison Radiator, which was shedding employees every year. The only good thing about living there was that it was rent-free.

Tim needed work and thought he could parlay his military experience into a job with the U.S. Marshals Service. In a story that he would tell over and over, McVeigh said he did very well on the written test, but was turned down because he was a "white male." Just as McVeigh felt the Army cheated him out of sniper school because of affirmative action, he thought the Marshals didn't consider hiring him because they only wanted women and African Americans. (This story is impossible to verify and likely untrue.)

McVeigh found a job in the Buffalo area that was a lot like his last one. With a pistol permit and a security clearance from the Army, he became a supervisor at Burns Security. Making a decent salary with few expenses, he found a new and risky way to spend money. He started betting heavily with a bookie on his beloved Buffalo Bills. He promptly lost $1,000 when the Bills lost their second straight Super Bowl, this time to the Washington Redskins, on January 26, 1992. (At about the same time, the Army demanded that he return, with interest, the $3,000 reenlistment bonus that he received in 1991, because he did not complete his commitment. This damaged his finances and contributed to his bitterness against the federal government and now, the Army.)

The job at Burns was grueling. The company had roughly 1,100 security guards in his area, and McVeigh had to keep track of them all. He frequently found himself filling in for absent guards—at the airport, the zoo, and various establishments around the city and suburbs. He often worked sixty or seventy hours a week, and the only benefit was the opportunity to spend time at the office with Andrea Augustine, the personnel manager.

McVeigh later told his lawyers that Augustine was the only woman he ever envisioned marrying. She was beautiful, with a dreamy bohemian streak, and he was immediately smitten. Augustine, however, was not. She lived with her boyfriend and showed no romantic interest in McVeigh. But she liked him as a friend, and they spoke on the phone nearly every night, sometimes for two or three hours, as she lay in bed next to her sleeping boyfriend. She had little curiosity about politics, so they talked about other things. He complained about his family—his "drunken" mother, "slut" sister, and "angry" father. Later, after he left the Buffalo area and lived on the road, he kept writing to her. Once, when he returned to Buffalo for a visit, McVeigh found out that she had moved. As Augustine said in an interview with McVeigh's investigators, "He got the address somehow, then bought a map and looked it up. Then he drove an hour to where I live and put a letter in my mailbox. That's a lot of effort to go through to find someone."

Indeed, McVeigh's behavior toward Augustine resembled stalking. This letter to her reflected the mix of longing and menace in McVeigh's approach.

> Hey gorgeous, ("Poof" goes to your head—I know.)
>
> I can take a hint, but here's my address anyway. If you ever need anything, let me know.
>
> i.e. 1) Someone killed/blown up/etc.
>
> 2) A "shoulder"
>
> 3) Refuge
>
> 4) Fertilization from good stock (if that clock starts ticking.) This one I like best.

McVeigh came of age before the term "incel"—involuntary celibate—came into wide use. Like the incels of a later day, McVeigh was unable to attract the sexual interest of women and responded with rage toward them. Augustine was simultaneously right next to him and out of reach. In those melancholy days after McVeigh left the Army, his resentments against Blacks (for taking his job opportunities) and women (for denying him companionship) festered and grew. McVeigh spent most days in his treasured Road Warrior vehicle, shuttling between guard locations. There, on the radio, he found a man whose views reflected and reinforced his own.

McVeigh started listening to Rush Limbaugh, who was in his heyday. He was carried on more than five hundred radio stations; he published his first book, *The Way Things Ought to Be*, which became one of the best-selling nonfiction books of all time. He also started a television program. Limbaugh's rhetoric—comparing feminists to Nazis, accusing Bill and Hillary Clinton of committing untold numbers of crimes—matched and encouraged McVeigh's views. McVeigh wrote to his boyhood friend Hodge, "As they say, 'Rush is right,' (double-meaning), and many people (opponents) consider his views extreme." McVeigh also helpfully informed Hodge of the local time and station for Limbaugh's television show.

Limbaugh's success persuaded McVeigh that there were lots of people who shared his own worldview. Later, McVeigh would talk about his belief that an "Army" of fellow believers was somewhere out there, but he admitted that he never figured out how to reach them. What McVeigh lacked was something that hadn't yet been invented. McVeigh needed the internet and social media—places where those of similarly extreme views could convene and plot together, as they did before January 6. Instead, McVeigh tried to use the analog tools of his time. He wrote letters—a handful to his local newspaper and his congressman and many to his friends, like Hodge, where he pressed his views. "What is it going to take to open up the eyes of our elected officials? AMERICA IS IN SERIOUS DECLINE. We have no proverbial tea to dump; should we instead sink a ship full of Japanese imports?" he wrote in a letter published in the *Lockport Union-Sun & Journal* on February 11, 1992. "Is a civil war imminent?" he continued. "Do we have to shed blood to reform the current system? I hope it doesn't come to that! But it might."

In June 1992, a restless McVeigh took a few days to drive to Decker, Michigan, to visit Nichols. They had not been in close touch since Terry left the service, but he welcomed McVeigh to the family farm. For McVeigh, the highlight of the trip was meeting Terry's brother James, who was as outspoken as Terry was withdrawn. James was big and bald; Terry was small, almost shrunken, and bespectacled. Like Terry, James became a kind of ideological tutor to McVeigh, introducing him to shortwave radio. James Nichols followed Mark Koernke, a University of Michigan custodian who was affiliated with the infant Michigan Militia—a paramilitary force that advocated armed defense against the government's incursions on their freedom. Neither James nor Terry ever formally joined what would become one of the biggest militias in the nation, but they shared most of the group's methods and agenda. (The influence of Koernke and the Michigan Militia endured for decades. In 2022, several members of the Michigan Militia were convicted in a plot to kidnap Gretchen Whitmer, the Democratic governor of Michigan. Koernke, who was still active in the movement, denounced the prosecution.) McVeigh never joined a militia, either, but after leaving Decker, he mailed away for membership in the Ku Klux Klan, which was then headquartered in Harrison, Arkansas.

James also introduced McVeigh to *The Spotlight*, and McVeigh became a subscriber and as dedicated a reader of that magazine as he was of *Soldier of Fortune*. Much later, McVeigh told his lawyers how much those publications meant to him. "In flipping through these items," he wrote in a letter, "you should realize that you are basically flipping through my world/my culture. This is the stuff I identify with—not just to look up to, like a fantasy—but stuff I know and live."

The Nichols brothers also introduced McVeigh to the first politician who ever drew his interest—Pat Buchanan, who was then waging a long-shot challenge to President George H. W. Bush in the 1992 Republican presidential primaries. Buchanan, whom Limbaugh endorsed, talked a lot about a concept that became central to McVeigh's world view, the New World Order. Bush had used the phrase in a speech, and Buchanan seized on it as a symbol of a purported desire to achieve a single global government. Buchanan saw in the New World Order an explanation for the decline that families like the McVeighs and Nicholses experienced—that shadowy elites, including the United Nations, were secretly manipulating events to their advantage. He found a receptive audience in men like McVeigh, who saw jobs like his father's going to foreign countries. McVeigh didn't think much about economics, but Buchanan's answer—protectionism—made sense to him.

Buchanan also made almost a fetish of gun rights—McVeigh's main cause—and the candidate even waved rifles at his rallies. Buchanan fancied himself a historian of sorts, and he was fond of comparing his own efforts with the rebellion of the Founding Fathers against the British—a trope that McVeigh would also employ. Considering the way Buchanan merged McVeigh's obsessions, it's no surprise that the young man was drawn to him. For Buchanan, like McVeigh, guns meant freedom. "What were the British coming for?" Buchanan said at one rally, where many attendees were armed. "The British were coming to capture the arsenal of the colonists, because before they could repress the colonists, they had to capture all their weapons and guns, and then they could put them under the boot of the British crown." Buchanan himself never came close to winning the presidency, but the appeal of his ideas—nationalistic, protectionist, gun-embracing—became central to Donald Trump's victory two decades later.

For McVeigh and others in the 1990s, it was expensive and inconvenient to steep themselves in right-wing extremism. They had to pay for magazine subscriptions; books like *The Turner Diaries* were available through advertisements in those magazines or at gun shows. Shortwave radio was a balky technology. (Rush Limbaugh, at least, was easy to locate on the radio dial.) In all, finding an education in this world took real commitment. Identifying a community of allies was even harder. Later, after McVeigh's time, the internet made it easy. The literature of the movement became simple to find with a few clicks on a computer or phone, and it was free. Social media, either through major platforms like Facebook or specialized sites like 4chan, allowed for instant connections with potential allies. (One study sponsored by the Department of Homeland Security found that social media was used in 90 percent of extremist plots in the United States.) More than any other reason, the internet accounts for the difference between McVeigh's lonely crusade and the thousands who stormed the Capitol on January 6, 2021.

In the fall of 1992, McVeigh finally moved out of his father's house and into a nearby apartment. His first purchase was a deluxe portable Radio Shack radio, which could receive ten shortwave bands, but only when the sun was down and reception was better. McVeigh became a devoted listener to William Cooper, a self-styled "patriot," whose program *The Hour of Our Time*, was broadcast out of his home in rural Arizona.

Cooper described himself as the head of an imaginary organization called the "Intelligence Service of the Second Continental Army of the Republic." Just as McVeigh always linked his own patriotism to the early days of the Republic, Cooper connected his "Army" to the Framers. He railed against the government's intrusions on the liberties that those patriots had fought for, chiefly the right to bear arms guaranteed by the Second Amendment. Later, Mike Fortier would give an interview to a right-wing newsletter, where he said, "There is this guy with a radio station in Arizona, Bill Cooper. He keeps calling people 'sheeple' and was mad that they ain't doing anything to change things. Well, we got to thinking, that's right, things need to change. Tim really responded to that." As McVeigh's travels increased in the year ahead, the Radio Shack radio, as well as Bill Cooper and Rush Limbaugh, were his constant companions.

The siege at Ruby Ridge—where an FBI sniper killed Randy Weaver's wife as she held their infant son—took place in August 1992, but it didn't come to McVeigh's attention until a couple of months later. "I read this Randy Weaver thing, and I said something is wrong here, so I think I went to shortwave to find out more," McVeigh told Jones. "So I started getting more of these publications, I looked into the back of *Spotlight*. I was starting to listen to daytime talk radio—Rush Limbaugh—started seeing most of their views were pretty much on track. Bought one of Limbaugh's books, sent it to my friend Steve [Hodge], who I could see was drifting in a liberal way, even though we had both been raised around guns."

Then, further disaster: on November 3, 1992, Bill Clinton was elected president of the United States. McVeigh was no fan of George H. W. Bush, but Clinton was a far measure worse. As 1992 drew to a close, nothing seemed to be going right. McVeigh had been promoted to an office job at Burns, but it only reminded him daily that Andrea was out of reach. He had no girlfriend and not much money. His letters to the editor, to the congressmen, and to his friends felt pointless. "I didn't have a love in my life. The job stresses were extremely high, political stuff was bothering me, where I was writing letters, and I really couldn't see a response," he told Jones. "I looked back through history and started studying literature I was getting from shortwave and *Spotlight*—and for a century people had been fooling themselves into seeing that a vote will help or writing letters will help."

In January 1993, the Buffalo Bills played their third straight Super Bowl. McVeigh again bet $1,000 on his team, and they lost, this time to the Dallas Cowboys. He was broke—and despondent and disgusted. A few days later, he decided that the time had come to settle his affairs in Buffalo. He quit his job at Burns and paid off his bookie. McVeigh hadn't settled on what to do next, but he started to disengage from the conventions of middle-class life. By this point, his friend Nichols had already been sued twice by credit card companies for running up $40,000 in charges he had no intention of repaying. (Nichols tried to defend himself with gibberish "constitutional" arguments that his brother James had fed to him. Terry lost the cases, but still refused to pay the damages.) Starting in 1993, McVeigh headed down the same path, walking out on about $10,000 in credit card charges. Both men used their cards to purchase gold bars, which they sold over time to raise cash. As 1993 began, McVeigh had $6,000 in gold bars, $3,000 in cash, and $6,000 in guns and ammunition. He sold almost all his other possessions (except the shortwave radio) and kept only what would fit in the Road Warrior. Whatever came next in his life was going to be different.

"So, I decided to hit the road and see what else was out there," McVeigh said.

CHAPTER 5

"They're Killing Feds. They Must Be Doing Something Right."

Shortly before McVeigh left the Buffalo area, he stopped in to see his friend Carl Lebron, a fellow supervisor at the Burns Security office. Lebron knew McVeigh was coming, so he planned ahead. He slipped a microcassette recorder into the pocket of his windbreaker. "I thought something was not right and wanted him to say what he was up to," Lebron later told the FBI. "It was bothering me what he was talking about."

McVeigh's dark hints about his plans and state of mind unnerved Lebron. It wasn't that Lebron was a liberal outraged by McVeigh's politics; far from it. The two men struck up their friendship when McVeigh noticed that Lebron brought a copy of *National Review*, the conservative magazine, to work one day. McVeigh was vague about his views, but Lebron sensed the darkness within him. *The government was going to take our guns. The banks are secretly in charge of the economy. UFOs are real.* (UFOs were a particular obsession of Bill Cooper's, McVeigh's shortwave favorite.) But what really concerned

Lebron was that McVeigh was itching to act. He was going to do . . . something. At one point, McVeigh had scolded Lebron, "This is just a hobby for you, reading these books. You're stomping your feet, but you're not *doing* anything about it." McVeigh, the implication seemed to be, would.

So, on Sunday, January 24, 1993, Lebron pressed record.

The previous week, just before Clinton was inaugurated, the Senate Judiciary Committee had held a hearing on the new president's choice to be attorney general, Zoë Baird. By that point, *The New York Times* had broken the story that Baird and her husband had hired a family nanny who was illegally in the United States. Baird had sought to explain the problem, but McVeigh was not impressed—because Rush Limbaugh wasn't. "Do you know what that Zoë Baird chick said—watch Limbaugh," McVeigh told Lebron as the tape rolled. "'I put my husband in charge of hiring the people to take care of my kids.' She testified that he didn't do a good job. Rush Limbaugh says, 'If that would have been a man up on the stand, and he woulda said, I put my wife in charge and she didn't handle it, he would have been laughed out of that courtroom. But a woman, hey, that's okay.'"

Limbaugh's dig resonated with McVeigh because it spoke to a broader complaint that he, and many others, had about the state of American society. Women like Baird were getting special privileges and dispensations that men like McVeigh were now denied. In McVeigh's view, the Baird story was like what was happening in the Army, where women were being allowed to serve without proving themselves the equal of men. It also resembled the reason the Marshals Service rejected McVeigh's job application and the Army didn't send him to sniper school. Black people were jumping the line ahead of white males like McVeigh. The world he once knew—the one where Tim's father walked into the same steady job in the same factory where his own father used to work—had vanished. For people like McVeigh, the pie was shrinking. And he blamed the government—especially the federal government—for reserving the best jobs for women and Blacks. Changes in gender, race, and the economy had undermined McVeigh's status in the world. He thought it was maddening that so many people out there couldn't see what was right in front of them. As McVeigh put it in a letter to his friend Steve Hodge, "Jesus, man, wake up!" But McVeigh was determined to be something more than "sheeple," Bill Cooper's neologism for human sheep. McVeigh would figure out a way to force the world to pay attention.

The recorded conversation between McVeigh and Lebron went on for thirty-one minutes. It meandered through the latest office gossip. (McVeigh said one colleague "has a little bit of Jew in him.") McVeigh complained about the Federal Reserve. "I believe if the American people knew what the banking system was, there would be a revolution by tomorrow morning," he said. As a result, McVeigh said he had cut his own ties with banks. He told Lebron that he had converted the money from his credit cards into gold bars, and that's the last his creditors would hear of him. "I've dropped out of the, uh, system. I didn't exist. The IRS didn't exist. AT&T didn't already exist."

McVeigh had told Lebron about his visits to the Nichols brothers, so Lebron asked if he was going to see them in Michigan. No, McVeigh said. "That's my mail drop, and I only walk in every few months to get my mail. That's the only way they can trace me."

In all, on this occasion, McVeigh never said anything specifically incriminating, so Lebron threw the tape in a drawer and basically forgot about it.

Asked later if he knew where McVeigh was going after their conversation in 1993, Lebron said he had no idea.

Over the next two-plus years, the Road Warrior—the Chevy Geo Spectrum with the turbocharged engine—was, in every real sense, McVeigh's home. For as much as a couple of months at a time, he made stops—in Michigan, in Arizona, in Kansas. But he was mostly on the road, alone with his thoughts and, for three hours a day, Rush Limbaugh. McVeigh was always a rather shy person, and he made few connections during his travels. But he took careful note of the people he did meet, and he sometimes reached back out to them months or even years later. For this reason, McVeigh's casual encounters on the road took on an unexpected significance.

Where was McVeigh going? And what did he want? On one level, he just drifted among the handful of people who would take him in. But there was also a terrible kind of momentum to his travels as the failures, frustrations, and outrages built up within him. What made McVeigh different from so many others who faced disappointments in their lives was that he became ever more determined to strike back.

In the meantime, in January 1993, he headed first to Florida—a common enough destination for Buffalonians in the middle of winter. McVeigh drove 1,400 miles to Fort Lauderdale, where his brother-in-law was running his contracting business. (McVeigh could cover so much ground because, as he later told his attorney Jones, he could drive for three straight days and nights without falling asleep at the wheel. All he needed was a supply of Rolaids and Pepto Bismol, because his diet of fast food ruined his digestion.) His older sister let McVeigh stay in a house they were vacating and gave him some construction work at $10 an hour. Characteristically, though, McVeigh was discontented after only a few weeks. As he recounted to Jones, his brother-in-law "appreciated how quickly I was able to pick up on the skills I needed, but I wasn't fitting in down there. It was in the Miami area, and it was even worse than Buffalo as far as traffic and rude people. A couple of times I almost smashed into people because they pissed me off so bad."

Shortly after McVeigh arrived in Florida, he set up a small booth at a gun show in Fort Lauderdale. He had a vague plan to try to make a living this way, but he had a very limited amount of material to sell—no guns, a little bit of ammunition, canteens, duffel bags, T-shirts, bumper stickers, and a big stack of *The Turner Diaries*. (He sent a price list to Steve Hodge with the message, "I'm trying to recoup some of my Superbowl bet losses!") Despite the modest inventory, McVeigh drew attention because he showed up in his Army camouflage uniform. He still had his crew cut, polished boots, and military bearing, and he told anyone who asked that he was a Desert Storm veteran, which was still a novelty at the time.

One shopper, who identified himself as Bob Miller, struck up a conversation with McVeigh. He was impressed with McVeigh's service in the war and because of his shabby merchandise, Miller felt kind of sorry for him, so he bought an electric clock in the shape of Texas for five dollars. As it happened, Miller said he was a part-time dealer as well, and he asked McVeigh if he wanted to share a table at another gun show in Coconut Grove. They did, and Miller made a confession. That name was just one he used at gun shows. He didn't want people tracking him down. Bob Miller's real name was Roger Moore. They agreed, in a casual way, to stay in touch. Moore was the first of McVeigh's road acquaintances who would come to play a significant, if unintentional, role in the Oklahoma City bombing.

In the meantime, McVeigh's Florida sojourn continued to go poorly. "Stresses were building up," he said. Between the new job and the gun shows, McVeigh hadn't been able to pay as much attention to the news as usual. Then, gradually, he became involved in the story that would change his life. "One night, I'm watching the news, and there is a raid in Waco. And at that time, I was so wrapped up in the job, and I wasn't really watching the news too much, once a night, but I had put it out of my mind. And then this Waco story hit me again."

"This Waco story" had deep roots. The Branch Davidians, a messianic offshoot of the Seventh-day Adventist church, was founded in 1959 and established a headquarters on a hilltop they christened Mount Carmel, near Waco, Texas. Over the years, the sect went through several power struggles and leadership changes. In 1987, a young man named Vernon Howell confronted the leadership of the group, and a gun battle ensued. Howell and seven of his allies were charged with attempted murder. Seven were acquitted, and the jury hung on Howell. The state chose not to retry him. In 1990, Vernon Howell legally changed his name to David Koresh.

Koresh cut an eccentric figure as a leader, but he drew little attention outside Waco. He separated husbands and wives and decreed that only he should procreate with the women. He predicted an apocalyptic end for life on earth. He decreed that the group's compound be built out of cheap plywood, because Jesus was returning soon and the walls wouldn't have to last long. Local news reports accused Koresh of statutory rape with children in the compound and asserted that the group had accumulated a stash of illegal weapons. This claim drew the attention of the Bureau of Alcohol, Tobacco and Firearms, which obtained a search warrant for the Mount Carmel property and an arrest warrant for Koresh on weapons charges. A local reporter who had been tipped about the raid asked a letter carrier for directions to the compound. The fellow happened to be Koresh's brother-in-law, so he gave Koresh, who was just thirty-three years old at the time, advance notice that federal agents would storm the place on the morning of February 28, 1993. The ATF assault was a fiasco. Four federal agents were killed, and sixteen were wounded; five Branch Davidians were killed and many more wounded during a two-and-a-half-hour gun battle. Koresh refused to surrender, and the FBI was brought in to try to bring him out. A siege, and a national news phenomenon, began.

The story had clear parallels to the Randy Weaver saga in Ruby Ridge, which had drawn McVeigh's attention when he was still in New York. "This Waco story hit me again, and Randy Weaver flashed in my head," McVeigh said. As he saw it, the feds had preyed on a group of outsiders who were minding their own business. The only crime that Weaver and Koresh had committed was owning their own weapons, which McVeigh believed was protected under the Second Amendment. The Weaver raid, back in August 1992, was bad enough, but now Clinton was president, and the Democrats were in charge. McVeigh's views about federal law enforcement hardened into a sinister anger. Recalling the TV scenes of the initial Waco raid, McVeigh said, "I saw the guys climbing on the roof and falling down, and I remember turning to my sister and she said something like, 'Oh, that's terrible.' And I said, 'Well, okay, they're killing feds. They must be doing something right.'"

McVeigh followed the news coverage for the next few days and then made a decision. "I wasn't finding myself in Florida," he said. "I was getting caught in the same old thing, not being happy where I was. So, I hit the road again." He got in the Road Warrior and drove the 1,300 miles from Fort Lauderdale to Waco to see for himself.

Michelle Rauch became perhaps the unlikeliest figure to find herself, years later, a witness at McVeigh's trial. In 1993, she was a twenty-two-year-old senior at Southern Methodist University, in Dallas. She was a reporter for *The Daily Campus*, the school paper, and she was itching to cover a big story. The siege at the Branch Davidian outpost was continuing day after day, and the press contingent in Waco was growing. Bob Ricks, an FBI agent, was giving daily briefings to the news media, but Rauch figured there must be more to the story. She asked her faculty adviser for permission to miss classes to go to Waco, which was a couple of hours away. He said no. So, she waited until spring break and convinced a friend to come along. Rauch had no press pass, so she improvised. She had an NBC luggage tag from her time as a summer intern at the local affiliate, and her friend had a pass to a Dallas Cowboys parade.

Just before Rauch and her friend reached the checkpoint to approach the compound, she noticed a handful of people on a small hilltop. Rauch had a nose for news, so she strolled over to talk to one of them. He was a tall, skinny man in rugged blue jeans, a plaid shirt, and a camouflage Army cap. He was selling bumper stickers that were arrayed on the hood of his car. FEAR THE GOVERNMENT THAT FEARS YOUR GUN. A MAN WITHOUT A GUN IS NOT A CITIZEN. He told Rauch that his name was Tim McVeigh. "I was out here to make a statement," he told her. A hand-lettered sign said the stickers were $1.50 a piece or four for $5.00. Business was slow.

As Rauch later reported in her story for the SMU paper, "McVeigh said he believes the government is greatly at fault in Waco and has broken constitutional laws. 'The government is afraid of the guns people have, because they have to have control of the people all the time. Once you take away the guns, you can do anything to the people,' he said." McVeigh's comments to Rauch represented an almost perfect distillation of his political philosophy, one with both deep roots and enduring appeal to many Americans. He regarded guns as instruments of freedom and any attempt to regulate them, especially by the federal government, as a form of oppression.

If anything, McVeigh downplayed his fury in his interview with Rauch. He wanted to get closer to the scene at Mount Carmel, but he was stopped at the checkpoint, about five miles away. "I just got incensed," he later told Jones. "How can these federal authorities just come into this state and close down roads at their whim and just take over?" After a couple of days at Waco, he decided to head west, to visit his Army friend Mike Fortier, in Kingman, Arizona.

The choice illustrated how small McVeigh's world was. Fortier was hardly a close friend. In the two years since Fortier left the Army, he had never seen McVeigh in person and rarely heard from him. But even though McVeigh had only a vague sense that Fortier had guns that McVeigh could sell at gun shows, he left Waco and drove the 1,100 miles to Fortier's mobile home in Kingman. McVeigh didn't have a lot of friends or a lot of options.

Fortier lived with his girlfriend, Lori, and they both had the long-haired, loosed-limbed look of surfers, even though they both grew up in the dusty confines of Kingman. Mike roughly shared McVeigh's politics, if only in the same lackadaisical way that he did most things. Mike and Lori were more interested in getting high than changing the world. Their political activities amounted to little more than raising the yellow Gadsden flag with the coiled rattlesnake and the words DON'T TREAD ON ME outside their home. Crystal meth was their drug of choice, and conveniently, their dealer lived next door. Mike had worked for a time in the lumberyard of the True Value hardware store in town, but he hurt his back and moved to an office job.

Fortier didn't even show up for work all that often, and as McVeigh later reported to his lawyers, with some amusement, "Mike and Lori mostly watched talk shows all day long." Their politics chiefly manifested itself as a kind of free-floating paranoia, often involving government surveillance. They did what they called "porch trolling." They turned off all the lights in the house, went to the porch, and watched the neighborhood with binoculars and a scanner. When McVeigh visited, they told him that stationary objects in the sky were spy satellites. They also used their daughter, a toddler named Kayla, to demonstrate their antiauthoritarian politics. Mike and Lori watched the television show *Cops*, which often showed the police breaking down doors and the like. On these occasions, they taught Kayla to say, "Bad cops! Bad cops!" They were among her first words.

Fortier didn't have much to sell at gun shows, and McVeigh, restless as always, only stayed in Arizona for a few days. He decided to drive 1,100 miles to go to Wanenmacher's, in Tulsa, which billed itself as the world's largest gun and knife show, to meet like-minded souls and see what he could buy and sell. As would become clearer in the months ahead, McVeigh was naturally reticent, even awkward, in these settings, and he had trouble making connections, especially since he didn't have a booth. Still, he ran into someone he knew—

Roger Moore, also known as Bob Miller, whom he had met at the gun shows in Florida. Miller's companion, Karen Anderson, chatted with McVeigh and felt sorry for him. As far as Moore and Anderson knew, McVeigh was making a threadbare existence at gun shows and mostly sleeping in his car. Moore later testified before the grand jury, "He seemed poor. And I had felt that I was very lucky to make the money and have the breaks that I had. So, she said, 'Do you mind if I invite him over for a couple of days?'" Moore said that would be fine. Moore and Anderson generally spent half the year on a ten-acre ranch in Royal, Arkansas, and McVeigh followed them on the 250-mile drive to their home on April 11, 1993. They arrived late at night, and McVeigh had one task to complete before he went to bed. He turned on his shortwave radio, found a stepladder, and used an alligator clip to attach an aerial to the gutter of Moore's house, to get better reception for Bill Cooper's nightly program of right-wing paranoia.

Roger Moore was born in 1934 and made his fortune during the Vietnam War. In 1966, he started a company in Florida that manufactured thirty-six-foot fiberglass patrol boats for the Navy. Over the next decade, he bought and sold five companies that did the same kind of work. He made enough on the deals so that, by the late 1970s, he never had to work again. He turned instead to his hobby—ammunition. He started a business called the American Assault Company (which was also known as the Candy Store), and he traveled the gun show circuit. He sold what is known as specialty ammunition, including tracer and incendiary rounds, as well as the dummy explosives used by paramilitary groups in training.

Moore led an unconventional life. He lived half the year with his wife, Carol Moore, in Florida, and half with his friend Karen Anderson, on the ranch in Arkansas. (The nature of his relationship with

Anderson was unclear.) As the FBI reported in its interview with Carol Moore, "she and Anderson are total opposites. Anderson is the outdoors type and really enjoys the ranch in Arkansas, whereas she [Carol Moore] does not enjoy the outdoors nor does she enjoy the lifestyle the ranch has to offer. Moore stated she and Anderson may be opposites, but they do get along very well and even take trips together." Roger Moore was a gun collector, as well as a dealer, and he kept a large stash of gold and silver bars as well as cash on the premises in Arkansas.

Roger Moore thought McVeigh would help around the ranch, but McVeigh didn't seem interested in doing chores. They talked politics, and McVeigh told Moore that he had visited Waco, to register his outrage at the government's conduct. Moore's views were fairly similar to McVeigh's, but he had no interest in those kinds of field trips. "You're nuts," he told McVeigh. "I wouldn't go near there with a ten-foot pole." After only a day, McVeigh became uncomfortable around the couple, and he may have worn out his welcome as well. As he later told his lawyer Stephen Jones, Moore was "exceedingly interested in only the money. Didn't give a damn about why he was selling it or what other people thought. He was preaching freedom and the freedom to sell, but in the end he was a dictator himself. He was kind of a prick."

It may be, of course, that Moore was kind of a prick. But he was another successful person, like McVeigh's brother-in-law and the new arrivals in Lockport, whom McVeigh disdained. McVeigh resented anyone who was making it in the new world. He had only arrived in Arkansas on Sunday night, but he suddenly announced midday Tuesday that he was leaving. Karen Anderson gave him $50 for the road. "I left from there determined that this wasn't the place to be," McVeigh said. Still, he would long remember that Moore kept a stash of riches—weapons, gold, and cash—in a house with little security.

McVeigh decided to next go to what he called his "mail drop" at the Nicholses' farm. He made an overnight stop at a motel in Junction

City, Kansas, next to Fort Riley, and then completed the thousand-mile journey to Decker, Michigan.

It was now mid-April 1993, and the siege at Waco had been going on since February 28. The FBI had cut all phone lines to the compound, except those used for negotiations with Koresh. He, in turn, demanded that one of his speeches be played on the radio to the public (it was), and he spent long hours berating the negotiators on the phone. A handful of followers were released over the first few days of the siege, but still about a hundred remained inside. All power in the compound was cut on March 8, restored the next day, and then cut for good on March 12. On March 22, to force a surrender, the FBI began playing loud music and noise around the clock, including Tibetan chants, rabbits being killed, Nancy Sinatra singing "These Boots Are Made for Walkin'," Mitch Miller Christmas carols, telephones ringing, and reveilles. Nothing worked. An impatient press corps asked increasingly hostile questions at the daily briefings. "We are going to get them . . . to bring them before the bar of justice for the murder of our agents," Bob Ricks, the FBI spokesman, said. "They're going to answer for their crimes. That's the bottom line to this whole thing, they're going to come out."

By the time McVeigh arrived at the Nichols farm, he was seething about the situation in Waco, and so were Terry and James. "We are saying, 'What is going on? People are just allowing this to happen,'" McVeigh recalled for Jones. "Our anger increased every time we heard something on the news, like, well, the federal government decided to employ psychological warfare today, they are blasting sound at these people's house, there are women and children there, they are keeping the lights on all night, they won't allow communication with the outside world.

"It's common sense—at least to me it was—that when you look at their place, it's their home," McVeigh went on. "They didn't ask these agents to come out to their home. Nothing could stop the federal juggernaut from taking these people in custody."

What could be done? McVeigh had a dispiriting memory of his own short visit to the scene at Waco. "I told them when I was down there, no one else was down there rallying," he said. He recalled that there was a crazy woman who had made a cross out of railroad ties and yelled, "This is the beast" at a government helicopter. Yes, she was a wacko, McVeigh told Terry Nichols, but she may have had a point. "The helicopter represented the federal government, which represented evil—not good, evil. Maybe not in the biblical sense she took it, but to me as the oppressors," he said.

So, McVeigh and Terry decided to make a stand. "Me and Terry decided to go down there, and maybe hook up with other people that may be down there," he said. "We had no way of knowing, but any action is better than no action."

The following morning, McVeigh was changing the oil on the Road Warrior in preparation for another long drive, this time a return to Waco, when Terry rushed out of the house and screamed for McVeigh to come inside and see what was on television.

It was April 19, 1993.

CHAPTER 6

"The First Blood of War . . . WACO"

Terry Nichols's life continued its downward spiral in the months after his marriage to Marife Torres, his mail-order bride. Lana Padilla, his ex-wife, had remarried and moved with their son, Josh, to Las Vegas. Terry and Marife tried to make another start there as well. Like Terry's first attempt in Vegas, this one ended in failure. However, while they were in Nevada, Marife gave birth to the baby she had conceived with another man in the Philippines. On September 21, 1991, Jason Torres Nichols was born, and Terry agreed to raise him as his son. But with no good options in Las Vegas, Terry, Marife, and Jason returned to the Nichols family farm in Decker, Michigan, as 1992 began.

After Nichols left the military, his politics had become more extreme, but in a somewhat different way than McVeigh's did. Nichols belonged to a distinctly rural tradition of right-wing extremism, which emerged from the enduring conflicts between farmers and banks. For generations, farmers have required loans to survive; their revenue typically comes in only during harvest season, so they need to borrow money during the rest of the year. This, of course, leads to conflict when farmers have trouble paying back their loans. In bad times, either because of economic conditions or ruinous weather, foreclosures abound. These legal proceedings—when banks go to court to seize family farms—are the focus of tremendous anger in agricultural communities.

This was especially true in Michigan. Thanks to creeping suburbanization, the value of land kept rising, which generally only meant higher taxes for small farmers. The prices of machinery, feed, and chemicals rose as well. So did the cost of complying with environmental regulations, which always expanded when Democrats were in office. In light of these challenges, many farmers simply gave up. Between 1985 and 2000, Michigan acreage lost to farming totaled more than the size of Rhode Island.

The Nichols brothers didn't give up: they fought back. Their rage manifested itself in a series of actions that were roughly associated with what was known as the Posse Comitatus movement, which asserted that the only legitimate form of American government was at the county level. To followers, the federal government was the enemy, largely because it served the interests of the banks and bankers (who were invariably described as Jewish). The first martyr in their cause was a North Dakota farmer named Gordon Kahl, who believed that Jewish bankers had extended loans to him knowing that he would default. In other words, he was a victim of a conspiracy, which included the federal government, to steal his land. In protest, he stopped paying federal taxes, and the Justice Department prosecuted and convicted him in 1977. While out on parole, Kahl killed two U.S. marshals who were investigating him. Later, in 1983, he was tracked down in Arkansas and died in a shootout with law enforcement agents. (*The Spotlight*, the favorite magazine of both the Nicholses and McVeigh, published articles for years lionizing Kahl and denouncing the federal agents who killed him.)

Kahl's heir in Michigan was Mark Koernke, the janitor at the university in Ann Arbor, who had established a shortwave presence as "Mark from Michigan." Koernke focused less on religion than Kahl—both his own and that of his enemies—but he was ferocious in his condemnation of the federal government, especially Democrats. Koernke adapted the Posse Comitatus message into one focused on advocacy for militias, private paramilitary organizations that would fight the predations of the federal government. In the early 1990s, Koernke was part of a swirl of activity on the extreme right, which included the founding of several militia groups in Michigan. There were multiple internal rivalries and factions—Koernke himself was not associated with the group that called itself the Michigan Militia—but the number of people involved kept growing. The militias were lauded in the right-wing press. "Citizen Soldiers: Fighting for the Right to Defend America," read the headline of one story in *Soldier of Fortune*. "Federal Power Abuses Spark Militias," read another in *The Spotlight*.

The rise of the militia movement in Michigan revealed another difference between McVeigh and the Nichols brothers. By temperament and choice, McVeigh was a loner, who confided his views and plans to only a handful of people. James and Terry Nichols were part of a genuine political and paramilitary faction in their home state. The precise contours of their involvement with the militias remain somewhat unclear; they appear never to have formally joined the Michigan Militia or any other such organization. But both Terry and James Nichols went to meetings, communicated with fellow members, listened to the same programs, and read the same publications. (McVeigh told Stephen Jones that he never went to a militia meeting in Michigan, but that he watched videotapes of meetings that James brought home; McVeigh said the meetings were boring and the members were "all talk.") By the mid-1990s, the militias claimed twelve thousand members in Michigan. That number was probably exaggerated, but it's still likely that there were thousands of people in Michigan who shared the Nicholses' thinking. The militia members were never a proletarian army, made up of a revolutionary lower class. In the mid-1990s and into the Trump era, they were like Nichols and McVeigh—middle-class, if tenuously so, small-business owners, struggling farmers. It was not a movement of people trying to overthrow the power structure, but rather one of people trying to hang on to their role in it.

Before Terry joined the Army, he was very much under the thumb of his older brother. But the Terry Nichols of 1992 was his own man, with his own anger and approach to the crises in his life. At one point, Terry thought he could start a new life with Marife in the Philippines, and they packed up their belongings and moved. But that experiment lasted only a month; Terry was outraged that the Filipinos thought he was rich just because he was an American. Back in Michigan, his economic problems mounted. He had always lived modestly, but the trips to the Philippines were expensive. He ran up about $60,000 in charges on various credit cards, and he used the incoherent rhetoric of the movement to excuse his debt. When Chase Manhattan Bank sued him for $19,739 in delinquent credit card payments, Terry appeared in court to defend himself, and his words were preserved on tape. "For the record, I appear here as a common law individual," he said. "Should the court insist that I answer any questions, I will only do so under duress, threat and intimidation. Doesn't the Constitution of the United States and the constitution of the state of Michigan hold any water in this court?" The court ruled that he had to pay, but Terry didn't.

At around the same time, Terry wrote a letter to a county clerk in Michigan renouncing his U.S. citizenship and returning his voter registration card. He was a "sovereign citizen," which was a term used by right-wing extremists of the era, based on a crackpot view of the Constitution that allowed them to avoid paying their debts and taxes. He said "the entire political system" was corrupt and declared himself a "nonresident alien, non-foreigner, stranger to the current state of the forum.” The language was drawn from various right-wing sources associated with Posse Comitatus. (Terry renounced his citizenship again in a letter to a judge a few months later.) Around the same time, James Nichols also appeared in court and renounced his citizenship, to avoid paying child support. When the judge threatened to jail him, James changed his mind and paid.

James was the real farmer in the family, and Terry helped out as much as he was able. He did odd jobs in the area but never held a steady job in Michigan. Like McVeigh, Terry nursed his grievances over long nights listening to the shortwave. This unsettled existence was why he had the time to head down to Waco with Tim. McVeigh's roots may have been in the economic wreckage of the industrial North, and Nichols's worldview was shaped by the farm crisis, but Waco tapped into their shared obsessions. The siege there reminded the two men of everything they loathed about the federal government—its arrogance, its oppressive power, its threat to private gun ownership. The long standoff at Mount Carmel seemed destined to end in a cataclysm. So, the two men were already outraged and ready for battle when Terry called McVeigh away from his oil change on April 19, 1993.

By this point, there were nine hundred law enforcement officials gathered outside David Koresh's complex in Waco. Scores of FBI and ATF agents mingled with Texas Rangers, National Guard troops, and local cops, as well as federal, state, and local prosecutors. All of them seethed with frustration and embarrassment as Koresh defied them. The scene outside the walls of the compound was under the control of law enforcement, but it looked more like a military occupation. There were seven Bradley Fighting Vehicles (McVeigh's former bailiwick) and two Abrams battle tanks, along with scores of other formidable vehicles, including four Combat Engineer Vehicles (CEVs). Three UH-60 Black Hawk helicopters monitored the scene from the air. (The siege was costing the government about $128,000 per day.) After the gun battle on February 28, federal officials knew that the Davidians were also heavily armed, with several automatic and semiautomatic weapons as well as night vision equipment. It was later established that Koresh had assembled more than a million rounds of ammunition.

The FBI officials in charge of the siege didn't have a lot of good options. The Davidians had 360-degree vision around their compound, with the potential to respond to any direct attacks. Individuals who had been released earlier in the siege said that there were many, perhaps dozens, of children inside. And there had long been unsubstantiated reports that Koresh was abusing the children, who clearly had no choice but to remain. On the other hand, the status of the adults was unclear. Were they Koresh's allies—or his hostages? And what about the possibility of a mass suicide, like the one in Jonestown, Guyana, two decades earlier? The situation was, as one leading FBI official on the scene put it, "a shit sandwich."

In mid-April, there were a series of meetings in Washington where the leadership of the Justice Department, including the new attorney general, Janet Reno, decided that the siege had to conclude. To that end, the agents on the ground came up with a plan to use CS gas, which is a supposedly nonlethal, nonflammable form of tear gas. (The Los Angeles police used CS gas during its 1974 showdown with the Symbionese Liberation Army, which had kidnapped Patty Hearst. That confrontation ended in a fire that killed six SLA members.) The FBI plan in Waco was to introduce the liquid CS into the compound in stages, one section at a time. This "restrained response" was designed to allow the Davidians ready access to other exits or unaffected areas.

At 5:55 a.m., on April 19, the fifty-first day of the siege, the first two Combat Engineer Vehicles advanced on the compound. The CEVs looked like tanks, and they were equipped with battering rams, to clear the way to the main building. On a loudspeaker, an agent began reading a speech that began "We are in the process of placing tear gas into the building. This is not an assault." Soon after a mechanical arm began pumping in the tear gas, the CEVs faced weapons fire from inside the building. Once the Davidians started shooting, the FBI escalated its plans. Though the agents never returned the gunfire, they used the seven Bradleys to launch canisters of tear gas into the building. For six hours, there was a kind of standoff; gunfire from the Davidians, more tear gas shells from the FBI.

Then, at 12:09 p.m., there were the first signs of flames inside the compound. Nine people, all adults, ran out of the building. In just two minutes, the fire, whipped by high winds, turned into a torrent, consuming the entire building. By the time the first firefighting units arrived, at 12:41 p.m., the compound had burned to the ground. Seventy-six bodies, including those of twenty-five children, were found in the wreckage of the compound. There were no survivors.

On that day, McVeigh was at the Nicholses' farm in Michigan, preparing to return to his vigil at Waco. "I was changing my oil in my car, getting ready for the trip, when it came on the radio, the place was burning down," McVeigh told Jones, "and I remember tears came into my eyes. And someone came out of the house and said, 'They've got it on TV, come in here, Tim,' and I ran in, and she's burning, and no one is doing anything. There's no fire equipment. They are just standing there, watching it burn."

The Davidians' flag, which resembled the Star of David, had flown over the compound throughout the siege. "The flag is flying and in maybe only ten minutes—it seemed like an hour, but it was probably only ten minutes—the flag finally broke free. And that was like more symbolism than you could have planned, the flag blew away," McVeigh said. Shortly thereafter, the law enforcement agents raised an American flag, a Texas flag, and a flag bearing the initials ATF on the charred flagpole. "Sure enough, the A.T.F. goes in and raises their flag over the ruins. Great, there are a bunch of charred babies laying there and you raised your flag—you conquered a lot, buddy. So, this just pretty much hammered me down, that I was going to do whatever I could to wake people up, and help people fight, because this is wrong," McVeigh told Jones.

McVeigh's reaction to Waco exceeded mere political outrage and became a psychological obsession. Over the next two years, he wrote dozens of letters to friends and family and invoked Waco in many of them. (He often mentioned his horror at the deaths of babies and children.) McVeigh ordered videotapes, books, and magazines about Waco, and he absorbed them all and often sent them on to others. As he wrote to his friend Steve Hodge, it was "that event which in my mind is the straw that broke the back of Lady Liberty, and drew the first blood of war, no longer of peacetime—WACO."

McVeigh had a lot of company in the conservative movement in his obsession with Waco. Among many on the right, it was widely viewed as decisive proof of the perfidy of the new Clinton administration. On April 21, Limbaugh referred to "the Waco invasion as orchestrated by this administration. Here is this administration's full-fledged character on display." (Limbaugh would always refer to the event as "the Waco invasion.") *The Spotlight* covered the story repeatedly, with headlines like "Government Villainy at Waco Surfaces" and "Protesters Plea: Don't Forget Waco." G. Gordon Liddy, the Watergate felon who became a national radio talk show host, was even more frenzied. Regarding ATF agents, Liddy advised his listeners to "kill the sons of bitches." He went on, "If the Bureau of Alcohol, Tobacco and Firearms comes to disarm you and they are bearing arms, resist them with arms. Go for a head shot; they're going to be wearing bulletproof vests."

Another extreme voice on the subject was William Cooper, McVeigh's shortwave favorite. He became nearly as obsessed with Waco as McVeigh was, and Cooper all but taunted his audience to act against the government. "Are you going to stand up on your own two feet, like a real man?" he said at one point. "How many more people are you going to allow to be jailed, persecuted, burned to death, murdered, because you are a coward? And that's basically what it boils down to, isn't it? Cowardice." In a way that few could imagine, McVeigh took up Cooper's challenge.

The Justice Department commissioned former senator John Danforth to conduct an independent investigation of the Waco siege, and he acknowledged that the standoff at Mount Carmel was "unprecedented in the annals of American law enforcement. . . . Never before have so many heavily armed and totally committed individuals barricaded themselves in a fortified compound in a direct challenge to lawful federal warrants." The FBI negotiated at length with Koresh, in 117 conversations that took place over sixty hours. Obviously, in retrospect, the Bureau should have kept talking, because the outcome was a humanitarian and law enforcement disaster. Still, it became an article of faith for McVeigh and his allies to assert that the denouement at Waco was worse than a blunder; it was an intentional crime of mass murder.

Not long after the fire, a right-wing documentarian named Linda Thompson produced a film called *Waco, the Big Lie.* McVeigh watched the videocassette many times and often referred to it in his letters. Thompson's key claim was that one of the Combat Engineer Vehicles used a flamethrower to intentionally start the fire that demolished the building. Danforth's report refuted that claim; the fire started nowhere near that CEV, which had no flamethrower anyway. Moreover, audiotapes from inside the compound, as well as an arson investigation, suggested that the Davidians themselves started the fire as part of a mass suicide. In addition, since at least seventeen of the seventy-six victims had been shot, and the FBI fired no weapons, that, too, suggests that the Davidians caused many of the deaths themselves. None of this excuses the FBI's tragic misjudgments, but it does offer some balance and perspective. McVeigh never acknowledged that Koresh himself bore considerable responsibility for the deaths at Mount Carmel.

For McVeigh and many others, the Waco raid became a turning point. It confirmed every dark suspicion they had about Bill Clinton's federal government. After the conflagration, McVeigh and Nichols chose not to go to Waco after all, but they had to decide what to do instead. McVeigh came up with at least an interim solution. As he told Stephen Jones, "Back in Michigan, I decide to do something. Well, what can we do, what is in our power to change things? We can mass copy letters and send them to representatives as well as people. We tried that, but we will continue to do that, even though it has had no effect. But maybe the key is the gun show circuit."

It was a reasonable choice on McVeigh's part. If he was looking for kindred spirits in the aftermath of Waco, the gun show circuit was his best bet.

The phrase "gun show" was almost misleading. The circuit consisted of mass events that resembled conventions more than flea markets. Some events featured thousands of distributors and tens of thousands of attendees. At these events, licensed gun dealers—commercial establishments—had to record and report all sales, but private dealers like McVeigh could buy and sell without any reporting to the government. (This was known as the "gun show loophole"; it still exists.) The exhibitors sold new, used, and antique firearms, ammunition, shooting supplies, knives, scopes, clips, reloading supplies, holsters, carry cases, hunting gear, concealment products, gun apparel, knives, tasers, stun guns, and pepper sprays, among other things.

Gun shows were also cultural events as much as commercial enterprises. They were celebrations of the gun as both a weapon and a symbol of political allegiance. Attendees were welcome to bring their own guns, though the weapons were supposed to be unloaded. "Guards can hold your ammo at the door so you don't have to walk through the parking lot unarmed," read the rules at the Wanenmacher extravaganza in Tulsa. At the big ones, there were explicitly political events, like panel discussions on such subjects as "What Do Bill and Hillary Have in Store for Gun Owners During a Second Term?" and "The Future of Militias: What Will the Feds Do?" Overall, as one study observed, "Political activities at gun shows represent views that start at the conservative and move right from there." The causes promoted at gun shows only began with Second Amendment rights, and they included closing the borders, avoiding taxes, and defending the rights of Christians. Confederate flags and memorabilia abounded. So did right-wing literature.

McVeigh was reticent and secretive by nature, but he felt at home at gun shows. (He later told his lawyers that he had been to gun shows in thirty states.) Sometimes he just prowled the aisles and sought to make deals with distributors at the tables, but more often he'd spend $50 or so and rent his own table. His inventory was never large or elaborate, mostly clothing and accessories. The one constant of McVeigh's sale items was *The Turner Diaries.* He bought copies by the box from the publisher; if any were left over at the end of a show, he'd just give them away. Later, when McVeigh would tell his lawyers there were potential allies out there, he based his view on what he saw at the gun shows—where thousands came not just for firearms, but for political solidarity. And that didn't even count all his fellow listeners to Limbaugh and Bill Cooper. But, in making his hesitant way around the tables at the shows, or waiting for customers to arrive at his own, McVeigh never figured out a way to meet more than a handful of his putative allies. Consequently, he was never very successful as a businessman or political organizer.

Not long after the Waco conflagration, McVeigh set up a table at a gun show in Tulsa. There he had a quick encounter that seemed inconsequential at the time but later took on special significance. A German national named Andreas Strassmeir—nicknamed Andy the German—browsed McVeigh's merchandise, which on that occasion was mostly fatigues and other military clothing. Strassmeir mentioned that he lived in a compound in Oklahoma called Elohim City, which McVeigh had never heard of at the time. Located about two hundred miles east of Oklahoma City, near the Arkansas border, Elohim City was a small religious community of a few hundred people, with a white supremacist orientation. The two men made a trade, with little or no money changing hands. McVeigh gave Strassmeir a shirt, a pair of trousers, and some gloves, and Strassmeir gave McVeigh a U.S. Navy combat knife with a sheath. They exchanged business cards, as was customary for these kinds of private exchanges at gun shows. Of course, they talked about Waco. "I remember we were in agreement," Strassmeir told the author Ben Fenwick. "Those people were Jesus Freaks or weirdos or whatever, but the government did not have the right to move in and kill them. That was the basic thing. I remember telling him, 'Hey, if you are in the area, come look me up.' He was a really nice guy."

McVeigh spent most of the summer of 1993 in Kingman, Arizona, where he rented a small house near his friend Mike Fortier, and he briefly held a job as a security guard. McVeigh then drove the 1,300 miles to Arkansas, where he met up with Nichols, and they looked at property they might buy together, perhaps to start a blueberry farm. They found nothing to their liking, and McVeigh, still with all his possessions in the back of the Road Warrior, followed Nichols back home to Michigan, where they spent the fall.

At the farm in Decker, Terry helped his brother, but McVeigh didn't do much of anything except listen to the radio, watch his mail-order videotapes, read his propaganda, and stew in his resentments. Then, on November 22, 1993, there was a sudden death in the Nichols farmhouse.

CHAPTER 7

Hillary Clinton's Face

Farm life starts early, but McVeigh was still lounging in bed at 9 a.m. on November 22, 1993. He had dropped in on the Nichols family homestead in Michigan a few days earlier, and he wasn't doing much except plotting his next move. As usual, he had been up late listening to the shortwave. In theory, McVeigh was willing to help out at the farm, but he lacked useful skills. He didn't know how the machines worked. All he knew how to do was split wood.

McVeigh was still groggy when he heard Marife Nichols's voice. "Jason! *Jason!* JASON!" McVeigh threw on a pair of pants, ran into the hall, and saw Marife kneeling over the body of her two-year-old son. He wasn't breathing. His neck was cold. "Go get Terry," McVeigh said, "and call 911." McVeigh started CPR, which he had learned in the Army. Terry raced up the stairs, and together they tried to resuscitate the boy. Terry did compressions, and McVeigh did breaths. McVeigh wanted to rush Jason to the hospital, but Marife and Terry decided to wait for the ambulance, which arrived eighteen minutes after being summoned, at 9:31. Jason was pronounced dead at the hospital.

What happened?

Marife told the medical personnel that when she went into Jason's room in the morning, he had a plastic bag around his head. She and Terry were thinking about moving to Utah, and they had stored some packing material in his room. Jason knew how to climb out of his crib, and Marife said he must have started playing with the bags. At the time, McVeigh was in his room, and Terry had started work on the farm. The local police conducted a brief investigation and closed it with the conclusion that there were "no signs of foul play."

Still, the story was peculiar, to say the least. Toddlers like Jason do sometimes accidentally suffocate, but it's rare. McVeigh's role appears to have been straightforward. He had no reason to harm the child, and Marife saw him emerge from the bedroom and try to administer CPR. McVeigh did give the first responders a fake name—Tim Tuttle—which was one he often used at gun shows. But that seems to have been his customary suspicion of authority, rather than an attempt to cover up a crime.

The real question centered on the role of Terry Nichols. He alone had a motive to want Jason, another man's son, out of the picture. (At this point, Terry and Marife had an infant daughter of their own, Nicole.) Terry said he was out of the house and working at the time that Jason suffocated, but that was never established with certainty. Neither Nichols nor McVeigh had a criminal record at the time, so the police had no reason to give the matter special scrutiny. In later years, Marife voiced her suspicions to relatives that Terry had something to do with Jason's death, but she never went further. The story of Jason's death remains a tragic mystery.

Even though it led to no criminal charges, and almost no investigation, Jason's death was another destabilizing event for McVeigh and Nichols. As 1994 began, the two men set out on the same aimless roundelay as in the previous two years. But their level of alienation and anger kept growing, thanks at least in part to Rush Limbaugh's characterization of Clinton's second year in office. He warned that a second revolution was coming "because people are sick and tired of a bunch of bureaucrats in Washington driving into town and telling them what they can and can't do." This attitude came through in McVeigh's letters to his younger sister, Jennifer, who was nineteen at the time. McVeigh, who had never before treated her as a peer, learned that she was feisty and opinionated, and he began to take her into his confidence. He was vague about his plans, but the gist was clear. "We are at war with the system, make no question about it. We have to fund our war efforts with, sometimes, 'covert' means. We operate no different than the American underground in Nazi Germany." He sent Jennifer *The Turner Diaries* as well as his favorite document from American history—the full Declaration of Independence, with the colonists' complaints about the king highlighted in yellow. "Now, Jen, compare these 'grievances' of yesteryear with events of our own time, in your own mind. You will now, maybe, understand better." McVeigh was focused on the Clinton administration: "You're living the conversion of a free Republic into a Socialist-Welfare State. This is what big government is all about." (Jennifer endorsed Tim's views. "It's come time for change, and I know it doesn't happen instantly but you can use all the help you can get," she wrote back. "I know you don't want me to be involved, but I want to be involved. Little sister can handle it—I'm a big girl now!")

McVeigh shared with Limbaugh a common right-wing obsession of the period, regarding the death of Vince Foster, a White House lawyer and longtime friend of the Clinton family. On July 20, 1993, Foster committed suicide in Fort Marcy Park, just outside Washington. Foster was suffering from depression, and a series of investigations established that he shot himself. Still, as months passed, a conspiracy theory arose that Foster had been murdered and the Clintons were somehow involved. Given his large audience, Limbaugh was the most important peddler of this lie. "Vince Foster was murdered in an apartment owned by Hillary Clinton and the body taken to Fort Marcy Park," Limbaugh told his listeners.

In a letter to Jennifer, McVeigh repeated the same theory about Foster's death. After making elliptical references to various alleged conspiracies in the government, he concluded, "Do not spread this info as you could (very honestly, seriously) endanger my life. You think Pres. Clinton's personal aide (Vincent Foster) REALLY committed suicide in that CIA-frequented Nat'l Park?!? (That's why I've been working so hard to cover my trail!)"

But it was a bill to ban assault weapons, which was working its way through Congress during 1994, that represented the greatest threat to McVeigh's worldview. Assault weapons—that is, short-stock semiautomatics, with magazines for multiple rounds—had figured in several recent mass murders at the time. In 1989, a teacher and thirty-four children were shot by an intruder in an elementary school in Stockton, California; in 1991, a gunman killed twenty-three people at a Luby's restaurant in Killeen, Texas; eight people were killed in a San Francisco law firm in July 1993. (Notably, as the roll call of mass shootings continued in subsequent decades, these horrors have been largely forgotten.) In 1994, Clinton and Congress planned a response to these murders, and McVeigh was outraged.

Most accounts of the Oklahoma City bombing describe McVeigh's motivation as a straightforward act of revenge for the Waco siege. Waco may have been a disturbing news story for most Americans, but it was an obsession only to a fringe element. Thus, associating McVeigh with Waco alone served to marginalize him, to make him seem like a freakish outsider. But opposition to the assault weapons ban was the mainstream position for Republicans in 1994. Limbaugh said the ban had been pushed "by people opposed to the Second Amendment." Just as the agendas of the January 6 rioters were close to those of most other Republicans in the Trump era, McVeigh's views were like those of many conservatives in the 1990s.

After Jason's death in the farmhouse, McVeigh and Nichols made another plan to move on from Michigan in early 1994. They had talked about where they might go, perhaps to a place where they would pool their assets, buy land, and live near one another. They wanted good weather—a mix of cold and warm—and an inviting political climate, which meant freedom from what they regarded as the excessive presence of government. As McVeigh later recounted, Arkansas, where they had already looked, had "insect problems, ticks and stuff." Idaho and Montana were too cold. Salt Lake City had a "high Mormon population, and they don't really welcome outsiders." Sight unseen, they settled on St. George, Utah, a small city near Zion National Park. Terry and Marife, along with their daughter, headed there to see if they could make another fresh start.

Before they did, however, McVeigh and Nichols made a seemingly trivial purchase, which turned out to be of enormous consequence. Though they had no reason to think that they were being monitored by the government—and they had not yet committed any crimes—the two men wanted to make sure that their movements and communications would not be tracked. Paranoia about government surveillance was common among militia members and their ideological allies. While together in Michigan, McVeigh and Nichols found an advertisement in *The Spotlight* for a telephone calling card, a product in common use at the time. The card operated on a debit system; the owner made payments in advance of calls being placed against it. They registered the card in a fake name—Daryl Bridges—at the Nicholses' address in Decker, Michigan. They sent a $50 postal service money order as the first deposit in the phone account. Both men used the card's pass code for long-distance calls. Over the next year and a half, they refreshed the account with six more deposits and made 685 calls.

The idea behind the purchase of the card, as McVeigh later explained, was to keep their phone calls secret from the government. It had precisely the opposite effect. Once the FBI identified the account, investigators were able to identify all the calls made by McVeigh and Nichols from November 1993 to April 1995. (The card itself was found in a search of Nichols's home after the bombing.) Even more important, the FBI could identify the landlines from which the calls were made as well as the numbers dialed. So, the card operated as a diary of McVeigh's and Nichols's travels as well as their contacts. The phone card records also refuted the conspiracy theories that swirled around the bombing case. For example, rumors about their supposed international connections abounded; but there were no calls to other countries on the *Spotlight* phone card. The two men were in touch with the people they called with the phone card—and *only* those people. If their numbers were not in the phone card records, McVeigh and Nichols were not in contact with them. For two men seeking to cover their tracks, the purchase of the phone card was a fateful mistake.

Nichols's move to Utah was a bust. He and Marife found nothing to their liking there and moved (again) to Las Vegas, where Terry's son and first wife lived. With Utah off the table, McVeigh stayed in Michigan long enough to see the Buffalo Bills lose their fourth straight Super Bowl, again to the Dallas Cowboys, on January 30, 1994. The next month, he left for Arizona, where he stayed with Mike Fortier for a while and then rented a small house in the town of Golden Valley, about ten miles from Kingman. He took a minimum-wage job at a warehouse for the True Value hardware store where Fortier worked. In the spring, Marife and baby Nicole went to the Philippines, and Nichols came to Golden Valley to stay with McVeigh for a couple of weeks. One night, McVeigh and Nichols cooked dinner for Mike Fortier and his girlfriend, Lori, and the three friends from basic training six years earlier had a reunion. They still had a lot in common, especially now that Clinton was in office. The peril of big government loomed larger than ever for the trio, and they brooded together about the chances for a crackdown against people like them.

McVeigh quit his job at the warehouse after only two months and decided to support himself full-time on the gun show circuit. He headed east to Arkansas for another visit to Roger Moore's ranch (and another 1,300-mile drive). McVeigh stayed a few more days than he did the first time, but the relationship between the two men remained prickly. Moore accused McVeigh of stealing his design for a flare to be sold at gun shows, and McVeigh indignantly denied it. He then drove up to New York, to visit his father and grandfather, then out to Las Vegas, where he served as best man to Mike Fortier, when he married Lori at the Treasure Island Hotel on July 25, 1994.

Throughout that summer, McVeigh was loosening his ties even further to conventional life, experimenting with drugs, credit card fraud, and burglary. Mike and Lori gave him crystal meth a few times, once mixed with orange juice in a Gatorade bottle and the other times to snort. The last time, Mike and Lori invited him to join in their lovemaking, McVeigh told his lawyers, but he couldn't perform sexually. He also tried pot and LSD. None of the drugs had much effect on McVeigh, and he was not tempted to seek them out on his own. McVeigh improved on Nichols's credit card scams. When Nichols applied for cards with no intention of paying the bills, he had used his home address, so the companies knew where to track him down. McVeigh, in contrast, opened his account through a post office box in Arizona and charged $5,000 for gold bars. Since he had used a post office box, it was harder for the credit card companies to find him, and McVeigh correctly figured they wouldn't bother. Also, in mid-1994, McVeigh and Fortier engaged in some minor theft in Kingman. Fortier's particular obsession was the United Nations. As Fortier later testified, "We both believed that the United Nations was actively trying to form a one-world government. To do this, they had to meet certain ends, one of them being they needed to disarm the American public, take away our weapons. We were calling this the New World Order. We spoke quite a bit about that." One night, Fortier and McVeigh broke into the local armory of the National Guard to see if they could find evidence of United Nations activity. They found none, but stole some farm tools while they were in the building.

Around the same time, too, McVeigh started experimenting with bomb-making, which he hadn't done since high school. In Michigan, he had seen James Nichols set off minor explosions with fertilizer in soda bottles—"pop bottle bombs," James called them. So, McVeigh borrowed books from the Kingman public library. These included *Improvised Explosives*, *The Black Medicine Book, Vol. I and II*, and *Armed and Dangerous: The Rise of the Survivalist Right* by James Coates. (He stole the Coates book.) As a result of his studying, McVeigh determined that the proper proportion of an improvised bomb was fifty pounds of fertilizer to a half gallon of fuel—a ratio he committed to memory.

McVeigh and Fortier started setting off fertilizer bombs in the desert outside Kingman. In 1994, this appears to have been mostly for entertainment—a fairly common form of fun for people who lived in that part of Arizona. With Lori as an audience, McVeigh and Fortier set off a pipe bomb and then bought a pair of seventy-five-pound bags of fertilizer from True Value to continue experimenting.

During the summer, McVeigh again ran into Roger Moore at the big gun show sponsored by *Soldier of Fortune* in Las Vegas. The tables were expensive—$200 apiece—and Moore took two of them. He gave McVeigh some space to sell his wares, but they had a final blowup during the show. McVeigh was haranguing possible customers about Waco and scaring them away. "Don't ever talk about that Waco shit at my table!" Moore told him. McVeigh left in a huff, vowing never to speak to Moore again. This confrontation with Moore was just the latest disappointment for McVeigh on the gun show circuit. It wasn't just that he was making very little money; the gun shows were failing to address McVeigh's frustrations with Clinton's federal government. Later, McVeigh summed up his problem by calling it "the offensive-defensive thing." He had read the articles and seen the videos about Waco, and he had sold bumper stickers and bought T-shirts. He had written his congressman and letters to the editor. But the government continued to roll over the people's rights, and no one ever *did* anything in response. (McVeigh made the same point in his recorded conversation with his former colleague Carl Lebron, back in Buffalo.) Terry Nichols, with the accumulated setbacks in his own life, had the same complaint. So, as McVeigh told Stephen Jones, "I decided we needed to turn the tide and go on the offensive, and that is when we started formulating a plan in the summer of '94."

By this time Congress had failed to pass any part of President Clinton's health care initiative, which had been led by Hillary Clinton. This created a measure of desperation on the part of Democrats for some legislative achievement to show to voters before the 1994 midterm elections. After furious lobbying by Clinton, the Senate passed the assault weapons ban by a vote of 52 to 48 on September 13. Clinton signed it the same day, and it went into effect immediately.

"In the midst of this frenzy, the assault weapons ban is signed," McVeigh wrote authors Michel and Herbeck, "a new class of criminal was invented where none existed before. Standing in front of a TV, I instantly was put into a criminal 'class' thru no action of my own. As the bumper sticker says, 'When guns are outlawed, I become an outlaw.' And so it was—my way of life threatened, my heritage, my income, maybe even my life (See Waco, et al.) I decided then and there that I couldn't sit back in the defense mode any longer. I had to take pro-active steps to prevent the loss of all I hold dear." Or as McVeigh put it more simply to Stephen Jones, the assault weapons ban was "the last straw."

From this point forward, McVeigh and Nichols committed themselves to the bombing project. First, the Nichols family—Terry, Marife, and their infant daughter, Nicole—moved to Marion, Kansas, which was in the same Flint Hills region of the state as Fort Riley, where he and McVeigh had been stationed together. Terry hired himself out as a ranch hand, which didn't pay much, but it came with a house for his family. The work was grueling, but there was plenty of space and few people.

McVeigh soon joined Nichols there. But first he took a leisurely route from Arizona, displaying his customary willingness to make very long drives, especially if a detour allowed him to check out a conspiracy theory. He stopped first near Homey Airport, in Nevada, which is better known as Area 51. For decades, the site had been the subject of rumors about unidentified flying objects. The lore drew McVeigh's interest but, not surprisingly, he didn't see anything of note on his visit. McVeigh then made his way to the airport in Gulfport, Mississippi, where *The Spotlight* had reported sightings of aircraft and vehicles with Russian and United Nations markings. "Top Russian War Equipment Pre-Positioned in America," one headline warned. This was related to a broader conspiracy theory, popular during the Clinton years, that "black helicopters" were menacing law-abiding citizens. The Gulfport rumor had an element of truth. In the early 1990s, a pair of local investors bought one thousand Soviet-bloc military trucks for $1.4 million at an auction in Berlin. They shipped them to Gulfport, with the hope of converting them into ambulances or dump trucks and selling them around the world, including to the United Nations. The plan came to naught, and most of the vehicles, with their hammer and sickle logos, sat rusting at a lot near the airport. McVeigh satisfied himself that the vehicles were not part of an invasion force or the New World Order and went on his way.

At last, in late summer 1994, McVeigh made it to Kansas, where he moved in with Nichols, Marife, and daughter Nicole. McVeigh had given up even the pretense of looking for a job. He was on a full-time mission to go on the offensive against the federal government. "We decided at the house that we wanted to take some action," McVeigh told Jones. "We knew we would have to prepare for it." So the two men started training as if they were going into battle. McVeigh and Nichols thought they had become lax since they left the military, so they wanted to work on their marksmanship. They started doing sharpshooting exercises out among the native grasses. The value of living in rural Kansas was that they could shoot guns without worry about being bothered. For extra motivation, McVeigh procured a life-sized silhouette as a target, and he pasted a photograph of Hillary Clinton's face on it.

CHAPTER 8

Assembling the Ingredients

By the fall of 1994, when McVeigh was twenty-six years old, he had been consuming right-wing media for nearly a decade. He started in high school, with the publications of the National Rifle Association. He moved on to *Soldier of Fortune* and *The Spotlight*, and he listened to Rush Limbaugh during the day and William Cooper at night. After Waco, he gorged on propaganda-style documentaries like *Waco, the Big Lie*. But throughout this period, *The Turner Diaries* remained his lodestar. So, when McVeigh decided, after the passage of the assault weapons ban, that he was going to go on the offensive, he knew he was going to do what Earl Turner did. To McVeigh's mind, the assault weapons ban was just like the "Cohen Act," which was the gun control law that set off Turner's fictional rebellion against the government. In the book, Turner's commanders assigned him to "take the offensive" against the federal government by detonating a truck bomb at the FBI building in Washington. As Turner described the plan, "We will then drive into the FBI building's freight-receiving area, set the fuse, and leave the truck." Turner's truck bomb exploded, killing hundreds of federal employees.

In the novel, Earl Turner's specific assignment was "the design and construction of the mechanism of the bomb itself." The book provides some detail on how Turner did it. His team stole forty-four 100-pound bags of ammonium nitrate fertilizer from a farm supply warehouse. "Sensitized with oil and tightly confined, it makes an effective blasting agent . . . to punch through two levels of reinforced-concrete flooring while producing an open-air blast wave powerful enough to blow the façade off a massive and strongly constructed building." Turner built a homemade detonator, which he could activate from the driver's seat of the truck: "We'll have to poke small holes in the walls of the trailer to run the extension cord and the switch into the cab."

McVeigh followed the plan in *The Turner Diaries*—his "blueprint." Still, the book, with all its specificity, did not tell McVeigh everything he needed to know. Where to get the fertilizer and how much? Where to store it in the meantime? Where to get the barrels to hold the fertilizer, and how many? What kind of fuel and how much? Where should they mix the ingredients and assemble the bomb? What kind of truck should they use—and how to get one? How exactly to design and use a detonation mechanism? And even broader questions—How many of these ingredients should be purchased, and how many should be stolen? How to finance the complex operation? Should McVeigh and Nichols solicit the help of other conspirators? When and where should they set off the bomb? And, of course, how should they avoid getting caught?

There was one more issue: What did McVeigh and Nichols hope to accomplish by setting off a bomb at a federal building? What was the point?

McVeigh's lawyers pressed him on this issue, and he had trouble answering. In part, the bombing was retribution for Waco, Ruby Ridge, and the assault weapons ban. He was tired of talk. "It's just the liberal view that all things in the world can be solved by discussion," he told Jones. "Well, the military taught me aggression. Negotiation can win, but the truth is, there are times when negotiations fail. I found out in history—the Declaration of Independence—repeated petitions have been answered only by repeated injury." McVeigh also said he hoped, just as Earl Turner did, that his bombing would inspire a broader rebellion against a corrupt federal government. By the fall of 1994, the plan for the bombing had a momentum of its own, and that was ultimately the most important reason for it; it was not the result of strategic or tactical thinking but rather an expression of rage. In a similar way, it may be that relatively few of the hundreds of people who invaded the Capitol on January 6, 2021, actually thought that they would overturn the election. As with McVeigh, the rage—as much as the result—was the point.

Terry, Marife, their daughter, Nicole, and Tim were now all living under one small roof in Marion, Kansas. That proximity created an immediate complication.

As McVeigh recounted to his lawyers, he told Terry that he was feeling close to Marife. Terry responded that if he ever learned that McVeigh had slept with Marife, he would have to kill him. Terry left for work on the ranch every morning, and one day, Marife appeared in McVeigh's bedroom and slipped into bed with him. They slept together a few times. (This was a pattern in McVeigh's life. He told his lawyers he had slept with eight women in total, three of them the wives of friends.) At the time, neither Marife nor McVeigh told Terry that they had slept together, though Marife did acknowledge it much later.

Apparently unaware of his wife's infidelity with his friend and partner, Nichols turned his attention to the bombing plan. Like McVeigh, Nichols had been drifting through life over the previous few years, and he, too, now brought a single-minded energy to the project. Since their marriage in 1990, Marife had pressed Terry to pay for repeated trips to her native Philippines. But after the assault weapons ban passed, and McVeigh and Nichols decided to build a bomb,

Nichols flipped the script. Instead of acquiescing to another trip to the Philippines himself, Terry told Marife to take Nicole there for the foreseeable future. He didn't want to be distracted by their presence in Kansas. Marife and Nicole remained in the Philippines for the next six months. With Marife out of the picture, Terry quit his job at the ranch, moved out of their house, and put their furniture in storage. He stayed in motels or slept in the bed of his pickup. Like McVeigh, Nichols was all in.

They settled one goal right from the outset. The bombing would take place on April 19, 1995. That would be exactly two years after the Waco conflagration as well as the anniversary of the Battles of Lexington and Concord in 1775. To McVeigh, the date would prove his patriotic bona fides. Just as important, it was about seven months away—just long enough to complete this complex undertaking.

The next challenge was also straightforward: the purchase of the fertilizer. Ammonium nitrate fertilizer is widely available in Kansas, where even large purchases rarely draw suspicion. In McPherson, a town near Marion, Nichols made two purchases of forty 50-pound bags for a total of 4,000 pounds. McVeigh bought a few more bags in other places in the area, which gave them nearly the same amount of fertilizer as Earl Turner used for his truck bomb in the novel. (Both men used fake names when making the purchases.) It was also simple to obtain several dozen 55-gallon barrels. Some of them were free from a milk cooperative, and others were $12 from a hardware store. Continuing to use fake names, McVeigh and Nichols rented storage sheds in the area for the fertilizer and barrels.

The bigger challenge was finances. Since McVeigh left Buffalo almost two years earlier, he had lived frugally, often sleeping in his car or at low-priced motels. He survived on fast food and candy and as a result had a perpetually sour stomach, which he calmed by chugging

Pepto Bismol and popping antacids. He had borrowed $4,000 from his father and made a few dollars at the gun shows, buying and selling whatever he could find—military clothing, ammunition, copies of *The Turner Diaries.* Both men had charged several thousand dollars in gold bars to their credit cards, and they had cashed in several bars to pay for the first loads of fertilizer. But once they made the decision, in the fall of 1994, to go forward with the bombing, they realized that they were going to need more money—for travel expenses, more fertilizer, fuel for the bomb, barrels, fuses, the truck itself. McVeigh considered robbing a bank. He even cased one in a nearby town in Kansas. But he quickly thought better of it. He didn't know how to rob a bank—how to extract a meaningful amount of money from a teller while avoiding security cameras and exploding dye packets. As McVeigh told Jones, "I was of the opinion that we should not jeopardize our security by robbing a bank because we could get caught, and we would never get to the main mission."

Where else were riches to be plundered? "I suggested Bob," McVeigh recalled. "Bob Miller" was the pseudonym for Roger Moore, who became rich as a boat-building entrepreneur and now sold ammunition at gun shows. McVeigh had visited his ranch in Arkansas several times, and he remembered the cash, gold, and guns on display. "He's pricked me a few times, he deserves it, he's rich anyway—the fat fuck," McVeigh recalled saying to Nichols. McVeigh and Nichols would finance their bombing project with an armed robbery of McVeigh's erstwhile friend. According to McVeigh, Nichols loved the idea. "He bit hook, line and sinker, wanted to go for it," McVeigh said.

Soon, though, McVeigh had second thoughts about his own participation in the robbery, because he thought Moore would recognize him. McVeigh could wear a mask, but Moore knew his voice, and McVeigh's long, lanky frame was recognizable as well. In contrast, Nichols and Moore had never met. Nichols thought it over for a day or two, then agreed to do the mission solo.

The two men began several weeks of intense preparation. Working from memory, McVeigh drew up a map of the Moore property, and he detailed how he thought Nichols should conduct the robbery. McVeigh knew that Moore possessed an abundance of weapons, so he drilled Nichols on what to do if Moore came after him with a gun. Nichols had to be prepared to shoot Moore first, and they planned for Nichols to have the right weapons with him. Because McVeigh would be an obvious suspect, they set the robbery for a time when McVeigh would have a solid alibi, at a gun show far away from Arkansas. They were heading toward an October date for the Moore action, when McVeigh decided to change plans.

Although McVeigh lived on junk food, his skinny frame absorbed any number of greasy hamburgers (and Peppermint Patties) without changing shape. Nichols, on the other hand, had a long-term interest in unrefined grains and natural food, and he was mostly a vegetarian. He drew the line at McDonald's, but he was willing to join McVeigh at the Pizza Hut in Marion. They'd eaten several meals there, when McVeigh noticed that there was the entrance to a quarry, owned by the Martin Marietta company, across the street. In his work on the ranch, Nichols had visited the quarry to buy gravel, which was mostly used to make concrete. The two men figured that the quarry used explosives to create the gravel. McVeigh had an idea. "Holy shit," he said. "Let's jump in the car in the middle of the night and do a recon."

Pizza Hut was long closed on the night in early October when McVeigh turned the Chevy onto the dirt road that led into the quarry. Even at a crawl, the car bounced on the pitted and uneven surface. Before too long, the two men came upon what they wanted. Hard against a hillside were a pair of steel-reinforced sheds known as magazines, which were used to store explosives. Later, back at Nichols's home, he conducted a test to see if his Makita power drill could open padlocks like the ones on the magazines. The experiment worked, so the two men decided to return to the quarry to loot the magazines. They chose a Friday night. "That way it would give us a whole weekend to clear the scene, because they wouldn't come into work until Monday morning," McVeigh told Jones.

It was 2 a.m. on October 2, in the middle of a rainstorm, when McVeigh and Nichols took two cars into the quarry. McVeigh drove his Chevy, and Nichols took his 1984 GMC pickup, which had a covered bed. Nichols brought his drill, and he used it to open the locks on the doors to both magazines. They had brought two vehicles in the hope that there would be too many explosives to fit in McVeigh's little sedan. Their hopes were fulfilled. In several hours of work, they loaded 300 sticks of dynamite and 350 pounds of blasting caps into their vehicles. (Blasting caps, which are also known as detonators, contain small explosive charges that are used to ignite larger explosives, like dynamite. Blasting caps are usually set off with fuses.)

The bounty from the quarry created a problem—what to do with the loot. McVeigh and Nichols knew that the crime would soon be reported, so they wanted to get the proceeds out of the vicinity as soon as possible. McVeigh later said he operated on a "tri-state system," meaning that he sought to get the explosives at least three states away from Kansas. He thought of his sometime home in Kingman, Arizona, so he and Nichols took their two vehicles west the day after the robbery. The trip nearly ended in calamity. On the highway in Amarillo, Texas, McVeigh was almost rear-ended by a mobile home. With his trunk full of explosives, a crash would have set off a massive blast. But the other vehicle missed McVeigh's Road Warrior by inches.

While still in Kansas, McVeigh had written to Michael Fortier telling him that he and Nichols had decided to take "offensive action" against the government. During the journey to Kingman, McVeigh (using the *Spotlight* phone card) called Fortier. He told Fortier to rent a couple of lockers for him to store explosives. Fortier agreed, but didn't follow through. McVeigh told his lawyers that he berated Fortier for his failure: "I'm, like, fuck—all talk, no action, you know. I told you to get it."

McVeigh stopped by Fortier's mobile home and spelled out his plan with Nichols. They were going to bomb a federal building. Would Fortier help?

"No—not unless there's a U.N. tank in my front yard," Fortier said, according to his later testimony. "Obviously if there was a U.N. tank sitting in my front yard, we would be at a state of war with the New World Order, and I feel that actions like that would be appropriate at that time, but not before."

Rebuffed by Fortier, McVeigh told Nichols to rent storage sheds for the explosives in Flagstaff, 150 miles away. But McVeigh quickly changed his mind and decided to bring the explosives to Kingman after all, and he rented a storage shed there. Proud of his stash, McVeigh brought Fortier to the shed, showed off the explosives, and told him about the robbery of the quarry. He also mentioned that he and Nichols were planning to replenish their finances by robbing "Bob," a gun dealer in Arkansas.

Nichols went to visit Josh, his twelve-year-old son from his first marriage, in Las Vegas, and McVeigh stayed with Fortier. The two men talked about McVeigh's plan in a way that reflected Fortier's role as a quasi-participant in the bombing conspiracy. Fortier listened, offered suggestions, but never actually did anything to move the plan forward. Fortier suggested a target—the IRS offices in Prescott, Arizona. McVeigh scoffed, preferring a much higher-profile objective. He briefly considered assassinating Lon Horiuchi, the FBI sniper who killed Randy Weaver's wife at Ruby Ridge, as well as Walter Smith, the federal judge presiding in the Waco prosecution, but he told Fortier that a bombing, like in *The Turner Diaries*, was his real goal.

McVeigh had already thought through much of the plan for the truck bomb. He would fill 55-gallon drums with a mixture of fertilizer and anhydrous hydrazine fuel—which is often used in race cars. (McVeigh's research showed that racing fuel produced a more powerful explosion than ordinary gasoline.) McVeigh drew a diagram for Fortier of how he was going to arrange the drums in the bed of the truck. He explained that he would drill a hole from the cab of the truck to the bed; he would thread a fuse through the hole, light it with a lighter, and leave—just as Earl Turner did. He said they had assembled all the fertilizer and blasting caps they needed, but they still needed to buy the fuel, and it would be expensive, about $1,200. He said the plan was to set off the bomb at about 11 a.m. on April 19, in the hope that a general uprising against the U.S. government would follow.

When McVeigh wasn't studying one of his books about bomb design, he talked about the project incessantly. He knew he wanted to project the explosion outward from the truck toward the building, so he needed a "shaped charge"—an arrangement that would direct the force in one direction. Eager to explain to Mike and Lori, he took fifteen soup cans from the Fortiers' kitchen cabinet and arranged them on the floor. Each can represented a 55-gallon drum with the fertilizer and fuel mixture. "You're going to use that many?" Lori asked. Yes, said McVeigh, and he thought a V-shaped design of the drums would do the most damage to the building.

For all that McVeigh made meticulous plans for building the bomb, he was curiously haphazard in choosing a target. He told Fortier that he never considered duplicating Earl Turner's attack on the FBI building in Washington. McVeigh had never been to Washington, but he knew that security there would be tight. Besides, he was more interested in the heartland—to shock and motivate the great masses of ordinary Americans. Earlier, he had passed by the federal building in Little Rock, but the plaza was too open to get as close as he wanted. Fortier talked about the federal building in Phoenix, but it didn't seem right, either. Ditto for Kansas City as Nichols had described it. McVeigh would be heading east in a few days, and he planned on checking out two other options—Dallas and Oklahoma City.

After Nichols returned from Las Vegas, the two men headed back to Kansas in Nichols's pickup, on a mission to buy racing fuel. They stopped in Wichita for Nichols to sell nine gold bars to raise cash and then pulled into Heartland Motorsports Park—a sprawling drag racing mecca in Topeka. Over its seven hundred acres, the track sold a wide variety of fuel, including for race cars. Near the pit stops, McVeigh approached Glynn Tipton, who worked for a company called VP Racing Fuels. McVeigh asked if he could buy a 55-gallon drum of anhydrous hydrazine fuel. To Tipton, something seemed off about the request, as McVeigh didn't appear to own a race car or have any legitimate need for the fuel. Tipton called his supervisor, Wade Gray, who had similar misgivings, especially because he knew that racing fuel could be used to make a bomb. By this point, McVeigh had wandered off, without leaving his name. The approach so unnerved Gray that he and Tipton called the Bureau of Alcohol, Tobacco and Firearms office in New Orleans to report that someone might be trying to build a bomb. The agent referred them to the Kansas City office of the ATF, and the two men made the same report. No one from the ATF ever followed up with Tipton and Gray.

At the Topeka racetrack, McVeigh heard that there was another track near Dallas where he might be able to buy racing fuel. To get to Dallas from Kansas is a straight shot south on I-35. About halfway through the journey, the highway passes through Oklahoma City, so McVeigh and Nichols stopped to check out the federal building there. Leafing through the local phone book's blue pages (which showed government listings), they found the address of the Murrah building* and noted that virtually all the federal agencies, including the hated ATF, were quartered there.

Nichols made two slow circuits around the building in his pickup, and McVeigh liked what he saw. Access to the back of the building was blocked by an underground parking garage, but the front was wide open, with a cutout in the curb that would allow a truck to park very close. The front wall was all black glass, which would crumble with a bomb, creating many casualties. There was a structural elevator tower that might prevent the whole building from collapsing, but overall it seemed like an ideal target. Better yet, McVeigh had read an article in *The Spotlight* that said Bob Ricks, the spokesman for the FBI in Waco, was an Oklahoma City native. (This was a mistake, though Ricks was now the head of the FBI field office in Oklahoma City.) Later, McVeigh told his lawyers that he was also drawn to the Murrah building because there were empty parking lots nearby, lessening the chance for collateral damage to nonfederal employees. There is no contemporaneous record that McVeigh thought that way, and reason to believe that he made it up later to try to lessen the magnitude of his crime.

Continuing to Dallas, McVeigh and Nichols had only the vaguest idea about the location of the federal building or the racetrack. When they stopped for directions, they checked the blue pages of the Dallas phone book. It appeared that there was no single federal building in town that housed a full array of government offices, so that settled the issue: the Murrah building would be the target. Eventually, they

* The building was named for Alfred P. Murrah (1904–1975), a longtime federal trial and appeals court judge.

found their way to what was then known as the MaryLou Racetrack in Ennis, about forty miles south of Dallas.

When they arrived, they had a bit of luck: it was raining, so racing was canceled, and that meant fuel salesmen were desperate for customers. In light of their failure in Kansas, McVeigh took additional steps for security. They had stolen a license plate in Kansas and affixed it to Nichols's pickup so they couldn't be traced. McVeigh left Nichols by the front gate and put on a do-rag so he looked like a biker. He then found the local outlet for VP Fuels, the same company where they had shopped in Topeka. Tim Chambers, the salesman, was more accommodating than his colleagues in Kansas. He didn't have anhydrous hydrazine, but he had a good substitute called nitromethane. Most of Chambers's customers only bought nitromethane in one- to five-gallon increments; it's usually used as a fuel additive to boost high-powered engines. But McVeigh said he wanted a 55-gallon drum. Chambers said it was $1,200. "What if I buy three?" McVeigh said. Chambers thought the quantity was odd; why did he want so much? McVeigh said his buddies had a motorcycle rally each year in Oklahoma City and always bought "nitro" to juice their engines. That was good enough for Chambers, and he knocked the price down to $925 per drum. He even threw in a hand pump. (Chambers did not think to report the transaction to the authorities. He never even asked McVeigh his name.)

McVeigh and Nichols drove the pickup back to Marion, Kansas, and stashed the drums of racing fuel with the fertilizer in the storage sheds. With the blasting caps and dynamite in storage in Arizona and the other main ingredients in Kansas, they had assembled the most important parts of the bomb. Over the next few days, Nichols drove McVeigh back to Kingman so he could pick up his car and the blasting caps. After they arrived, McVeigh learned that his grandfather had died. Ed McVeigh had introduced Tim to guns, and the two had been Tim's only uncomplicated, loving relationship in his family. The loss of his grandfather was another event that untethered Tim from the bonds of everyday life. He had no one, and nothing, to live for, except his mission to attack the federal government.

Nor did McVeigh or Nichols have a fixed residence. Back in Kansas, they arranged to meet up at the small state park at Geary Lake, a recreation area just off the main road between Marion and Junction City. Little more than a fishing hole with a few picnic tables, it offered a convenient place for Nichols and McVeigh to spend nights in the back of Nichols's pickup. On the afternoon of October 30, McVeigh had a surprise for Nichols: a shot in the face with pepper spray.

They were both still planning for Nichols to rob Roger Moore, but they had a disagreement about how he should pull it off. Nichols thought he could neutralize Moore with pepper spray. "I kept trying to tell him that if you've ever been hit with pepper spray, it's not that powerful, and [Moore] is big," McVeigh told Jones. "He doesn't have stamina, but if he gets his hands on you, he'll break your neck. He was so convinced I felt I had to show him before he got himself killed. So, in the park I turned around and without him expecting it, I blasted him in the face with pepper spray. It hit him in the side of the face and didn't even blind his eyes. That showed him right there that it was ineffective."

Instead, they bulked up Nichols's armor and weaponry. In a couple of days, Nichols went to Arkansas for his mission at Roger Moore's ranch. McVeigh headed to Lockport to settle his grandfather's affairs and then to a gun show in Ohio to establish his alibi.

CHAPTER 9

The Desert Rat

Roger Moore's geese and ducks usually woke him around dawn at his ten-acre ranch in Arkansas. But on Saturday, November 5, 1994, he managed to sleep until around 8:30. He threw on a pair of sweatpants, skipped breakfast, and wandered to his barn. Before he reached the door, a voice called to him from behind.

"Lay down on the ground."

"What?" said Moore.

"Lay down on the ground."

Moore turned around. Later, he was asked in the grand jury what he saw.

"A horrible picture," Moore testified.

There was a man in a strange and terrifying outfit. He wore a black ski mask, Israeli combat boots, and two pairs of Vietnam-era combat fatigues, covered by a long field jacket. In his hand was a sinister weapon—a pistol-grip shotgun with a circular garrote wire attached to the muzzle. The weapon can kill in several ways. With the garrote placed around a victim's neck, he can pull away, and the wire can cut the carotid artery; the gunman can pull the wire and strangle the victim; or the gunman can pull the trigger and blow off the victim's head.

Moore lay down on the ground.

The gunman then placed the muzzle to the back of Moore's head and told him to crawl to the house, which he did. "He was polite. He didn't hurt me," Moore testified. "I was very surprised. I opened the door. I crawled in. And he said, 'Lay flat.'"

Moore had two immediate thoughts. The first was *This is the kind of thing that Tim McVeigh would do.* McVeigh had been to the house, and he was crazy and reckless. But the second thought was *This isn't Tim McVeigh.* This man was shorter, thicker, with a deeper voice. The man with the gun was Terry Nichols.

Once Moore was on his belly on the living room floor, Nichols restrained Moore's hands and feet with plastic zip ties. Then he duct-taped Moore's eyes and threw a jacket over his head. Nichols asked if there was anyone else in the house, and Moore answered (honestly) no. After Nichols looked around to make sure, he began to collect the bounty promised by McVeigh.

Nichols took seventy-six guns, eight of them handguns, the rest long guns and rifles. Many of the long guns were in custom-made cases. Nichols also grabbed several 35mm cameras and tripods; forty or fifty pre-Columbian jade statues and gold dolls from Costa Rica; a box of unmounted gems from Ceylon; a thousand ounces of silver coins and bars; Gold Eagle coins worth a total of $3,000; and $8,700 in cash.

Collecting the loot took about ninety minutes. As Nichols was leaving, he said to Moore, "Don't worry about the guns. They are going to gangs. Now, don't move. My buddy is outside and coming back for the rest of it." There were no gangs, and no buddy outside, and when Moore finally wriggled free of his bindings an hour or so later, Nichols was long gone.

Before cell phones and email, news traveled slowly, even among co-conspirators. During the weekend of the robbery, McVeigh was at a gun show in Akron, the place he had chosen to give himself a solid alibi. After the show, he drove to Lockport to see his father, who told him, "Somebody has been trying to call you—Terry." As McVeigh later told Jones, "I thought, 'What the fuck—he must be in jail or something.' Well, I got ahold of him and it turns out everything went fine, and he was just so elated he was trying to call me." McVeigh was perturbed at Terry for calling Bill McVeigh; he didn't want his father's number connected to any of their activities. But both McVeigh and Nichols were delighted by Nichols's success. Suddenly, they were flush, with a lot more cash and valuables than they needed to finance the bombing. As a first step to sharing the wealth, Nichols mailed McVeigh $2,000 in cash taken from Moore.

After the robbery, the two men laid low, hoping that any heat from the police would dissipate. Then they took different paths. The robbery energized McVeigh, giving him new confidence and resources to make the bombing a reality. Nichols seemed almost traumatized by what he had done. He had never committed a violent crime or fought in a war. He didn't repudiate the bombing project, but he wanted, increasingly, to leave it to McVeigh. Nichols wanted to avoid the police—and perhaps McVeigh as well.

McVeigh stayed for a couple of weeks in Lockport, where he helped his father prepare his grandfather's property for an estate sale. Bill McVeigh noticed that his son's politics had taken on an even darker edge. When they were watching the news, Bill saw Tim's hatred for Bill Clinton. Whenever Clinton appeared, Tim would mutter, "Someone should kill that son of a bitch," Bill told defense investigators.

"Tim was obsessed with Waco. He was convinced that it was all the government's doing—a conspiracy." Also in this period, Bill learned that Tim refused to pay taxes to the federal government. Tim used his father's computer to type a document that Tim sent to his sister. "ATF, all you tyrannical mother fuckers will swing in the wind one day for your treasonous actions against the Constitution of the United States," it said. "Remember the Nuremberg War Trials. But . . . I only followed orders. Die, you spineless cowardice [sic] bastards." Around the same time, McVeigh wrote in a letter that he believed in the Constitution "in every bit of my heart, soul, and being." As the legal historian Jared A. Goldstein has observed, right-wing extremists have long wrapped their views in twisted interpretations of the Constitution. This was as true for McVeigh as it was for the January 6 insurrectionists.

After the robbery in Arkansas, Nichols returned to Kansas and stashed the guns in one of his storage lockers near Marion. (He mailed McVeigh the combination to the lock.) Nichols then went to Las Vegas, to visit his son, Josh, and ex-wife, Lana Padilla.

After seeing Josh, Nichols used some of the proceeds from the robbery to visit his wife and daughter in the Philippines. On November 22, Lana Padilla drove him to the airport for the first leg of his journey. As Nichols was getting out of the car, he gave Lana the keys to his pickup and told her to give them to his friend Tim McVeigh if he asked for them. Then he pointed to a brown paper bag on the floor of the car. "This package is for you," he said. "If I'm not back in sixty days, open it, and follow the instructions." When Terry walked toward the terminal, Josh ran after him for a final hug, and he returned to his mother in tears. "I'll never see my dad again!" he told her.

Disturbed by Josh's last exchange with his father, Padilla defied Terry's wishes and opened the package the following day. The contents made it clear that Terry was in a fatalistic frame of mind. There were two envelopes. The one addressed to Padilla included the combination to a storage locker he had rented in Las Vegas. It also said there was a secret package hidden in Padilla's home—"located in kitchen behind utensil drawer between the dishwasher and stove." The second envelope was addressed to Jennifer McVeigh, and it contained another envelope intended for Tim. Padilla opened that one, too.

The letter gave McVeigh instructions on how to empty all the storage lockers in Kansas, followed by: "Your [*sic*] on your own. Go for it!! Terry." Then, scribbled at the bottom. "As far as heat—none that I know, this letter would be for the purpose of my death."

After reading these messages, Padilla went to her kitchen and pulled apart the utensil drawer. In a Walmart plastic bag was $20,000 in cash, mostly in hundred-dollar bills. She then went to the storage locker and found the gems, gold, and silver from the Moore robbery—along with a note that said their value was $36,000 to $38,000.

For Padilla, the turn of events was baffling and disturbing. Nichols, the father of their child, was obviously contemplating his imminent death, even if she didn't know why. She also couldn't explain how the sporadic low-wage jobs he had held in recent years could yield tens of thousands of dollars in cash and valuables. And he was telling McVeigh, "Go for it!!" But go for what? And Nichols was feeling no "heat"—meaning no attention from the police. But why would Nichols be concerned about the police? Padilla could only wonder, and she couldn't ask Nichols because he was unreachable in the Philippines. She didn't share her concerns with the police, either.

It's not clear why Nichols thought he was facing his death at that moment. He may have thought something would happen to him in the Philippines. (In earlier trips, he had been spooked by the number of locals who thought all Americans were rich.) Or he may have worried that he would be arrested for the Moore robbery. Or he may have thought that he'd be arrested or killed in the bombing conspiracy. In any event, the truth behind Nichols's letters in the package was more sinister than Padilla could have imagined. The plot to bomb the Murrah building was far along. By providing McVeigh with access to the storage lockers containing the bomb ingredients, Nichols was helping McVeigh pull off the bombing even if Nichols himself never made it back to the United States. To be sure, the letters showed that Nichols was the secondary figure in the conspiracy; they presupposed that McVeigh could assemble and detonate the bomb by himself. But at that moment, Nichols was still playing a part, even though he was thousands of miles away.

While Nichols was in Las Vegas and then in the Philippines, McVeigh was slowly making his way west. After leaving Lockport, he went to Michigan, where, on this visit, he avoided James Nichols. (McVeigh found James overbearing, as did his brother Terry.) McVeigh stayed with a different friend, Kevin Nicholas, whom he had met when Nicholas was a farmhand for the Nichols family. McVeigh never told Nicholas about the bombing plot, though he made his obsession with Waco clear. As for his ultimate plans, McVeigh was cagey but boastful in his narcissistic way. "Someday you will hear about me," he told Nicholas. McVeigh then went to the storage locker in Kansas where Nichols had stashed Roger Moore's guns. "I got to Kansas, I opened up the storage, and I almost shit my pants," McVeigh told Jones. "I couldn't believe all the guns Terry had gotten. I should have known, the greedy son of a bitch."

McVeigh knew he couldn't sell all seventy-six guns by himself, and Nichols was still in the Philippines, so he decided to recruit Fortier as a partner. McVeigh called Fortier from Kansas and tantalized him with the prospect of making as much as $10,000, but he didn't say how. McVeigh then set off for Arizona with three of the guns to show Fortier some of the merchandise, as well as two large boxes of blasting caps from the robbery of the quarry. In the second week in December, McVeigh checked into a motel in Kingman and asked Lori Fortier to bring him some Christmas wrapping paper. There, she wrapped the two boxes of blasting caps like they were gifts. He said he was going to sell them for $2,500 apiece.

Fortier told McVeigh that he was game to help sell the guns from the Moore robbery. He asked his boss at True Value hardware for a couple of days off, and McVeigh took Fortier in the Road Warrior on the familiar thousand-plus-mile drive from Arizona to Kansas to pick up the rest of the guns. McVeigh had already shared his plan for the bombing with Fortier, including the April 19 date—now about four months away—but he filled in a lot of details as they made the long drive. "He told me they picked that building because that was where the orders for the attack on Waco came from," Fortier later testified. "He told me that he was wanting to blow up a building to cause a general uprising in America hopefully that would knock some people off the fence and urge them into taking action against the federal government." On December 16, after they spent the night in a motel in Amarillo, McVeigh pointed to a Ryder truck on the highway. He said he wanted to use a bigger version, a twenty-footer, which said "18,000 pounds" on the side. McVeigh said he was thinking of remaining in the truck when the bomb went off. He wanted to make sure no security guards jumped in and tried to stop him. He'd have his Glock .45 handgun with him, and he'd shoot anyone who got in his way. "It sounds like you're thinking of committing suicide," Fortier said. "If that's what it takes," McVeigh replied.

Near the end of their long trip to Kansas, McVeigh insisted on a four-hour detour—a 250-mile trip to Oklahoma City. He wanted to show Fortier the Murrah building—the target for the bombing. When they arrived, they pulled off the highway and made two slow circles around the building. Fortier made an observation that impressed McVeigh. "He pointed out something I had already seen, but I was proud of him for noticing it too," he told Jones. "The elevator shaft could prevent it from collapsing, because it had structural integrity. And I said, 'Yes, I've seen that. Good job of noticing.'"

When they stopped in one of the parking lots that faced the front of the building, they worried that someone might notice them. "I was freaking," McVeigh said. "We talked for about two minutes, and he said, 'I'm getting nervous. Let's leave.' So I said, 'Okay,' and we drove away."

McVeigh steered them a couple of blocks to a quiet alley. There he explained how the attack would go down. A few days before the bombing, he and Nichols would take two vehicles from Kansas into Oklahoma City. They would stash one in the alley for a getaway and return to Kansas in the other. Then McVeigh would rent a Ryder truck in Junction City, and he and Nichols would assemble the bomb from the ingredients in the various storage sheds. On the morning of the bombing, McVeigh would drive the truck to the Murrah building, light the fuse, and walk to the getaway car stashed in the alley. (McVeigh told Fortier that it was unclear whether Nichols would come with him on the day of the bombing.) Fortier asked why McVeigh wanted to park the getaway car so far away from the Murrah building. McVeigh said he needed at least one building between the target and the car. That was the only way to preserve the getaway car, because the explosion was going to be so enormous.

From Oklahoma City, McVeigh and Fortier drove to the airport in Manhattan, Kansas, where Fortier rented a car for his return to Arizona. Then the two men went to the storage locker near Nichols's home in Kansas, where Nichols had stashed the guns from the Moore robbery. They split the seventy-six guns roughly in half, and McVeigh took Fortier to his favorite Pizza Hut for a tutorial on how to sell at gun shows. Then they went their separate ways—Fortier to Arizona and McVeigh to Michigan, where he was hoping to sell his share of the guns and the Christmas-wrapped blasting caps. This, however, would be McVeigh's last thousand-mile journey in the Road Warrior.

McVeigh was about thirty miles outside of Decker when he tried to turn left into a gas station and a pickup truck plowed into his trunk. Miraculously, the blasting caps did not explode, but the car was totaled. The destruction of the little Chevy devastated McVeigh. "This was actually a psychological downfall here because it was like the last straw, because that car had been the only thing I could rely on for seven years," he told Jones. "That was kind of, like, this is it, there is nothing else—one of many things like that, like my grandfather dying." McVeigh summoned his friend Kevin Nicholas to rescue him and his cargo—the blasting caps and the guns. McVeigh and Nicholas went to a few gun shows in Michigan, where they sold some of the guns, and McVeigh thought he had a deal to sell the blasting caps to a gun dealer named David Paulsen, but it fell through at the last minute. While in Michigan, McVeigh bought a barely functioning used Pontiac station wagon to replace his beloved Road Warrior. He attached an Arizona license plate that he had taken off an abandoned car in Kingman.

In mid-January 1995, despite his grim forebodings, Nichols returned from the Philippines with his wife and daughter and made it to Kansas. He connected with McVeigh at their customary rallying spot, the Geary Lake state park, outside Junction City. Relations between the two men were deteriorating. Nichols was irritated that McVeigh had told Fortier about the Moore robbery; Nichols didn't know if he could trust Fortier with that information. But McVeigh vouched for Fortier, and besides, that was the only way he could figure to sell so many guns.

Again, Nichols and McVeigh went their separate ways. Tired of living out of cars and motels, Nichols tried to put down some roots in Kansas for Marife and Nicole. He rented a small house in the town of Herington, which was midway between Marion and Junction City. McVeigh pressed on to Arizona to see if Fortier had sold his share of the guns. His stoner friend had done almost nothing. Fortier said his back was bothering him, so he hadn't sold any guns at all. This infuriated McVeigh, who had promised Nichols a share of Fortier's sales. McVeigh was sleeping in the station wagon in the desert near Kingman. The Fortiers invited him to move back into the extra bedroom in their mobile home, but things were tense between them, too.

McVeigh thought Fortier was lazy, and Fortier, increasingly, thought McVeigh was nuts.

McVeigh was more committed than ever to the bombing project, but he was torn about how to proceed. At one level, he knew that he would probably need some help to assemble a nearly five-thousand-pound truck bomb in Kansas, transport it to Oklahoma City, detonate it, and escape. The job seemed too big for one person. But could he count on Nichols—or Fortier? Were the two of them more trouble than they were worth?

Nichols had been in on the plan from the beginning, but McVeigh couldn't be sure he would stick with it. At times, Nichols seemed more interested in money than the cause; plus, even though his marriage to Marife was troubled, he had two kids he wanted to watch grow up. Was he willing to take the risks involved with going through with the bombing? Fortier was an even bigger question mark. Unlike Nichols, Fortier had never committed to taking a real role in the bombing. McVeigh thought he was too drug-addled to be reliable, and he was, in his way, devoted to his wife and daughter. Mike and Lori knew all the details of the plan, and they never discouraged McVeigh, even when he said during this visit that the death toll might include women and children. As McVeigh later recounted to Jones, "I told them, 'Children may die. There may be a pregnant woman working there, or there may be someone walking down the street, or someone may have taken their child to work with them. Do you understand that?' And Mike said, 'Yeah, I know, it's part of life.' But reality hit them more than they thought." McVeigh recognized that he would have to do the lion's share of the work himself.

Through February and March, McVeigh roused Fortier enough for them to sell some of the Moore weapons at gun shows in the region—in Reno, Tucson, and St. George, Utah. But McVeigh's real energy was devoted to completing the remaining tasks for the bombing. With the ingredients in hand, his thoughts turned to the rental of the Ryder truck. He was going to use cash for the rental, but he would need some form of identification, too. He didn't want to use his own name, since he figured the authorities would quickly identify the truck as the source of the explosion. Fortier said he knew a "rough and tumble" guy in Kingman who might be willing to go to Las Vegas, mug a stranger, and take his wallet. The mugger would keep the cash and credit cards, but give any identification cards to Fortier, who would in turn pass them to McVeigh. He could then rent the truck in the name of the mugging victim. McVeigh approved the plan, but in typical fashion, Fortier let a couple of weeks pass and did nothing to make it happen.

McVeigh came up with an alternative. He answered an advertisement in the back pages of *Soldier of Fortune* for blank identification sets—phony driver's licenses. When the forms arrived, he used the Fortiers' typewriter to create a license in the name of Robert Kling. He chose the name because he served in the Army with a soldier by that name whom he somewhat resembled; he invented an address in South Dakota and provided a birth date of April 19—a macabre inside joke. McVeigh destroyed the typewriter ribbon that he used. He was going to use Lori's iron to laminate the card, but she worried that he was going to ruin the iron. So she offered to laminate the card for McVeigh.

As the date for the bombing drew near, McVeigh took on an almost messianic view of his mission. His letters hinted at a coming apocalypse. In Michigan, he had come to know an older woman named Gwenn Strider, who was related to the Nicholses' former farmhand Kevin Nicholas. From Kingman, he wrote Strider a letter about his approach to life: "Hell, you only live once, and I know you know it's better to burn out than . . . rot away in some nursing home. My philosophy is the same. In only a short 1–2 years, my body will slowly start giving way—first maybe knee pains, or back pains, or whatever, but I won't be 'peaked' anymore. Might as well do some good while I can be 100% effective! Sorry I can't be of more help, but most of the people sent my way these days are of the direct-action type, and my whole mindset has moved from the intellectual to . . . animal. (Rip the bastards heads off and shit down their necks! and I'll show you how with a simple pocket knife.)" He signed the letter, "Seeya, The Desert Rat."

On March 25, he wrote a final, cryptic letter to his sister Jennifer. He said she shouldn't write any more letters back to him. "If one is already en route, Don't send another. Send no more after 01APR, and then, even if it's an emergency—watch what you say, because I may not get it in time, and the G-men might get it out of my box, incriminating you."

Fortier noticed the grim turn in McVeigh's demeanor and decided he needed to protect himself. In those last weeks, McVeigh had urged Mike to leave Lori and travel the country with him, like "a couple desperados." Mike wanted no part of it. The Fortiers agreed to care for a relative's children, and as April began, McVeigh moved out of their home into a motel. McVeigh was clearly disgusted with Fortier and started giving him reading assignments, starting with *The Turner Diaries*, to try to jolt him into joining forces with him. Fortier thought he was getting too many "negative vibes" from McVeigh and worried that McVeigh might find it easier to kill him and his wife, since they knew so much about the bombing plot. On the night of April 12, Fortier's last visit to McVeigh's motel room, Fortier brought a gun with him to protect himself. McVeigh called Fortier a weakling and a coward, but he dismissed his old friend without violence.

The next morning, McVeigh went to the storage shed in Kingman and filled his station wagon with the blasting caps from the quarry robbery. He raced the 1,100 miles to Kansas and placed the caps with the fertilizer and racing fuel in the storage sheds so that all the bomb ingredients were together. With less than a week to go, he had only to rent the truck, assemble the bomb, and deliver it to Oklahoma City.

CHAPTER 10

The Final Days

In the final days before April 19, McVeigh made ever more meticulous plans for the bombing—except for one thing. He was almost disdainfully casual about what he would do *after* he destroyed the Murrah building.

McVeigh did make a couple of half-hearted efforts to reach out to possible allies who might shield him in the aftermath. He left a few messages for Richard Coffman, who worked for the National Alliance, the right-wing organization that published *The Turner Diaries.* Coffman never called him back. McVeigh also called Andreas Strassmeir, the German émigré who lived in Elohim City, and left him a message. But Strassmeir didn't return the call, either. These calls later generated speculation that Coffman or Strassmeir (or others) were McVeigh's accomplices. But there was never any evidence that either Coffman or Strassmeir did anything to facilitate the bombing or even that they spoke to McVeigh on the eve of the bombing. And McVeigh himself always insisted that Nichols and the Fortiers were the only ones he told about his plans for the Murrah building—and the overwhelming evidence establishes that McVeigh was telling the truth.

At this point, as McVeigh completed preparations for the bombing, he saw himself on a kind of existential journey, where he was going to let fate take over after he completed his mission. His lawyer Stephen Jones asked him why he didn't make clearer plans to escape. "This is hard to pin down in my head," McVeigh said. "There is a little bit of giving up involved there. There is a little bit of, I had nowhere to go, no allies to continue anything with. I would not want to go to a friend that did not know anything about it, because that would put their lives in danger. One thing that never came to me was a purpose after this besides a solo war, which I did not have the resources for. So, since it did not come to me, I said, 'Let's just let fate play this out. Let's see what happens.'" There is, in McVeigh's absence of planning for a next act, a similarity to the attitudes of many rioters in the Capitol on January 6, 2021. Rather, to the extent the rioters could articulate it, the mission—the fight—was the end in itself.

McVeigh saw his mission as one of illumination rather than revolution. "If I step back and look at the entire incident, I believe with 99 percent surety that I could have gotten away clean from this and continued on if I had anywhere to go. But as Mike fell out and then Terry fell out, I determined that the best way was to continue on as the Paul Revere–type messenger instead of the John Brown–type revolutionary." In other words, after the Murrah building bombing, McVeigh planned to leave the fight to others whom he would inspire.

When McVeigh left Kingman by himself on Wednesday, April 12, he originally intended to make the 1,100-mile drive straight to Kansas, but he decided to detour to Oklahoma City again. He was driving the Pontiac station wagon with Arizona plates—the car he had purchased in Michigan after the Road Warrior died. He wanted to make sure that there weren't construction projects or scaffolding blocking the space next to the Murrah building. On this circuit of his target, McVeigh didn't stop, preferring just to slow down and satisfy himself that there was room to park a truck. He swung by the alley where he planned to park the getaway car and found the space clear. He made it to Kansas on Thursday, April 13, six days before the all-important anniversary of Waco.

With Nichols's status on the project unclear, McVeigh tried to do as much as possible on his own. He spent Thursday running among the various storage sheds they had rented in the Flint Hills region and pulling all the ingredients together. As McVeigh intended when he left Arizona, the fertilizer, blasting caps, racing fuel, and all the smaller pieces, like fuses, were now "in one basket"—specifically shed number 2 in the Herington storage facility. Even though McVeigh and Nichols had made a lot of money from the Moore robbery—both in stolen cash and in the proceeds from the sales of the guns—McVeigh was still living as if he were broke. He planned to spend Thursday night in the Pontiac at Geary Lake State Park, in Junction City. Just as he pulled in, the station wagon overheated and stalled out. Continuing with that car was untenable, so he decided to make a change on Friday morning.

McVeigh recalled that when he was stationed at Fort Riley, he had gotten the Road Warrior repaired at a Firestone dealer in downtown Junction City. He thought he could find the place again, so he used some lake water to get the car running, and he coaxed it ten miles to the dealer, on Eighth Street. The mechanic took a quick look and said the gasket was blown, and it would cost $500 to fix it. McVeigh said that was more than the value of the car, so he asked where he might find a used car. McVeigh started making calls from the pay phone to find a car, when he was interrupted by the owner.

"Tim, I've got a car for you," Tom Manning said.

It had been almost five years since McVeigh was in the building, but Manning, the owner of the dealership, remembered him and his Road Warrior.

Manning took McVeigh around back and showed him a 1977 Mercury Grand Marquis. The car was an enormous land yacht, a four-door artifact from the days when carmakers didn't worry about gas mileage. The car had once been bright yellow, but it had faded a great deal in almost two decades, and several panels had rusted entirely. "It's not pretty but it runs real good," Manning said. He told McVeigh the price was $350 plus the Pontiac station wagon as a trade-in.

"Can I Jew you down?" McVeigh asked, according to Manning.

The Mercury was older and barely more functional than the Pontiac; among other defects, the radio and gas gauge were broken. In the end, Manning relented. "Just give me $250—to hell with the rest," he said. Since Manning recognized McVeigh, it wouldn't have made sense for him to use the fake "Kling" identification card with the address in South Dakota. So, for the bill of sale, McVeigh showed Manning his real driver's license, which came from Michigan, and asked for the record to be mailed to him at 3616 North Van Dyke Road, Decker, Michigan—the Nichols family farm. While Manning's mechanic refreshed the Mercury's transmission fluid and found a new spare tire, McVeigh used his phone card to make a couple of calls.

McVeigh had already researched where he could rent a Ryder truck—a place called Elliott's Body Shop, about three miles away on a hillside outside downtown Junction City. McVeigh called, gave his name as Bob Kling, and said he needed a truck that would carry five thousand pounds. Vicki Beemer, the office manager, consulted a chart and said he needed a twenty-footer. McVeigh asked for the truck on Sunday, April 16, but Beemer said Elliott's would be closed for Easter Sunday. So, McVeigh reserved one for Monday, April 17. He said he'd be paying cash.

From the same phone, McVeigh called Nichols at home in Herington. They arranged to meet in a couple of hours—at noon in the park at Geary Lake.

McVeigh then returned to the dealer and moved his handful of belongings—a couple of bags of clothes and a set of jumper cables—

to the Mercury. He transferred the Arizona license plates from the Pontiac to the Mercury, fastening the plate with two screws at the top. Then he headed to Geary Lake to meet Nichols.

McVeigh and Nichols had not had a real conversation in months, since around the time of the Roger Moore robbery the previous November. With the bombing a few days away, they had to take stock of where they were and how, or even whether, they were both going to proceed.

According to McVeigh, Nichols was his usual sour, withdrawn self, worried as always about money. Marife had come back with him from the Philippines, and he said she was giving him a hard time. She hadn't uprooted herself from Cebu City to live in a broken-down house in a bedraggled town in the middle of nowhere. McVeigh listened quietly but with little patience. He wasn't interested in their marital drama. McVeigh just wanted to get on with the plan.

It's difficult to know what Nichols was thinking. His lawyers later argued that he had the same fear as Fortier—that McVeigh might kill him because he knew too much about the bombing plan. But unlike Fortier, Nichols was in no position to go to the police or FBI and blow the whistle. Nichols had bought and stored much of the fertilizer, stolen the blasting caps from the quarry, and robbed Moore. If Nichols went to the authorities, he would have had to incriminate himself in several crimes. And though he was not nearly as outspoken as McVeigh—and not a letter writer—Nichols shared the same grievances against Clinton and the federal government. In any event, after about a two-hour conversation, they made their deal. Nichols agreed that on Sunday, April 16, he would take his pickup on the 250-mile trip to Oklahoma City at the same time as McVeigh drove the Mercury to leave it at the parking place in the alley. Nichols would then drive them both back to Kansas. Then, once McVeigh had rented the truck, Nichols agreed to help McVeigh mix the explosives in the barrels. But as for the bombing itself on Wednesday, McVeigh was on his own.

McVeigh had been content to sleep in the back of the Pontiac station wagon, but the back seat of the Mercury was too cramped. He needed a motel room, and Nichols gave him the cash for one. The meeting at the lake ended inauspiciously. The battery died in the Mercury, which McVeigh had bought just that morning, and Nichols had to give him a jump start. Then McVeigh headed back into Junction City, to get a new battery at Walmart.

At around 4 p.m., McVeigh swung by the Dreamland Motel to register. The Dreamland was a regional landmark of sorts, with its distinctive sign—a five-cornered red star—visible to motorists passing through Junction City on I-70. Lea McGown, the motel owner, was a local institution herself. A German immigrant with a strong accent and big personality, she kept a tight rein on her place, leaving the premises for only two days a year, Christmas and Easter. The nearby presence of Fort Riley guaranteed a steady stream of customers, but she had no patience for loudmouths or deadbeats.

The moment that McVeigh registered at the Dreamland was momentous, though it did not seem that way at the time. He had spent at least the previous seven months, since Clinton signed the assault weapons ban, singularly focused on the plan for the bombing. He'd assembled the ingredients and was ready to begin final preparations. But Nichols had told him earlier that day that he would be on his own for the critical moment in Oklahoma City. Now, with a certain weariness, McVeigh accepted the idea that he was going to get caught or die in the process. He wasn't going to hide anymore. He had planned to use the name Kling throughout the final days and wear a disguise when he rented the truck and checked into the motel. But that plan had already fallen apart when Tom Manning recognized him as he bought the Mercury. At the Dreamland, McVeigh didn't bother with a disguise, and when Lea McGown asked him his name for the motel registry, he said Tim McVeigh. For his home address, McVeigh listed 3616 North Van Dyke Road, Decker, Michigan—the Nichols family farm. As he told Jones, "I'm sure subconsciously it was like giving up because I know for a fact giving them a composite"—that is, the chance to prepare a sketch of him—"was giving up."

As always, though, McVeigh was looking for a bargain. The posted rate was $24 per night, but McVeigh said that since he was planning to stay for four nights, why couldn't she cut the rate to $20? McGown agreed and took McVeigh's prepayment of $88.95 in cash.

McGown had a sixth sense for trouble, and McVeigh raised her suspicions. With his crew cut and neat clothes, he looked like one of the soldiers she saw all the time. But his car—the Mercury—was a total wreck. The contrast between the man and his car was peculiar. Therefore, she gave him room 25, the one closest to the office, so she could keep an eye on him. (Ever thrifty, McVeigh thought the Mercury was now running well with the old battery, so he returned the new battery to Walmart for a refund.)

On Saturday morning, April 15, McVeigh drove to Elliott's Body Shop, to complete the transaction for the Ryder truck. He had already spoken on the phone to Vicki Beemer and given his name as Kling, maintaining the fiction. This time he told Eldon Elliott, the owner, that he would need the truck on Monday, April 17, and he would drop it off in Omaha on Friday, April 21. Elliott asked if "Kling" wanted to buy insurance; otherwise, he would be liable for any damage to the truck. Considering what was going to happen to the truck, McVeigh had to suppress a smile, and he declined the coverage. "I won't need any," he said. "I'm a good driver." Eldon accepted McVeigh's $280.32 in cash, which included $15 for a hand truck, and he told McVeigh the truck would be waiting for him on Monday.

With the transaction complete, McVeigh was at loose ends for the rest of Saturday. He wandered around Junction City for several hours before he made it back to the Dreamland. At around 5 p.m., he placed an order from the Hunam [*sic*] Palace restaurant, a favorite from his Army days; he even remembered the phone number. He ordered moo goo gai pan for $7.25 and added egg rolls for $2.00 to make the $8.00 minimum for delivery. He gave his name as Kling, which showed how careless he had become. He was Kling to rent the truck; McVeigh to book his room; Kling to order food delivered to his room. He was making it easy for the authorities, when the time came, to show that McVeigh and Kling were the same person. When the deliveryman, a twenty-two-year-old named Jeff Davis, came to his room with the food, McVeigh gave him $10 and told him to keep the change.

The tension between McVeigh and Nichols flared again on Sunday, April 16. They had planned to meet in the morning at the Geary Lake park so they could caravan in their separate vehicles to Oklahoma City to stash the getaway car. But Nichols didn't show. Fuming, McVeigh drove the twenty miles south to Herington, where he tried Nichols from a pay phone at a Dairy Queen.

"Where the hell are you?" he yelled. Nichols explained that Marife had wanted to go to church on Easter morning, so he had taken her. But now Nichols was ready, so he told Marife a phony tale that McVeigh's car had broken down in Omaha, and he was going to pick him up. In truth, Nichols drove his pickup to meet McVeigh for the four-hour drive to Oklahoma City. McVeigh told Nichols about the broken gas gauge on the Mercury, so he didn't really know how much gas he had in the tank. Because the banged-up engine probably got lousy gas mileage, McVeigh told Nichols that he would be making two stops for gas. At the second stop, planning ahead, McVeigh stuffed a blue paper towel in the gas cap. If the paper was gone when he returned to the car after the bombing, he would know that someone had siphoned the gas.

McVeigh made it to Oklahoma City, and he wedged the Mercury into the alley a few blocks from the Murrah building. In light of the secluded location, he doubted that anyone would tamper with or tow the grungy old car, but he didn't want to take a chance. He scrawled a note and left it on the dashboard: "NOT ABANDONED. PLEASE DO NOT TOW. WILL MOVE BY APRIL 23. (NEEDS BATTERY & CABLE.)" McVeigh took care to place the note to cover the vehicle identification number on the dashboard so the car could not be tracked without breaking into it. Just before he walked away to reunite with Nichols, McVeigh made another fateful decision: he removed the license plate from the Mercury. Driving a getaway car without a license plate was an invitation to be stopped by the police. Why did he take that chance?

"There were two things working here," McVeigh told Jones. "There was a somewhat conscious effort in my mind that I was pretty much going to be caught anyway. Second, I did not want to leave my plate on the car in case in the three days before the bombing a police officer ran the plate to find the abandoned car's owner. So, therefore, I took the plate off and backed it to within about two inches of this brick wall." In other words, he removed the license plate, but he still wanted to make it difficult for a casual observer to notice it was missing.

After McVeigh parked the Mercury in the alley, he went to the spot where he had arranged for Nichols to pick him up. At first Nichols didn't show, and McVeigh worried that he had stranded him, but eventually Nichols's pickup pulled into view. They stopped at McDonald's for dinner, then drove north to Kansas, where Nichols took McVeigh back to the Dreamland in Junction City.

Now carless, McVeigh had little to do on Monday morning, April 17. He spent time trying to memorize the number on the phony South

Dakota driver's license that he had procured from the ad in *Soldier of Fortune.* He was hoping that he could just recite it when he rented the Ryder at Elliott's later that day. If he didn't have to display it, there was less chance for anyone to discover it was fake.

In the afternoon, he took a cab from the Dreamland to a McDonald's that was about a mile away from Elliott's Body Shop. In some ways, McVeigh was still trying to cover his tracks, and he didn't want a record of a cab going directly to Elliott's. When he arrived at the body shop, he wore a cap, but didn't disguise himself, as he had once planned to do. Even that morning, he thought about going in with a scruffy beard, but then he gave up on the idea. "I also that morning specifically shaved off some rough beard I had been growing for five or six days, to purposely hide my clean-shaven look. That way, wearing a hat and being scruffy, no one would have a clue that I had a military appearance. But I said, 'The hell with it, I'm just going in flat-top, and let's see what they can do with that.'"

The office at Elliott's was busy when McVeigh arrived. When he was called on, he had his patter ready for the people behind the desk. He said he had split with his girlfriend and was going to drive her stuff to Omaha. He'd visit his parents in South Dakota later. As he hoped, he never had to present the fake license, just recite the number. They gave him the keys to a twenty-foot Ryder truck, and he went on his way to the Dreamland.

After McVeigh pulled into the motel, he parked by the swimming pool. Irritated by and suspicious of McVeigh, Lea McGown asked her son to tell McVeigh to move the truck to a spot out front, by the big sign. The conversation worried McVeigh, because it meant that the son was now another witness who could tie him to the Ryder truck. Originally, McVeigh had planned to park the truck overnight at the local Walmart so the folks at the Dreamland wouldn't associate him with it. "But I drove it to the motel," he told Jones. "This was the final step in the conscious effort that I wasn't going to get away anyway." It's true that McVeigh behaved in Junction City almost as if he wanted to get caught. Toggling back and forth between a real and fake name was hardly the mark of a sophisticated criminal. After the fact, with his customarily high self-regard, McVeigh said it was all on purpose, like he was on a courageous journey to his doom. That may be; it may also be that his actions were the result of incompetence.

McVeigh didn't leave the motel again Monday night, preferring to dine on MREs—military meals ready to eat—which he had thrown in his bag. The plan for Tuesday, April 18, was to mix the bomb. He was going to meet Nichols at 6 a.m. at the storage unit in Herington, where all the bomb ingredients were waiting—if, that is, Nichols decided to show up.

CHAPTER 11

The Blood of Patriots and Tyrants

At about 4:30 a.m. on Monday, April 17, Lea McGown took up her customary vigil at her Dreamland Motel and peered out toward the darkened parking lot. She saw a light in the cab of the Ryder truck and the figure of her guest Tim McVeigh hunched over the steering wheel. He looked like he was reading a map, which he was. She looked again at around 5:30 a.m., but McVeigh and the truck were gone.

Wired for a big day, McVeigh had risen early to make yet another journey on Route 77. Ever since he was stationed at Fort Riley, key moments of his life had taken place along this quiet two-lane blacktop that passes through the Flint Hills. From Junction City, it was thirteen miles to Geary Lake State Park, nineteen more to Herington. On this day, for the final time of his life, McVeigh would make a circuit through those familiar locations, in anticipation of his world-changing plan for the following day.

McVeigh told Nichols they should both report for duty in Herington at 6 a.m. McVeigh would park the Ryder truck at the storage facility, then walk across the street to the Pizza Hut, where Nichols would park his GMC pickup. (They didn't want the Ryder truck and pickup to be seen together.) The two men would then walk back across the street and start loading the bomb ingredients into the Ryder truck.

McVeigh arrived at Pizza Hut right on time, but Nichols didn't show . . . and didn't show. After about a half hour, McVeigh gave up and started work by himself. He backed the Ryder up to the door of unit 2 at the storage facility, pulled down the ramp from the cargo bay, and used the hand truck to load. It was hard work. He started with the light stuff—about a dozen empty 55-gallon drums, then the blasting caps from the quarry robbery. Then the main ingredients: about seventy 50-pound bags of fertilizer, and the three 55-gallon drums of racing fuel, which each weighed about 400 pounds. There were also fuses and other miscellaneous tools and ingredients.

Finally, sometime after 6:30, Nichols straggled in, but McVeigh sensed something was off. The first thing Nichols did was to suggest that they close the storage shed, go to Geary Lake, and come back later. "Something didn't sound right in his voice, whether he was going to back out, had second thoughts," McVeigh told Jones. McVeigh rejected Nichols's idea. "I started, I'm going to finish, you can help or not," he said. Sheepishly, Nichols went to park his pickup at the Pizza Hut and returned to help McVeigh finish loading the truck.

McVeigh left a few items in the shed—the Arizona license plate that he had removed from the Mercury, a rifle from the Moore robbery, his beloved shortwave radio, some ammunition, clothes, and a sleeping bag. The rough plan called for McVeigh to retrieve his belongings after the bombing on Wednesday. They locked the shed with a combination lock; neither one wanted to have a key that might link them to the contents. But McVeigh wasn't sure he would ever make it back to Kansas after the bombing; he told Nichols that if he didn't return, Nichols should just remove everything from the shed and clean it out.

Just as McVeigh and Nichols were finishing loading the Ryder, a man in a pickup truck pulled into a veterinary clinic that was next door to the storage facility. McVeigh watched him and thought, "I hope this person does not come over as they do in the country and say hi." He had a handgun in a shoulder holster. "If someone discovers us now, he's got to be put out," he told Jones. But the man never approached the truck. With all the ingredients in the Ryder, McVeigh headed back north toward Geary Lake. Nichols followed in his pickup.

Two days earlier, on Easter Sunday, Rick Wahl, a sergeant assigned to Fort Riley, had taken his eleven-year-old son fishing at Geary Lake State Park. They cast their lines from the bank, but figured they'd do better if they rented a boat and a depth finder. Thus equipped, they returned to the lake around 9 a.m. on Tuesday, April 18. When they arrived, they noted a curious sight toward the end of the dirt road that circles the lake.

A large Ryder truck was parked next to the water. Right behind it was a GMC pickup. The park was a modest fishing hole with a few picnic tables. What was a Ryder truck doing there? With a pickup no less? Why were they so close together? It was a windy day, and the fishing was disappointing, so Wahl and his son didn't stay long. But the sight of the vehicles was unusual enough that it stuck with Wahl.

This final meeting at Geary Lake was when all of McVeigh's research paid off. He was barely out of high school when he first encountered *The Turner Diaries*, which planted the idea of a truck bomb in his head and gave basic instructions about how to build one. Over the years, McVeigh never strayed too far from that basic concept. At first he educated himself about bomb-making, studying books like *The Poor Man's James Bond* and *The Anarchist Cookbook*. But then he delved deeper into the subject, first as he watched James Nichols blow up tree stumps in Michigan and then as he borrowed actual bomb-making guides from the library in Kingman. McVeigh's life had built to this moment. He knew exactly what to do.

"We immediately started to mix" at the lake, McVeigh told Jones. The idea was to prepare twelve barrels of fertilizer and fuel. McVeigh hefted the 50-pound bags of fertilizer, and Nichols, using the hand pump that they'd bought with the fuel outside Dallas, poured in the "nitro"—the nitromethane racing fuel. (He used a funnel made from a Gatorade bottle.) McVeigh had learned that the best ratio was five parts solid to two parts liquid—seven 50-pound bags of fertilizer and seven 20-pound buckets of fuel per 55-gallon drum. As McVeigh had demonstrated for Lori Fortier with soup cans in Kingman, he arranged the barrels in a V-shape in the cargo bay, with the tip pointed toward the passenger side—toward the Murrah building—to focus the effect of the blast.

About midway through the process, McVeigh recognized a problem. He was running out of nitro. But he improvised a backup plan. He told Nichols to siphon diesel fuel from his pickup. They then poured the diesel into the remaining fertilizer bags to make an ANFO bomb—which stands for ammonium nitrate–fuel oil. This is a much more common type of explosive, frequently used on farms to blow up tree stumps and rocks. It's less powerful than a nitro bomb, but still packs a considerable punch. The ANFO served another purpose. "I knew chemical traces would be taken at the scene of the crime to determine what the explosive was made out of," he told Jones. "I figured if we put diesel in there it would throw them off, at least a little bit, if not completely. Sure enough, that is what happened." Speaking with his attorney later, McVeigh lamented that he had run out of nitro, rendering the bomb a little less powerful. "What I am saying is there could have been more damage than was done," he said.

They were down to the final tasks. Nichols nailed wooden blocks to the floor of the cargo bay, to keep the barrels from sliding as McVeigh drove the Ryder to Oklahoma City. Nichols used his drill—the same one he had used on the locks at the quarry—to make two holes in the back of the cab to the cargo bay. McVeigh then threaded the fuses through the holes. (The truck bomb in *The Turner Diaries* had the same kind of holes in the cab for the fuses.) To make sure the bomb went off, McVeigh connected two fuses—one that would last two minutes, the other five minutes. McVeigh had one more task. He was filthy, covered in residue from the mix. He had brought an extra set of clothes, including clean boots. He carefully removed what he was wearing and placed it all in a bag that he would dump along the way to Oklahoma City. (Nichols disposed of the empty bags of fertilizer.) McVeigh decided to keep one article of clothing: his T-shirt, which he would wear the following day as well. He had designed it himself and had it printed at a gun show. On the front was a drawing of Abraham Lincoln, with the words "Sic semper tyrannis"—which was what John Wilkes Booth yelled after he shot the president, meaning "Thus always to tyrants." On the back of the shirt was a drawing of a tree, and a quotation from Thomas Jefferson: "The tree of liberty must be refreshed from time to time with the blood of patriots and tyrants."

They finished at the lake around noon and said their goodbyes, unsure if they would ever see each other again. "You know," Nichols said as they packed up, "I found out something today. Marife is leaving, she's going back to the Philippines." McVeigh rolled his eyes, indicating that he had heard this song before. "Well, this time she is going back for good," Nichols protested. "We've decided to end it." McVeigh knew that Nichols's commitment to their project had been wavering, and he wondered if the grim news about his marriage had prompted him, in a fatalistic way, to help build the bomb.

Nichols added that he was going to leave some money for McVeigh in the Herington storage unit as well as a phone card he had bought at a truck stop. (Ironically, if the two men had used truck stop phone cards all along, instead of the one they bought by mail from the ad in *The Spotlight*, it would have been much more difficult for the authorities to track them.)

"Good luck," Nichols said, and they parted.

But as McVeigh drove away in the Ryder, Nichols shouted for him to stop. He pointed out that diesel fuel was leaking out of the side of the truck. McVeigh's last-minute improvisation to use ANFO had created a problem. The fuel was seeping out of the fertilizer bags into the cargo bay and then dripping outside. McVeigh thought of buying kitty litter, to absorb the spill, but they thought he shouldn't be seen inside a store at this point. Instead, he just decided to hope the leak would stop. He pulled out of the park for the last time and headed south toward Oklahoma City, about four hours away.

After about an hour, McVeigh stopped to see if the fuel was still leaking. It was. After another hour, he stopped again at a gas station. He opened the rear gate to check on the load. The barrels hadn't moved, but the bags were soaked and dripping. He figured there was nothing he could do, so he just locked the truck's rear gate and side door. "We were thinking that even if we parked in front of the building, if you have some Rambo looking in there, it would create problems," he told Jones, "so we put locks on there that would defeat them long enough for the load to go off."

McVeigh switched to I-35, the main interstate between Kansas and Oklahoma. By late afternoon, McVeigh began thinking about where to spend the night. He had planned to park at a truck stop near Oklahoma City, but he worried that the fuel leak would draw attention. "I don't even know where to park the truck now without somebody coming up to say, 'Hey, you're leaking fuel,'" he said. When McVeigh reached Guthrie, Oklahoma, which was just thirty miles north of Oklahoma City, he remembered a McDonald's and a Best Western just off the exit. He parked with the leaking part of the truck close to the building, blocking the view of the problem. He got something to eat at McDonald's and thought about spending the night in the motel. But when he entered the lobby, he saw there were people in line ahead of him, and he didn't want anyone there to see him. Besides, he had destroyed the phony "Kling" driver's license when he was back at the Dreamland, so he would have had to check in using his real name. Thinking better of the whole idea, McVeigh spent the night of April 18 in the cab of the Ryder truck in the McDonald's parking lot.

In the weeks leading up to April 19, McVeigh completed one project for the post-bombing period. He collected a group of political writings to take with him on the mission. He wanted to convey why the bombing had taken place, and the collection would explain it. As McVeigh said to Jones, "The paperwork was to give a reason why I did what I did in case I got caught in the blast or something." Still, it wasn't clear—even to McVeigh—how he was going to use the papers. Perhaps, if he got away, he might mail the collection to a newspaper or television network. Perhaps, if he was caught, he would just leave it in the Mercury and wait for it to be discovered. All McVeigh knew for sure was that he wanted to assemble the writings as a cross between a will and a manifesto.

By the time McVeigh left on his final trip to Oklahoma City, the legal-sized envelope was about a quarter-inch thick—with a few dozen pages inside. Some were photocopies, some were quotations and comments in McVeigh's distinctive hand. There was a page photocopied from *The Turner Diaries*, which McVeigh had marked with a yellow highlighter: "The real value of our attacks today lies in the psychological impact, not in the immediate casualties. More important, though, is what we taught the politicians and the bureaucrats. They learned this afternoon that not one of them is beyond our reach." (This would have been a fitting message from the January 6 rioters to the politicians in the Capitol who refused to anoint Trump the winner of the 2020 election.) Much of the material related to McVeigh's idea of patriotism. There were quotations from the Founding Fathers (Patrick Henry and Samuel Adams) and their influences (John Locke). There was a copy of the Declaration of Independence, with McVeigh's handwriting at the bottom: "Obey the Constitution of the United States, and we won't shoot you." There was harsh criticism of the Waco raid, which McVeigh called "a cruel sadistic crime"—proof that "the U.S. government has declared open warfare on the American people."

The items reflected McVeigh's hope that the bombing would prompt others to revolt against the government. There was one of the bumper stickers that he had tried to sell at Waco. It said WHEN THE GOVERNMENT FEARS THE PEOPLE, THERE IS LIBERTY. WHEN THE PEOPLE FEAR THE GOVERNMENT, THERE IS TYRANNY. Beneath it, McVeigh scrawled: "Maybe now, there will be Liberty!"

In addition to the envelope, McVeigh's only possessions that final night were his wallet with his Michigan driver's license, the handgun in his shoulder holster, a knife, and a business card that was McVeigh's creepy idea of a joke. When he had taken the two Christmas-wrapped boxes of blasting caps to Michigan several months earlier, he thought he had a deal to sell them for $2,500 each to a gun dealer named Dave Paulsen. But Paulsen backed out, and McVeigh decided to vent his long-gestating anger by leaving behind Paulsen's business card. This, McVeigh knew, would cast suspicion on Paulsen, even though he knew nothing about McVeigh's plans. In the parking lot in Guthrie, McVeigh set his watch alarm for 7 a.m. on April 19 and went to sleep.

McVeigh was already awake and ready to go by the time his watch buzzed. He got good news when he stepped outside to inspect the truck. There was residue from the leak on the yellow exterior, but the flow had stopped. He set off for Oklahoma City, being careful to obey the speed limits—going neither too fast nor too slow—to avoid being stopped by the police. McVeigh had thrown the "Kling" rental agreement in the back with the barrels, so he had no proof of his right to drive the truck. If he was stopped, McVeigh told Jones, he would have to "take care of whoever pulled me over." No one did.

McVeigh had planned to detonate the bomb at 10 a.m.—to catch the full complement of federal workers after they had settled into their offices—but he made it to Oklahoma City faster than he expected. Even after he got caught in a bit of late rush hour traffic around 8:45 a.m., he was going to arrive at the Murrah building about an hour early. From his repeated visits, he knew the tangle of highway exits that would get him to NW 5th Street, which ran along the front of his target. He recalled a Firestone dealer a few blocks away from the Murrah building. As he told Jones, he "parked the truck, turned around in my seat, used my Bic lighter, and lit the five-minute fuse." He put in a pair of earplugs and pulled a black cap low over his forehead. It was almost 9 a.m.

When he was a half block from the Murrah building, he stopped at a red light. It had been a little awkward twisting his body to light the five-minute fuse, he said, "so I determined I had better light the two-minute at the light, instead of fumbling in front of the building. So, I turned around at the red light and lit the fuse."

To McVeigh, the traffic signal seemed to take a very long time to turn green.

When it did, he eased the truck into the small indentation in the sidewalk, which was there to facilitate drop-offs without blocking traffic. There were no other cars by the building, so McVeigh took care to line the truck exactly parallel to the sidewalk. "I set the parking brake, dropped the key behind the seat so that if any Rambo jumped in the truck or something, he could not get it started or move it or anything," he said. "Opened the door, locked it, shut the door behind me." He took the envelope with the political writings with him.

Trying to avoid calling attention to himself, McVeigh walked at a normal pace toward the YMCA building, which shielded the alley where he had parked the Mercury. When he was out of view of anyone in front of the building, he began jogging—and worrying. "In my mind, I'm thinking it didn't go off yet, something is wrong," he told Jones.

McVeigh spied the Mercury in the alley, and broke into a jog again when—

AP IMAGES/RICK BOWMER

The bomb went off at 9:02 a.m. on April 19, 1995, destroying about a third of the Murrah building.

ZUMA/SHUTTERSTOCK

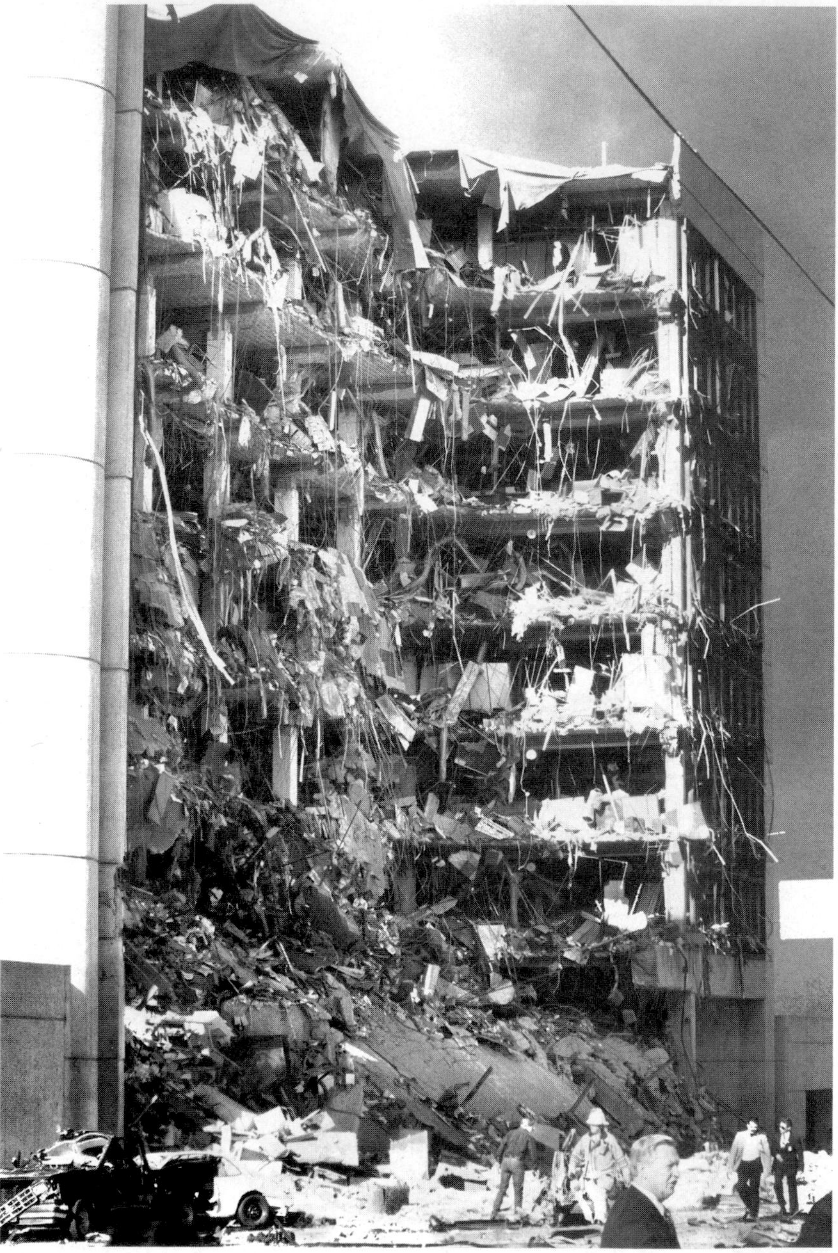

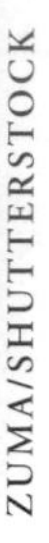

Most of the 168 victims were killed by debris, not by the explosion itself.

ULLSTEIN/TOPFOTO/CHARLES PORTER IV

Aspiring photographer Charles Porter IV rushed to the scene and saw firefighter Chris Fields cradling Baylee Almon, who did not survive. This heartland Pietà became a symbol of the horror and tragedy of the bombing.

AP PHOTO/JUSTICE DEPARTMENT

This truck axle was blown hundreds of feet through the air and nearly destroyed this Ford Festiva. The identification number on the axle led investigators to the Ryder truck rented in Junction City, Kansas.

ORLIN WAGNER/AP/SHUTTERSTOCK

From the moment Terry Nichols was arrested, he wore this blank and bewildered expression.

REUTERS/LEE CELANO

Michael Fortier, McVeigh and Nichols's stoner Army buddy, looked this way in the first days after the bombing, but prosecutors made sure he cleaned up when he became a key witness for the government.

The most famous perp walk of the twentieth century: FBI agents lead Timothy McVeigh from the courthouse in Perry, Oklahoma, on April 21, 1995. McVeigh's stone-faced image left an indelible impression.

AP PHOTO/RICK BOWMER

Merrick Garland gave a press briefing after representing the government in Timothy McVeigh's first court appearance. He was ultimately called back to Washington to supervise the floundering investigation of the Unabomber.

AP PHOTO/KATHY ROBERTS

McVeigh's lead lawyer, Stephen Jones (right), and his second-in-command, Rob Nigh, invited a photographer to take this photo in the El Reno prison in Oklahoma so that newspapers would have another picture of McVeigh besides the sinister-looking image of the perp walk.

AP PHOTO/DAVID LONGSTREATH

Michael Tigar (seated) combined scholarly erudition and down-home folk wisdom in leading the defense of Terry Nichols.

GETTY IMAGES/AFP/DOUG COLLIER

Stephen Jones (left) and Richard Burr (right), who handled death penalty issues for the defense, clashed over legal strategy and Jones's high media profile.

AP PHOTO/ED ANDRIESKI

Joseph Hartzler (on scooter) led the McVeigh prosecution team, which included Larry Mackey (striped tie, on left), Beth Wilkinson, and Scott Mendeloff (light suit, behind Hartzler).

The Oklahoma City National Memorial & Museum opened in 2000. On the site of the Murrah building, the memorial features 168 commemorative chairs to honor those killed in the bombing. The chairs of the 19 children who were killed are smaller than the others.

CHAPTER 12

The Oklahoma Standard

Florence Rogers was known to her employees as Mother Goose. She was sixty in 1995, a good deal older than the thirty-three people who worked for her at the Oklahoma City branch of the Federal Employees Credit Union, and she took a maternal interest in their lives. Located on the third floor, the credit union was a social crossroads in the Murrah building. Rogers called it the "credit union kitchen table," because so many people stopped by to chat, or take out a few dollars, before they went to the fourth-floor cafeteria for lunch.

April 19 was Rogers's first day in the office after a week's vacation. She had taken a cruise with her sister, and she'd brought photos to share with her colleagues. She arrived around 8 a.m., to give herself a little time to set up for a meeting with her direct reports at 8:30 a.m., before the credit union opened to the public at 9:00. The credit union had just installed a new boardroom, and Rogers was looking forward to meeting with her staff there for the first time. But the printer in the boardroom wasn't working, so she decided to hold the meeting in her office instead.

Rogers was a stickler in one way—office attire. At the time, casual clothes were beginning to infiltrate the corporate world, but Rogers wanted no part of the trend. For her staff, which was almost all women, she insisted on dresses, suits, and makeup. Whenever she heard a woman on her team say, "Mother Goose, I don't feel good," her first response was usually "Well, go put on some lipstick, and see how you feel after that." On this Wednesday morning, one staff member thought that they were dressed in colors reflecting the holiday they had just celebrated. "Look at all of us," Claudette Meek, a vice president, said as the seven staff members gathered their chairs in a half circle around Rogers's desk. "We look like a basket of Easter eggs, don't we?"

The remark prompted Rogers to note the tidy outfits, and she spread out her vacation photos on the desk, near her collection of ceramic geese. As it happened, the seven—including two vice presidents, the chief teller, the credit card manager, the head of marketing, and the office manager—were all women. (The comptroller, the only man who directly reported to Rogers, was absent that day.) At the last minute, Rogers's administrative assistant joined, too.

The group had completed their first agenda item, and Rogers turned to look at her computer to find the second one. When she did, at 9:02 a.m., "a tornado-like concussive force hurled me away from my desk and flung me against the wall like spaghetti in a toddler's hand," she recalled in an interview. When Rogers came to her senses, the scene was hellish. The air was choked with concrete dust and smoke. Boulders and twisted wires were everywhere. A cement pillar had destroyed her office chair, and a steel beam was on the floor beside her. Her desk was intact, and as she looked toward her colleagues, she saw that they were gone. Her desk was hanging over the edge of what was left of the floor.

The seven colleagues who were on the other side of the desk had disappeared, having fallen into the abyss where the front third of the building had been. They all died. (The conference room was destroyed; if the meeting had been held there, Rogers would have died, too.) The bombing killed eighteen of the thirty-three people who worked for Rogers at the credit union. The eighteen who died left fourteen children without a parent.

Gabreon Bruce had just turned three months old, so his mother, Daina Bradley, wanted to get him a Social Security card. Bradley, who was just twenty years old, was unfamiliar with the bureaucracy, so she took a family delegation to the Murrah building. She brought her three-year-old daughter, Peachlyn; her mother, Cheryl Hammon, forty-four; her sister Falesha Bradley-Joyner, twenty-three; as well as her baby. They wanted to beat the rush, so they arrived around 8 a.m., but there was already a line at the Social Security Administration, which was on the first floor.

Daina's mother did most of the line-waiting so Daina could sit elsewhere and keep her kids from fussing. Her mother brought her the paperwork to sign, when Daina noticed a flash of light, before everything went dark. She heard voices, but then she began floating in and out of consciousness. Daina could hear her children screaming, but she had no idea where they were or how to reach them.

Andy Sullivan was chief of orthopedics at the University of Oklahoma Medical Center, which was about a mile away from the Murrah building. He heard the bomb go off, went to the roof of the hospital, and saw the smoke rising. He put on scrubs and rushed to the scene, but he was told he was needed back at the hospital, to help care for the wounded. Then, around 11 a.m., he received a call from a colleague on the scene. A woman was trapped under the rubble, and there appeared to be no way to extricate her except to amputate her leg. Could Andy get an amputation set—sterile instruments for removing a limb—and rush to the scene? Sullivan left his wallet and wedding rings behind, carrying only his driver's license. If he was trapped in the building, or buried under a collapse, he wanted to be identified.

The missing portions of the building's nine floors had collapsed into a kind of pyramid, which became known as "the pile." When Sullivan reached the scene, he grabbed a hard hat and began picking his way around the pile to find the colleague who had summoned him. Sullivan crawled around live electrical wires, through puddles of water, and over miscellaneous debris. Even with a portable generator powering special lights, it was hard to see through the dust. Finally, he reached Daina Bradley, who had a huge concrete beam across her leg. She was lying in about six inches of water, and her face was covered with so much dust that it looked like Kabuki makeup. Sullivan removed his helmet to slide in on his belly to the tiny space beside Bradley. It was clear to Sullivan that there was no way to save her except to amputate her leg.

As Sullivan was explaining the situation to Daina, they received word that there was another bomb in the building and were told to evacuate immediately. Bradley screamed not to be left alone, but Sullivan and his small team hustled out of the darkness. It took forty-five minutes for the all-clear after the bomb scare. When they returned, Sullivan devised a plan. He would do a through-the-knee amputation; any other type of amputation would have involved cutting through bone, which he didn't have the time or equipment to do.

Daina refused—she wanted to save her leg. But Sullivan insisted she would die of exposure and shock if he didn't amputate right away. She relented.

Sullivan had to lie on top of Bradley to get access to her knee. He improvised a tourniquet, tightened it, and injected her with a drug called Versed, which operated as an anesthetic, albeit an imperfect one. Sullivan took a deep breath, said a prayer, and began cutting with a scalpel. Bradley screamed and thrashed. Sullivan kept cutting, but he couldn't get all the way through. The scalpel was getting too dull. Frustrated, Sullivan reached into his back pocket for his pocketknife, which happened to be new, and completed the amputation. Firefighters removed Bradley from the rubble.

Bradley's mother and her two children died that day. Daina Bradley and her sister, who also suffered terrible injuries, survived.

Baylee Almon celebrated her first birthday on April 18. The next day, Aren Almon, who was a single mother, took Baylee to day care, as she did most days. Baylee went to America's Kids, the day care on the second floor of the Murrah building. Capacity at the day care was thirty children, but there had been a recent change of management, and some parents removed their kids. On the morning of April 19, twenty-one children, all preschoolers, came to play and learn.

Visitors could look above the main entrance to the Murrah building and see kids' artwork taped to the black glass of America's Kids. Next to the window were four cribs for the youngest children; the infants would look out the window and often reached for the clouds that hurried by in the steady Oklahoma wind. America's Kids opened at 7 a.m. and served breakfast at 8 a.m. At 9 a.m., on this Wednesday, it was song time, and the group was singing the Barney song—"I love you, you love me"—when the bomb struck.

The first responders to the scene had to pick their way through flames before they even arrived at the building. In the parking lot on 5th Street, the force of the blast had set several cars on fire; their gas tanks and tires had exploded, giving some observers the impression that there were more bombs. The spot where McVeigh had parked the truck was now a seven-foot-deep hole. Amid the smoke and fire, the responders could scarcely see what was in front of them. But when they began to see and hear victims, many were children. Because of the location of the day care center, some of the first victims to be found were the youngest. The firefighters on the scene brought out so many children that they began to line up their small bodies on the sidewalk, in a kind of temporary morgue. A priest arrived on the scene and began blessing the dead, and people started calling the improvised morgue "the church."

A police sergeant named John Avera had already helped two women escape from the wreckage when he returned to try to find more. He found a baby without any signs of life. At a minimum, the child's left arm and leg were broken. Avera sprinted with the baby toward the back exit of the building, through the parking garage. Avera shouted, "I have a critical infant! I have a critical infant!" He found a firefighter, who pointed to a nearby ambulance. Avera walked that way, and the firefighter, Captain Chris Fields, took the baby—Baylee Almon—from his arms.

At that moment, a twenty-five-year-old bank employee and aspiring photographer named Charles Porter IV came upon the scene, pointed his camera, and clicked the shutter. That afternoon, Porter took the film to a local Walmart to be developed, and when he picked it up, the clerk began to cry when she looked at one picture in particular. At the suggestion of a friend, Porter took that picture to the local office of the Associated Press, where the photo editor put it on the AP wire.

The picture showed Baylee Almon sprawled in Fields's arms. Baylee's head is bloodied, and her right arm and both legs are limp. The sun illuminates Fields's red helmet, but his face is otherwise in shadow. This heartland Pietà became a symbol of the nightmare of April 19. Baylee was pronounced dead at the hospital.

The horror that befell Florence Rogers's colleagues, Daina Bradley and her family, and Baylee Almon was repeated in the experiences of hundreds of other people. As best as could be determined after the fact, there were about six hundred people inside the Murrah building's nine floors on April 19. (There would have been more, but the Small Business Administration had recently moved out, leaving the sixth floor almost vacant.) Of these, 163 were killed, including 15 of the 21 children in the day care center. (All three teachers in the day care, as well as all the infants in the cribs, were killed.) Four people died nearby—three in office buildings across the street and one in the parking lot. One rescuer, a nurse named Rebecca Anderson, was killed inside the building when she was struck by falling debris. (The number of wounded has never been determined with precision because many people sought care from private doctors to leave room in hospitals for the most seriously injured.) At 7 p.m. on April 19, a fifteen-year-old girl named Brandy Liggons was found alive and freed hours later. She was the last survivor.

The bomb damaged 324 buildings in a fifty-block area of downtown Oklahoma City. The explosion was felt fifty-five miles away and registered 6.0 on the Richter scale. According to the state of Oklahoma, as a result of the bombing, 30 children were orphaned and 219 lost one parent. About 7,000 people lost their workplaces downtown. The state estimated that 360,000 Oklahomans (in a state of about 3.2 million at the time) knew someone personally who worked in the Murrah building.

On the morning of April 19, virtually the entire power structure of the state was gathered at the Myriad Convention Center, about five blocks from the Murrah building, for the annual Oklahoma City Prayer Breakfast, sponsored by Mayor Ron Norick. Governor Frank Keating, who had just won in the Republican landslides of the previous November, joined 1,200 guests who ate biscuits and gravy until their pagers starting going off. In short order, those leaders, as well as thousands of Oklahomans acting on their own, began one of the largest volunteer efforts in American history. They gave blood; they comforted victims' families; they hosted responders from around the world; they donated money and time. Eventually, the local response to the bombing became known as the "Oklahoma Standard," which remains a statewide goal for compassionate response to tragedy.

In one way, though, the local and national response to the bombing missed the mark. In the immediate aftermath of April 19, 1995, and even to this day, the bombing has often been described as "the deadliest terrorist assault on U.S. soil" until the attacks on the World Trade Center and the Pentagon on September 11, 2001. As the FBI still puts it in its official history, the bombing was "the deadliest act of homegrown terrorism in U.S. history." It was not; indeed, the bombing was not even the deadliest terror attack in Oklahoma history. In June 1921, a white mob in Tulsa conducted a pogrom and killed about three hundred Black residents of the city's Greenwood neighborhood. In the aftermath of the Oklahoma City bombing, the Tulsa race massacre was scarcely mentioned.

The initial efforts at the bomb site were led by Oklahoma City firefighters, who focused on extricating survivors. But an investigation of the bombing itself began as well. The first clue—and the most important—literally fell out of the sky.

Then as now, the Regency tower stands as an anomaly in downtown Oklahoma City—a twenty-four-story white stucco apartment building that would not look out of place on Manhattan's Upper East Side. On April 19, it was surrounded by empty lots and a handful of low-rise commercial buildings. It was located a little more than a block away from the Murrah building on 5th Street.

Richard Nichols (no relation to Terry) was a maintenance worker at the Regency. On April 19, he arrived at work at about 7 a.m., but shortly before 9, his wife, Bertha, came by to pick him up in their Ford Festiva, so that he could accompany her and their nephew Chad to a doctor's appointment. Bertha went inside to hurry Richard along, and when they stepped back out to the sidewalk, they heard the explosion. They rushed to protect Chad in the back seat, when they heard a strange whirring sound, and then a giant piece of metal crashed into the hood of the car. The force of the impact pushed the car ten feet up onto the curb. Miraculously, Chad suffered only a bump on his head, and Richard and Bertha were unhurt. The metal object stood out amid the broken glass on the street. Richard identified it right away: a truck axle.

The first law enforcement official to examine the axle was Mike McPherson, a bomb technician with the Oklahoma City Police Department. All vehicles made in the United States have a vehicle identification number (VIN), which is usually stamped on the dashboard. Because car thieves and chop shops often remove VIN numbers to make the vehicles harder to trace, manufacturers and insurers devised a response. The carmakers stamp a confidential vehicle identification number (CVIN) on a hidden piece of metal in each car. The CVIN is usually the last eight digits of the seventeen-digit VIN.

McPherson found the CVIN on the truck axle, scribbled it on a business card, and passed it to an FBI agent named Jim Elliott, who called the number in to the National Insurance Crime Bureau in Dallas. The Bureau traced the number to the Ryder truck rental company, based in Miami. The FBI made an emergency request to Ryder to identify the vehicle, and the company reported that the number belonged to a twenty-foot 1993 Ford truck that was currently out on a rental from Elliott's Body Shop in Junction City, Kansas. By 3 p.m., this game of telephone led to Scott Crabtree, an FBI agent who was assigned to Salina, Kansas. He was told to rush to Junction City, about fifty miles away, and secure the rental documents for the Ryder truck. Crabtree called ahead, and when he arrived at Elliott's Body Shop, the agreement was waiting for him.

Crabtree learned that the truck had been rented on Monday, April 17, by Robert Kling, who gave an address in South Dakota and a birth date of April 19, 1970. Crabtree spoke to three people at the shop—Eldon Elliott, the owner; Vicki Beemer, the office manager; and Tom Kessinger, a mechanic. Kessinger had the best recollection of the fellow named "Kling." He also remembered that a second man had arrived at the shop with Kling. The FBI scrambled to bring a sketch artist to Junction City, to get renderings of the two men.

Raymond Rozycki, a visual information specialist for the FBI—that is, a sketch artist—was told to rush to National Airport, outside Washington, to get on a Bureau plane to Kansas. Bad weather prevented the plane from getting to Junction City, so it landed in Kansas City. Rozycki was driven to Fort Riley, where the FBI had set up temporary headquarters. Kessinger was waiting for him when Rozycki arrived around midnight. Sketching was a purely analog process in those days. Rozycki had a series of books with faces—white faces, Black faces, even some famous faces, like those of Al Capone and John Dillinger. (His superiors directed Rozycki to bring his "Middle East book," with Arab-looking faces, given the early assumption that the bombing was an act of an Islamic terrorist.) Kessinger leafed through the books and described his recollections to Rozycki, who worked only with a pencil and eraser. They went back and forth as Rozycki refined his work. Kessinger was a lot more sure of the first customer than the second. The first guy looked military, with a brush-top crew cut, five ten or five eleven, with a slender build. The second guy was beefier, and the only thing Kessinger remembered clearly was that he was wearing a baseball cap with a wings-type design on the sides. They worked together until around dawn on Thursday, when Kessinger was happy with the two sketches Rozycki had produced. For the sake of simplicity, they called the two men in the sketches John Doe Number 1 and John Doe Number 2.

On Thursday, April 20, the FBI scrambled a team of agents to fan out from Elliott's Body Shop in Junction City to see if anyone had seen a Ryder truck. In the early afternoon, as part of a census of local hotels, Special Agent Mark Bouton visited the Dreamland Motel and spoke to the owner, Lea McGown. As it happened, she did remember a guest with a Ryder truck. She checked her records and found the name: Tim McVeigh, from 3616 North Van Dyke Road, in Decker, Michigan. McGown remembered him particularly well because he had a clean-cut appearance and a junky car—a "Mercury," according to his registration form. Bouton showed McGown the sketch of "Kling," who was John Doe Number 1. That sure looked like McVeigh, McGown said.

It was only the day after the bombing, and the pieces were coming together—perhaps. Kling rented the Ryder truck. McVeigh rented a room and had a Ryder truck. But did McVeigh rent *the* Ryder truck? Who were Kling and McVeigh—and were they the same person? And more to the point, where had he (or they) gone?

CHAPTER 13

So Is Mine

The lawmen of the Oklahoma Highway Patrol are called troopers, not officers, and in their lonely drives on the state's byways, they wear the same kind of round hats as park rangers. The vibe is more Western sheriff than city cop, and so it was with Charlie Hanger. His barrel chest stretched his OHP uniform to bursting; he looked like he was wearing a bulletproof vest even when he wasn't. He never used two words when one would do, preferring to let his presence do the talking.

Still, even though Hanger had enjoyed his two decades on the force, he was ready for a change on April 19, 1995. He had long been based in the town of Perry, population about five thousand, the seat of Noble County, in north-central Oklahoma. Perry had some agriculture, ranching, and oil—a common mix in rural Oklahoma—but it was known to most people in the state only as an exit on I-35, the main north–south artery leading to Kansas. Hanger's shift began at 7 a.m., and he started the day by making the short drive to the local headquarters of the highway patrol in Morrison. He wanted to deliver a letter to remind his chief that he wanted a new assignment, away from Perry. He was still in the office when news of the bombing hit. The OHP called a 10-653—a major statewide emergency—which meant that troopers were supposed to stay off their radio transmitters for anything except calls relating to the bombing. Hanger was ordered to rush to a temporary command post in Oklahoma City. He turned on his lights and siren and peeled out south on I-35.

But after only about twenty minutes, Hanger received a new command. He should not go to Oklahoma City after all and instead resume his routine patrol on I-35. This was disappointing, because Hanger didn't want to be sidelined in the most important investigation of his lifetime. Instead, he crossed over the median and began driving north, toward the Kansas border, at normal speed. As he was heading that way, he received a call to help a couple of women whose minivan had broken down. He waited with them for a tow truck to arrive and then went on his way. At that point, he remembered that he had to complete a report about an accident that had taken place over the weekend several miles north of where he was on I-35. He floored the accelerator on his cruiser, and soon his speedometer hit 100 miles per hour.

Hanger was going so fast in the left lane that he almost missed the Mercury in the right lane. In a quick look, it appeared that the car lacked a license plate, but Hanger wasn't sure. He slowed down to let the Mercury pass. No plate. Hanger turned on his lights and siren to pull the Mercury over. It was 10:17 a.m. The mile markers on I-35 showed that they were seventy-five miles north of Oklahoma City.

Just when McVeigh had started to worry that the bomb was not going to go off, he heard the explosion. It was 9:02 a.m. He was in the alleyway, close to where he'd parked his Mercury, and the force of the blast blew bricks off the side of the building beside him. One nicked him on the leg. A power line collapsed in front of him. He took out his earplugs and heard alarms everywhere—car alarms, store alarms, police and fire sirens. McVeigh reached his car and did a quick walk around to see if the tires or windows had been damaged by debris from the bombing. He checked that the paper towel was still on the gas cap. The car appeared undamaged.

McVeigh got in the Mercury, turned the key . . . and nothing. The engine was turning over, but it wasn't catching. He waited thirty seconds and tried again. Still, no luck. He had driven the Road Warrior Chevy for so long that he didn't remember how old junkers like this Mercury worked. Thinking logically, he figured that he needed to get fuel to the carburetor. He pumped the gas pedal five times. The battery was only sounding weaker each time. "Finally, it catches," he told his lawyer Stephen Jones. "I let it warm up for maybe thirty seconds, and I put it in drive. Beggars couldn't be choosers when I got this car."

When McVeigh emerged from the alley, the streets of downtown Oklahoma City were swarming with emergency vehicles. He did his best to avoid them and make his way to the highway. He wanted to know what was going on with the bombing, but he had no working radio in the car. So, he just kept his eyes open, even looking above to see if a helicopter was following him. McVeigh made it to I-35 without any interference. Once he got on the highway, he weighed whether to stop at a rest area. "I was tossing around whether I should pull over in there and throw away the little things I had on me—the gloves I was wearing that Terry had given me, that maybe had traces of diesel on them, my ear plugs, the note that I had in the dash of the car that said it needs fixing," McVeigh said. But he decided to press on, believing that he could clean out the car when he reached the storage facility in Herington. "If I get that far, I'm pretty much free and clear, and I can sit back and think," he said. "Right now I have to keep on the move."

Careful to stick to the speed limit, McVeigh kept going north. He noticed the trooper's car stopped next to a minivan—this was Hanger with the two women—but he passed by without incident. About fifteen minutes later, though, "I looked in my rear view and saw this state trooper car flying up to me in the passing lane without his lights on, just flying." A moment later, the trooper's car pulled back to even with McVeigh's. "He looks at me, I look back over at him," McVeigh said. "I had my hat off at this time, knowing that my haircut lends itself to a clean-cut appearance, and nine times out of ten that will get the respect. They will think I'm law enforcement or some type of security guard, et cetera, with this haircut."

The haircut gambit didn't work, however, and the Oklahoma trooper turned on his lights and siren to summon McVeigh to a stop. For McVeigh's lawyers, this traffic stop was a puzzle. At this point, McVeigh knew that he had just set off a bomb that (presumably) killed many people. He was stopped by law enforcement. He had a gun in his holster. Why didn't McVeigh just kill the trooper then and there? After all, McVeigh said he would have killed the man at the Herington storage facility if he had come over when McVeigh and Nichols were loading the Ryder truck. Wouldn't it have made even more sense to kill the trooper and get on his way?

McVeigh gave his lawyers a legalistic answer: "He was a state trooper, as opposed to federal law enforcement, and I have no problem with state law enforcement." Many right-wing extremists, past and present, describe themselves this way. From the Reconstruction Era to George Wallace in the 1960s to Gordon Kahl in North Dakota in the 1980s to the Capitol rioters in 2021, hostility to the federal government has been the touchstone of the movement. Indeed, many state and local law enforcement officials have been involved in extremist activities. In sparing Charlie Hanger's life, McVeigh was operating in accord with the broader principles of his movement.

Alternatively, the real answer of why McVeigh didn't kill Hanger may be simpler. In Iraq, McVeigh could fire a projectile from a Bradley and strike a target far off in the distance. In Oklahoma City, he could put in his earplugs and set off a bomb that targeted faceless federal employees whom he would never see. But McVeigh never had the guts to kill a man face-to-face.

For Hanger, this was a routine traffic stop—almost. Because of the 10-653, the radio was reserved for matters relating to the bombing, so Hanger did not call in a report on his radio. He operated on his own. Based on his training, Hanger opened his door and stood behind it as he shouted for the driver to get out of the car.

The stop was peculiar in one way. The driver of the Mercury pulled over as requested, but he parked way off to the right, with his two right wheels on the grass next to the shoulder. Nervous behavior, Hanger thought. (He was right. McVeigh pulled way over because he didn't want to be accused of blocking traffic.) It took three shouted requests for the driver to get out of the car. Again, a little strange. (Right again. McVeigh was delaying as he weighed his options.)

Instead of reaching for the gun in his holster, McVeigh stepped out of the Mercury and walked toward Hanger. At that point, of course, Hanger didn't know his name.

McVeigh's hands were in view, so Hanger felt no threat, but he was still suspicious. They were about ten feet from each other.

"You don't have a license plate," he said.

The man looked down at his car and said, "I just bought the car." Hanger wondered why he had to look for the plate if he knew he didn't have one.

"Registration and bill of sale?"

McVeigh said the seller was still filling out the paperwork.

"Do you have a driver's license?"

The man was wearing a light blue windbreaker, and when he reached into his right rear pocket for his wallet, the jacket tightened, and Hanger saw the outline of a shoulder holster. McVeigh handed Hanger the license for Timothy James McVeigh, of Decker, Michigan. (The name meant nothing to Hanger because McVeigh's name had not yet surfaced in connection with the bombing.) Hanger was more concerned about the holster than the license.

Hanger spoke very deliberately. "I want you to slowly unzip that jacket and pull it back," he said.

As McVeigh did as he was told, he said, "I've got a weapon."

Hanger immediately moved forward, spun McVeigh around, and told him to place his hands on the back of the Mercury.

"My weapon is loaded," McVeigh said.

Hanger placed his own handgun to the base of McVeigh's skull.

"So is mine," he said.

Hanger reached into McVeigh's holster, removed the SIG Sauer .45 caliber automatic handgun and tossed it on the grass. Hanger frisked McVeigh and found a fully loaded ammunition magazine and a knife and scabbard on his belt. Hanger threw the ammunition and knife on the side, too. He then placed McVeigh in handcuffs, told him he was under arrest for carrying a weapon without a permit and read him his Miranda rights. Hanger placed McVeigh in the front seat of his cruiser, as was customary. There were no cages in Oklahoma Highway Patrol cars, so suspects were generally placed in the front seat.

When Hanger gathered the gun, ammunition, and knife from the side, he looked in the gun's chamber and saw a Black Talon "cop killer" bullet. He asked McVeigh why he needed to carry a loaded weapon. McVeigh said it was his constitutional right to do so. McVeigh tried to talk his way out of the arrest, saying, "I have a permit in New York, and if I have a permit in New York, which is a pretty socialist state, then I must be pretty trustworthy." But Hanger wasn't buying.

With the radio off-limits, Hanger had to use his primitive cell phone to inform the dispatcher of the arrest. He provided McVeigh's name, driver's license information, VIN number on his car, and serial number on the gun. The checks came back clean. McVeigh was not wanted and had no criminal record. Neither the car nor the gun had been reported stolen. Hanger inventoried the contents of the car—including a sealed legal-sized envelope—and asked McVeigh if he wanted to pay for a tow or leave the Mercury where it was. McVeigh said to leave it.

It was about a half-hour drive to the Noble County Courthouse in Perry, and McVeigh made small talk with Hanger on the way. He asked about the cruiser—a 1993 Ford—and Hanger's handgun—a 9mm. It was not quite a routine arrest; Hanger had never arrested someone who was carrying a gun on his person, as opposed to in his car. "You should be careful," he told McVeigh. "You could get killed if someone sees that." But the encounter was hardly extraordinary. The charge was just a misdemeanor. Hanger took McVeigh to the fourth-floor lockup in the courthouse, where he was fingerprinted, processed, and given an orange jumpsuit. There was a television in the office, and all the coverage was about the bombing. Everyone who passed through was talking about it. (Later, McVeigh told his lawyers that he chuckled to himself when he heard a clerk say of the bombing, "You know, this is going to make the national news.") The jail staff recalled that the only odd thing about the new prisoner's behavior was that he didn't say a word about the big news of the day.

Louis Freeh was the director of the FBI, but he used to be a special agent—a street agent—and he never let anyone forget it. In high-profile cases like the Oklahoma City bombing, Freeh used his experience as an excuse to micromanage. His involvement from the beginning of the case illustrated the mixed blessing of his background. Freeh's interest guaranteed a massive commitment of resources to the case, but it also brought the complication of decision-making from on high.

Freeh's first big decision was whether to make public Rozycki's sketches of John Does Number 1 and 2. Of course, the point of sketches is to prompt members of the public to provide tips to law enforcement. On the other hand, given the amount of attention the bombing was receiving, the sketches were guaranteed to generate hundreds of false leads. Some in the FBI believed the Bureau should wait until the investigation was further along before releasing the sketches. Freeh didn't hesitate. On the afternoon of Thursday, April 20, just hours after Rozycki completed the sketches, the director ordered their release to the public. Not surprisingly, the sketches circulated around the world and received enormous coverage in the news media.

The sketches even made an impression at the jail in the Noble County Courthouse, where McVeigh was spending his first day in jail, in a cell with four other inmates. McVeigh had never been arrested before, and he was trying to understand the system. "I mostly was just getting the feel of where I was, never had been in a cell before," McVeigh told Jones. In one respect, McVeigh was relieved, because it was clear that he wasn't being charged in the bombing, but he was still wondering what was happening. When was he going to have a chance to make bail? When would bail even be set? "I started asking, 'Isn't there some law that says I have to be booked within 48 hours and be charged?'" He was told the Oklahoma law was seventy-two hours.

McVeigh arrived in the courthouse too late on Wednesday to see Judge Dan Allen, the only one on duty. In the normal course, his case would have been heard Thursday morning, and he would have been released on a low bond, given the minor nature of the charges. But on that morning, Judge Allen's son had missed a bus to Stillwater, twenty-five miles away, and the judge had to take him. That ate up most of the morning. Then in the afternoon, the judge had to deal with a complex divorce, involving accusations of domestic violence. That took up the rest of the court day on Thursday.

At first McVeigh was only hearing snatches of news coverage on the radio and television in jail. "There were rumors they have recovered an axle," he told Jones. "They thought it's Middle Easterners at first and all this, and I'm listening to the progress." But he did get a glimpse of the John Doe Number 1 sketch on Thursday night, and he saw how much it resembled him. McVeigh devised a plan to brush off the connection. "I heard the height on John Doe 1, and I thought good, that's the first excuse I'll use when they start cracking a joke about my flat top," he told Jones. "Sure enough, not an hour after the composite drawing came out, one guy says, 'Man, that is an awful lot like you,' and I said, 'The height is way off, like four inches different.'"

For advice, McVeigh turned to the only sources available to him: the other four inmates, who were also awaiting hearings on minor charges. He got the name of a bail bondsman, but the bondsman wouldn't accept a collect call. McVeigh heard the names of two local lawyers, but he couldn't reach them, either. The sketch and the passage of so much time were making McVeigh nervous. He wanted to get out of there and back on the road. Finally, though, on Friday morning, April 21, McVeigh got good news. He would be taken downstairs to the courtroom, where he would finally receive his bail hearing and the chance to go free.

The release of the sketches had the predictable effect: a torrent of false tips. In the immediate aftermath of the bombing, many people called the FBI to report that they had seen a man with the distinctive crew cut leaving a Ryder truck and walking away from the Murrah building. Whether these were well-intentioned errors or pleas for attention, they were all wrong; McVeigh wore a cap on the morning of April 19. The sheer number of clues stressed the FBI's resources, so that it was difficult for the Bureau to follow up on useful information.

Still, the evidence came together quickly. Shortly after tying the truck rental to Elliott's Body Shop in Junction City, Kansas, the FBI determined that the South Dakota driver's license that Robert Kling presented at Elliott's was a fake; no such address existed. On Thursday, when they found that McVeigh had registered at the Dreamland in Junction City with his Ryder truck, the Bureau set up surveillance at the address on his license: 3616 North Van Dyke Road, Decker, Michigan—the home of James Nichols. Then the agents located James's brother Terry at 109 South 2nd Street in Herington, Kansas, and set up surveillance there as well.

But the most important new clue came when the agents inspected the phone calls McVeigh had made from room 25 at the Dreamland. Two calls were to the Hunam Palace restaurant in Junction City. The owner of the restaurant had kept the order slip; the customer in room 25 had ordered food under the name of Robert Kling. Since "McVeigh" had registered for that room—but then ordered food as "Kling"—this established that Kling and McVeigh were the same person. McVeigh had rented the truck used in the bombing. But where was he now?

By Friday morning, the FBI had begun to impose some order on the investigation. Southwestern Bell had donated space to the FBI as an investigation headquarters in one of its buildings near the Murrah site. (The bomb blew out windows in the building, but it was otherwise functional.) Working from a conference room there the previous day, investigators had run a check on McVeigh's name in the database of the National Crime Information Center (NCIC), which catalogues most arrests in the United States. The search turned up nothing. On Friday morning, though, investigators decided to dig deeper and do what was then called an "off-line" search of NCIC. Off-line searches, which involved laborious reviews of records on paper, sometimes produced more information than conventional NCIC searches—and this one did. The off-line search, which was conducted in Washington, revealed that on the morning of the bombing, someone in Troop

K of the Oklahoma Highway Patrol had run a background check on the name Timothy James McVeigh.

The assignment to follow up went to Mark Michalic, an agent with the Bureau of Alcohol, Tobacco and Firearms, who was part of the team in the conference room. (When the bomb went off, Michalic would have been in his office in the Murrah building if he had not stopped to have coffee with a friend.) Michalic had questions about the lead from the off-line search: Who ran McVeigh's name on Wednesday? Why? And what was Troop K?

Michalic checked with an old friend named Ace McAllen, who was an OHP trooper. McAllen called back and said the OHP computer did not show any search for McVeigh's name. Michalic pushed back. "C'mon, computers don't lie," he said. "How many troops you got riding that county?" McAllen said there were just two. Michalic asked McAllen to track one down. When McAllen called back, he said, "I got Trooper Charlie Hanger, who remembers hooking up an old boy that morning and taking him to Noble County jail."

This was getting interesting. The two dozen or so investigators in the conference room began to cluster around Michalic, who quickly found a number for the Noble County Sheriff's Office. When someone answered, Michalic heard everyday life in the background—people talking across the room, banging coffee cups, business as usual. He asked to speak to the sheriff, Jerry Cook, a notably voluble figure in Oklahoma law enforcement.

"Is this Sheriff Cook?"

"Well, you can call me Sheriff Kook today," Cook told Michalic, and Cook launched into a monologue about his administrative and budget headaches. When Michalic was able to get a word in, he said, "Oklahoma Highway Patrol arrested an old boy on the morning of the bombing, and they said they stuck him in your jail. Can you check on that?"

Michalic heard yelling through the phone line as Cook asked his staff to check whether the fellow was still locked up. The investigators' conference room, in contrast, had now gone totally silent.

After a seemingly interminable wait, Cook came back on the line. "Yeah, Mark," he said. "We got the guy here. It's the guy that Charlie brought in."

Michalic now spoke slowly, his voice almost shaking: "Okay, Sheriff, can you give me his name?"

"Yeah," Cook replied. "It's Timothy James McVeigh."

Michalic shouted, "We got him! We got him!" and the Oklahoma City conference room erupted in cheers.

When the noise died down, Cook said McVeigh was being taken to his arraignment at that very moment. Michalic told Cook, "Sheriff, you tell your deputies to spin that old boy around and put him in your hotel. There are going to be some federal boys there to see you shortly."

CHAPTER 14

The Vise Closes

Sometime on the morning of Friday, April 21, McVeigh felt the atmosphere change in the Noble County Courthouse. Up to that point, things had been fairly casual. He was in a cell with other inmates; he traveled in the elevator with just one guard; his hands were cuffed in front of him when they were cuffed at all. He was treated like what he appeared to be: a prisoner held on a minor charge who was going to be released at any moment.

Then, suddenly, as McVeigh was waiting his turn before Judge Allen, everything was transformed. "I was leaning on the counter on my arm, just shooting the breeze," he told Stephen Jones, "and one of the clerks comes out of the back room, and her eyes just like go in the back of her head when she sees me. And as soon as I saw her reaction, without her saying anything, I knew that somebody had called that place." A deputy sheriff approached him and said, "'Oh, McVeigh, yours has been postponed, I've got to take you back upstairs.' You could hear it in his voice."

For the first time, McVeigh was placed alone in a cell, one that was nicknamed "Palestine." McVeigh's cell was across from the only women's cell on the floor. He had spoken to the woman in the cell before, and now she called out to him.

"Do you know what all this is about?"

McVeigh shook his head.

"Can you read my lips?"

McVeigh nodded.

She mouthed the words "They think you're the bomber."

The tradition at the FBI had been for the special agent in charge (SAC) for a region to be responsible for all investigations, large and small. For major cases, FBI director Freeh changed the practice so that he placed handpicked surrogates in charge. For the Oklahoma City bombing, Freeh layered in Weldon Kennedy, the Phoenix SAC, over Bob Ricks, who ran the Oklahoma City office. The practical effect of this move was to allow Freeh himself to take day-to-day control. Since the buck stopped with him, Freeh wanted to be as hands-on as possible.

By that Friday, Kennedy had arrived in Oklahoma City, and so had a battalion of other Bureau personnel, including Danny Coulson, the Dallas SAC. With Kennedy's approval, Coulson and Ricks, who were old friends, decided that Ricks would run the investigation—finding out who did the bombing—and Coulson would control the crime scene—collecting the evidence that would allow Ricks to do his job. A picture began to emerge. The discovery of the axle suggested that a bomb had been placed in a Ryder truck that was rented in Junction City, Kansas. Fragments from blue barrels were all over the scene, so the truck bomb had likely been assembled in barrels. "Robert Kling" rented the Ryder truck in Junction City. McVeigh stayed with a Ryder truck in room 25 at the Dreamland Motel. Kling ordered Chinese food to room 25. Kling and McVeigh appeared to be the same person. And as of Friday morning, the investigators knew that Charlie Hanger had arrested McVeigh seventy-five miles away from Oklahoma City about ninety minutes after the bombing. And

McVeigh was, at that moment, still locked up in the Noble County Courthouse in Perry. Also: McVeigh looked just like the sketch of Kling, who rented the truck—that is, John Doe Number 1.

Considering all this, Kennedy—and Freeh—told Danny Coulson to get up to Perry as fast as he could and bring McVeigh back into custody.

Coulson and a small team of agents scrambled an FBI helicopter at the Oklahoma City airport. When they arrived, they found that the model was open-sided; that is, without doors. Coulson's colleague Dave Williams, who had an aversion to copters, blanched. "Don't worry," Coulson reassured him, "half of all helicopter trips end without a crash." The helicopter stopped first at McVeigh's Mercury, which was still parked by the side of I-35. Leaving a couple of agents to begin processing the vehicle for evidence, Coulson and his team flew on to Perry.

Ordinarily, the park in front of the Noble County Courthouse looks like an idyllic slice of small-town America, with a gazebo, tall shade trees, and picnic benches. By late afternoon on April 21, however, word had leaked that there was a bombing suspect in the courthouse, and hundreds of people had gathered, baying for blood. As the agents were hustling into the building in their FBI windbreakers, one elderly man called Coulson aside. "We want to tell you that if you have any problem with the evidence, just put him out back, and we'll take care of him," the man said. Coulson passed on the offer.

Inside the courthouse, a pair of agents named Jim Norman and Floyd Zimms summoned McVeigh from his cell to a small conference room. He was asked if he had any idea why they had come to talk to him. "That thing in Oklahoma City, I guess," McVeigh said. He then asked for an attorney, ending the interview. The agents pushed him a little, telling him that the evidence against him was strong, that his confederates were talking (they weren't), and that he could help himself by cooperating with the investigation. By this point, McVeigh thought of himself as a prisoner of war, and he only provided the FBI with the equivalent of name, rank, and serial number.

As the end of the workday neared, Judge Allen still hoped to go through with McVeigh's arraignment on the state charges from Hanger's arrest. Coulson said the FBI wanted to take McVeigh on the bombing charges. (Freeh was calling Coulson's cell phone, demanding, "Get him the hell out of there!") Allen insisted on proceeding, and a deputy sheriff brought McVeigh back downstairs to the courtroom. For the first time he was restrained in a leather belly strap with handcuffs and chains attached—"the full Hannibal Lecter," as McVeigh put it. The judge set bail for $5,000, which was meaningless because the feds were about to take him away and file new charges based on the bombing.

Coulson now faced the issue of how to get McVeigh past the crowd in front of the courthouse and away from anyone else who wanted to harm him. McVeigh himself had the same concerns. He asked for a helicopter to land on the roof of the courthouse, which wasn't possible. "You remember what happened with Jack Ruby," McVeigh told the agents, referring to the man who shot Lee Harvey Oswald after he was arrested for assassinating President John F. Kennedy. The FBI helicopter was at an airfield about twenty-five minutes away from the courthouse, and Coulson had no way to get him there. Jerry Cook, the sheriff, had an idea. He'd lend Coulson his wife's minivan. Thinking it was the best he was going to do, Coulson had the soccer mom vehicle pulled up for the man who would soon become the most notorious criminal suspect in America.

By 6 p.m., a full contingent of the national media had joined the crowd in front of the courthouse. Coulson wasn't just worried about the fury of the crowd. He didn't know if McVeigh was involved in a broader conspiracy. There was at least the possibility of a John Doe Number 2, and perhaps others, out there as well. McVeigh's co-conspirators might have wanted to silence him—or to attack the people who arrested him. It was just a short walk from the courthouse door to the two-tone minivan, but Coulson wanted McVeigh totally surrounded by law enforcement officials.

McVeigh's walk from the courthouse to the van—which was only about twenty steps—became an emblematic moment in the story of the Oklahoma City bombing. Coulson wanted a fast pace, so in the endless repetitions on television, McVeigh's journey was usually shown in slow motion, which always adds a sinister edge. McVeigh was still in his orange jail jumpsuit. His brush-top crew cut was just as distinctive in real life as it was in Rozycki's sketch. But it was McVeigh's expression that so many people remembered, even decades later. The hoots of the crowd were clearly audible, but McVeigh ignored them; he looked fierce, determined, unapologetic—which is exactly what he was.

When the van arrived at the airstrip in Perry, and McVeigh was about to be transferred to the helicopter, Coulson put his hand on McVeigh's back. "Tim, I expect you to act like a gentleman on the helicopter ride," he said. "I don't expect any trouble from you. Act like a gentleman, and you'll be treated as a gentleman. If not, then you will be very sorry. Do you understand me?"

McVeigh nodded. "Yes, sir, I understand," he said.

In the day or so after Hanger arrested him, McVeigh affected an insouciant attitude, one befitting a man who knew he would soon be released. But once McVeigh recognized that he was a suspect in the bombing, he flipped a switch. He knew this moment was likely to come, and he had planned for it. The bombing was an act of advocacy, and McVeigh's behavior after his arrest would demonstrate that he was a soldier and a patriot, who had acted for the good of his country and in defense of the Constitution.

The helicopter lifted off at 6:10 p.m., and the pilot began a steady route south, toward Oklahoma City. The Bureau had arranged for McVeigh's arraignment and initial detention to take place at Tinker Air Force Base, a mammoth facility just inside the city limits. The base offered greater security than the federal courthouse downtown, which was, in any event, just a block away from the Murrah building and also damaged in the bombing. The pilot began the trip several hundred feet in the air, but Coulson immediately ordered him to change course. Worried that the chopper would make an easy target for a McVeigh ally (or adversary) with a missile, Coulson ordered the pilot to skim the treetops for the whole route. (It's harder to shoot down a helicopter that's flying close to the ground.) McVeigh said nothing during the entire stomach-churning ride.

The U.S. Attorney's Office in Oklahoma City—itself damaged in the bomb—scrambled to put together a brief complaint charging McVeigh with use of an incendiary device to damage the Murrah building. The question of a defense attorney was more complicated. In ordinary circumstances, an indigent defendant like McVeigh would be represented by the local federal defenders' office. And for that first appearance, Susan Otto of the defenders did appear for him. But the defenders' office had suffered especially heavy damage in the bombing, making McVeigh's lawyer also potentially his victim—an untenable situation. Recognizing the potential problem, Otto recruited John Coyle, a veteran Oklahoma City defense lawyer, to come with her, at least for McVeigh's initial appearance. Later, they could sort out who would defend him over the long haul.

The buildings at Tinker are low-slung and vast, built on the scale of the B-52 bombers that are serviced there. When Coyle arrived on Friday night, he was placed in one of those big rooms for his first conference with McVeigh. Determined to speak in a more intimate setting, Coyle demanded a human-sized conference room, which was provided. McVeigh was starting to recognize the enormity of his predicament. Still, he was clear with his lawyers from the beginning about one point: he was the one who set off the bomb at the Murrah building. The arraignment finally took place late Friday night, and McVeigh was ordered held without bail.

For his first night in federal custody, he was transferred under heavy guard to the Federal Correctional Institution in El Reno, about forty miles away. The prison had made hasty preparations for his arrival. Eighteen inmates (including Gene Gotti, John's brother and a fellow Gambino family gangster) had lost relatives in the bombing. To avoid the chance for reprisals, they had to be transferred elsewhere. Two years earlier, administrators had shuttered an old cell block that had opened in 1934. The structure, known as Arkansas 2, once housed as many as 180 inmates on four tiers, but it had become obsolete. Operating on the fly, those in charge decided to reopen it for a single inmate—McVeigh. Fourteen officers were assigned to supervise him around the clock. New rules were established for the rest of the prison. Whenever McVeigh left his cell, the entire complex went into lockdown. No inmates were allowed out of their cells, even for work details or meals, until McVeigh was safely back inside his own. If McVeigh left to take a shower or meet with his lawyers, he was surrounded by three to five guards. A lieutenant was stationed outside his cell twenty-four hours a day.

The investigation kept accelerating. The FBI obtained a search warrant for McVeigh's Mercury, which had been sitting by the side of I-35, and agents found his envelope of right-wing literature. The references in the material to the Waco raid, exactly two years before the bombing, suggested that McVeigh was acting on the anniversary. McVeigh's T-shirt, with its allusion to the Lincoln assassination and violent political rebellion, made a similar point. By the day after the bombing, the news media had reported that the bomb was likely delivered in a Ryder truck from Junction City, Kansas, and that McVeigh was a suspect. This led to more tips. Rick Wahl, the Army sergeant who was fishing with his son, called the FBI and said he saw a Ryder truck at Geary Lake shortly before the bombing. Carl Lebron, McVeigh's former colleague at Burns Security, who had surreptitiously recorded a conversation with him, saw the sketch of John Doe Number 1 and reported to the FBI office in Buffalo that it looked like McVeigh; Lebron said further that McVeigh's hatred of the federal government made him even more suspicious of a connection. Crucially, Lebron also told the FBI that he had received mail from McVeigh at an address in Kingman, Arizona. This was the first lead that connected McVeigh to Mike and Lori Fortier.

But the most important leads came from the Michigan driver's license that McVeigh had used at the Dreamland Motel. The address on the license was the Nichols family farm in Decker, where the FBI promptly set up surveillance. Among the Nicholses' neighbors, it was well known that James Nichols held extreme right-wing views, and so did his brother Terry. The FBI quickly tracked down Terry's ex-wife, Lana Padilla, in Las Vegas, and she reported that Terry was close friends with Tim McVeigh. She also provided the FBI with Terry's address in Herington, Kansas. By Friday, April 21, the FBI was staked out in front of the shabby little house that Terry and Marife had moved into just a few weeks earlier.

The reactions of McVeigh and Nichols to the bombing and its immediate aftermath reflected the differences between them. McVeigh was icily serene; he had a job to do, and he had done it. He had known there was a good chance that he would be caught, and now that he had been arrested, he was going to use the legal process to advance his political agenda. Nichols, on the other hand, was flailing and panicking. Unlike McVeigh, he desperately wanted to avoid being caught, but he was as inept at covering his tracks as he was at everything else in his life.

On the day of the bombing, Nichols did his best to be seen out and about in Herington, visiting several stores. He wanted witnesses to the fact that he was nowhere near Oklahoma City on that Wednesday. He also spread a good deal of fertilizer on his small lawn, trying to find an innocent use for the stash he had accumulated in planning the bombing. By Friday, however, Nichols heard on the news that his brother's farm in Decker was being surveilled, and then he started to see law enforcement officials watching his own house in Herington. In response, Nichols made the worst possible decision: he showed up at the local police station and asked why he appeared to be under suspicion. Intending to talk his way out of trouble, Nichols did the opposite.

After establishing that a police car had followed his pickup as he went on a shopping trip with Marife and their daughter, Nichols drove to the Herington Police Department—the city's tiny police department. In the car before he went inside, he made a confession to Marife: He had not gone to Omaha to pick up McVeigh on the previous Sunday. He had collected McVeigh in Oklahoma City. This was only the beginning of Nichols's shifting tales about his behavior.

Inside the police station, Nichols asked why his name was on the news and why people were following him. The local cops summoned the FBI agents who had been trailing Nichols. The agents didn't arrest Nichols, but they had him sign a form acknowledging that he had received his Miranda warnings. Nichols said he had only seen McVeigh once in recent months. He admitted that he had picked up McVeigh in Oklahoma City the previous Sunday, but said it was for an innocent purpose: to retrieve a television that McVeigh had borrowed. Nichols admitted further that he had told his wife that he had gone to Omaha, not Oklahoma City, to get McVeigh. Why had Nichols lied to his wife if he was just picking up a television? Nichols didn't have much of an answer to that question.

Nichols said he knew that McVeigh was "hyped" about Waco—

and Nichols acknowledged that he, too, had grievances with the federal government and refused to pay taxes to the Internal Revenue Service. “In my eyes, I didn’t do anything wrong,” Nichols told the agents, “but I see how lawyers can turn things around.” Nichols said McVeigh had told him that he was planning “something big” in the previous weeks, but he had no idea what it was. They had mostly gone their separate ways because McVeigh didn’t like Nichols’s penchant for practical jokes. Nichols at first denied, and then admitted, that he had purchased fertilizer, which he said he planned to sell as plant food at gun shows. Why had he lied about the fertilizer? “Because it would make me look guilty to a jury,” he said.

With Freeh prodding the agents long-distance to keep the conversation going, the interrogation of Nichols lasted well into Friday night. Late in the evening, the agents in Herington received a fax from the agents in Las Vegas who had been questioning Lana Padilla, Nichols’s ex-wife. Padilla had given the agents the letter that Nichols left for her to give to McVeigh when Nichols went to the Philippines. The letter encouraged McVeigh to “Go for it!!” What, the agents wanted to know, did that mean? Go for what? Nichols had no explanation. Toward the end of the interview, Nichols signed a form allowing the agents to search his home and car. He was then held in custody as a material witness in the bombing investigation.

The search of Nichols’s home, which began the next day, was a bonanza. It turned out that Nichols was a pack rat, which is an unfortunate quality in a criminal who doesn’t want to be caught. Nichols had failed to throw out the receipt for his purchase of forty 50-pound bags of fertilizer on September 30, 1994, just days after Clinton signed the assault weapons ban. For the purchase, Nichols had used the name Mike Havens—which, the agents found, he had also used for the purchase of two thousand pounds more fertilizer a few weeks later. In central Kansas, these were not unusual quantities of fertilizer for farmers to buy—but Nichols didn’t have a farm. Two tons of fertilizer was an enormous quantity if Nichols planned on selling them in one-pound bags at gun shows—which was the story he told to the FBI. The search also revealed that Nichols had kept blasting caps. An innocuous-looking Walmart receipt for the purchase of an oil filter on April 13 had both McVeigh's and Nichols's fingerprints, which meant that Nichols had lied when he said he had not seen McVeigh for months before April 16. The agents found guns that had been stolen from Roger Moore in Arkansas and the drill that, according to subsequent tests, had been used to open the locks in the quarry robbery the previous year.

But the most important discovery in Nichols's home was the phone card that Nichols and McVeigh had purchased, under the name Daryl Bridges, from an advertisement in *The Spotlight.* By 1995, phone cards were widely available for purchase in gas stations and convenience stores; if Nichols and McVeigh had paid cash for those kinds of cards, then used them and disposed of them, their calls would have been nearly impossible to track. But because they thought they were being clever by patronizing an advertiser in a right-wing magazine, they delivered proof of their actions to their pursuers. As fortunate as this misjudgment was for the FBI, it was catastrophic for McVeigh and Nichols.

By the morning of Saturday, April 22, just three days after the bombing, McVeigh and Nichols were in custody, and the case against them (especially McVeigh) looked strong. Investigators had a great deal more work ahead of them, and their efforts would span the country. The massive crime scene had to be scrutinized in painstaking fashion for evidence about the bomb itself. McVeigh's home, upbringing, and adult life in the Buffalo area had to be examined; likewise, Nichols's roots in Michigan—and the role of his brother James. With the phone card as a guide, agents would have to reconstruct McVeigh's peripatetic travels across the country—from New York to Arkansas to Michigan to Arizona, among other places. The investigation of Michael Fortier in Kingman remained a key open question—and so did the matter of John Doe Number 2.

Even at this early date, the broad outlines of the criminal case were in place. On the other hand, the political fallout from the Oklahoma City bombing was just beginning.

What did it mean that a pair of right-wing zealots were the lead suspects in the case? Who or what inspired them? How, if at all, were more mainstream conservatives responsible for the extremists on their side? Did the blame for the Oklahoma bombing belong exclusively to the individuals who could be charged in a court of law, or did the public figures who motivated them deserve a measure of culpability as well? Most of all, simply, who *are* these people? Those questions remain relevant today. In 1995, one of the first people to address them was the president of the United States, Bill Clinton.

CHAPTER 15

"Fighting This All My Life"

For Bill Clinton, the Oklahoma City bombing was personal from the beginning. "I was in the White House, and they told me what had happened in Oklahoma City, and they told me that a lot of kids had been killed in the day care center and that a Secret Service man, Al Whicher, had been killed, who had been on my detail," he recalled in an interview with me in 2022 while sitting in the Midtown Manhattan office of his foundation. "I liked him, and he wanted to move. He wanted to go to Oklahoma City because he had young children and he thought it would be a good place to raise his family—and obviously relatively safe as opposed to running around into India and Bangladesh and places with me. And I was just heart-broken. For me, he became like a metaphor for all the other people that died. And I realized that for a moment I was just like everybody else. I was just a guy that knew somebody I cared about who died."

The bombing took place at a precarious moment in Clinton's presidency. In the previous midterm elections of November 1994, Republicans won a historic victory. The GOP picked up eight seats in the Senate and fifty-four seats in the House of Representatives to take unified control of Congress for the first time since 1952. Newt Gingrich, the leader of the Republican resurgence and the new

Speaker of the House, dominated the news and American politics. He was presenting himself as a kind of prime minister—the head of government—with Clinton as little more than a caretaker of foreign policy. On the evening of April 18, hours before the bombing, Clinton held a prime-time news conference, which only one network chose to cover live, a sign of his diminished status. Forced to defend his role in the altered dynamic of Washington, Clinton insisted, "I am relevant. The Constitution gives me relevance." (Even years later, the reaction to the press conference still rankled Clinton: "The press made fun of me, but I didn't say 'I was relevant.' I said, 'the Constitution makes the President relevant.'")

On the morning of April 19, the president was in the Oval Office for a photo opportunity with the Turkish prime minister, Tansu Çiller, when Mike McCurry, the White House press secretary, whispered to him that CNN was reporting that a bomb had destroyed the federal building in Oklahoma City. A few moments later, Leon Panetta, the chief of staff, slipped Clinton a handwritten note: "Half of federal building in O.K. City blown up—expect heavy casualties. Called Janet Reno—she has dispatched FBI."

After his visitor was ushered out, Clinton moved his team to the Situation Room in the basement. He spent much of the day trying to learn what was going on—the extent of the damage and the number of casualties. He reached out quickly to Frank Keating, the governor of Oklahoma. Keating was a conservative Republican and an ideological adversary of the president's, but they had been undergraduates together at Georgetown. They were rivals in campus politics, but friends as well, and they collaborated well in the crisis.

On that first day, Clinton had a lot of questions—about the possibility of further attacks, about the federal death penalty statutes, about security in nearby airports. He also wanted to know what proposals his administration had on the shelf to propose to Congress as antiterrorism measures. Clinton heard the news about an Arab

American from Oklahoma City who had been detained on his way to London and then Jordan, but there was no further information about him. At the time, no one at the White House recognized at first that it was the second anniversary of the Waco raid. (Over at the Justice Department, Reno, who shouldered much of the blame for Waco, immediately noticed the significance of the date.)

On the question of who committed the bombing, Clinton vowed to say nothing publicly, to avoid prejudicing the investigation. "I knew I needed to make a statement that condemned the violence without assuming that it was an act of an Islamic terror network, which is what a lot of people did," he recalled. Still, those around Clinton at the time were surprised at the certainty with which he expressed his private view about who was responsible.

"This was domestic, homegrown, the militias," he said to his staff. "I know these people." As Clinton recalled many years later, "I said, 'You guys have got to understand.' I told them, 'I've been fighting this all my life.'"

Clinton's view emerged from long familiarity with right-wing extremism. Throughout his twelve years as governor of Arkansas, Clinton had seen the movement up close. His state had long been home for some of the worst of these zealots, and Clinton dealt frequently with the fallout from their rage. Clinton's long political career in the state, combined with his extroverted nature, made it seem like he knew everyone in Arkansas. As a result, right-wing terror often had a personal dimension for him.

McVeigh had closely followed the story of Gordon Kahl, the notorious tax protester, who came to a violent end on Clinton's watch. After Kahl killed two federal marshals in North Dakota, he fled south to the small northwest Arkansas town of Smithville, in Lawrence County. Acting on a tip, on June 3, 1983, federal, state, and local law enforcement confronted Kahl at the home where he was hiding out. In the ensuing gun battle, both Kahl and the local sheriff were killed. As Clinton recalled, "Kahl murdered a sheriff in Lawrence County who was my campaign county coordinator, Gene Matthews."

Then there was Richard Snell, who was among the most notorious criminals in Arkansas history. He belonged to a white supremacist group called the Covenant, the Sword, and the Arm of the Lord (known as the CSA), which was based in western Arkansas, near the Oklahoma border. On November 3, 1983, Snell killed William Stumpp, a pawnshop owner in Texarkana, in the mistaken belief that Stumpp was Jewish. On June 30, 1984, during a routine traffic stop in the town of De Queen, Snell shot and killed a Black Arkansas state trooper named Louis Bryant. As Clinton remembered in 2022, "He was a Black state trooper whose brother-in-law Ralph was on my security detail in Arkansas as the governor. So, I felt like I knew him, too. His brother-in-law was unbelievable. I took a keen interest in Snell's case. He was a mean mother." On the way to Bryant's funeral, where Clinton spoke, four more state troopers were killed in a horrific automobile accident. Bryant's murder, and the carnage that followed, remained a haunting memory for Clinton. Snell was sentenced to death, and the date for his execution happened to be April 19, 1995. There were theories that McVeigh planned the bombing as a kind of protest on behalf of Snell, but McVeigh told his lawyers that he had never heard of Snell.

Also, during Clinton's governorship, the Ku Klux Klan was headquartered in Harrison, in the north-central part of Arkansas. (McVeigh obtained his KKK membership by mailing a form to Harrison.) The Klan was a small but visible presence in the state, and in his first term as governor, Clinton had to navigate a planned KKK rally in Little Rock. "They wanted to do a big march and scare the shit out of everybody in Little Rock," Clinton remembered. "They were going to have a march on University Avenue in front of the University of Arkansas at Little Rock, where they knew there were a lot of people who hated them." Clinton recognized the Klan's right to free speech, but he also wanted to make sure there was no violence. He arranged for an overwhelming police presence at the march. "The Klan folks were blown away," Clinton said. "They got down there and there were all these people who said, 'We're just here for your protection. You're entitled to protection.' And so there was a totally uneventful, boring demonstration."

Later, the CSA, which had been Richard Snell's organization, established a 244-acre compound on the remote Bull Shoals Lake in the Ozarks, just south of the Missouri border. Drawing inspiration from *The Turner Diaries*, the group amassed an arsenal of weapons and talked of taking the fight to the government. Federal prosecutors obtained a search warrant for the compound and an arrest warrant for the group's leader, Jim Ellison, on weapons charges; the stage was set for the kind of explosion that would later take place in Waco. But Clinton counseled caution. "I immediately said, 'Okay here's what we're going to do. We're going to say nobody can go in and out except to get food or medicine,'" he remembered in 2022, "and then they'll send the wives and the kids out, and we just won't let them go back. And slowly but surely then when they would complain, we'd say, 'Send the children out with the women, and we'll let them off.' So slowly we got that done and finally they gave up." The FBI, led by Danny Coulson (who would later take McVeigh into federal custody), arranged for Ellison's peaceful surrender.

In short, Clinton recognized the kind of anger that might lead someone to bomb a federal building. "I saw what I had seen in Arkansas in the fifties and sixties—how if you could turn anything into politics and make it an 'us and them' war, it was very powerful in the short run, but the consequences could be devastating," he said. "If people feel their identity is in danger of being dislodged, then nothing else matters." Clinton's first political memory, when he was eleven years old, came from Governor Orval Faubus's refusal to allow nine Black students into Little Rock Central High School. Most of Clinton's friends and classmates in Hot Springs were either supporters of the governor's or indifferent, but young Bill, encouraged by his free-spirited mother, always supported civil rights. Clinton never forgot the faces twisted with rage as many of his fellow southerners resisted integration. The memories of their fury at the government, especially the federal government, remained with Clinton. That kind of anger never disappeared from American life, but Clinton believed that it was especially virulent in the early 1990s—in Gingrich's sneering contempt and Limbaugh's roiling bombast. So, too, Clinton speculated, in the origins of the Oklahoma City bombing.

In thinking about his initial public statement, Clinton believed that he needed first to express righteous fury against the perpetrators, whoever they might be. Within moments of the first reports of the bombing on CNN, Don Baer, the chief speechwriter, and his colleague Jonathan Prince began drafting a statement for Clinton. Later, the pair was summoned to the Situation Room. Their draft referred to the perpetrators as "cowards," but Clinton inserted an adjective to give the statement more punch. He ducked into a cubbyhole office to make a phone call to run the remarks past the first lady, and then went to the briefing room to deliver the statement.

"The bombing in Oklahoma City was an attack on innocent children and defenseless citizens," Clinton said. "It was an act of cowardice, and it was evil. The United States will not tolerate it. And I will not allow the people of this country to be intimidated by evil cowards." The government's response to the bombing, he said, would be "swift, certain and severe." At around the same time, Attorney General Janet Reno announced that the government would seek the death penalty against the persons responsible for the bombing.

Behind the scenes, the pressure for a break in the investigation was intense. Rahm Emanuel, who was then the White House adviser with responsibility for the Justice Department, made the point in a characteristically earthy way. On the afternoon of the bombing, he called Jamie Gorelick, the deputy attorney general, and sputtered, "Are you paying attention to this? It looks like you're not paying attention. Why aren't you doing anything? Don't you realize that this is a big fucking deal?" On the day after the bombing, Thursday, April 20, Clinton hosted a state dinner for the president of Brazil. The president spent much of the evening huddled with Gorelick (also in evening wear), talking about the investigation. McVeigh was taken into federal custody the next day, ending for a time the talk of a Middle Eastern angle.

At this point, Clinton realized he needed to leaven his anger with empathy. Dozens of bodies were coming out of the wreckage every day. (Alan Whicher was one of six Secret Service employees killed in the blast. The Department of Housing and Urban Development lost thirty-five employees, the most of any agency.) More to the point, the story of the America's Kids day care center was coming into focus. The death toll of children had not yet reached the final total of nineteen, but Clinton saw that these losses would be the most wrenching for the American people. For his Saturday radio address, the White House gathered a handful of children of federal workers in the Washington area, and the president and first lady did a joint talk with them. "We want children to know that it's okay to be frightened by something as bad as this," Bill Clinton told them.

The following day, Sunday, April 23, turned out to be one of the most consequential of Clinton's presidency. A crowd of eighteen thousand had gathered at the Oklahoma City Fairgrounds for a memorial and prayer service. Those who were there remember a grave silence after Clinton arrived. The only sounds were muffled sobs. Many of the victims' families held teddy bears, which became symbols in the aftermath of the bombing. Clinton had worked on his speech through the previous night and during the trip on Air Force One, even though his remarks lasted only nine minutes.

The mission in Oklahoma City played to Clinton's strengths. He was a naturally empathetic person; his political success rested in significant part on his ability to feel others' pain. Plus, as a longtime governor, Clinton had a lot of experience offering comfort—to victims of natural disasters or violent crime. He had spoken at many funerals. So, he talked simply, never presuming to know the depths of sadness of those who had lost so much. He said he spoke to "represent the American people. . . . Today the nation joins with you in grief. We mourn with you." But in addition to those sentiments, Clinton began to explore a theme that would come to define his reaction to the bombing. "This terrible sin took the lives of our American family, innocent children in that building only because their parents were trying to be good parents as well as good workers; citizens in the building going about their daily business," he said, adding pointedly, "and many there who served the rest of us—who worked to help the elderly and the disabled, who worked to support our farmers and our veterans, who worked to enforce our laws and to protect us. Let us say clearly, they served us well, and we are grateful." (Speaking to his aides shortly after the service, Clinton recalled ruefully that he had sometimes lapsed into criticism of "federal bureaucrats," but he never did so again after Oklahoma City.)

His speechwriters had canvassed favorite members of the clergy over the previous few days, looking for appropriate passages of scripture to quote. Clinton knew plenty himself from his Southern Baptist boyhood. For the task of the investigation, he drew on Proverbs: "Let us teach our children that the God of comfort is also the God of righteousness: Those who trouble their own house will inherit the wind. Justice will prevail."

But this, ultimately, was a time for hope, not vengeance. He recalled that when he met with the children in the White House the previous day, one had suggested that trees should be planted to honor the memory of the children who had been lost. So that morning, before they left for Oklahoma, he and the first lady had planted a dogwood on the White House grounds—"with its wonderful spring flower and its deep, enduring roots." He concluded: "My fellow Americans, a tree takes a long time to grow, and wounds take a long time to heal. But we must begin. Those who are lost now belong to God. Someday we will be with them. But until that happens, their legacy must be our lives."

The public reaction to Clinton's speech was overwhelmingly positive, and they remain the most praised remarks of his presidency. Only a week after he had to plead for his own relevance, an NBC/*Wall Street Journal* poll showed that 84 percent of Americans approved of his handling of the Oklahoma City bombing. On the same Sunday as his speech, he gave an interview to *60 Minutes* where he outlined a series of proposals for Congress to expand the government's power to investigate terrorists. They soon passed almost without opposition.

Spurred by his new political Svengali Dick Morris, Clinton pressed his political advantage. His goal was no less real for being unspoken—to tie responsibility for the bombing to the fervor of his political opponents, especially Rush Limbaugh. (On that point, Clinton didn't know how right he was—that McVeigh was an avid Limbaugh fan.) "We hear so many loud and angry voices in America today whose sole goal seems to be to try to keep some people as paranoid as possible and the rest of us all torn up and upset with each other," Clinton said on the following Monday, April 24, in a speech to the American Association of Community Colleges in Minneapolis. "They spread hate. They leave the impression that, by their very words, that violence is acceptable. . . . I'm sure you are now seeing the reports of some things that are regularly said over the airwaves in America today. Well, people like that who want to share our freedoms must know that their bitter words can have consequences, and that freedom has endured in this country for more than two centuries because it was coupled with an enormous sense of responsibility." Afterward, his advisers told reporters (unconvincingly) that Clinton wasn't referring to anyone in particular. In addition to Limbaugh, Clinton had a special grievance with G. Gordon Liddy, the former Watergate figure, who had become an inflammatory talk show host. He had particularly drawn Clinton's ire when he said he used drawings of Bill and Hillary Clinton for target practice. (Prison officials in El Reno denied McVeigh access to television, but he did have a radio. While incarcerated, he became a fan of Liddy's program.)

Limbaugh's response to the Oklahoma City bombing, and to Clinton's speech, established a pattern that has recurred for decades following acts of right-wing domestic terrorism. Limbaugh took offense: "Make no mistake about it: Liberals intend to use this tragedy for their own political gain," he said after Clinton spoke, citing "irresponsible attempts to categorize and demonize those who had nothing to do with this. . . . There is absolutely no connection between these nuts and mainstream conservatism in America today." Whether it was the Oklahoma City bombing, mass shootings, other violence by right-wing extremists, or the January 6, 2021, insurrection, Limbaugh, Gingrich, and their allies always responded the same way. They made dutiful condemnations of the attacks themselves, accompanied by refusals to accept any responsibility for inspiring them.

Logorrheic as always, Gingrich in 1995 couldn't help but make Clinton's case for him. He made the ritual expression of sadness about the attack, and even made a late-night visit to the scene of the bombing, but he also persisted in demonizing the federal government. He had come to power by asserting that the government had "created a culture of poverty and a culture of violence which is destructive of this civilization." Even after the bombing, he wasn't backing away. On *Meet the Press* two weeks after the bombing, he said, "We have to understand that there is, in rural America, a genuine—particularly in the

West—a genuine fear of the federal government and of Washington, D.C., as a place that doesn't understand their way of life and doesn't understand their values." The new Speaker's incessant demands to "cut bureaucrats" suddenly had a sinister edge, because those individuals now had human faces—the victims inside the Murrah building.

Before the bombing, when Clinton had complained about Limbaugh and Gingrich, the president had sounded like a whiner, but with the backdrop of the bombing, his critique gained heft. He decided to press his advantage the next month in a speech at the Michigan State University graduation—a site chosen because the state's militia, and native son Terry Nichols, had been implicated in the bombing. On May 5, Clinton addressed these Michiganders directly:

> I want to say this to the militias. . . . I am well aware that most of you have never violated the law of the land. I welcome the comments that some of you have made recently condemning the bombing in Oklahoma City. I believe you have every right, indeed you have the responsibility, to question our government when you disagree with its policies. And I will do everything in my power to protect your right to do so. But I also know there have been lawbreakers among those who espouse your philosophy. I know from painful personal experience as a Governor of a State who lived through the coldblooded killing of a young sheriff and a young African American state trooper who were friends of mine by people who espoused the view that the Government was the biggest problem in America and that people had a right to take violence into their own hands.
>
> So, I say this to the militias and all others who believe that the greatest threat to freedom comes from the government instead of from those who would take away our freedom: If you say violence is an acceptable way to make change, you are wrong. If you say that government is in a conspiracy to take your freedom away,

> you are just plain wrong. If you treat law enforcement officers who put their lives on the line for your safety every day like some kind of enemy army to be suspected, derided, and if they should enforce the law against you, to be shot, you are wrong. If you appropriate our sacred symbols for paranoid purposes and compare yourselves to colonial militias who fought for the democracy you now rail against, you are wrong. How dare you suggest that we in the freest nation on earth live in tyranny! How dare you call yourselves patriots and heroes! I say to you, all of you, the members of the Class of 1995, there is nothing patriotic about hating your country or pretending that you can love your country but despise your government.

"Nothing patriotic about . . . pretending that you can love your country but despise your government"—this became one of the most quoted lines of Clinton's presidency. And it was an apt capstone to his rhetorical victory over his political adversaries in the aftermath of the bombing. But it was also the end of Clinton's engagement with the forces behind the bombing. In the way of the modern presidency, Clinton began responding to new news cycles, albeit those where his hand had been strengthened by his deft handling of the aftermath of the bombing. In demonstrating that he was, in fact, head of state, Clinton showed that he was head of government as well. In the fall, when Gingrich engineered a shutdown of the federal government in a dispute over the budget, it was the Speaker who wound up looking petty and inept.

After warning the country of the threat from the militias, Clinton turned over the matter of the Oklahoma City bombing to the Justice Department. The approach of the leaders there, chiefly a lawyer named Merrick Garland, would turn out to be different from the president's, with clear implications for how the American people would view the legacy of this shattering event.

CHAPTER 16

Merrick Garland's Case

A new attorney general of the United States makes a statement by choosing which predecessor's portrait to hang next to the entrance to his private office. Democratic appointees tend to go with Robert F. Kennedy, but Merrick Garland selected Edward H. Levi, a Republican, whom President Gerald Ford placed in charge of the Justice Department after the chaos and corruption of the Nixon years. Levi was independent and incorruptible—a role model for Garland.

Levi also had old-fashioned notions about lawyerly discretion, which meant that he kept a modest public profile. This, too, commended him to Garland when he took over as attorney general in 2021. By temperament and conviction, Garland was a reticent, cautious person, who believed that lawyers should confine their speechmaking to the courtroom. He felt the same way in 1995, when he supervised the prosecution of McVeigh and Nichols. Reflecting on that role in an interview with me in 2022, Garland immediately recalled the "Dancing Itos."

"That was exactly what we wanted to avoid," he said.

The criminal trial of O. J. Simpson for murdering his ex-wife and her friend began in January 1995 and by the time of the bombing, in April, it had become a televised national obsession. One reflection of the mania was a goofy feature on Jay Leno's *Tonight Show*: black-robed dancers who were made up to look like Judge Lance Ito, who was presiding over the trial. Decades later, the thought of this undignified spectacle repelled Garland—and served as a photo negative of how he wanted to proceed. Even at the time, Garland's colleagues noted his fixation with everything O.J.-related and his desire to avoid any association with the proceedings in Los Angeles. (The taste left by the Simpson case turned especially sour for Garland when the former football star was acquitted in October 1995.)

At the time of the bombing, Garland's title was principal associate deputy attorney general (pronounced p-dag, in DOJ argot)—which hardly did justice to his importance in the department or his place in the Washington legal firmament. He was forty-two years old and one of the two undisputed legal stars of his generation. Raised in the Chicago suburbs, Garland was the valedictorian of his high school class, a summa cum laude graduate of Harvard College, an editor of the law review at Harvard, a law clerk for the revered appeals court judge Henry Friendly and then for William Brennan on the Supreme Court. John G. Roberts Jr., who was two years younger, had an extremely similar résumé: valedictorian of his suburban Chicago high school class, Harvard College summa, editor of the Harvard law review, and clerk for Friendly. Roberts went on to clerk for William Rehnquist on the Supreme Court and ascended through the ranks of the Justice Department in Republican administrations just as Garland did under Democrats.

After his clerkships, Garland joined the Justice Department during the Carter administration, as a special assistant to Attorney General Benjamin Civiletti. When Carter lost, Garland moved to the eminent Washington law firm of Arnold & Porter, quickly making partner, but then made an unconventional career move in 1989. As a big-firm lawyer, Garland had never spent much time in courtrooms, so he took a dramatic pay cut and joined the U.S. Attorney's Office in Washington as a trial lawyer. He did the range of felonies, including murder cases, until Bill Clinton won the presidency, and Jamie Gorelick, the new deputy attorney general (and Garland's Harvard College classmate), asked him to be her own deputy—her eyes and ears around the Department.

As p-dag, Garland was a political appointee, and he was a nominal Democrat, though he was never terribly political. Even then, Garland was a kind of throwback, a link to the days when the Justice Department was led by people like Ed Levi. Garland was a lawman—a prosecutor—but also a law man—a figure with a deep respect for and confidence in the rule of law. Temperamentally, if not politically, he was a conservative, a man who preferred to see an orderly world and tried his best to create one.

The deputy attorney general and her staff worked out of a suite of offices on the fourth floor of the Justice Department building, and that's where Garland was on the morning of April 19. He received word of the bombing on his beeper and then turned on CNN. He went upstairs to brief Attorney General Reno, whose office was directly above Gorelick's, and then raced across Pennsylvania Avenue to the command center inside FBI headquarters. There, Garland monitored reports from the investigation on the ground in Oklahoma City, including the breakthrough discovery of the Ryder truck axle at the scene. But there was news elsewhere, too. "So, all day there were bomb scares from all over the country," Garland recalled. "Every person who wanted to be part of this was phoning in a phony bomb threat. Courthouses all over the country were reporting bomb threats. Stories of trucks being seen going to Omaha and all different places." They all had to be checked out.

Later, one focus of criticism of the bombing investigation was that it settled too quickly on McVeigh and Nichols as the perpetrators and thus discounted other suspects. The opposite was true. The Bureau devoted massive resources to the search for a broader, or even different, conspiracy. The reason was simple. Given the massive damage to the Murrah building and the number of casualties, investigators were skeptical that McVeigh and Nichols could have pulled it off alone; more important, they feared that co-conspirators, if they existed, planned to launch similarly devastating attacks elsewhere.

Like many others, Garland at first suspected that the bombing might have been an act of international terrorism. There were similarities between the strike on the Murrah building and the first attack on the World Trade Center in New York on February 26, 1993, a little more than two years earlier. That bomb, which weighed about 1,300 pounds, was also detonated with a fuse and transported to the target location in a rented Ryder truck (albeit a smaller model than the one from Junction City). The first suspect in the World Trade Center case had been arrested a few days after that bombing, and it became clear that it was carried out by a cell of Islamic militants based in New York. In February 1995—just weeks before the Murrah bombing—Ramzi Yousef, the mastermind of the Trade Center attack, had been arrested in Pakistan. Moreover, it was clear by April that a related terrorist cell had planned a series of additional bomb attacks—on the Holland and Lincoln Tunnels, and the United Nations building, in New York. It was not unreasonable to ask whether the attack on the Murrah building had the same, or at least a similar, pedigree.

Still, those suspicions led the FBI to make an immediate blunder. On the day after the bombing, Ibrahim Abdullah Hassan Ahmed, a thirty-two-year-old American citizen who was born in Jordan, flew from his home in Oklahoma City to Chicago, planning to go first to London and then on to Amman. The FBI questioned him in Chicago, allowed him to fly on to London, but then decided that Ahmed needed to answer more questions. The Bureau asked the authorities in London to send Ahmed back to the United States, which they did. After further questioning, Ahmed was released without being charged. It later appeared that the only reason he was stopped was because he fit an absurdly broad profile—he had an Arabic name, was between twenty and forty, and was flying from Oklahoma City to the Middle East. Some news reports about him said he had bomb-making material with him, but that was untrue. He was a victim, albeit briefly, of the hysteria of the moment. No apologies for his detention were ever forthcoming. As Garland and Louis Freeh, the FBI director, were ready to acknowledge, in the period immediately after the bombing, they were not going to take any chances.

On Friday morning, forty-eight hours after the bombing, it became clear that the law enforcement team on the ground in Oklahoma City needed help. The U.S. attorney there had just been elevated to a judgeship, and there was no confirmed replacement. The federal courthouse, which included the prosecutors' offices, was damaged and unusable. Many of the victims in the Murrah building worked for law enforcement agencies, and their leaders were all itching to take part in the investigation. Turf battles had started. Before his political career, Governor Keating had been an FBI special agent, the U.S. attorney in Oklahoma City, and a senior Justice Department official under George H. W. Bush, so he had a better understanding than most about these conflicts. Someone needed to be in charge.

On Friday morning, Reno passed the word to Gorelick: get a senior person on the ground in Oklahoma. Gorelick sent Garland. He barely had time to rush home for some clothes and head to a small airstrip in Virginia, where he boarded an FBI plane. In those days, the planes in the Bureau's fleet only had enough range to reach Indianapolis. When Garland's plane landed there, someone handed him a brick-like cell phone and told him the attorney general was on the line.

"We found him," Reno said. "He's at a jail in Oklahoma. You're going to be doing the initial hearing tonight."

The plane pressed on to Oklahoma City, and Garland went straight to Tinker Air Force Base. "We see this huge crowd of people outside, and you never know what that's going to mean," he said. "Turned out it was angry, but it wasn't the mob. It was the press corps, because they had not been allowed to go inside. It was an Air Force base, and it was ringed with barbed wire, and there were MPs [military police] with bayonets, and they weren't letting anybody in."

Garland went inside the small courtroom, which was usually used for courts-martial. He recognized Danny Coulson of the FBI, who had brought McVeigh from Perry in the helicopter. "Where's the public? Where's the press?" Garland asked. Coulson said this was an Air Force base, and the military police had their rules—no press or public inside. Garland said that approach was a nonstarter. "We don't want to do it that way. The case is going to be bad enough with conspiracy theories," he told Coulson. "The defendant is going to complain he didn't get an open hearing. The law requires an open hearing." Coulson had a brief confrontation with the MPs, and eventually the Air Force backed down. A press pool was selected for the dozen or so seats, and Garland went ahead with the arraignment—a brief proceeding.

This gave Garland his first close-up look at McVeigh. "I sat across the table from killers when I was an AUSA," he recalled, "but I had never seen such a stone-cold face." McVeigh was held without bail and sent for his first night in the federal prison in El Reno.

It was around midnight by the time Garland made his way to what remained of the Murrah building. The scene was still illuminated so searchers could continue their work around the clock. What Garland had seen on television didn't prepare him for the real thing. "It was like a war zone—the destruction was so massive," he said. He was struck by how rescue workers had come from around the country to help; one of the first teams he met happened to come from the suburban Maryland town where he lived with his family. Like so many others, Garland was haunted by the thought of the day care center that had been on the second floor. When Garland arrived, there were still tiny broken toys and ripped little backpacks visible in the debris. Garland and his wife had two daughters who were close in age to the kids who had perished. Even decades later, in his office as attorney general, Garland teared up at the thought of that first night in Oklahoma City.

Garland took charge of the legal side of the case the next morning. The O. J. Simpson case was already on his mind. In that unfolding drama, the defense had pointed to a series of blunders made by Los Angeles police and prosecutors. The issue of law enforcement competence and misconduct was much in the air, and Garland knew that the public—and prospective jurors—would be watching the bombing case through that filter. Garland didn't want agents to take any chances that a judge might later find their searches unlawful and suppress the evidence they discovered. So, Garland set up shop processing search warrants for nearly every step the agents took in the investigation. It was tedious and perhaps unnecessary, but Garland, acting in character, made sure that the proprieties were observed.

Garland's assignment in Oklahoma City was open-ended, and he found himself wanting to remain. The pain in the city was as great as the response from the community was inspiring. It seemed like the whole state had mobilized to do what it could, whether it was help dig through the rubble or make sandwiches for the rescuers. The investigation was massive and complex, and its reach quickly extended from the bombing site to Michigan, Kansas, Arizona, New York, and beyond. Managing such a complex undertaking suited Garland's fastidious temperament.

The first significant legal proceeding in the case against McVeigh took place on April 27, and Garland appeared as lead prosecutor. In a preliminary hearing, it's almost impossible for the government to lose. The prosecution need only show probable cause that the defendant is guilty, and hearsay evidence is admissible. This means that the government can prove its case by calling a single FBI agent who summarizes everything investigators have found. Because of the damage to the federal courthouse (and for security reasons), the hearing was held in a makeshift courtroom inside the El Reno prison. Just before the proceeding, John Coyle and Susan Otto asked to be relieved as McVeigh's defense lawyers because of their connections to victims of the bombing, but Magistrate Judge Ronald Howland insisted they stay on at least for this one day.

Garland's strategy for the preliminary hearing established the model for the prosecution effort that would follow. He pared the case down to its essentials and let the evidence speak for itself. There were no histrionics. Garland called a single witness, Jon Hersley, the new lead FBI agent on the case. He testified about the discovery of the truck axle at the scene and the connection to the rental at Elliott's Body Shop in Junction City, Kansas. He displayed the sketch of John Doe Number 1, which looked just like McVeigh, and Garland elicited that McVeigh had stayed at the Dreamland Motel on the nights leading up to April 19. He told of Charlie Hanger's arrest of McVeigh about ninety minutes after the bombing. McVeigh's shirt contained bomb residue. Garland rested his case after Hersley's testimony, which lasted less than thirty minutes on direct. Garland's summation was deadpan in the extreme. "You have heard evidence, Your Honor," he said, "more than sufficient to establish that during and in relation to a crime of violence the defendant used and carried a destructive device—that is, a bomb." On the issue of bail, he said, "Your Honor, as everyone knows, he faces the possibility of the death penalty in this case and enormous incentive to flee. The government represents no condition would prevent a person in that situation from fleeing." To no one's surprise, Judge Howland ordered McVeigh to be held over for trial and refused to release him on bail.

The Garland template—a narrow, focused case, including only the evidence necessary to meet the government's burden of proof—made sense from a law enforcement perspective. If one believes, as Garland did, that the government's burden in a criminal case is limited to proving a specific defendant guilty of a specific crime, then it was the appropriate way to proceed. (Not coincidentally, the Garland template was also different from the sprawling mess that was the Simpson prosecution.) Still, it is worth noting that Garland's agenda in the aftermath of the bombing was very different from Bill Clinton's. The president sought to raise the alarm about the political and media culture that produced McVeigh; Clinton recognized the broader threat that McVeigh's worldview represented and tried to warn the American people about it. Both the Garland and Clinton approaches made sense from their own perspectives. But as the president's attention turned to other subjects, Garland's view of the Oklahoma City bombing became the only one on display.

Accordingly, thanks to the way Garland organized the prosecution, the idea took hold that the bombing was just about Tim McVeigh and Terry Nichols. In limiting their mission that way, Garland and his subordinates actively discouraged the idea that McVeigh and Nichols represented something broader—and more enduring—than just their own malevolent behavior. This was a dangerously misleading impression. Clinton saw that the bombing was the product of more than just a pair of twisted minds, but also the result of the poisonous rhetoric of Rush Limbaugh, Newt Gingrich, and the right-wing zealotry machine. Convicting McVeigh and Nichols, while necessary, would do little to stop the forces that propelled their terrible mission. In the years after 1995, those forces endured, flourished, and burst forth, among other places, at the Capitol on January 6, 2021.

Garland remained in Oklahoma City for weeks. He wanted to stay longer and remain the lead prosecutor in the case. But Gorelick insisted that he return to deal with a different crisis—the Unabomber.

At that point, no one knew who the Unabomber was—and that was the problem. The first bomb appeared in 1978, when a package with the address of a Northwestern University professor was found in a Chicago parking lot. It exploded when a police officer opened it. (He suffered minor injuries.) A year later, another bomb was sent to a different Northwestern professor, and the graduate student who opened it also suffered minor injuries. Later in 1979, a bomb was placed in the cargo hold of an American Airlines flight from Chicago to Washington, D.C. The device malfunctioned, failing to explode but emitting smoke, which caused the pilot to make an emergency landing. Because the bombs appeared to be made by the same person—who carved the letters *FC* on one component in each bomb—the FBI set up a task force to investigate the UNABOM case, code-named for UNiversity and Airline BOMbing targets. From 1979 to 1987, there were nine more bombings, which resulted in one death and several serious injuries.

The Unabomber was silent for the next six years, and the FBI made no progress in catching him, but the mysterious villain started up again after Bill Clinton took office. A geneticist at the University of California at Berkeley was injured by a bomb on June 22, 1993, and two days later, a computer scientist at Yale lost several fingers to a bomb. In December 1994, an advertising executive in New Jersey was killed. On April 24, 1995—five days after the Oklahoma City bombing—a mailed bomb killed the president of the California Forestry Association in Sacramento.

As far as Gorelick and the other leaders of the Justice Department were concerned, the crowning insult from the Unabomber came during the last week of June. The Unabomber first wrote a letter to the *San Francisco Chronicle* warning that the "terrorist group FC, called Unabomber by the FBI, is planning to blow up an airliner out of Los Angeles International Airport some time during the next six days." The letter, which the FBI authenticated, set off days of chaos in Los Angeles and around the country as the authorities increased screenings at airports. Later in the same week, an editor at *The New York Times* received a letter that said the first letter was "one last prank to remind them who we are. But, no, we haven't tried to plant a bomb on an airline (recently)." The Unabomber wasn't just killing people and disrupting the national economy; he was making the FBI and the Justice Department look inept.

"After all those years, the FBI was nowhere in the investigation, and Jamie said I had to come back to Washington and get my arms around this thing," Garland said.

The investigations of the Unabomber and the Oklahoma City bombing unfolded simultaneously, with implications for how each was perceived. From the start, the Unabomber was characterized—correctly—as a lone wolf. This impression was reinforced when the government met the Unabomber's most audacious demand. In a series of letters to *The New York Times* and others in 1995, the Unabomber vowed to cease his bombing campaign if the *Times* and *Washington Post* published a thirty-thousand-word manifesto. After deliberations at the highest level of government, Freeh and Reno advised the papers to publish the manifesto, in the hope that the public attention would lead to his capture. The *Post* published the manifesto on September 19, 1995, and it showcased an idiosyncratic ideology that borrowed from both the left and right. (The style and content of the work reminded David Kaczynski of his brother Ted, who lived an isolated existence in the Montana woods. Ted Kaczynski was arrested as the Unabomber in his tiny cabin on April 3, 1996.)

At the time, and especially in later years, the two crimes, and especially the two lead defendants, came to be seen in similar ways. Kaczynski and McVeigh were perceived as evil eccentrics whose views and actions emerged from the bizarre circumstances of their individual lives. But this was not accurate. Kaczynski was a genuine loner, a teenage math prodigy who evolved into an anti-technology fanatic. He followed no one and had no followers. Garland limited his description of McVeigh to the acts charged in the indictment; because McVeigh and Nichols were the only ones charged in the Oklahoma City bombing, that left the impression that McVeigh, like Kaczynski, also represented no one except himself. In fact, McVeigh belonged to a thriving and enduring political movement in the United States. Both before and after his crimes, McVeigh's views on guns and race were widely shared. Kaczynski didn't have even a platoon of supporters, but McVeigh was right when he told his lawyers that he had an "Army" of allies, even if he never figured out how to rally his troops.

McVeigh himself recognized this important distinction. After Kaczynski was arrested in 1996, *Time* magazine devoted much of an issue to him and McVeigh. In a letter to Stephen Jones, McVeigh wrote, "Time, unfortunately, has failed to recognize the stark difference between the Unabomber and the OKC bombing. Namely, the Unabomber has approximately one sympathizer (Al Gore), whereas the OKC bombing represents a massive feeling of disenchantment and growing unrest in the country." McVeigh was making the point that a lot of right-wingers in the United States believed that violence was an appropriate response to political grievances. He had a lot of company in that view. Donald Trump made the same point in a tweet late in the day on January 6, 2021, following the riot at the Capitol: "These are the things and events that happen when a sacred landslide election victory is so unceremoniously & viciously stripped away from great patriots who have been badly & unfairly treated for so long."

Back in Washington, after Garland helped salvage the Unabomber investigation after being denied the chance to try McVeigh, he received a splendid consolation prize. In September 1995, Clinton nominated him to a seat on the United States Court of Appeals for the District of Columbia Circuit, the second most important court in the country, though he was not confirmed until March 1997. (In 2001, President George W. Bush nominated Garland's doppelgänger, John Roberts, to be Garland's colleague on the same court; as with Garland, it took two years for Roberts to be confirmed.) Garland's judicial nomination left the leadership of the Justice Department with a quandary. If Merrick Garland wasn't going to try the case of *United States v. Timothy McVeigh*, who would?

CHAPTER 17

The Case Against Clutter

There was one major loose end before the case could move forward with new prosecutors. At the preliminary hearing, Garland had made much of the resemblance between McVeigh and the man in the sketch who was known as John Doe Number 1. But Garland skated by the issue of the second sketch—of John Doe Number 2. The close resemblance between McVeigh and John Doe Number 1 made the issue of Number 2 more pressing. If one sketch was right, shouldn't the other one be accurate, too? But the FBI had no clue about the identity of John Doe Number 2.

Of course, if McVeigh had another person with him when he rented the Ryder truck at Elliott's Body Shop, that didn't mean that McVeigh was innocent. But if prosecutors wanted to provide a jury with a coherent picture of the bombing conspiracy, they had to have some explanation for the man in the second sketch. Who was he? Investigators ruled out the most obvious suspect—Terry Nichols—almost right away; the sketch looked nothing like Nichols. But if Nichols was not John Doe Number 2, did such a person even exist? And if he didn't exist, why did the mechanic at the rental counter say that he did? How could the same eyewitness be so right about one person and totally wrong about another?

Louis Freeh, the director of the FBI, was obsessed with the issue of John Doe Number 2. Micromanaging, he vowed to find John Doe 2—personally. He played hunches, and he wanted fast follow-up. The FBI immediately compiled a huge dossier on every aspect of McVeigh's life, including in the Army. Reviewing this material, Freeh saw a photograph of one of McVeigh's Army buddies, and the director decided that the fellow looked like John Doe Number 2. Freeh demanded that Bob Ricks, the special agent in charge in Oklahoma City, personally track down this individual, and Ricks did—only to discover he was the town drunk of his Oklahoma burg and incapable of bombing anything.

Freeh's spare-no-expense approach to the bombing investigation sometimes created more problems than it solved. The magnitude of the crime led civilians to provide tips (nearly all useless) to FBI field offices all over the country and even the world. Collecting and organizing that material pushed the Bureau's archaic computer systems beyond their capacity, with consequences that later turned out to be damaging to the court case against McVeigh. The effort to find eyewitnesses sometimes went from thorough to excessive. For example, Sergeant Rick Wahl reported that he had seen a Ryder truck at Geary Lake in Kansas when he had gone fishing with his son on the day before the bombing. Freeh wanted follow-up. To do so, agents set up a roadblock by the entrance to the park on Route 77 and stopped every car to ask the occupants if they had seen a Ryder truck there on April 18. The civilians wanted to help, and once they were asked, many of them reported that they had seen a Ryder truck by the lake. They provided dozens of leads, all of which had to be checked out, and later turned over to the defense as possible exculpatory evidence. But the leads turned out to be false, which was a predictable outcome of collecting evidence with this kind of dragnet.

One of the more consequential tips came from a man who said he saw two "Middle Eastern–looking" men hurry away from the Murrah building shortly before the bombing. The witness said the pair entered a brown pickup with smoked windows and a smoke-colored front bug guard. The witness also gave a detailed description of their clothing—white shirts, jeans, black boots, and black hats. Both before and after this witness's story became public, FBI agents spent a great deal of time with the witness and tried to check out his account, which had abundant problems. First, it was peculiar, to say the least, that this individual had such a specific memory of something that was inconsequential at the time—just two men walking away *before* the bombing. Second, he gave inconsistent accounts of where the pickup was driven. In the end, the FBI concluded that the witness was either mistaken or lying. But a local television news reporter named Jayna Davis kept pursuing this "Middle Eastern" angle and gave it enduring life.

The matter of John Doe Number 2 was different. Three people had been involved with the rental of the Ryder truck at Elliott's Body Shop in Junction City. "Robert Kling" had visited the shop twice—once to fill out paperwork, and then again to pick up the truck. Tom Kessinger, the mechanic at Elliott's Body Shop, had the best memory of what happened, and Raymond Rozycki, the FBI artist, had relied on Kessinger's descriptions to produce the sketches. Kessinger gave precise descriptions of two men who picked up the truck on the 17th. The first clearly matched McVeigh. The second person—John Doe Number 2—was also distinctive. He was a white male with a beefy build, dark brown hair and eyes. Kessinger noticed the point of a tattoo partially visible under the sleeve of the man's black T-shirt. The man was also wearing an odd-looking baseball cap, with blue and white wings on the sides. In light of such a detailed description, John Doe Number 2 hardly seemed like a figment of Kessinger's imagination. At first, Eldon Elliott told investigators that only one person picked up the truck, but when he heard Kessinger's version, he agreed that there were two, though he couldn't describe Number 2. Vicki Beemer, the office manager, didn't remember much at all.

The sketch of Number 2 generated literally thousands of tips, especially after McVeigh was arrested. Most of them simply described people who looked like the man in the sketch, and they could easily be discounted. (Sightings of purported John Doe Number 2s were reported in Kansas, Arizona, New York, and several other states.) Many of the identifications conflicted with known facts. One tipster saw McVeigh and John Doe Number 2 in a twenty-foot Ryder truck on April 16 in Tulsa; but "Kling" didn't pick up the truck until April 17. Another saw McVeigh and John Doe Number 2 at a diner in Herington, Kansas, on the morning of the bombing—but that's a four-hour drive from Oklahoma City. Most of the other sightings were simply improbable. One witness, who was in the Murrah building at the time of the explosion, said she staggered out and saw McVeigh and John Doe Number 2; she claimed that McVeigh asked her how many people had been killed. Another saw McVeigh and John Doe Number 2 shortly after the bombing pointing at blood-covered victims and laughing. Other tips were too vague to be useful, like the person who claimed to see McVeigh and John Doe Number 2 driving on I-35 three days before the bombing. The FBI checked out virtually all the tips, producing an enormous drain of resources. Eventually, the tips were also provided to the defense as possible exculpatory evidence. In all, the investigation of the Oklahoma City bombing was a case study in the fallibility of eyewitness identification.

Baffled and frustrated by the failure to locate John Doe Number 2—a quest that was becoming something of a national joke—the FBI tried a different approach. In late May, agents asked Eldon Elliott to produce records of all the trucks his shop had rented in the period around the bombing. This was a manageable task because the shop mostly did repairs and rented few trucks. Agents were determined to track down all the people who rented any kind of truck from Elliott's Body Shop.

In early June, agents found Michael Hertig, who rented a truck on

April 18, the day after McVeigh rented the one used in the bombing. Like many customers at Elliott's, Hertig was a soldier assigned to Fort Riley who had been transferred to another base. He rented a truck to take his belongings. With his crew cut and military bearing, Hertig bore a rough resemblance to both McVeigh and the sketch of John Doe Number 1. Probing further, the agents asked Hertig if he had brought anyone with him to rent the truck. Yes, his friend Todd Bunting. It took the agents some time to locate Bunting, but when they did find him, they almost wept with gratitude. He looked exactly like the sketch of John Doe Number 2—brown eyes and hair, beefy build. They asked Bunting to roll up his sleeve and saw a tattoo of a Playboy bunny; the bunny's foot dipped below the sleeve of his T-shirt. Was he wearing a hat when he went into Elliott's? Yes—a Carolina Panthers cap, with what looked like blue and white waves on the sides. In other words, Todd Bunting was the man Kessinger thought was John Doe Number 2.

What happened became clear: Kessinger had made an understandable mistake, mixing up McVeigh's rental with one that took place the next day. Presented with photos of Hertig and Bunting, Kessinger quickly acknowledged his error. But real life is not as tidy as fiction. Eldon Elliott, who had first insisted that McVeigh was alone, never agreed that Todd Bunting was the actual John Doe Number 2. And the issue of John Doe Number 2 is still often portrayed as one of the lingering mysteries of the Oklahoma City bombing. But to the FBI, the interviews of Hertig and Bunting closed the matter. McVeigh rented the Ryder truck by himself on April 17, 1995; there never was a John Doe Number 2.

Jamie Gorelick, the deputy attorney general and Garland's boss, took charge of the talent search for the prosecutors who would try McVeigh. It's customary for the local United States attorney to prosecute crimes that take place within his or her jurisdiction, but Gorelick ruled out that option from the beginning. Patrick Ryan, who was about to take office as the new United States attorney in Oklahoma City, had been a civil litigator, with no experience trying criminal cases. Besides, his office only had a handful of prosecutors, and they were preoccupied with getting their damaged facilities back up and running. In addition, Gorelick was a meritocratic snob. She wanted an elite team for this high-profile assignment, and she didn't trust the Oklahoma prosecutors with that kind of responsibility. (The resulting tension between the outsiders and locals in the Justice Department would endure.)

After Main Justice, as the headquarters of the department is known, put out the word that Gorelick and Garland were looking for experienced outsiders to try the case, they were inundated with applicants. Again, the O. J. Simpson case figured prominently in the process. Gorelick wanted prosecutors who would not seek the fame and notoriety that came with the assignment. Leslie Caldwell, who came from the U.S. Attorney's Office in Brooklyn, was a top candidate. She had won cases against some of the most ruthless criminals in New York and never sought personal glory. But Gorelick had a different idea of the perfect candidate. She figured that the case was going to be tried in Oklahoma or somewhere nearby, and she wanted someone from "the heartland."

One application caught her eye from the outset. Joe Hartzler had been a summer associate at Gorelick's firm when she was in private practice. She remembered his diligence and midwestern reserve, which would be an important qualification if this was going to be the un-O.J. prosecution. He even had a boyish cowlick that dipped over his forehead, giving him, even on the brink of middle age, a Tom Sawyer look. Then forty-three, Hartzler had grown up in central Ohio, gone to college at Amherst, and then graduated first in his class at the law school at American University. After a clerkship on the D.C. Circuit, he followed his then-girlfriend, now-wife to her home state of Illinois. Hartzler joined the storied U.S. Attorney's Office in

Chicago. He investigated public corruption—the bread and butter in the Northern District of Illinois—but he'd also prosecuted bombing cases, which were a relative rarity in the federal system. Those prosecutions led to convictions of several members of the FALN—the Puerto Rican nationalist group—for a terrorist campaign in Illinois. When Garland checked out Hartzler with contacts in Chicago, he received glowing reports; Hartzler was said to have an "affidavit face"—a look of extreme trustworthiness. After a decade in the office, Hartzler had been promoted to chief of the criminal division—a position of great responsibility for a line assistant.

But there was a problem. Starting in the mid-1980s, Hartzler started having trouble walking—his right foot dragged, and he kept stubbing his toe. On a trip to Amsterdam, he tripped on the cobblestones. A series of tests back in Chicago solved the mystery. In 1988, when Hartzler was thirty-six, he was diagnosed with multiple sclerosis. He kept the secret for a while. He hoped for rainy days so he could bring an umbrella to work and use it like a cane. Eventually, though, there was no hiding what was happening. He couldn't use a wheelchair because he lacked the arm strength to propel it forward. He couldn't make it across the grass to his sons' soccer games, so he got an electric scooter, which eventually became his full-time mode of transport. In 1990, seeking a different pace and a greater income, he joined a Chicago law firm. Two years later, though, the Hartzlers thought a departure from Chicago would be best for the family finances and Joe's condition. He joined the U.S. Attorney's Office in Springfield, Illinois, in the center of the state, where the workload was more manageable than in Chicago. When the bombing happened, Hartzler was working on a real estate fraud case involving some resort property in Arkansas. It was a worthy enough prosecution, but hardly the kind of headline-making investigation he was used to leading in Chicago. The Oklahoma City bombing would be the case of a lifetime for a prosecutor, and Hartzler was more than tempted.

He called a family meeting with his wife and three sons, who were thirteen, ten, and six at the time. Joe said he was looking at a two-year commitment to the case. He wouldn't be gone all the time—he could return to Springfield on weekends—but it would mean a lot of time away from home. Alex, the oldest, was skeptical. He pointed out that lots of people could prosecute the case, but only one person could be their dad. Adam, the sports nut in the family, took a different view. "Alex! Dad's a lawyer. This is like playing in the NBA. This is being on the Bulls!" Alex was convinced, and the family gave Joe the go-ahead to seek the job.

It came down to a final interview with Janet Reno and Jamie Gorelick, who played good cop/bad cop with Hartzler. Reno waxed dreamily about living amid the farms of central Illinois. Gorelick wanted to know what Hartzler would do if the defense asked for a change of venue. It was a tough issue. The powerful local victims' lobby wanted the case kept in Oklahoma City, but it would be difficult to persuade a judge that McVeigh could get a fair trial there. Hartzler said a move to Tulsa might satisfy the judge and the victims. Gorelick also addressed the main issue. Hartzler's qualifications were not in doubt. But Gorelick herself had a close relative with MS. Stress is known to aggravate the condition. Could Hartzler really take on this responsibility, including all the travel?

All Hartzler could say, with his heartland earnestness, was yes, and that was good enough. On May 22, 1995, Hartzler was named lead counsel for the prosecution.

Hartzler quickly learned that his job was as much political as legal. The Justice Department press release announcing his appointment said, "Hartzler will lead the joint team, which is composed of federal prosecutors from Oklahoma City and around the country." No one told him how to do that, especially since it was clear that the Oklahoma City contingent viewed him as an interloper. Garland was still supervising the investigation from Washington, and he and Hartzler spoke almost daily, but when it came to day-to-day operations, Hartzler was on his own.

Hartzler had a different problem with the FBI. The investigation now involved dozens of agents gathering evidence all over the country. They all clamored for Hartzler's attention, and they all wanted their evidence showcased in the trial. Hartzler didn't even have time to look at his email. The work was overwhelming. He needed a second-in-command who could establish a system for digesting the mountain of information that was coming his way every day. Hartzler's boss in Springfield suggested Larry Mackey, who had been an AUSA—assistant U.S. attorney—in the Central District of Illinois before he moved to a similar job in Indianapolis. Mackey was both tremendously organized—not a skill all prosecutors possessed—and a workaholic. Hartzler explained the problem to Mackey simply: "I am fucking drowning." Mackey signed on.

Three more lawyers joined the team in short order. Scott Mendeloff came from the U.S. Attorney's Office in Chicago, where he and Hartzler had tried a crooked judge together. Beth Wilkinson was detailed from Gorelick's staff in Washington; earlier she had been an assistant U.S. attorney in Brooklyn and a captain in the Army. Aitan Goelman, the junior member of the team, was recently out of law school and a lawyer at Main Justice. He was brought to Oklahoma City to shadow Hartzler and pick up day-to-day assignments from him.

Hartzler figured the best way to keep the lawyers out of each other's way was to give them clear assignments. For himself, he had overall supervision of the case, but also the Arizona portion. Even at this early stage, Hartzler knew that McVeigh had spent a lot of time with Michael and Lori Fortier, making them potentially the best witnesses for the prosecution. Mackey was to create a system to organize the evidence, but also handle matters relating to Terry Nichols, especially the possible testimony from his ex-wife, Lana Padilla. Mendeloff took Kansas—the witnesses from Elliott's Body Shop, the Dreamland Motel, and Geary Lake. Wilkinson, who as an assistant U.S. attorney had won a conviction of a narcoterrorist for bombing an Avianca jetliner, had the scientific evidence and the crime scene; it would be her job to present the now famous Ryder truck axle to the jury.

That left the Oklahoma prosecutors. Hartzler assigned them the job of dealing with the victims. It was, at one level, an enormous job, just because there were so many victims, including the injured as well as the families of the dead. From the beginning of the case, Reno vowed that the Justice Department would keep the victims closely informed about the progress of the investigation. Some were also likely to be witnesses in the trial, especially in the death penalty portion. But there was no disguising the fact that the local prosecutors were being shunted aside from the substantive part of the investigation. Pat Ryan, the new U.S. attorney, resented the way Hartzler and his team had been imposed on him. Hartzler dutifully reported the complaints back to Garland—and Ryan complained himself—but Garland didn't waver in his support of Hartzler. Just win the case, Garland counseled. That would salve any wounded egos.

Hartzler soon realized that a big part of his job was saying no. No more lawyers; no more investigators; no more tests on the evidence; no more witnesses. The prosecutors had a strong case against McVeigh. It was not complicated. McVeigh rented the truck and bombed the Murrah building. That was the case that Garland wanted presented to a jury, and Hartzler entirely agreed. In the prosecutors' makeshift offices in the former Southwestern Bell office space, Hartzler scrawled out a sign that summed up his philosophy (and Garland's) and taped it to his door: DO NOT BURY THE CRIME IN CLUTTER!

CHAPTER 18

"*This . . . Is CNN*"

The story of how McVeigh's defense team came together was very different. There were even disputes about how the lead lawyer was hired. Rancor, distrust, stress, competition as well as a proudly guilty client—all made this family unhappy in its own way.

In the period immediately after McVeigh was arrested in Perry, and through the preliminary hearing at the makeshift courtroom in the El Reno prison, he was represented by Susan Otto, of the federal defenders, and John Coyle, the Oklahoma City lawyer. Both had misgivings from the start. Since Otto's office was damaged by the bombing, she was effectively a victim of the attack and didn't think it appropriate to participate in the defense for the long haul. Coyle had several long talks with McVeigh and heard him boast that he had set off the bomb. But the mounting death toll weighed on Coyle. Several days after the bombing, one of the victims was identified as Mike Weaver, a lawyer for the Department of Housing and Urban Development, who was a friend and occasional golf buddy of Coyle's. That was too much for him. Coyle called David Russell, the chief judge of the federal district court in Oklahoma, and asked to be relieved of the assignment to represent McVeigh.

This left Russell with a dilemma. Representing McVeigh was a plum assignment, but also a controversial one, especially in Oklahoma, which remained in a state of collective shock. Russell had received some advice. A prominent Oklahoma lawyer named Stephen Jones had written him a letter recommending a former lawyer in his firm, Robert Nigh, for the job of defending McVeigh. Nigh had gone on to work as a public defender in Tulsa and then in the lead role of the legal aid office in Lincoln, Nebraska. Nigh was an obscure out-of-state lawyer, and Judge Russell understandably ignored Jones's recommendation. But the letter planted a seed in Russell's mind. What about *Stephen Jones* as McVeigh's lawyer?

So, after returning to his office from a business trip to Dallas late on the evening of Friday, May 5, Jones found a note from his receptionist taped to his chair: "Mr. Jones, Chief Judge Russell desires you call him. He wants to talk to you." The message gave the judge's office and home numbers. When Jones and the judge connected that evening, Russell asked Jones to represent McVeigh. Jones officially took on the assignment the following Monday.

Later, after relations between Jones and his colleagues on the McVeigh defense team turned rancorous, some lawyers on the team asserted that Jones hadn't really been recommending Nigh, who was clearly an unsuitable choice as lead defense counsel. He was putting his own name in front of Russell, in hopes of being appointed. According to this theory, Jones longed for the attention that a case of this magnitude would bring. Jones rejected this hypothesis. He had known Judge Russell for years, as he knew most of the top echelon of the Oklahoma legal world. If he had wanted the McVeigh assignment, he would simply have asked for it. Jones later said that he only reluctantly accepted the McVeigh assignment because of his ethical obligations as an attorney. The conflict between the two versions served mostly to demonstrate the level of distrust between Jones and some of his colleagues. And the hostility between Jones and McVeigh himself would turn out to be even worse.

The office that Jones returned to on that May evening was in one of the very few tall (fourteen-story) office buildings in Enid, Oklahoma, population about fifty thousand. Enid resembled Junction City, Kansas, in that it functioned largely as a civilian adjunct to a military installation. In Enid, it was Vance Air Force Base, where most military pilots receive their initial training. The clear skies and flat terrain provide a forgiving setting for novices in the cockpit. The only obstacles in Enid are nine enormous grain elevators, now largely abandoned, which are taller than anything between Oklahoma City and Denver.

Jones was born in 1940 and raised in the Houston suburbs during the post–World War II boom in Texas. When Jones came of age, Texas was still a one-party Democratic state, but his town was a harbinger of the region's future—a Republican stronghold. A high school debater, Jones caught the political bug and went to work for the state Republican Party after graduating from the University of Texas. In 1963, Jones wrote fan mail to Richard Nixon, who had just lost the race for governor of California and moved to New York to practice law. The former vice president flabbergasted young Jones by writing back with an offer: come to New York to work as a researcher as Nixon plotted his political comeback. Jones spent about a year with Nixon before toiling for the next three as an aide to various Republican congressmen on Capitol Hill.

Jones returned to Oklahoma with a singular goal—to win a seat in Congress. He chose to settle in Enid, the eighth largest city in the state, where he had no previous ties, because he thought the area offered him the best chance to run for office. And Jones did run for office—over and over. In the 1970s and '80s, Republicans were coming to dominate Oklahoma politics, but Jones never caught the wave. He ran four times, starting in 1974 as the Republican nominee for state attorney general; he lost with 32 percent of the vote. His political career ended sixteen years later, when he was routed, with just 17 percent of the vote, in a U.S. Senate race against David Boren, the incumbent Democrat. The common touch eluded Jones. A regal Anglophile, with a gray comb-over atop a six-foot-plus frame, Jones bought his suits on London's Savile Row and favored such pretentious expressions as "sanctum sanctorum" for his office. He lived with his wife and four children in a house in Enid modeled on George Washington's Mount Vernon. The house had a name—Elmstead—rather than an address.

In part, Jones's political career fizzled for honorable reasons. Shortly after he started practicing law, at the height of the Vietnam War, he represented a University of Oklahoma student who was charged with a felony for waving the Vietcong flag at a rally. Jones's law firm, reflecting the politics of the state, threatened to fire him if he kept the client. Jones refused to drop the young man and was dismissed by the firm. Jones took the protester's case to federal court, won his client's freedom with a First Amendment defense, and went off to practice on his own. He represented several more activists, including the notorious 1960s radical Abbie Hoffman, and built a reputation for doggedness and fearlessness. He tried cases all over the state, winning often, and represented a variety of clients—Republican politicians, oil and gas interests, the occasional death row prisoner. By the mid-1990s, Jones was making about a million dollars a year, but he had never garnered the attention that would have come with political success. Since his Nixon days, Jones had dwelled on the periphery of renown, but no closer. That all changed with the offer of the McVeigh case from Judge Russell. As Jones wrote later, with barely contained glee, "I was about to get a cram course in dealing with the media multitudes, from the New York City heavyweights—the Dan Rathers, the

Barbara Walterses, the Diane Sawyeres—down to Mr. J. D. Case, who wrote, very influentially, for the McCurtain County Gazette in Idabel, Oklahoma (population 6,500)."

Starting on Monday, May 8, Jones spent most of the week with McVeigh at the El Reno prison outside Oklahoma City. Jones knew from his brief conversations with Coyle, McVeigh's original lawyer, that McVeigh would admit to the bombing. But rather than jump right into those details, Jones began their conversations by asking McVeigh to provide his intellectual autobiography. What did he believe, and why? This gave McVeigh the chance to show off what he had learned from *The Turner Diaries*, *The Spotlight*, Rush Limbaugh, and Bill Cooper on shortwave.

McVeigh claimed that he was acting out of patriotism, out of faith with the nation's Founders. He was defending the Constitution, especially the Second Amendment, against the depredations of a power-mad federal government. McVeigh dazzled Jones by reciting from memory large chunks of the Declaration of Independence, especially the parts about the duty to rebel against a tyrannical government. Then there were the assault weapons ban, Ruby Ridge, and Waco—his *casus belli*, as Jones would say, the causes that pushed him into direct action against the government.

Jones would ultimately plow this ground with McVeigh many times, and like most defense lawyers, he never passed judgment on his client—at least not in front of him. But in this first week, Jones couldn't resist asking a few questions about the subject that would remain the touchstone of the Oklahoma City bombing case: the day care center, where nineteen children perished. To this day, these deaths remain central to public memory of the event, even more so than the overall toll of 168 lives.

So, Jones asked: Did you know there was a day care center in the building? Can you justify killing children? How do you feel about their deaths now?

McVeigh never flinched. He made a plausible case that he did not know there was a day care center in the Murrah building. He had done only cursory research into which federal agencies were housed there, and during his short visits to the scene, he said he never noticed children's artwork taped to the inside of the black glass on the second floor. But McVeigh was always quick to add that even if he had known about the day care center, he would have bombed the building anyway. He told Jones that in Ruby Ridge and Waco the federal government had "set the rules for engagement" and declared that women and children were not off-limits. In Ruby Ridge, FBI snipers had killed both Randy Weaver's fourteen-year-old son and his wife, while she was holding their infant son. Moreover, McVeigh said, "More children were killed in Waco than in the bombing." (Twenty-five children died in the Waco conflagration.) To put it another way, McVeigh told Jones, the "kill ratio" of child-to-adult victims was 1:5 in Waco, whereas in Oklahoma City it was 1:10, so his actions were not as "inhumane" as those of the federal government. McVeigh's rationalization for murdering the children in the Murrah building provided a useful reminder of his soulless fanaticism.

In one way at least, McVeigh's arrest gave him what he always wanted—an attentive audience. Jones's initial round of interviews was just the beginning. McVeigh loved to talk, and he had a lot to say—about his background, his motives, his plan for the bombing, and its execution. Through McVeigh's long months on the road before April 19, 1995, he had been hoping to find his "Army" of fellow warriors, but even at gun shows, McVeigh never had the gumption or charm to recruit anyone.

This, in the end, was the most important difference between McVeigh and the right-wing extremists who came after him. McVeigh had an analog radicalization—the product of reading books and magazines and listening to the radio and shortwave. His contacts with prospective allies were stilted and cumbersome. In a letter to the author Lou Michel, McVeigh described how Clinton's signing of the assault weapons ban in 1994, following the Brady Bill in 1993 (which mandated federal background checks for some firearm purchasers), was the "trigger" for his decision to bomb the Murrah building. "I decided then and there that I couldn't sit back in the defense mode any longer—that I had to take a pro-active step to protest the loss of all I held dear," he wrote. "As the gun show/gun world frenzy was 'amped up' even more, rumors abounded that 'Brady II' was on a fast track," with even more restrictions on the ownership of guns and ammunition. Gun show "rumors"—that was the only way McVeigh learned what his allies were thinking.

The digital radicalization of McVeigh's descendants—the mass shooters in stores and synagogues, the would-be kidnappers of the Michigan governor, and the insurrectionists at the Capitol—was much faster and more efficient. The substance of their concerns was similar to McVeigh's, especially in the shared obsession with guns and the Second Amendment. Likewise, the possibility of a "great replacement" of white Americans by immigrants of color was another factor. The internet allowed these ideas to spread at the speed of light. Several of the right-wing mass shooters who came after McVeigh were in their late teens, almost a decade younger than McVeigh when he bombed the Murrah building. These twenty-first-century extremists found incendiary information on the internet a lot faster than McVeigh tracked down paper copies of *The Turner Diaries* and *The Spotlight*. Their transformation—and their crimes—happened faster, too.

Even more important, social media allowed like-minded extremists to gather and scheme in a way that made the peddling of gun show rumors look archaic by comparison. The right-wing mass shooters of recent years drew from many of the same sources and connected over many of the same websites. Robert Bowers, who killed eleven people in a Pittsburgh synagogue in 2018, used the social media website Gab. Patrick Crusius, a fan of *The Turner Diaries* who killed twenty-three people in an El Paso Walmart in 2019, posted on the online message board 8chan, as did John Earnest, who killed one and injured three at a Poway, California, synagogue. In 2022, Payton Gendron, who killed ten Black people in a Buffalo supermarket, used the instant messaging platform Discord. (In Gendron's manifesto, he said he would post a livestream of his shooting spree to 4chan, an online cousin to 8chan.)

Nor did extremists in later years have to search out obscure corners of the internet to see their ideas in circulation. Tucker Carlson of Fox News served as a major proponent of the great replacement theory, which was cited by the Pittsburgh, Poway, and Buffalo mass shooters. Several of the plotters to kidnap Michigan governor Gretchen Whitmer in 2020 met on Facebook and then used private Facebook group chats to plan the attack. Communications on Facebook were also central in the conspiracy to swarm the Capitol to overturn the 2020 presidential election. Nor, of course, did gun shows disappear in the post-McVeigh era. Thanks to the relaxation of gun safety laws in recent years, especially in Republican-controlled states, the shows offered more and bigger guns than they did in the 1990s. And the right-wing political advocacy at these events complemented the extremism available on the internet.

Even though the internet and social media emerged years after McVeigh's time, his goals and tactics were aligned with those of his successors. They all wanted to build a movement and spread the word. In the El Reno visiting room, McVeigh had a captive audience of his attorneys, and Jones was determined to accommodate him. As Jones wrote in a memo to McVeigh, "I think for the foreseeable future we ought to try to see you every day."

In prosecutions of indigent defendants in the federal system, especially capital cases, defense attorneys are provided some latitude in hiring co-counsel and experts at government expense. In normal circumstances, the Justice Department and the courts impose limits on overall expenses. But Garland decided from the beginning of the Oklahoma City bombing investigation that he would give the defense essentially an unlimited budget. Garland didn't want to risk a defense claim, perhaps years in the future, that McVeigh's rights had been compromised by insufficient resources to conduct a defense. Jones took full advantage, and then some, of this largesse.

Jones's law firm usually had only a handful of lawyers. But Jones used the McVeigh case, in effect, to re-create the firm at government expense; less an all-star team than an Enid alumni association. Rob Nigh came on as Jones's de facto second-in-command, but the defense team also came to include such former Jones colleagues as Bob Wyatt, Mike Roberts, Jim Hankins, and Julia Sims. But the Enid alumni were only the beginning of the team Jones assembled. He also recruited a separate team for death penalty issues, which included Dick Burr and Mandy Welch, a husband-and-wife duo from Texas, and Randy Coyne, a professor at the University of Oklahoma Law School, who had written a casebook on the subject. There would eventually be more than a dozen lawyers, but that was just the beginning. Jones hired a forensic psychiatrist, a polygraph expert, and several scientific experts on ballistics, explosives, and related matters. At least a half dozen private investigators also came and went over the course of the case. Jones and his colleagues didn't get rich, but the case offered comfortable sinecures; the federal government paid him and the other lawyers $125 per hour when Jones's usual rate was $175, and the others generally charged less. In October 1996, a few months before McVeigh's trial began, Jones arranged for a group photo of the defense team. There are twenty-five people in the photo, and Jones noted, with lawyerly precision, that two lawyers were absent.

The big cast of defense lawyers allowed Jones to keep his promise to McVeigh of a visit every day, including weekends. (The lawyers memorialized these talks in memoranda that were shared with the full team; they are now on file at the Briscoe Center at the University of Texas.) The conversations ranged over a variety of subjects—for example, McVeigh liked sharing his favorite cartoons from Gary Larson's *The Far Side*—but one thing was clear from the beginning. McVeigh had an extraordinary memory, and he was remarkably consistent in recounting the complex tale of the bombing. He could recall the precise routes of his security guard rounds in Buffalo or how much and where he bought fertilizer in farm supply stores in Kansas. He remembered every motel where he stopped during his many cross-country journeys; he remembered storage locker numbers; he remembered the items he bought and sold at gun shows. Always polite, never evasive, McVeigh recounted his life story from his roots near Buffalo to his fateful encounter with Trooper Charlie Hanger on I-35.

However, there was one subject on which McVeigh wavered: whether to plead guilty. The bombing was a political gesture—an act of protest against Bill Clinton's federal government. Like the protagonist of *The Turner Diaries*, McVeigh hoped that his action would set off a broader rebellion. For that reason, he wanted to claim credit for the bombing and explain his reasons. McVeigh often cited a favorite quotation from a dissenting opinion by Justice Louis Brandeis: "Our Government is the potent, the omnipresent teacher. For good or for ill, it teaches the whole people by its example." The government had taught by example in Ruby Ridge and Waco, and McVeigh meant the bombing as a response in kind. From the beginning, then, he talked with Jones about the possibility of taking a plea.

Still, for all that McVeigh wanted to take credit for the attack, he recoiled at the idea that the government might "win" the case against him. He never expressed fear of the death penalty, but he didn't seek it out, either; McVeigh wasn't suicidal. He liked the idea of an acquittal that would demonstrate the incompetence of the government. McVeigh tore into the weaknesses in the government's case, even though he knew (and his lawyers knew) that he was guilty. He particularly enjoyed pointing out contradictory, or simply incorrect, eyewitness testimony. He chuckled at the witnesses who put him in places he never was or saw things that never happened—like McVeigh in his distinctive crew cut leaving the scene of the crime, when he was wearing a hat at the time. McVeigh's ambivalence about his own case would present an ongoing problem for Jones's attempt to defend him.

Jones saw McVeigh's attitude as a public relations problem. From the beginning, Jones was obsessed by news coverage of McVeigh's image and his own. Jones's first important step with the press was a bizarre manifestation of his priorities. At this point, McVeigh had no access to a telephone, but Jones was concerned that once he did, McVeigh was going to start making collect calls to journalists—to Mike Wallace or Peter Jennings—and take credit for the bombing. This, Jones worried, would amount to signing his own death warrant. McVeigh hadn't talked to any journalists yet, but he might. What was Jones to do?

It's fairly common for criminal defendants to want to get their side of a story out in public. They're itching to respond to what they regard as unfair coverage, or they think they have a good story to tell. And the customary response from their lawyers is simple: shut the hell up and let us do our jobs. This is especially true early in an investigation when the government has not yet provided any discovery material and the defense team has not fully debriefed the client or conducted its own inquiries. In these circumstances, silence is usually the best option.

Jones made a different choice, one which reflected recurring themes of his representation of McVeigh. First, McVeigh exercised an extraordinary degree of control over his own defense. He came to regard his lawyers, who appeared dutifully before him every day, as supplicants as much as advisers. He told them what to do, and they often did it. In this case, McVeigh wanted his story out to the public. Second, Jones had a near obsession with the press and devoted enormous amounts of time talking to and cultivating reporters. Jones insisted that these conversations were in McVeigh's interest, as Jones tried to shape news coverage to his client's advantage. Some of his defense colleagues thought Jones just liked hobnobbing with journalists, the more famous the better. Later, one disgruntled lawyer on the defense team devised a combination protest and mockery of Jones's media obsession. Every time Jones took a call from a reporter, this lawyer played a short sound clip from his computer for the team to hear. It was James Earl Jones's famous tagline, "This . . . is CNN."

As practically the first order of business for the defense, Jones and McVeigh came up with a press plan. Jones told Pam Belluck, a reporter for *The New York Times*, that McVeigh "claimed responsibility for the Oklahoma City bombing." This was, of course, an enormous scoop for the *Times*, which played the story on the front page on May 17. Citing "people who have talked with him in jail since his arrest," Belluck wrote, "the Federal Building in Oklahoma City was chosen as a target because it housed so many Government offices and because it was more architecturally vulnerable than other Federal buildings." Further, the story went on, "Mr. McVeigh has also said he had not known there was a day-care center in the building and was surprised when he learned from newspapers that children had died in the bombing." Belluck's source recounted that "Mr. McVeigh said he had been motivated in part by anger at the Federal Government's actions" in Ruby Ridge and Waco.

The story was accurate about McVeigh's role and motives, and Belluck honored Jones's request not to identify him by name. The question, of course, was whether the story—a confession to the bombing—served McVeigh's interest. Realizing the magnitude of the disclosure, Jones took an unusual step the day after the story ran. While he was with McVeigh in the visiting room at El Reno, he scribbled an after-the-fact authorization for his client on a legal pad. Dated May 18 at 6:10 p.m., the document stated,

> My attorney STEPHEN Jones has had and continues to have my Authorization TO TALK OFF the record AND on background to NY Times regarding the following subjects:
>
> 1. My Responsibility
> 2. That I am saddened children were killed 4/19/95
> 3. Assault on Waco
> 4. Lexington & Concord 4/19/1775 . . .
>
> I have read *The New York Times* story of 5/17/95. It is consistent with what I authorized him to tell NY Times . . . I am satisfied with this Act.

McVeigh initialed each sentence in the document and then signed it.

With his guilt announced by his attorney in the nation's leading newspaper, McVeigh's defense could now begin.

CHAPTER 19

The Biggest "Get"

McVeigh was proud that he bombed the Murrah building, and he wanted the world to know how and especially why he did it. It was Stephen Jones's obligation to honor his client's wishes while at the same time preparing a defense for him at trial. Ultimately, and perhaps inevitably, the paradox of defending a client who didn't want to be defended would lead to a breach between the two men. But for many months, they found a common interest: public relations. McVeigh wanted his own story out there, and Jones, ever the aspiring politician, wanted attention.

Jones had the good fortune to represent McVeigh at the height of what were known as the "booking wars" of the 1990s. Network news stars battled each other for the biggest "gets"—exclusive interviews—of the moment. The competition spawned an entire industry of source cultivation, which involved the stars themselves as well as their assistants, usually young women, who were called bookers. Jones reveled in the attention of the stars and bookers and spent an enormous amount of time with them. Jones controlled something that all the journalists wanted—the chance to meet McVeigh in person—so the lawyer initiated a series of meetings between journalists and McVeigh at El Reno.

The meetings were off the record, meaning the journalists agreed not to report, or even take notes on, what McVeigh said. (Jones and his colleagues did take notes.) The journalists also agreed not to ask McVeigh questions about the case against him. Jones justified the press offensive as attempts to humanize McVeigh for people who knew him only as the grim-faced figure in the orange jumpsuit from his perp walk in Perry. When Jones first met McVeigh, he found him thinner, younger, and friendlier than he expected, and the lawyer believed that the journalists would come away with the same impression.

Jones brought dozens of journalists to meet with McVeigh. Many were famous, like Barbara Walters and her ABC colleague and rival, Diane Sawyer, but there were also print reporters for major newspapers and even local news figures from the Oklahoma City area. For the reporters, these meetings were auditions as well as audiences, because they all wanted the real "get"—an on-the-record, on-camera interview with McVeigh. Many sought to ingratiate themselves. Walters, who arrived at El Reno in a stretch limousine, advised McVeigh that it would sound better if he said, "I am not guilty" rather than "I will plead not guilty." (Later McVeigh told Jones that he liked Walters. "She was a person—normal," McVeigh said. "She didn't act like a Hollywood snob. But she's dangerous.") A reporter from the *Los Angeles Times* boasted to McVeigh that "he has been in Oklahoma City for the last two months; in contrast, *The New York Times* simply comes in when there is a hearing and then leaves."

So, what did the journalists discuss with McVeigh? Jones's colleagues took especially detailed notes of a long visit by Scott Pelley of CBS News, who asked McVeigh about his visitors (about one a week), his cell (about eight by five feet), his reading habits (five newspapers a day, plus books), and other media (radio allowed, but not television). "Tim mentioned a recent *New York Times* article which indicated that Tim does his own dishes, therefore he is asexual," the report states. "Tim was chastising the press in general for making generalizations about his character without the facts." McVeigh and Pelley also traded stories about the Gulf War, which Pelley had covered.

Jones made trips to New York and Washington, to be courted by the news celebrities. Afterward, in a report to his team, Jones wrote, "Larry King is definitely out, and I was not impressed with Mr. [Peter] Jennings of ABC. He appeared to be a name dropper, he was 30 minutes late, and he appeared somewhat arrogant." Tom Brokaw of NBC, who took Jones to lunch at the 21 Club, "is a pleasant person, and we had a nice lunch, but I sense that an interview by him with Tim would not be productive and we have already encouraged Jennifer and Bill [McVeigh's sister and father] to give an interview with Jane Pauley of NBC News. I see no reason to 'kiss' NBC twice." Dan Rather of CBS "is extremely impressive, was personally attentive, very professional, and is very eager for the interview." Diane Sawyer "is a very beautiful woman, and obviously highly intelligent." Still, Jones concluded that "Barbara Walters is clearly the most impressive. She spent approximately 3 to 3-½ hours with me. . . . I think she will treat our client with sympathy and not attempt to cross examine him."

Jones did allow one of the journalists who was granted an audience with McVeigh to write about the meeting. David Hackworth, who wrote for *Newsweek*, was a decorated soldier who had turned into a prominent and opinionated writer about war. He claimed always to speak for the grunts in the military, not the brass. Both McVeigh and Jones figured correctly that this perspective would lead Hackworth to have some sympathy for McVeigh, who was, if nothing else, a model grunt. "Looking into McVeigh's eyes in the El Reno prison, I realized that my gut feeling was right," Hackworth wrote. "He has what a lot of soldiers, good and bad, have: fire in the belly." McVeigh told Hackworth the Army "teaches you to discover yourself. It teaches you who you are." Hackworth explained, "To warriors, the military is like a religious order. It's not a job. It's a calling. Not too many people understand that calling or have what it takes. McVeigh apparently did. . . . The Timothy McVeigh I talked with didn't seem like a baby killer."

Jones counted the Hackworth story in *Newsweek* as a success in softening McVeigh's image. Still, Jones's investment of so much time in courting journalists irritated some of his colleagues on the defense team, who regarded the process as more about Jones's ego than McVeigh's defense. But Jones also did use his ever-growing public profile to plant doubts about the government's case. There was, for example, the matter of the extra leg. In the weeks after the bombing, the medical examiner in Oklahoma undertook the massive task of identifying all the bodies that had been recovered from the wreckage of the Murrah building. Most of the victims were killed from the collapse of the building rather than from the explosion itself, and many bodies were mutilated and torn apart in gruesome ways. According to Fred Jordan, the chief medical examiner, a "traumatically amputated left thigh and lower leg" were recovered on May 30. "The leg has not been matched to any of the known victims or survivors," he said.

Jones embraced the news and suggested the leg belonged to the real culprit in the bombing. "There may be a logical explanation for the leg, but none comes to mind," Jones told *The Washington Post* (and several others). "There are no persons unaccounted for. It could have been a drifter nobody knows anything about. It could have been the individual that drove the vehicle used in the explosion. The third possibility is that this person was with the person driving the vehicle." Jones asserted that the discovery of the leg meant that the government had "rushed to judgment" to charge McVeigh and Nichols in the bombing.

On and off the record, Jones insisted to reporters that the conspiracy was much broader than the one identified by the government. This was a complicated argument for him to make, because he had all but confirmed McVeigh's involvement, as he did in Pam Belluck's article in the *Times*. So, Jones wasn't telling reporters that McVeigh was innocent, only that he was part of a bigger web of intrigue that the government would have uncovered if it had cared to look. Jones was never specific or consistent about who participated in this grander conspiracy, but he didn't have to be. The idea was to sow doubt and uncertainty, not to prove an alternative.

Jones's theories broke down roughly into two strands, and they have shaped the way the Oklahoma City bombing has long been perceived. Jones played into the political preconceptions of the left and right. The extremes on both sides share a distrust for official explanations, and Jones tailored arguments for each one. For conservatives, Jones blamed the bombing on foreign terrorists, which would have the effect of lessening the responsibility of the right-wing movement to which McVeigh belonged. This argument usually took the form of extrapolating from Terry Nichols's marriage to Marife, his mail-order bride from the Philippines. As Jones later wrote, the Philippines was "a hotbed of fundamentalist Muslim activity, and if Ramzi Yousef had used the Philippines as a base, and Terry Nichols made numerous visits there, who knew who might have been recruited? Or who might have recruited whom?" Yousef was the brains behind the 1993 World Trade Center bombing. There was never any evidence that Nichols and Yousef met, but they were both apparently in the Philippines at the same time, and that was enough for Jones to drop portentous hints of a connection.

For liberals, Jones suggested a right-wing plot that extended well beyond McVeigh and Nichols. This idea was more plausible and was at least tethered to some actual evidence. Richard Snell, the Arkansas white supremacist, was executed on the morning of April 19, 1995. His final words were "Look over your shoulder. Justice is coming." Snell had been a visitor to the right-wing compound known as Elohim City, in rural Oklahoma, near the Arkansas border. A few days before the bombing, McVeigh used his phone card to call Andreas

Strassmeir at Elohim City, apparently to find a place to hide after the bombing. But they never connected.

Out of this tangle of facts came Jones's theory that McVeigh was tied to a broader circle of right-wingers, especially those in Elohim City, and that the bombing was a form of retribution for Snell's execution. Again, there was never any evidence connecting McVeigh to Snell, or that McVeigh and Strassmeir met more than once, but the web of connections was enough for suspicion.

This pattern of conspiracy theories tailored for the right and left has continued, both regarding the Oklahoma City bombing as well as for subsequent acts of right-wing terrorism. The right, for example, has never given up on trying to blame Oklahoma City on foreigners. In 2005, Dana Rohrabacher, a Republican congressman from California, issued a report from his Oversight Subcommittee called "The Oklahoma City Bombing: Was There a Foreign Connection?" It stated, "There is serious, yet in some cases circumstantial, evidence that suggests a possible Middle Eastern connection to the Oklahoma City bombing." In fact, no such legitimate evidence existed, and the report cited fringe sources to suggest that "a small group of recent Iraqi émigrés living in the Oklahoma City area helped McVeigh bomb the Murrah building." A 2012 book called *Oklahoma City: What the Investigation Missed—And Why It Still Matters*, by Andrew Gumbel and Roger G. Charles, made the left-leaning critique. The authors stated that the investigators failed "by taking their eye off the radical right at a time when advocacy groups were sounding the alarm." By focusing on McVeigh and Nichols, they argued, "the search for other suspects, or a larger conspiracy, came to be viewed as a risky fishing expedition."

In recent years, the right has continued to deny the existence of violence and extremism in its ranks, often attempting instead to blame "false flag" operations—that is, left-wing terrorism that is camouflaged to embarrass the right. This claim has been made about virtually all the mass shootings by white supremacists, including those in El Paso, Pittsburgh, and Buffalo. In 2018, Marjorie Taylor Greene, before she was elected to Congress, agreed on Facebook with the view that the mass shooting that killed seventeen people in Parkland, Florida, "was a false flag planned shooting." (Alex Jones made the notorious claim that the Sandy Hook school shooting in Connecticut in 2012 was faked.) The most prominent example of the effort to divert attention from the right-wing roots of extremist action came after the January 6, 2021, attempted insurrection at the Capitol. Notwithstanding the overwhelming evidence that supporters of Donald Trump staged the riot, some conservatives, including many voices on Fox News, tried to attribute the violence to a false flag operation led by the left-wing group antifa. As Rush Limbaugh said, the riots "undoubtedly included some antifa Democrat-sponsored instigators." But these imaginings cannot obscure the truth—that from McVeigh to the present, a meaningful part of the conservative movement in the United States has engaged in violence.

Stephen Jones anticipated and spurred the tradition of providing false explanations for right-wing violence. As the months after McVeigh's arrest passed, Jones became more outspoken about the purported secrets at the heart of the Oklahoma City bombing case. His theory evolved from suggesting that the government had failed to seek the truth about the bombing to insisting that the government was undertaking an active effort to deceive the public and courts about what happened in Oklahoma City. In a speech at the University of Oklahoma, he used language that would become familiar decades later from conservatives in the Trump era.

Jones spoke of how liberal elitists on the coasts looked down on authentic Americans in the heartland. "There are today a large number of individuals whom people on the two coasts would refer to as the far right, the fringe group, the militia community," Jones said. "At least in the interior of the country, the views of these individuals on subjects as diverse as taxation, the jury system, government regulations, police power, the schools, the family, gun control, corruption, and citizen militia represent not the fringe but increasingly the mainstream." Jones said there was a "polarization between impenitent federal officials and disenfranchised social groups such as bankrupt farmers and ranchers and a dislocated working class." Jones was making a chilling point. He was saying—correctly—that a lot of people shared McVeigh's views. The kind of violent anger that manifested itself in the bombing would continue to find expression in other crimes, too. Subsequent events vindicated Jones's prediction.

But then Jones, as was his habit, veered from legitimate insight into conspiratorial insinuation. "It is hardly possible to exaggerate the importance of this case and what it means for our country," Jones concluded. "Someday when you know what I know and what I have learned, and that day will come, you will never think of the United States in the same way."

To which the prosecutors responded: *Say what?*

Sitting around their bunkerlike quarters in the former phone company building in Oklahoma City, the prosecutors seethed. Abiding by Merrick Garland's directive for public silence, they refrained from sparring with Jones in the news media, or even responding to him. But Jones's suggestions of broader conspiracies rankled the prosecutors. For starters, they wondered, what did any of this have to do with whether Tim McVeigh and Terry Nichols conspired to bomb the Murrah building? What about McVeigh's rental of the truck? And Nichols buying all that fertilizer? What about the right-wing literature in the car? And if there were other conspirators in Elohim City or the Philippines, why didn't their numbers show up on McVeigh and Nichols's phone card? Jones's claim about the Philippines particularly rankled. Nichols and Yousef were there at the same time, but so were 70 million Filipinos. And information that would make you "never think of the United States in the same way"? What did that even *mean*?

Still, the prosecutors of McVeigh and Nichols had one important opportunity. When McVeigh was taken into federal custody on April 21, he was charged in a complaint, a bare-bones set of allegations prepared in haste by Garland and the local U.S. Attorney's Office. In order to bring McVeigh and Nichols to trial, the prosecutors had to prepare an indictment for the grand jury to issue. Sometimes, when prosecutors want to limit the amount of information they disclose, they write short indictments, which inform defendants of the charges against them but otherwise provide little information about the government's evidence. On the other hand, prosecutors often write "speaking" indictments, which lay out the evidence in some detail. Because of Stephen Jones's press offensive raising questions about the case against McVeigh, Hartzler and his team were determined to write a speaking indictment—which would show how powerful the evidence against McVeigh was.

Larry Mackey, Hartzler's second-in-command, who came from the U.S. Attorney's Office in Indianapolis, took charge of the indictment-writing process, along with Jon Hersley, the lead FBI agent. The idea was to refute Jones's theories by loading the indictment with as much specific evidence as possible. According to the indictment, the bombing conspiracy began on September 13, 1994, the day that Clinton signed the assault weapons ban. Mackey then laid out all the purchases of fertilizer and rentals of storage sheds and the fake names that McVeigh and Nichols used—Shawn Rivers, Mike Havens, Terry Havens, Joe Kyle, Ted Parker, and eventually Robert Kling. The indictment revealed the quarry robbery in Kansas and Nichols's letter to McVeigh that urged him to "Go for it!!" It was a powerful, detailed summary of facts—as opposed to Jones's vague hints. The indictment also provided a reminder of the magnitude of the crime: five of its fifteen pages were devoted simply to listing the names of those killed in the bombing.

The indictment was also the first official acknowledgment that the government was seeking to execute both McVeigh and Nichols. Reno had said from the beginning that the government would seek the death penalty, but that almost wasn't legally possible. Virtually all death penalty cases are prosecuted in state, not federal, courts; it was not until Clinton's crime bill in 1994 that killing a law enforcement official was made a capital crime. So, the counts charging McVeigh and Nichols with killing the nine federal agents in the Murrah building carried the death penalty. The murders of the other 159 victims could only yield life sentences.

The filing of the indictment on August 11 marked a major milestone in the investigation, and the prosecutors, who were wary of doing anything that the public would see as conflicting with the solemnity of their mission, allowed themselves a small celebration in the privacy of their offices. The initial public reaction was good. The consensus was that the case looked strong. Stephen Jones had a different reaction. He saw—correctly—that the prosecutors had made a serious blunder.

CHAPTER 20

The Fortiers Flip

As soon as McVeigh was arrested for the bombing on Friday, April 21, agents fanned out across the country to find out what they could about him. Buddies from the Army, security guard colleagues in Buffalo, and Bill McVeigh, Tim's father, all mentioned Tim's friendship with Mike Fortier. Before the first weekend was out, agents appeared at the door of the trailer home that Mike and Lori Fortier shared with their young daughter in Kingman, Arizona.

Fortier was still using meth and looked it. He had scraggly, unwashed hair, glassy eyes behind dirty glasses, a goatee, and an earring. The Fortier home still flew the Gadsden flag—DON'T TREAD ON ME—which served as an unofficial banner for the militia movement. Fortier could mouth the basics of the political views that he and McVeigh shared—he also subscribed to *The Spotlight*—but Fortier cared more about getting high than changing laws. His world was small. He worked at the local True Value hardware store (when his bad back allowed) and bought meth from his next-door neighbor.

Now, suddenly, Fortier was in the middle of a major terrorism investigation. He had watched the television reports of the FBI search of the Nichols homestead in Michigan, and he was terrified that agents in black raid gear would break down his door to search his home, too. On Monday, April 24, Fortier tried to negotiate with the agents by his door: If they were going to do a search, would they let him stay? No deal, said the agents, who secured a warrant that day. Mike, Lori, and Kayla Fortier retreated to a local community college while the agents searched their premises.

On that day, agents also started asking Mike Fortier questions about his friend Tim McVeigh. Panicking, Fortier lied—over and over again. He admitted that he and McVeigh were friends and that McVeigh had visited him in Kingman. But Fortier insisted that they never talked about bombing anything. Fortier knew that he still possessed some of the guns that Nichols had stolen from Roger Moore in Arkansas. He would have to explain their presence in his house. He said that McVeigh had given them to him. Where? Desperate to hide his trip to Oklahoma City with McVeigh to case the Murrah building, Fortier said he had only gone to Kansas to meet McVeigh. How had he made the trip from Arizona to Kansas? Fortier said he had hitchhiked the thousand miles—a preposterous story. The agents could tell Fortier was lying, but at that point they didn't know how or why. Aiming to increase the pressure on Fortier, the FBI dispatched Danny Coulson, the Dallas special agent in charge, to lead the investigative team in Kingman.

The news media beat Coulson to Arizona, and the Fortier mobile home had a fleet of TV trucks by its front door. Coulson didn't have enough evidence to arrest Fortier, but he wanted to point out the stakes of the case to him. Coulson arranged for the local sheriff to retrieve Fortier for a talk. (While the mobile home was empty, FBI agents placed court-authorized audio bugs inside; they also tapped the Fortiers' phone.) A fiery bantam with abundant self-confidence, Coulson thought he could scare the young stoner into cooperating.

Coulson and Fortier faced off in a tiny conference room. Fortier tried talking politics.

"We're at war," Fortier told Coulson. "You don't understand."

Coulson was having none of it. "No, we're not," he said. "If we were at war, I would have killed McVeigh, and I would have killed you, because I have the capability. You may be at war with your country, but your country is not at war with you."

"Well," Fortier answered. "It's about the Constitution."

"Oh, you're right," the FBI agent responded. "It is about the Constitution, and we're going to investigate you under the Constitution, and the Attorney General has said this is a death penalty case. And I can put every agent in the FBI on you, and we're going to indict you under the Constitution."

Coulson leaned in to the tiny table where they were sitting, their knees nearly touching. "And then we're going to convict you under the Constitution, and we'll handle your appeal under the Constitution," Coulson went on, his voice lowering to nearly a whisper. "And one day we're going to strap you to a gurney, and we're going to stick a needle in you, and kill you under the Constitution."

Fortier's eyes widened, and he didn't have much to say in response.

"I want you to get a lawyer, and I want you to come up with a proffer, and you need to go see our commanders in Oklahoma City," Coulson went on. "You need to get on our side, not his side. It's life or death, your decision." Fortier was intimidated, but for the time being he stuck to his story that he knew nothing that connected McVeigh to the bombing.

The following morning, Coulson bought breakfast for Fortier's mother, who still lived in Kingman. "Your son is a mass murderer, and he's going to face the death penalty," he said. Fortier's mother said she knew her son, and he would never be involved in something like this bombing. "Ma'am, I've arrested thousands of men, and their mothers all thought they were innocent, and none of them were. Your son is going to die by execution." By this point, the FBI had the results of the search warrant. Inside the Fortier mobile home, agents found bomb-making guides, right-wing literature (including *The Turner Diaries*), and several guns, but nothing that could tie Fortier directly to the bombing. (The audio bug in the house and tap on the phone also produced little of interest.)

Coulson's threats didn't do the job—at least not yet. The Fortiers fled with their daughter to Nevada for a couple of days, but when they returned, Fortier had decided not to flip. A CNN crew landed him for a short interview. "I do not believe that Tim blew up any building in Oklahoma," Fortier told the reporter. "There's nothing for me to look back upon and say, 'Yeah, that might have been. I should have seen it back then.' There's nothing like that."

The FBI had not yet interviewed Lori Fortier, but the agents figured she had to know something about McVeigh, too. They also thought pressure on Lori might move Mike off his denials. So, the prosecutors stepped into the Fortier story and escalated the pressure. In Kingman, agents served Mike and Lori with subpoenas, which summoned them to testify before the grand jury in Oklahoma City.

Neither Fortier had a lawyer at that point, and after the couple made the long drive to Oklahoma City, the public defenders' office assigned a veteran local attorney named Mack Martin to represent Lori, who was going to be the first to testify. Like most people in Oklahoma City, Martin had been transfixed and horrified by the bombing. Earlier, the public defenders had approached Martin to defend McVeigh, and the lawyer rejected the idea immediately. He simply knew too many people who had died. But since the public defender told Martin that Lori Fortier was a minor witness, he figured he would take the assignment.

Lori came to Martin's office in Oklahoma City, and unlike her husband she decided to tell the truth—at least to her lawyer. Petite and girlish in her early twenties, and expecting her second child, Lori scarcely looked like Martin's idea of a figure in a terrorism case. But after Martin chatted with her for only a few minutes, he realized that Lori was not a minor witness at all—and her husband was an even bigger one. Contrary to what Mike had told the FBI (and CNN), Lori told her lawyer that they had both long known of McVeigh's plan to bomb the Murrah building. She told Martin that she watched McVeigh pull soup cans from her cabinets to show her how he planned to arrange the bomb barrels in the back of the truck. She admitted that she used her iron to laminate the fake mail-order driver's license in the name of Robert Kling that McVeigh used to rent the Ryder truck. Plus, she knew that Mike's story of hitchhiking to Kansas was a lie. Mike had driven to Kansas with McVeigh, and they had stopped in Oklahoma City, where McVeigh showed Mike where he would park the truck to set off the bomb and where he planned to stash the getaway car. Eyes wide at the story he was hearing, Martin immediately placed a call to the public defenders' office. In a clear understatement, he said Mike Fortier was also going to need a lawyer.

The public defenders' office summoned Michael "Mac" McGuire to represent Mike Fortier. Even more than most people in Oklahoma City, McGuire was traumatized by the bombing. On the morning of April 19, just before a planned court appearance, he headed to his usual parking space, which was in the garage of the Murrah building. But the spot was crowded by cars on either side, so McGuire went to a different garage—where he heard the explosion. McGuire saw dazed victims covered in blood wandering the streets. A couple of weeks later, when he got the call to represent Mike Fortier, McGuire still wasn't over the shock. Still, like his friend Martin, McGuire figured he'd just ask his new client a few questions and then usher him into his grand jury appearance.

Everything changed as soon as McGuire and Fortier sat down together for the first time. "Mr. McGuire," Mike Fortier said, "I know the whole plan to blow up the building."

McGuire nearly threw up. He had barely recovered his equilibrium from the bombing itself, and now, suddenly, he was representing someone in the heart of the conspiracy. He felt shocked and overmatched, with what seemed like the entire federal government investigating his new client. McGuire did manage to make a phone call to the U.S. Attorney's Office to inform them that Mike Fortier would not be testifying in the grand jury anytime soon. When would Fortier be ready? McGuire said he didn't know because he was just sitting down with him for the first time. (Prosecutors often agree to delay grand jury appearances, though not indefinitely.) The FBI agreed to hide the two Fortiers in a hotel in Oklahoma City while McGuire talked to Mike and helped him decide what to do. Testify? Take the Fifth? Risk being indicted?

Mike Fortier was finally off drugs, and he was starting to realize the magnitude of McVeigh's crime—and his own connection to it. As McGuire became more panicky—the lawyer couldn't eat or sleep, thinking about Fortier and the bombing all the time—Fortier himself became calmer, almost serene. He reverted to what he once was—the thoughtful high school chess champion. Still, Fortier didn't come clean all at once. Like a lot of witnesses, he unveiled the truth a bit at a time, grudgingly acknowledging what he had done. McGuire discovered there was an enormous amount of ground to cover, starting with the time when Fortier, Nichols, and McVeigh went through Army basic training together. McGuire used page after page from large tablets of white paper to sketch out Fortier's account from their first meeting in the Army to the last time McVeigh said goodbye to him in Kingman.

While debriefing Fortier for several weeks, McGuire made a plan. He wouldn't let Fortier testify before the grand jury, but he'd agree to a lengthy proffer session with prosecutors, also known as a "Queen for a Day." Based on the rules for proffers, prosecutors couldn't use Fortier's statements against him, but rather consider his statement as a basis to decide what to do with him. The stakes for the proffer were enormous. In a worst case, prosecutors could turn around and charge Fortier as a co-conspirator of McVeigh's and seek the death penalty. In a best case, they could give Fortier immunity. More likely, the proffer could lead to some sort of plea bargain for Fortier. This was why McGuire worked so hard to get the full story out of Fortier. Only if prosecutors thought Fortier was telling the full truth about his own actions, as well as McVeigh's, would they cut a favorable deal with him.

Throughout this process, McGuire was guided by a favorite quotation from Sun Tzu: "If you know the enemy and know yourself, you need not fear the result of a hundred battles." By the time McGuire approached prosecutors, he felt like he and Fortier knew themselves—that is, Fortier was prepared to tell the full truth. But McGuire knew far less about the other side of Sun Tzu's admonition. What did his enemy—the Justice Department—want out of Fortier? McGuire had no idea.

Neither, in all candor, did the Justice Department itself. The decision of what to do with the two Fortiers was the most perplexing one the prosecution team faced in the period leading up to the trial.

By the summer of 1995, Hartzler and his team thought the case against McVeigh was strong. They had McVeigh renting the Ryder truck at Elliott's Body Shop, in Junction City, Kansas, and then spending the night at the Dreamland Motel. They had Charlie Hanger's arrest of McVeigh at a time and place that showed he could have left the Murrah building when the bomb went off. They had bomb residue on McVeigh's shirt. They had the right-wing literature in his car that provided a motive. And thanks to the extraordinary work of an FBI analyst named Fred Dexter, the prosecutors had cracked McVeigh and Nichols's *Spotlight* phone card, which showed all the places they contacted to buy the ingredients for the bomb.

But was it enough? The McVeigh case lacked what prosecutors sometimes call a narrator—an insider who can explain what the defendants did and why. In the federal system, most complex cases feature at least one person who pleads guilty to some charges and agrees to testify against his former associates. As Hartzler and his FBI team settled in to listen to Fortier's proffer, the question before them was whether they would use him as their narrator of the case against McVeigh.

One matter was settled quickly. All of the prosecutors and agents believed Fortier. McGuire's weeks of preparation had paid off. Fortier had dropped the half-baked political assertions and spelled out a clear and chilling narrative. And his testimony was even more devastating to McVeigh than the prosecutors had expected. Fortier would testify that McVeigh planned the bombing for months. He had drawn diagrams of how he planned to arrange the bombs in the truck. He had traveled with Fortier to Oklahoma City and shown him how he planned to execute the bombing. Fortier described the alley near the Murrah building where McVeigh stashed the getaway car.

In short, if the jury believed Fortier, the case would be over. He was enough for a conviction all by himself. What was more, Hartzler and the others saw genuine contrition in Fortier. He realized that even though he did not exactly assist McVeigh's bombing plan, he could easily have stopped it. If Fortier had made a single call to the FBI before April 19, 1995, McVeigh could have been identified and arrested, and 168 lives could have been saved. It turned out that Fortier had a conscience after all, and it was haunted by his failure to act.

But using Fortier as a star witness created problems, particularly in the fevered atmosphere of the Oklahoma City bombing case. From Janet Reno on down, the leaders of the Justice Department had promised to pay an unprecedented degree of attention to the victims of the bombing—the survivors and especially the families of those who had been killed. The bombing heralded a new era in American law enforcement, when the voices of the victims of crime were heard and frequently heeded.

The Constitution says nothing about the rights of victims. The Bill of Rights only addresses the rights of criminal suspects and defendants. A political movement to give victims a voice in the criminal justice system began in the 1970s, largely as an outgrowth of the women's movement. Feminists established the first rape crisis centers, to give victims both support and a voice in the prosecution of their attackers. In the next decade, Mothers Against Drunk Driving invoked the testimony of family members and survivors of car crashes to transform the national perception of drunk driving. Later, victims began to demand a formal role in the criminal justice system. In 1991, the Supreme Court, reflecting this change in mood, overruled a pair of recent precedents and allowed victim impact testimony in death penalty cases. In *Payne v. Tennessee*, the Court said that "reminding the sentencer that just as the murderer should be considered as an individual, so too the victim is an individual whose death represents a unique loss to society and in particular to his family." By the time of the Oklahoma City bombing, the testimony of victims' friends and family members had become a standard part of death penalty cases.

The Oklahoma City bombing case accelerated the transformation of the victims' role. For one thing, there was the matter of numbers. With 168 killed and hundreds more injured, the victims' lobby in the case was enormous, dwarfing that in any previous criminal case. Of course, too, the victims were tremendously sympathetic, given the horror of the crime. Moreover, the bombing took place at a time of increasing crime all over the country, which was prompting a national backlash against the rights of defendants. The previous September, President Clinton had won passage of the assault weapons ban largely by characterizing it as an anticrime measure, which also funded 100,000 new police officers and expanded the number of federal crimes eligible for the death penalty. In political terms, then, the victims in the Oklahoma City bombing were walking through an open door.

The victims wanted a hard line. The Justice Department was already seeking the death penalty for McVeigh and Nichols, but the victims wanted more—specifically, no plea bargains for anyone else implicated in the bombing. So, as Hartzler weighed what to do with Mike Fortier, he had to contend with the demands of the victims as well as those of Mac McGuire, Fortier's lawyer.

Hartzler had another problem. It wasn't clear what crime, if any, Fortier had committed. In a moral sense, Fortier's crime was easy to define. He had failed to make the one phone call that could have prevented the Oklahoma City bombing. But criminal law doesn't usually cover omissions; Fortier may not have violated any statute by failing to blow the whistle. But what did he do? In order to be guilty of conspiracy, the law required the government to prove that Fortier committed an "act in furtherance" of the conspiracy. Fortier had listened to McVeigh's plans and rode along with McVeigh to Oklahoma City, but it wasn't clear that Fortier had committed any "act" at all. For example, when McVeigh asked Fortier to rent a storage shed for him in Kingman—which would have been an act in furtherance of the conspiracy—Fortier didn't do it.

Plus, there was still another complication. In fact if not in law, Mike and Lori Fortier were a package deal. They wanted a legal resolution that covered both of them. Lori also knew about the plot to bomb the Murrah building, and she was not as close to McVeigh as Mike was. But the problem was that Lori had committed an "act" in furtherance of the bombing conspiracy. In late 1994, McVeigh was leaving Kingman and wanted to hide in his car some of the blasting caps that he and Nichols had stolen from the quarry in Kansas; Lori had gone to McVeigh's motel room in Kingman and wrapped the caps in Christmas wrapping paper. Then, more consequentially, shortly before the bombing, Lori had used her iron to laminate the fake "Robert Kling" driver's license that McVeigh used to rent the Ryder truck.

Thus, the prosecutors' dilemma when it came to the Fortiers and the bombing conspiracy: Lori was technically guilty, and Mike was technically innocent, but in any real sense, he was more culpable than she was. And Mike was vowing not to plead guilty to anything unless Lori received immunity.

Defense attorneys like McGuire often have to wage two-front wars. They must battle their clients to get them to face the grim realities of their situation; and they have to fight prosecutors to get the best deals for their clients. Fortier was willing to work hard with McGuire to tell the full story of the bombing plan, and Mike repeated the details in his proffer for the prosecutors. But when it came to pleading guilty, Fortier stalled and hedged. He didn't help McVeigh plan the bombing, he told McGuire, why should he have to plead guilty to anything?

McGuire saw Fortier's point—sort of. But the lawyer knew how tough it would be to persuade a jury that Fortier deserved to walk free. Even if Fortier had some decent arguments for his innocence, McGuire did not want to go to trial in any kind of case related to the Oklahoma City bombing. The stakes of such a loss might literally be life-or-death. A plea bargain was the only realistic option.

In some respects, McGuire's negotiations with Hartzler were easier than those with his client, and they made a deal. Fortier would plead guilty to four counts: conspiring with McVeigh and Nichols to transport, and then transporting, stolen firearms (from the robbery of Roger Moore in Arkansas); lying to the FBI in his initial interviews; and "misprision" of a felony—withholding information about a crime. Fortier faced a maximum of twenty-three years in prison, but it was clear that, if he cooperated fully and truthfully, he would receive a good deal less. Just as important, Hartzler agreed to give Lori immunity. She would remain free to raise the two Fortier children while Mike was locked up. The deal was not an easy sell to the victims, but it gave prosecutors two major trial witnesses. Mike Fortier would be the narrator, but Lori would turn out to be just as powerful. Lori would testify about watching McVeigh's soup can demonstration and ironing the lamination on the Kling license. She didn't want Tim to do it himself and ruin her iron and ironing board. A veteran trial lawyer like Hartzler knew that kind of peculiar detail had the ring of truth and would stick in jurors' minds.

Still, Mike Fortier agonized about making the deal, not least because once he pleaded guilty, he would have to begin serving his sentence. Weeks passed. Hartzler pressed. Over a final breakfast at a pancake house, Fortier told his lawyer he would plead guilty, which he did on August 10, 1995, four months after the bombing.

The following day, the grand jury returned the indictment, which was the crowning achievement of the prosecutors' first few months of work. The speaking indictment spelled out McVeigh's and Nichols's actions in greater detail than had ever before been made public. But very much unintentionally, the indictment also contained a gift for the defense, which Stephen Jones spent the rest of the case exploiting.

Before the indictment was released, it was reviewed by probably a dozen Justice Department lawyers, all of them experienced prosecutors, including Garland himself. The first count charged McVeigh and Nichols with conspiracy to use a weapon of mass destruction. Specifically, the indictment stated that the two men "knowingly, intentionally, willfully, and maliciously conspired, combined, and agreed together and with others unknown to use a weapon of mass destruction." Three words jumped out at Jones: *with others unknown*.

The words, as all the experienced prosecutors knew, were boilerplate, part of virtually every conspiracy prosecution brought by the federal government. The idea was that the indictment should leave open the possibility that some minor figure might appear later in the case; he or she would be one of the "others unknown." None of the prosecutors who reviewed the indictment noticed or commented on the words. They read right through them. But Jones, to his credit, read the words and claimed they proved his point. The indictment prepared by the prosecutors acknowledged that McVeigh and Nichols had conspired "with others unknown"—which is what Jones had been saying all along.

In truth, the government acknowledged no such thing, and the evidence never established that McVeigh and Nichols conspired with anyone else. Rather, the prosecutors made a careless error in drafting the indictment, and they spent the rest of the case paying the price. The consequences were long-lasting. Even long after the McVeigh case was over, Jones and others used the "others unknown" language to suggest that the government had never really solved the Oklahoma City bombing case. Needlessly, the mystery—which was really no mystery at all—lingered.

CHAPTER 21

Tigar, Burning Bright

No one in Oklahoma had ever seen anything like Terry Nichols's preliminary hearing. Nichols was also being held at the El Reno prison, and his hearing, like McVeigh's, took place in the makeshift courtroom there. What made Nichols's case different was his lawyer—Michael Tigar, law professor, legal celebrity, and cracker-barrel intellectual, who dominated the proceedings even before anyone uttered a word.

It's a custom for everyone to rise when the judge takes the bench, but Tigar put his own spin on the practice. He stood up when the judge entered, but he also went to his feet when his client was brought from a holding cell to the counsel table. He always made this gesture of respect to a client, not least because it made prosecutors look petty for failing to do the same. Tigar was a student of courtroom dynamics—he'd written several books on the subject—and he believed in the value of studied gamesmanship. Nichols himself didn't notice Tigar's gesture, because he remained in the same nearly catatonic stupor he'd been in since he was arrested. Nichols was, in every sense, smaller than McVeigh—in stature, in ambition, and in understanding what he had gotten himself into with their partnership. Tigar made a point of appearing to consult with his client, but it was mostly for show. Nichols just sat there. Except in size, McVeigh and Nichols came to resemble George and Lennie from John Steinbeck's *Of Mice and Men*—the quick-witted schemer and the reclusive dolt.

Like McVeigh, Nichols had no chance of winning the relief he sought at this stage in the proceedings—release on bail or dismissal of the case. The charges were too serious and the evidence too strong. But Tigar had an agenda beyond the immediate result. One of his courtroom maxims was that a lawyer should be able to sum up a client's legal position in a single sentence. Tigar came quickly to a motto for Nichols: *He was building a life, not a bomb.* Nichols was married, the loving father of two children, with a job as a hardworking, law-abiding ranch hand. The unspoken implication concerned what Nichols was not: a rootless, angry loner like Tim McVeigh. For the bombing case, Tigar had a second sentence about his client: *Terry Nichols wasn't there.* When McVeigh set off the bomb, Nichols was home in Herington, Kansas, far from Oklahoma City. As Tigar began the long march to a jury verdict in Nichols's case, he was going to keep sending those two messages.

Tigar developed his themes as he cross-examined the government's preliminary hearing witness, FBI agent Errol Myers. He used Myers to put helpful facts about Nichols on the record.

"You know that Mr. Nichols has a clean record, isn't that right?"

"Yes."

"He's honorably discharged from the service of his country, correct?" (Tigar always chose his words with care—"service of his country," not "the Army.")

"Yes."

Tigar got Myers to agree that lots of people in farm country have fertilizer and fuel pumps, and sometimes they use fertilizer as an explosive.

"Do you know that farmers blow stumps?"

"I have heard about it and read about it."

Tigar pointed out that no one dragged Nichols into the local police station.

"Mr. Nichols walked in, didn't he, to the police station in Herington, Kansas, right?"

"Yes, he did."

"That was a voluntary act on his part, right?"

The agent said it was.

Tigar went through some of the information that Nichols provided to the agents on that day. "That information that Mr. Nichols provided you with—that checked out, didn't it?"

"Yes."

Of course, there was a great deal of incriminating information that Tigar chose not to elicit from the FBI agent. Kansas was farm country, but Nichols didn't own a farm, so he had no legitimate need for hundreds of pounds of fertilizer, much less a reason to use phony names to buy it. In Nichols's voluntary interview with the authorities after the bombing, Nichols also told a series of lies, especially about his relationship with McVeigh.

Tigar really came into his own when he made an argument to the judge. Most contemporary lawyers aim for a conversational tone in courtrooms, but Tigar, at fifty-four, remained proudly old-school. He performed, trading off personas as he believed circumstances warranted. One moment he was a cornpone country lawyer, as when he dismissed Nichols's political views as common in a combative, contemporary world: "I grew up in a small town as a Baptist, but then I went away to Berkeley, Your Honor"—where the political battles were rougher. So, too, like a good Baptist, Tigar could invoke the Bible, as when he informed the judge, "The guilty flee where no man pursueth but the righteous are bold as a lion"—a paraphrase of Proverbs 28:1.

Tigar was most at home as the international scholar of the law, who could conjure just the right precedent from any era or continent. During his argument that Nichols should be released on bail, Tigar cited a Judge Learned Hand decision from 1950, a Justice Robert Jackson opinion from the same year, and he was just getting started. "Judge, you know, back in the eighteenth century when we had the Revolutionary War, tens of thousands of people lost their lives—a hot war," Tigar intoned, "and after they got done, they went and wrote a Bill of Rights. . . ." But Tigar was going back even further. "Lord Coke's treatise on bail and mainprize said that the capital felonies, of which there were quite some number in England until the Romilly Act of 1832 . . ."

Listening to Tigar's rapid-fire disquisitions, the judge begged for mercy on behalf of the court reporter: "Could you slow down just a bit? I know he's about to tear his hair out."

One could almost see the thought bubbles above others in the courtroom: *Who is Lord Coke? And what the hell is mainprize—to say nothing of the Romilly Act?* (Edward Coke, who died in 1634, was an English jurist of the Elizabethan era. "Mainprize" is an archaic term for a form of release similar to bail. In 1832, England reduced the number of crimes eligible for the death penalty.)

The question was, of course, whether Tigar's great curlicues of erudition did his clients any good. Not on this day; Nichols was ordered held without bail pending trial. Overall, though, Tigar's scene-stealing acuity augured a more promising outcome.

Michael Tigar and Stephen Jones, the lead counsel for the two defendants, differed in background, temperament, political views, and approach to the case. While Jones had struggled, largely without success, for public attention, Tigar had been famous since he was barely out of his teens. Not surprisingly, they couldn't stand each other.

Tigar always had a romantic, even grandiose, view of the law (and himself). When he was twelve, he announced he wanted to be a lawyer. His father, an aircraft worker and a union leader in his plant near

Los Angeles, gave him a copy of Irving Stone's book *Clarence Darrow for the Defense*, and told him, "This is the kind of lawyer you have to be." The figure of Darrow ran like a leitmotif throughout Tigar's life. With a fleshy face, bushy eyebrows, and pants hitched well above his waist, Tigar in middle age even started to look a little like Darrow.

Born in 1941, Tigar spent his formative years in Berkeley when the campus was, in effect, creating the 1960s. At the college radio station, Tigar both covered and joined the early days of the movements for free speech and against the Vietnam War. He was a prodigy and a show-off. At Berkeley's law school, he was editor in chief of the law review and valedictorian of the class of 1966. One day Tigar informed his contracts professor that he thought a decision from Quebec was relevant to the class discussion. The professor asked him to read it, and Tigar proceeded to do so, somewhat haltingly. The professor urged him to speed up, and Tigar apologized, adding, "It's just that I'm translating from the French as I go along."

While Tigar was still a law student, he was selected for a clerkship with Justice William J. Brennan Jr., the great liberal on the Supreme Court. Because Tigar had a high profile as a student journalist and activist at Berkeley, some conservative columnists attacked Brennan for hiring him. Brennan, in response, asked Tigar to write a summary of all his political activities, which Tigar refused to do. Brennan withdrew the clerkship offer. Instead, Tigar became a protégé of Edward Bennett Williams, a legendary figure in the Washington bar. Together they tried some of the major cases of the era, defending the former Lyndon Johnson aide Bobby Baker, Congressman Adam Clayton Powell Jr., and former Texas governor John Connally. Tigar also conducted what amounted to a side law practice for his clients in the antiwar movement. At age twenty-eight, Tigar argued and won a case in the Supreme Court on behalf of a draft resister.

In 1984, Tigar moved to Austin to become a professor at the University of Texas law school, but he maintained an active law practice with an eclectic collection of clients. He represented John Demjanjuk, a Ukrainian immigrant who was accused of being a Nazi concentration camp guard; Texas Republican senator Kay Bailey Hutchison, in an election law controversy; and an Army officer facing discharge and prison because of a lesbian relationship. (She was acquitted.) Notwithstanding Tigar's left-wing politics, then, it was consistent with his iconoclastic career that he would accept the assignment to defend Nichols. During his Texas years, Tigar began to dress like an ersatz rancher—with oversized silver belt buckles and cowboy boots. For Tigar, in or out of the courtroom, preening was as natural as breathing. To explain his decision to represent Nichols, he quoted (from memory) the English sage John Ruskin: "There is no snare set by the fiend for the mind of man more dangerous than the illusion that our enemies are also the enemies of God."

At first, it seemed like Terry Nichols was less likely to be implicated in the bombing than his brother James. When McVeigh registered at the Dreamland Motel on the Friday before the bombing, he had used a Michigan driver's license with the Nichols farm in Decker as his home address. On the afternoon of April 21, when McVeigh was charged in the bombing, FBI agents descended in force on the farm. It didn't take much asking around the area to learn that James—who was living on the farm—shared McVeigh's politics. (James liked to say the federal government was based in Washington, D.C.—which stood for "District of Criminals.")

There was much to raise suspicions about James's role. An FBI search of his property showed he had a collection of firearms, and neighbors confirmed that he sometimes set off small bombs in nearby fields. The link to McVeigh, the radical right-wing politics, the experience with explosives—he looked like a suspect in the bombing. Under prodding from Louis Freeh, the FBI decided to take an unusual step. Agents arrested James as a "material witness"—a person who was of importance to the investigation and also a flight risk. These warrants are controversial. They allow the government to lock people up for indefinite periods even if they are never charged with a crime. But Freeh and Garland thought the stakes of the case justified James's detention. He was held in the federal prison in Milan, south of Detroit.

After a few days, James found a local attorney to challenge his incarceration—and force the government to justify why he was being held. The prosecutors had little. James had no criminal record, there was no specific evidence tying him to the Murrah building bombing, and his explosives were like those used by many farmers to remove tree stumps. (He had purchased a lot less fertilizer than his brother Terry.) James had alibis for April 19 and the days leading up to it; he clearly was not John Doe Number 2, who was a major focus for the FBI in this period. James was released after thirty-two days in custody, but he remained an object of FBI attention for months. Still, investigators never found any evidence that James was involved in the bombing, or even knew about it in advance. Unlike Fortier, James was never anywhere near Oklahoma City, as far as prosecutors could tell. Hartzler decided to leave James alone. (James Nichols died of natural causes in 2017.)

Terry Nichols was another story. As Tigar said in his bail hearing, on the day after the bombing, Nichols had made the foolhardy decision to go to the police station near his home in Herington and ask why his name was being mentioned on the news. His presence there led him to submit to eight hours of questioning from FBI agents. His story was so garbled—and obviously false in places—that he guaranteed his own arrest. The search of his home turned up an abundance of incriminating evidence—including fertilizer residue, the drill used in the quarry robbery, and the phone card he shared with McVeigh. Still, Nichols had one enormous advantage over McVeigh as a defendant. As Tigar never tired of pointing out: *Terry wasn't there.*

It was undisputed that Nichols spent April 19 in Herington. On that day, he went on a series of conspicuous errands, so there were several people in town who could vouch for his presence. As a technical legal matter, it didn't matter whether Nichols set off the bomb, if he participated in a conspiracy to do so with McVeigh. But Tigar knew that jurors' instincts sometime conflicted with the instructions they received from judges. And if Terry Nichols wasn't there . . . he wasn't there. Tigar was far less present in the news media than Stephen Jones was, but Tigar made the point every time he made a public statement about the case: Terry Nichols wasn't even in the state of Oklahoma on the day of the bombing.

Tigar had another advantage over Jones. McVeigh was a demanding, opinionated client, whose agenda did not always align with Jones's. Sometimes McVeigh wanted to put out his message about the evils of the Clinton administration more than he wanted to win an acquittal; at other times, he helped Jones to find ways to discredit the government's case. Terry Nichols demanded nothing. He sat in his cell, he wept, he stared into space. He would answer questions from Tigar and his team, but Nichols let his lawyers go about their business without interference.

That began with a quest to get the case out of Oklahoma—and away from Oklahoma judges.

After the indictment, the case against McVeigh and Nichols was randomly assigned to United States District Judge Wayne Alley, who was even more headstrong than most federal judges, a notably self-confident group. He was sixty-three years old at the time and had spent most of his career as an Army lawyer, where he rose to brigadier general and became a military judge during the Vietnam War. (He presided over Lieutenant William L. Calley's appeal in the case of the My Lai massacre.) After retiring from the Army, Alley became dean of the University of Oklahoma law school, before President Ronald Reagan named him to the federal bench in 1985.

The federal courthouse in downtown Oklahoma City stands one block south from the Murrah building, with an underground parking garage separating the two structures. The explosion on April 19 vaporized the glass front doors to the courthouse, and Judge Alley's courtroom and chambers on the third floor were heavily damaged. Plaster fell from the ceiling, and light fixtures were left hanging. The skylight in Alley's courtroom shattered, covering the floor with an inch of broken glass. Alley was out of town that day, but a member of his staff was injured in the explosion. After the bombing, judges and other court personnel were offered counseling.

Tigar recognized—correctly—that there was no way either defendant could get a fair trial in Oklahoma City. The city, even the whole state, was convulsed with grief and anger; everyone in the courthouse, including the judges, was a victim of the bombing. It wasn't a matter of shifting the case from Alley to another judge. The case had to be moved out of Oklahoma altogether. The law on recusal states that a judge "shall disqualify himself in any proceeding in which his impartiality might reasonably be questioned." Tigar demanded that Alley recuse himself and shift the case out of Oklahoma City, and Stephen Jones joined him in the request—at first.

The defense motion for recusal and change of venue provided an early point of conflict within the Justice Department. Hartzler and his team wanted to concede that the defendants had a point. Alley and his staff were victims of the crime charged in the case. Alley's presence on the case, and a jury of Oklahoma City residents, might give McVeigh and Nichols legitimate grounds for appeal if they were convicted, requiring a second trial. This was especially true in a death penalty case, where appeals courts were usually more fastidious about guaranteeing procedural fairness. But Pat Ryan, the local U.S. attorney, wanted the trial kept in Oklahoma City. He was part of the community that felt almost proprietary about the crime; they regarded any move out of Oklahoma City would be a kind of repudiation. Local pride was at stake. Garland engineered a compromise. The government would ask Alley to voluntarily recuse himself, but the Justice Department would not formally join the defense motion for a change of venue.

Alley was determined to remain on the case. In a forty-six-page opinion, he said he could be unbiased. He said he had scrutinized hundreds of precedents in high-profile cases, and the bombing case did not resemble the ones where recusals or changes of venue had been ordered. "In each case where recusal was mandated, the presiding judge had taken some action, made some comment, or had some substantial relationship with the parties or witnesses, such that a reasonable person knowing all the facts would question the judge's impartiality," he wrote.

Still, Alley did give the defendants a victory of sorts. "Jury selection from a pool in the Oklahoma City area would be chancy," he wrote, in a serious understatement. As a result, Alley said he would agree to a change of venue, but only to Lawton, a military town of about eighty thousand people ninety miles from Oklahoma City. Alley said Lawton would be far enough removed to provide a "detached and dispassionate" deliberation of the evidence in the case. He ordered the trial to begin in Lawton in May 1996—a little more than a year after the bombing.

Alley's ruling was preposterous in every respect. It would have been farcical for him to preside over the trial. He and his colleagues in the local judiciary were traumatized victims of the bombing, even if they refused to acknowledge it. The fact that Alley had no previous relationship with McVeigh or Nichols was irrelevant. As a close neighbor of the Murrah building, Alley was confronted with the effects of the bombing every day. In a system with hundreds of federal judges, there was no reason to allow one so compromised to preside. Lawton was no answer, either. It was in the same media market as Oklahoma City, so the jury pool was completely consumed by news of the bombing. And Lawton was such a small town that there was no way it could provide hotels and other infrastructure for the hundreds of people who would necessarily be involved in or covering the trial.

Not for the last time, Tigar and Jones disagreed about what to do in response to Alley's ruling. Jones wanted to live with the decision and try the case in Lawton. As a prominent Oklahoma lawyer, he didn't want to rock the boat by insisting on a move elsewhere. Tigar wanted to fight on. The federal rules usually allow appeals only after a trial has concluded, but in extraordinary circumstances a party can seek a "writ of mandamus" in the middle of a case. A writ of mandamus amounts to a real embarrassment for a trial judge, and Jones didn't want to take that chance with Alley. Tigar didn't care about offending Alley, so he went ahead with seeking the writ on behalf of Nichols alone.

Tigar won a smashing victory. The Tenth Circuit Court of Appeals took the case away from Judge Alley. "We hold that a reasonable person could not help but harbor doubts about the impartiality of Judge Alley," the three-judge panel wrote. The court also rejected Lawton as a site for the trial. The chief judge of the Tenth Circuit in effect decreed that the litigation would have to start over from scratch. A new judge from outside Oklahoma City would take over the case and decide where the trial would take place. The chief judge then provided the final lead player in the drama of the Oklahoma City bombing trial by assigning the case to a veteran federal judge in Denver named Richard Matsch.

CHAPTER 22

The Necessity Defense

McVeigh had an idea to share with his defense team. Even though it was a Saturday in the summer of 1995, Stephen Jones was making good on his promise to have someone visit McVeigh every day at the El Reno prison. Jones's assistant Rob Nigh drew the duty on this day. McVeigh had been thinking about the movie *Clear and Present Danger*, which was based on the novel by Tom Clancy. "In the movie, the bad guys deliver a bomb with a helicopter, but they drop it on a truck, to make it look like it was a truck bomb," McVeigh told Nigh. "We could say someone did the same thing here—that it was really a helicopter bomb." Nigh dutifully reported McVeigh's idea to Jones in a memo, with the deadpan evaluation: "(Sounds like the perfect defense.)"

Nothing came of McVeigh's fake-helicopter theory, but it shows he was committed to the notion that he was in charge of his own defense. The problem was that McVeigh could never decide how, or even whether, he should be defended. From his first meetings with his lawyers, even before Jones took charge, McVeigh acknowledged—boasted, really—that he had set off the bomb at the Murrah building. He was realistic about the likely outcome of the trial. As he put it to Jones at one point, he thought there was a 50 percent chance he'd get a death sentence, 49 percent chance he'd get a life sentence, and a 1 percent chance he'd be acquitted. The prospect of conviction, or even execution, didn't seem to bother him too much. His problem was the government. The whole point of his actions was to damage the federal government, and he didn't want to see his enemy vindicated in the courtroom. McVeigh's challenge, then, was to figure out a way to take credit for the bombing, set off a broader rebellion, and simultaneously win his case. In a meeting with Mike Roberts, one of his defense lawyers, McVeigh spelled out his goals for the trial:

1. That the truth of the bombing come out.
2. That he be acquitted.
3. That he embarrass the government.
4. That after all the evidence is heard, the case remain a mystery.

McVeigh's agenda was both contradictory and impossible. There is often a mistaken assumption that criminals' goals make sense—that their ambitions, while nefarious, have a kind of holistic logic. But McVeigh was acting out of a perverse, but genuine, political conviction. In a similar way, it made little sense for the rioters on January 6 to believe that they would overturn the 2020 election. But their passion, as real as McVeigh's and as similar in motivation, drove them forward.

During his rambling sessions with his attorneys, McVeigh heard an idea that gave him hope: the necessity defense. The defense applies when a defendant violates a criminal statute in an emergency situation to prevent greater harm. This was it, McVeigh decided. Clinton's federal government had created an emergency with Waco and the assault weapons ban, so McVeigh had to take action. He instructed his lawyers to research the necessity defense and prepare to present it to the jury at trial.

Jones sent more than a dozen lawyers and investigators on visits to the prison, but McVeigh bonded most closely with one of them—Randy Coyne. They were an unlikely pair. Coyne was a hippie of sorts, whose great passion in life was jazz drumming. (He majored in music in college and spent a couple of years as a band instructor in Massachusetts before going to law school.) After a clerkship in Washington, he found a job teaching at the law school of the University of Oklahoma, where he developed a specialty in the death penalty, which he passionately opposed. In light of his background and politics, as well as his shaggy looks, Coyne never fit in very well in his adopted state. His alienation from his surroundings was reflected in a macabre sense of humor. For years Coyne represented Roger Dale Stafford, a notorious Oklahoma outlaw, who had been convicted of killing six people at a Sirloin Stockade restaurant in Oklahoma City. Two days after Stafford was finally executed, Coyne sent the prosecutor a five-dollar gift certificate to Sirloin Stockade.

Jones hired Coyne to handle death penalty issues, but he became the de facto legal director of the McVeigh defense, responsible for handling pretrial motions. Coyne also became McVeigh's confidant, and the two shared a jokey repartee despite the grimness of the circumstances. McVeigh would often scrawl wisecracks on legal papers and send them to Coyne. On a copy of his mug shot after his arrest in Perry, McVeigh wrote, for Coyne's benefit, "Busted, dude!"

McVeigh expressed his enthusiasm for the necessity defense to Coyne. "I'm extremely excited about it. It fits right into what I want to do. It's very possibly our best defense," McVeigh said, according to Coyne's memo to the defense team. "Chances of me living are pretty slim. Why not use the necessity defense and get the message out? Let them face me and allow me to tell them the truth. It will keep my family's respect. Whether I live or die doesn't necessarily make a difference. And it would be great to see the prosecutors try to respond. Wouldn't they shit their pants?"

As McVeigh understood the necessity defense, it meant he had to prove that his actions were a response to "imminent" harm. Coyne had given a law dictionary to McVeigh, who used it to study the meaning of the word. "'Imminent' is not the same as 'immediate,'" McVeigh told Coyne. "'Imminent' means 'likely to occur at any moment'; 'impending.' If you look at the pattern of federal law enforcement and their mindset, it's imminent that someone else is going to die soon." As always, McVeigh drew an analogy between his own actions and those of the patriots in Lexington and Concord on April 19, 1775: "Did the colonists have to fire on the British that day? The key is that they saw that there was an established pattern, a historical pattern. They knew what was taking shape, and they took action. That was 'necessity.'" McVeigh elaborated on the "necessity" for his attack in a cryptic message to his lawyers: "(1) logic; (2) the founding fathers; (3) basic tenets of democracy; (4) shock value, analogous to Hiroshima; (5) American history; (6) declaration of independence."

This litany was a familiar one for later right-wing extremists, like those who stormed the Capitol in 2021. Alex Jones, Congresswoman Lauren Boebert, and the leaders of the Proud Boys and Oath Keepers all invoked the American Revolution as justification for their actions. As with McVeigh, this rhetoric was based less on actual knowledge of the issues in 1776 than on the convenient use of certain words—like "rebellion," "tyranny," and "1776" itself—that suited contemporary obsessions. For both McVeigh and his heirs, the invocation of 1776 was based not on any real insight about or even knowledge of the causes of the American Revolution. Rather, the Revolution simply supplied useful buzzwords and, more important, a rationale for the use of violence.

Jones, Coyne, and others on the defense team indulged McVeigh for months regarding the necessity defense. They researched the use of the defense in the United States and even around the world and wrote detailed memos on the subject. They all reached the same conclusion. As Coyne put it in one memo, "there was no way a court would allow the issue to go to the jury to balance the evils" between

Waco and Oklahoma City. Amber McLaughlin, one of Jones's Enid firm alums, wrote a thirteen-page memo that concluded, "The limitations of the defenses of necessity and duress will prevent us from being able to assert either one of them at trial." The handful of cases where the defense had been successfully used explained why it was a nonstarter for McVeigh. For example, in a South Carolina case from 1991, a defendant was convicted of driving with a suspended license when he went to call for help for his wife, who was pregnant and experiencing intestinal distress. He had no telephone at home. The appeals court overturned his conviction because the trial court forbade him from raising a necessity defense. To invoke the defense, the court said, the defendant must reasonably believe that there was an imminent threat and that he had no realistic alternative to the action that he took. Moreover, the defendant's behavior must create no more substantial danger than the situation he is attempting to address.

No lawyer could, with a straight face, argue that McVeigh had a "necessity" to bomb the Murrah building and kill 168 people in order to prevent future violence by the federal government. The argument was worse than nonsensical; it was offensive. The idea that Jones and his team even deigned to research the issue demonstrated the way they coddled and indulged McVeigh. The "necessity defense" episode illustrated how the intense public focus on the case invested McVeigh with a kind of celebrity status; as a result, his opinions, even on legal issues, had to be taken seriously. The vast number of lawyers on his team meant that every silly idea could be explored. In a normal case, even one involving the death penalty, a defendant raising such an idea would have been told to stop wasting his lawyer's limited time.

Still, the ultimate rejection of the "necessity defense" left the question unresolved: What *was* McVeigh's defense going to be in front of the jury?

McVeigh rejected two more plausible but still problematic defenses. The first was some sort of defense based on insanity or mental disability. To explore this possibility, Jones hired Seymour Halleck, a psychiatrist from the University of North Carolina, who had gained some renown when he testified for the defense in the case of Susan Smith, who was charged with drowning her two children in a car. (Smith was convicted, but avoided the death penalty.) Halleck interviewed McVeigh and reported to Jones that McVeigh was "extremely self-centered and narcissistic. He has an extremely hard time seeing the world from another person's perspective." There had been "a marked absence of love in Tim's life." In prison, though, McVeigh was "eating well, sleeping a fair amount, and enjoying the attention that his legal team is directing toward him. He does not seem clinically depressed." McVeigh had no history of mental illness or delusional behavior. Considering all this, the chances for a successful insanity defense for McVeigh were close to nil. Halleck saw McVeigh for what he was—a right-wing extremist who made a conscious, considered decision to bomb the Murrah building. McVeigh also made clear to his lawyers that he didn't want to claim he was insane—because he wasn't.

McVeigh was likewise against the idea of blaming the bombing on family dysfunction. As McVeigh stated, and Bill McVeigh acknowledged, Tim's father was often frustrated and quick to anger. But there was never any claim that Bill had physically abused Tim. It was true, too, that McVeigh's mother left town with his sisters, leaving Tim behind as a teenager. Owing at least in part to the pressure from Tim's arrest, his mother's mental health took a turn for the worse. Now living in Florida with her second husband, Mildred Frazer, as she was known, had become irrational and paranoid. She claimed the FBI had bugged her wristwatch and a neighbor had poisoned her air conditioner. Shortly before Tim's trial, Frazer was involuntarily committed to a mental facility. Still, it was not clear what, if anything, Tim's family background had to do with his crime. McVeigh forbade his lawyers from blaming his family for his own decisions. As he said to one of his lawyers, who was proposing to do so, "If that's your role, see ya."

Stephen Jones had a different idea about how to defend McVeigh. It involved, in effect, conducting his own prosecution of his client.

From the moment McVeigh was caught, he was open and consistent about his role in the bombing. He drove the truck and lit the fuse at the Murrah building and did most of the planning himself, though Terry Nichols was an active, if junior, partner. Mike and Lori Fortier knew about McVeigh's plan but did nothing overt to bring it to fruition. No one else played any role in the conspiracy. That's what McVeigh told Jones in May of 1995, when they spoke for the first time, and he repeated the story in detail over many sessions in subsequent months.

Jones didn't buy it.

He didn't believe that McVeigh and Nichols could pull off such an audacious and complex plan by themselves. He didn't think they had the money or expertise. Jones thought others had to be involved. (Jones acknowledged that the phone card that traced their calls represented a problem for his theory.) Still, the lawyer explored, and seemingly believed, nearly every conspiracy theory about the bombing: McVeigh rented the truck with John Doe Number 2. He walked away from the bombing scene with a partner who escaped—or the partner was killed in the explosion and left behind the extra leg. Mike and Lori Fortier were part of the plot, and so was Roger Moore, the Arkansas gun dealer robbed by Nichols. Contradictions didn't bother Jones. He said McVeigh worked with right-wing terrorists based in the compound in Elohim City, Oklahoma—and with Islamic terrorists based in the Philippines. The cultivation of these theories was one reason why Jones spent so much time with journalists, so that he could plant these ideas and also benefit from the reporters' own explorations.

At one level, Jones's strategy made sense. He had no obligation to prove to the jury exactly what happened. If he succeeded in muddying the facts so that the jury rejected the government's proof, that would be a victory. As it happened, though, Jones did not regard the conspiracy theories as mere litigation tactics. To this day, he believes them, though he has never spelled out his version of the real Oklahoma City bombing conspiracy. "I don't accept the official version. I think it's shot full of holes," he said long after the bombing. "If you study the Oklahoma City bombing case carefully, you come up with probably 8 to 10 people that are involved." (He's never named them.)

It would have been one thing if Jones simply raised these theories as part of his duties as a zealous advocate. But he did something more. For month after month, Jones accused McVeigh of lying to him about the roles of others in the bombing conspiracy. In effect, Jones went to war with his client. "He was protecting the others," Jones said later. "It was a shield to the others." McVeigh insisted he wasn't lying. There were no "others." In light of this conflict, Jones launched his own investigation, which was designed to discredit McVeigh and uncover the truth. McVeigh tolerated this—at first.

In addition to working his sources among the journalists covering the case, Jones and his team undertook a systematic examination of McVeigh's own version of the story. In the late summer of 1995, after Jones had investigated the case for several months, he hired a court reporter and conducted a transcribed interview of McVeigh. In the cramped conference room of the El Reno prison, Jones began by administering an oath to McVeigh to tell the truth. Since this was just a private deposition, the oath had no legal effect, but it was meant to impress upon McVeigh the seriousness of the undertaking. "And I will state for the record that I'm taking this statement as Mr. McVeigh's attorney to assist me in the defense of him and that I intend the contents herein to be an attorney-client work product to be covered by the work product privilege and the attorney-client privilege—is that correct?"

"Yes," McVeigh said.

What followed was about eight hours of questioning over two days, when Jones asked McVeigh, in effect, to tell his life story, with a special emphasis on the plan for and execution of the bombing. By this point, the lawyer had heard his client tell pieces of this story many times. But this time, McVeigh recounted it as a consecutive narrative. He started with his childhood and concluded in Perry, Oklahoma, on April 21, 1995, just before he thought he was going to be released on bail—and wound up, instead, on the FBI's helicopter to Oklahoma City.

The interrogation was a bravura performance by McVeigh—comprehensive, detailed, and consistent with the story he had told from the beginning. But Stephen Jones still wasn't buying. He still believed that McVeigh was covering for others. "I'll take a lie detector," McVeigh told his lawyer. Deal, said Jones.

On August 31, 1995, a polygraph examiner named Tim Domgard, from Lincoln, Nebraska, went to the El Reno prison to administer a test to McVeigh. According to Domgard's report, the purpose of the examination was "concerning his truthfulness concerning the involvement of other individuals involved in the bombing." The examiner "initially asked McVeigh why he wanted to take the test knowing that he didn't have to take the polygraph test. McVeigh responded indicating that he wanted to clear the air with his legal counsel."

McVeigh began by giving a long summary of the events leading up to the bombing, much as he did in the interrogation by Jones. His story was the same. He and Nichols had no additional conspirators. After about two and a half hours of that recitation, Domgard moved to direct questions:

1. Were you born in Lockport, New York?
A. Yes.

2. Are you twenty-seven years old?
A. Yes.

3. Do you plan to try to lie to me on this test?
A. No.

4. Have you been completely truthful with me since we've been talking?
A. Yes.

5. Is your first name Timothy?
A. Yes.

6. Other than the people discussed, was there anyone else involved with you in the planning of the bombing?
A. No.

7. Is your last name McVeigh?
A. Yes.

8. Other than Terry Nichols, was there anyone else involved with you in the execution of that bombing?
A. No.

9. Were you born in the year 1968?
A. Yes.

10. Do you know who that leg belongs to?
A. No.

11. Are you attempting to keep any information from me regarding the involvement of another individual?
A. No.

"Upon analysis," Domgard's report stated, "there were indications of deception noted to the relevant questions: #6, 8, and 11." The polygraph said that McVeigh had lied about the involvement of others in the bombing. Domgard then asked the same questions a second time. The results were the same, though somewhat more ambiguous. At that point, Domgard told McVeigh that there was "absolutely no doubt in my mind" that McVeigh was protecting someone's identity. McVeigh scoffed at his failure, telling Domgard that he thought his lawyers were going to "have fun for the next year"—because they'd be wasting their time looking for conspirators.

In fact, McVeigh was furious about the polygraph. Three days later, he vented to Randy Coyne: "I failed it like a motherfucker." In his memo to the defense team about this meeting with McVeigh, Coyne wrote, "Tim maintains that he told the truth during the exam and attributes the indications of deception to his strong emotional feelings." McVeigh didn't like Domgard, finding him smug. "I think he played me." It is true that polygraphs are fallible, and the results were indeed perplexing, even internally contradictory. According to the test results, McVeigh told the truth in the narrative when he denied having co-conspirators, but he lied in the specific questions when he denied having co-conspirators.

In his meeting with Coyne, McVeigh, with characteristic bravado, proposed three options for follow-ups. He could be asked the same questions with "sodium pentothal, hypnosis or torture." (Sodium pentothal is a purported "truth serum.") Another option, McVeigh and Coyne agreed, was "just to drop it, forget about it." In the end, the polygraph served mainly to widen the breach between McVeigh and Jones. "I'll drop it if Stephen does," McVeigh told Coyne. "I can't have attorneys who think I'm lying."

CHAPTER 23

Matsch and the Victims

When the judges of the U.S. Court of Appeals for the Tenth Circuit assigned the McVeigh and Nichols case to the Denver-based district court judge Richard Matsch, they told him to select a fairer location for the trial than Oklahoma City. Not surprisingly, Matsch chose Denver. Judges like to sleep in their own beds.

Denver also made sense for reasons beyond the judge's convenience. The city is the biggest in the Tenth Circuit, which consists of six states in the desert West, and thus has the widest jury pool. Like all Americans, residents of the Denver area had been exposed to a great deal of publicity about the bombing, but they didn't have the same visceral connection to the case as Oklahomans did. Careful examination of prospective jurors, known as voir dire, could be relied upon to screen out undue bias.

Matsch (as in *make*) was also a logical choice to preside. In demeanor and background, he fit the judicial archetype, not least because Matsch had been a judge for most of his adult life. Matsch looked like a lawman from the Old West—with his droopy mustache, lean frame, and cowboy boots under his robe—and there was something heroic about him, too. With just a couple of young clerks to help him, he faced the baying demands of squadrons of attorneys on both sides and ruled with a cranky but admirable evenhandedness. At the same time, Matsch illustrated that he was, in one important respect, behind the times.

At legal conferences in the Denver area, Matsch was a familiar sight—sitting alone at meals. He didn't want to create an impression of possible bias by any kind of socializing with lawyers who might appear before him. The practice reflected a starchy, perhaps excessive, sense of rectitude, topped by a dollop of misanthropism. Matsch loved law—people, less so.

Born in Burlington, Iowa, in 1930, Matsch had an austere boyhood, where he was required to work every day in his father's grocery store, which was downstairs from the apartment where the family lived. He excelled under this disciplined regime, which he adopted as his own. He went to the University of Michigan for college and law school, graduating in 1953. After a couple of years in the Army, he settled in Denver, where he worked briefly for the city government, as an assistant U.S. attorney, and in private practice. In 1965, at the age of only thirty-five, he was appointed to preside over bankruptcy cases. He spent the rest of his life as a judge—first in the bankruptcy court and then, starting in 1974, as a federal district judge. He was appointed by Richard Nixon, but Matsch had no obvious political leanings. He wanted things done quickly, fairly—and his way. He had a portrait of General George S. Patton in his chambers.

Matsch and his wife raised five children in the Denver area, then moved to a thirty-acre farm near Boulder. The judge awoke at 5:30 every morning to clean the horse stalls and then board a bus to downtown Denver. He preferred the bus to a car, so he could do his judicial work in each direction. Matsch had a special fixation with promptness—tardy lawyers could expect to be locked out of his courtroom—and he was brusque to the point of rudeness with lawyers who didn't meet his standards. In 1992, Matsch suffered a devastating family tragedy. His twenty-four-year-old daughter, Elizabeth, died on a volcano in Hawaii when she stepped into a crevasse filled with superheated steam. Some wondered if the experience would soften the judge's hard edges. It didn't.

Matsch had experience with right-wing extremism. In 1987, he had conducted the trial of two white supremacists (avid readers of *The Turner Diaries*), who were convicted of killing the Denver radio host Alan Berg. (The Oliver Stone movie *Talk Radio* was loosely based on the case.) As with others in the Oklahoma City bombing story, Matsch's behavior was shaped by the O. J. Simpson trial. Like many judges, Matsch was appalled at the way Judge Lance Ito allowed Simpson's criminal case to drift for months as the attorneys and witnesses preened inside and outside the courtroom. Even in ordinary circumstances, Matsch presided with surly impatience, but the post-O.J. hangover prompted the judge to take preemptive steps to make sure he would remain in total control.

The first to feel the effects of Matsch's agenda were the families of the bombing victims. All judges warn spectators against outbursts in the courtroom, but Matsch went further. The judge came of age when criminal trials were seen as binary contests between prosecution and defense, with the victims regarded as barely tolerated outsiders. In this respect, Matsch was to learn that times had changed. When he was first assigned to the case, he heard motions in the Oklahoma City courthouse, where he saw enough to spirit the trial out of there. In his opinion moving the trial to Denver, Matsch ruled that the whole state of Oklahoma had been infected with bias against the defendants. "The public sympathy for victims is so strong that it has been manifested in the very courthouse where these motions were heard, when on the first day of the hearing a T-shirt was sold bearing the following inscription: 'Those Lost Will Never Leave Our Hearts

Or be Forgotten April 19, 1995 United States Court Western District of Oklahoma,'" he wrote. "The 'Oklahoma family' has been a common theme in the Oklahoma media coverage, with numerous reports of how the explosion shook the entire state, and how the state has pulled together in response. . . . Pride is defined as satisfaction in an achievement, and the people of Oklahoma are well deserving of it. But it is easy for those feeling pride to develop a prejudice." Many of the victims' families howled with outrage at this decision, but Matsch was just getting started on limiting the role of Oklahomans, especially the victims, even in Denver.

Considering the number of dead and injured, "the families," as they were known, were an enormous group, numbering well over a thousand people. On orders from Attorney General Reno, the U.S. Attorney's Office in Oklahoma City devoted a great deal of time and effort to providing counseling and keeping them informed of developments. Similarly, in the period leading up to the trial, Joe Hartzler and his prosecution team returned from Denver to Oklahoma once a month to brief the families on the progress of the case. Of course, not all of the families had the money or inclination to trek to Denver for every pretrial hearing, but several dozen did make the effort and became, by default, the spokespersons for the whole group.

During one early hearing, almost out of the blue, without consulting the lawyers on either side, Matsch made a startling announcement: anyone who wanted to testify at the trial, including during the penalty phase, had to leave his courtroom immediately. Matsch was enforcing the "rule on witnesses." The idea is that potential witnesses may be influenced by what they see in the courtroom, so they should only be present during their own testimony. But judges often display some flexibility in applying the rule, especially when, as here, there might be a penalty phase as well as a trial. After all, in a penalty phase, family members would be testifying about the pain from the loss of loved ones, which is not something likely to be influenced by other testimony.

Surprised and flummoxed, Hartzler, as lead prosecutor, tried to talk Matsch out of it. "We had hoped to allow victims to hear the pretrial hearing and guilt phase, because they really will not be affected," he told Matsch in court.

"How do you know that?" the judge snapped back. "They can be affected by just seeing the defendants in court." Matsch held firm. The victims had to go—right away.

Suddenly, the families faced a tough choice. Sacrifice watching the trial and preserve the chance to testify—or remain in the courtroom and give up the opportunity to tell the jury about their ordeals. On the day of Matsch's ruling, most stayed in the courtroom, but all the families, both in Denver and back in Oklahoma, were furious. On the courthouse steps in Denver, they denounced the judge, and their anger filled newspapers and television news, especially in Oklahoma. "It's a slap in the face to the family members," said Marsha Kight, whose twenty-three-year-old daughter died in the bombing.

Matsch believed his ruling on spectators as witnesses would be the last word on the subject. His long experience led him to believe that he alone controlled his courtroom. The ascendant victims' rights movement would show him otherwise.

With the defense team up and running in 1996, Stephen Jones began acting less like McVeigh's defense attorney and more like his secretary of state. Jones convinced himself that McVeigh was in the center of an international web of intrigue, so the lawyer traveled the world in an attempt to make the case. As he later wrote, "Chasing pieces of the puzzle took me all over the world in 1996." The impetus for this work was provided by a former CIA agent, who purportedly told Jones, "The government just isn't interested in uncovering a foreign plot. It has its perpetrators, and it doesn't want anyone or anything complicating its case."

Jones and his team went to China, the Philippines, Macau, Hong Kong, Germany, Scotland, England, Wales, Northern Ireland, Syria, Jordan, Israel, South Korea, and Washington, D.C. (with some repeat visits). Of course, the cost of these adventures was borne by U.S. taxpayers. Notwithstanding Jones's claims of a Justice Department cover-up, Garland decreed from the beginning that his prosecutors should not challenge any of Jones's expenses. Likewise, Judge Matsch, who had final authority over Jones's budget, also allowed the defense an unlimited expense account. Jones took full advantage. For the Philippines corner of his investigation alone, he hired a Chicago-based lawyer at a major American law firm, who in turn directed Jones to retain a pair of private investigators in Manila. Dissatisfied with the initial reports that showed no link between the bombing and anyone in the Philippines, Jones went to Manila himself in a visit he characterized as "very Graham Greene, as if 'Our Man in Havana' had been transposed to the Far East."

As for the results of these forays, they produced more insinuations than evidence. Jones was particularly obsessed with Terry Nichols's journeys to the Philippines, where he had met and courted his mail-order bride, Marife. Jones heard about a man named Edwin Angeles, who had been arrested in the Philippines as a possible associate of Ramzi Yousef, who was behind the first World Trade Center bombing. Later, Jones claimed that Angeles had told the local police that "he met Terry Nichols. Or someone I think is Terry Nichols." As it turned out, Angeles said he had met an American whom he knew as "the Farmer." A sketch of "the Farmer" looked somewhat like Nichols. Considering these tenuous connections, Jones later asked in his book, "Was it unreasonable to think Terry Nichols had gone to the Philippines to find somebody to teach him how to make a bomb?" (Actually, based on this "evidence," it was.)

As Jones teased out purported connections between his client and right-wing extremists in Elohim City a few dozen miles from

Oklahoma City, or Islamic terrorists eight thousand miles away, McVeigh himself was stewing. The premise of Jones's journeys was that McVeigh was lying to him about the bombing. From day one, McVeigh insisted that there was no broader conspiracy than the one he hatched with Nichols. Over and over, McVeigh denied that he received any help from "Andy the German" in Elohim City, Nichols's acquaintances in the Philippines, or anyone else. True, McVeigh had failed Jones's polygraph, but in light of the fallibility of such tests, that itself proved almost nothing. And the phone card evidence was powerful corroboration of McVeigh's account. If there were other conspirators, why was there no record of McVeigh or Nichols dialing them?

After Matsch moved the trial out of Oklahoma City ten months after the bombing, McVeigh was taken to a federal lockup in Englewood, Colorado, about a dozen miles from Denver. (McVeigh asked for his subscriptions to *Reader's Digest* and *Soldier of Fortune* to be transferred with him.) The Colorado prison was newer than his quarters in El Reno, and the accommodations somewhat more comfortable. But since most of Jones's defense team was based around Oklahoma City, it was harder to provide McVeigh with the daily in-person attention he had been receiving since his arrest. The longer gaps between attorney visits allowed McVeigh's anger at Jones to simmer. Why wouldn't his lawyer believe him? What was the point of all these trips around the world?

After the trial was moved to Colorado, Jones added yet another lawyer to his team—Jeralyn Merritt, a veteran Denver defense attorney who had long experience dealing with Matsch's prickly demeanor. Starting in May 1996, Merritt began making regular visits to McVeigh in Englewood, and she heard him give the same detailed recounting of the bombing conspiracy that he had long provided to others. "I said I had spoken a little to Stephen, but that all I knew was that he had 'done it,'" Merritt wrote in a memo to the defense team after her first meeting with McVeigh. "I told him that I would like to hear him tell me about it. He started with politics and began by complaining that no one had criticized Truman when he dropped the bomb on innocent women and children. He said that there was no point in bombing the Oklahoma building at night, because then all the damage would just be to property, and the government would just build it again. He said this is the nineties, and you 'can't make a statement without a body count.'"

The defense team was fracturing. Merritt joined the McVeigh lawyers who found their client's account credible. (Randy Coyne, the Oklahoma law professor, did, too.) Sure, they argued, there were ambiguities in the evidence, including possible eyewitnesses who saw McVeigh with others. However, the accounts of the purported eyewitnesses conflicted with those of *other* purported eyewitnesses, not just McVeigh's version. Jim Hankins, another alum of Jones's Enid firm who was working on the case, made the case for McVeigh's veracity in a lengthy memo to Jones. "Every single fact that Tim McVeigh has told us checks out. His story is entirely consistent with what he has been telling us and based upon the facts that we know are true," Hankins wrote. Yet Jones's strategy assumed that McVeigh was hiding his real co-conspirators. This, Hankins wrote, "places Tim in a vicious Catch-22. . . . The central premise appears to be that Tim was not acting alone and that he has not been truthful with us because he denies that he was not acting alone. . . . I simply don't think it is fair to use Tim's denials of the complicity of others to bootstrap a theory that others must be involved because he is trying so hard to protect them."

Hankins's analysis was irrefutable—but Jones tried to refute it. The lead defense lawyer remained committed to the idea of the broader conspiracy—and to the belief that McVeigh was lying about it. In every sense, Jones was a long way from Enid. He was traveling the world, usually with Ann Bradley—his paralegal and aide-de-camp. He was in daily contact with the most famous journalists in the country (as well as a lot of obscure ones). In his conversations with the reporters, Jones offered tantalizing hints about what he discovered on the road—and he welcomed their conjectures as well. The change in circumstances contributed to a kind of grandiosity on Jones's part. The story that his client and the government were both telling—that McVeigh and Nichols acted alone—was too simple, too straightforward. Jones needed a conspiracy worthy of his own exalted self-conception, even if no such conspiracy had existed.

As Jones traveled the world, Matsch worked his way through the legal issues necessary to set a trial date. McVeigh and Nichols won the change of venue to Denver, but the government won most of the other motions—like a challenge to the constitutionality of the federal death penalty law—and the case was largely on track. Unbeknownst to Matsch, however, the victims' rights movement was preparing to hand him a surprise.

Prodded by the victims' families, the prosecutors appealed Matsch's order that barred penalty phase witnesses from watching the trial. The Tenth Circuit upheld Matsch's judgment, which ordinarily would have ended the matter. But the victims' cause had so much bipartisan support that Congress mobilized, in a matter of weeks, to pass a law on their behalf. Cosponsored by Bill McCollum, a Florida Republican, and Chuck Schumer, then a congressman from Brooklyn, the Victim Rights Clarification Act ordered federal judges to allow witnesses in the penalty phase of a capital case to attend the guilt phase of the trial. In other words, Congress overruled Matsch's order on witnesses. What was more, the law directed Matsch to allow a live closed-circuit feed of the trial to be shown in a facility in Oklahoma City. (The video and audio would not be available to the news media, only to the victims' families.) Cameras were otherwise barred from federal trials, but the law made an exception for this single case. (President Clinton was so supportive of the bill that he signed it while on a trip to Finland, rather than wait until he returned to Washington.)

Matsch was furious about the congressional interference in the operation of his own courtroom—and he muttered on the bench that he thought the law might be unconstitutional—but he didn't want to delay the trial by challenging the new law. In any event, prosecutors had an even bigger problem to manage than Matsch's pique. On October 25, 1996, Matsch granted the defendants a severance—that is, separate trials for McVeigh and Nichols.

It was a close legal question, which related to Nichols's nine-hour interview with the FBI just after the bombing. In that statement, Nichols incriminated McVeigh in planning the bombing. Since Nichols would likely not testify in a joint trial, McVeigh's lawyers would have no chance to cross-examine him about his statements to the FBI. As a result, according to Matsch, McVeigh would be unfairly prejudiced by the introduction of Nichols's statement to the FBI. The prosecutors argued that any prejudice against McVeigh could be cured by a jury instruction from Matsch, but the judge argued that would not be enough. "Timothy McVeigh will be profoundly prejudiced by a joint trial of this case," Matsch said in his opinion. "His lawyers cannot question Terry Nichols or cross-examine the FBI agents on what they say Terry Nichols said and they cannot control the cross-examination by Terry Nichols or follow up on any suggestions or inferences of guilt of Timothy McVeigh resulting from it."

The prosecutors were shocked—and shattered—by Matsch's ruling. The reasons were mostly personal. The government's lawyers had put their lives on hold to travel first to Oklahoma City and then to Denver to try the case. (Hartzler and Scott Mendeloff came from Illinois; Larry Mackey, from Indianapolis; Beth Wilkinson and Aitan Goelman, from Washington, D.C. The team did add Sean Connelly, a brief-writing whiz, who was based in Denver. Jamie Orenstein, a later addition, came from New York.) By October 1996, most had been away from their families for about a year. The prospect of two trials, rather than one, meant that they were probably looking at another year.

Matsch granted the separate trials largely based on McVeigh's arguments, but the real winner in the ruling was Nichols. The case against him was much weaker than the one against McVeigh. As his lawyer Tigar never tired of pointing out, *Terry Nichols wasn't there* in Oklahoma City. In a joint trial, the government could expect Nichols to suffer from some guilt by association with McVeigh; not so in a separate trial.

The government did receive one piece of good news as 1996 came to an end. Matsch set a trial date for *United States v. Timothy McVeigh* of March 31, 1997—that is, if McVeigh's defense team didn't disintegrate by that point.

CHAPTER 24

The Defense Implodes

By the beginning of 1997, the Oklahoma City bombing had nearly disappeared from the news. Merrick Garland's plan—to turn the McVeigh case into the *un*–O. J. Simpson case—had succeeded. The prosecutors gave no interviews and rarely spoke in public except during their appearances before Judge Matsch. As a result, Joe Hartzler and his colleagues never became household names. Likewise, senior Justice Department officials like Garland maintained a similar silence about the case. The investigation had not produced evidence of a criminal conspiracy beyond the one charged in the indictment of McVeigh and Nichols, so those officials spoke of no broader threat. They didn't talk about the political context of the case or the people and forces that inspired the two defendants—nothing about the militias, the white supremacists, the gun rights extremists, the shortwave radio ranters, or even (especially) Rush Limbaugh. As Hartzler, following his boss, put it in the sign on his office door, DO NOT BURY THE CRIME IN CLUTTER! To Garland and Hartzler, anything that wasn't admissible evidence specifically against McVeigh and Nichols was "clutter."

A quarter century later, Garland became attorney general and supervised the investigation of the insurrection at the Capitol on January 6, 2021, and of Donald Trump's removal of documents from the White House after his presidency. He followed the playbook he wrote for the Oklahoma City bombing case. The Justice Department rolled out hundreds of cases against individual rioters, but Garland never said anything specific about who or what inspired the street-level lawbreakers. Garland himself, as well as his prosecutors, said virtually nothing in public about the investigations. "We follow the facts and the law wherever they may lead," he said at the Justice Department podium. "The best way to undermine an investigation is to say things out of court." This is a debatable point. Prosecutors, especially high-level figures like the attorney general, are allowed to speak publicly about the meaning and importance of their work. But as in 1995, Garland as attorney general took the obligation for public silence to an extreme. (In my interview with him, Garland not only refused to draw any comparisons between McVeigh and the Capitol rioters, he refused even to utter the words January 6.) As attorney general, Garland followed his own example, not that of Bill Clinton.

Garland's clutter, though, was Clinton's gold. In his speeches after the bombing, the president raised an alarm about what McVeigh and Nichols represented, not just what they did. Clinton spoke plainly about the dangers of the militia movement and its enablers in the media. The right-wing extremists of the 1990s employed the same kind of violent imagery that their successors would use more than twenty-five years later. Before Oklahoma City, Limbaugh spoke of how close the nation was to "the second violent American revolution," just as Donald Trump told his armed supporters on the Ellipse on January 6 to march to the Capitol and "fight like hell." On both occasions, actual violence followed broadcast incitement. Clinton believed that this kind of language had real-life consequences, but that wasn't the kind of conclusion that could be tested in a court of law. In contrast, Garland and others in the Justice Department refused to tie the bombing case to contemporary politics, believing that such analyses could only confuse a straightforward criminal trial. Thanks to the reticence of Garland and his colleagues, as well as the tunnel vision of the journalists covering the case, the impression lingered that McVeigh was an aberration, a lone and lonely figure who represented only himself and his sad-sack codefendant. This notion, as history would show, was mistaken.

Stephen Jones, in contrast, did his best to maintain the media's interest in the bombing trial, but that proved challenging. In the first months after the bombing and McVeigh's arrest, Jones welcomed a steady stream of journalist supplicants to the El Reno prison in Oklahoma and granted them off-the-record audiences with his infamous client. The journalists were happy to have the opportunities—who wouldn't want to meet the most notorious man in the country?—but the conversations were of limited value because they couldn't report anything McVeigh said. (Also, he said little of importance, because Jones put the bombing off-limits as a topic.) In his own conversations with the journalists, Jones dropped dark hints about what he was discovering during his travels. He had made a similar point publicly in his speech at the University of Oklahoma. But then . . . nothing. Jones had no new facts to deliver, no story to tell.

As the March 31, 1997, trial date drew near, the defense team grew brittle with tension. It was one thing for Jones to travel the world, following vague hunches, when the trial was a year away, but as the day approached when he would have to put on a defense in a courtroom, something close to panic ensued. Jones's own media habits became less discriminating. He became preoccupied with the work of J. D. Cash, a Tulsa banker who dabbled as a journalist for the *McCurtain Daily Gazette*, which was published in the small logging town of Idabel, Oklahoma. Cash published such dubious scoops as one placing McVeigh in a Tulsa topless bar eleven days before the bombing, boasting to a stripper that "on April 19, 1995, you'll remember me for the rest of your life!" (The story didn't check out.)

Still, Jones's issues with the news media paled next to his problems with his client. McVeigh was becoming impossible. He was full of demands for his lawyers and complaints when they didn't respond instantly. (Frustrated with Jones, McVeigh snubbed him by handwriting a letter to Beth Wilkinson, one of the prosecutors, asking for certain documents in discovery. Hartzler sent the letter back, saying that the government would only correspond with lawyers.) At the same time, McVeigh wouldn't answer Jones's questions or read the documents the lawyers sent him. Even as the trial approached, McVeigh wouldn't engage on the question of what his defense would be before the jury. He clung to the idea of the necessity defense—the idea that Waco compelled him to bomb the Murrah building—even as his lawyers told him it would be impossible to sell. McVeigh played on the splits that had developed within the defense team. Dick Burr, the death penalty specialist, and Randy Coyne, the Oklahoma law professor, seethed at what they regarded as Jones's showboating for the media—and McVeigh joined in their complaints about the lead defense counsel. Still, that left the question: What would be McVeigh's defense?

As the trial approached, McVeigh became haughty and preemptory with his lawyers, even drafting jury addresses for them. McVeigh spelled out one possible theory in a memo to Jerri Merritt, the Denver lawyer on the defense team. He proposed language for a summation:

> "If you believe the scenario that has been presented by the government, then you must find my client guilty. If, however, the government's theory, as presented, seems incomplete, implausible, inaccurate, or incredulous, then you should find my client Not Guilty. Please consider the language of the indictment: '. . . others unknown . . .'"

> As in the O.J. case, where they played the "race card," this is our version (to which people are receptive these days): "play the conspiracy card."

At one level, in this message, McVeigh was just picking up on the point that Jones had made about the faulty phrasing in the indictment, which suggested that "others unknown" had participated in the bombing. In this memo, McVeigh approved the idea of blaming "others," as long as they were not identified by name.

But McVeigh's draft also offered an insight into his fellow right-wing extremists, who were "receptive" to conspiracy theories. Long before McVeigh, like-minded extremists evinced hostility to official or authorized interpretations of events. Extremism is defined, at least in part, by aversion to accepted wisdom. In the 1950s, Robert Welch, the founder of the John Birch Society, made his name on the right by claiming (falsely and absurdly) that Dwight Eisenhower was a secret Communist agent. In McVeigh's time, he heard Limbaugh and others warn of imminent government seizures of weapons and Bill Cooper, his hero on shortwave radio, inveigh against government conspiracies to suppress information about UFOs. The predilection for conspiracy theories endured long after the 1990s. For a modern analog, there was Donald Trump, who advanced dozens of conspiracy theories over the course of his career, most notoriously that Barack Obama was not born in the United States. (McVeigh and Trump each voiced the debunked belief that Clinton's aide Vince Foster did not commit suicide.) In light of this long tradition, it's no surprise that McVeigh thought a defense based on "the conspiracy card" might succeed.

Mostly, though, McVeigh was emphatic about what his defense would *not* be. In his distinctive left-tilted block printing, he wrote a memo to "All Attorneys assigned to U.S. v. McVeigh" on November 24, 1996:

> As official notice, let it be known that I do not approve of a trial strategy in which Terry Nichols is attacked, blamed, or otherwise implicated in any crime. Further, I do not approve of pointing the finger of responsibility at anyone else who I know is not responsible and who is in no way deserving of such scrutiny. I have relayed this wish orally for 18 months—not only concerning Terry Nichols, but also addressing the "foreign" investigations and the "neo-Nazi" investigations.

This approach sought to shut down most of the work that Jones had been doing for a year and a half. McVeigh didn't want Jones to blame Islamic terrorists based in the Philippines or neo-Nazis based in Oklahoma—because neither theory was remotely close to true.

Jones recognized that McVeigh never came to terms with a fundamental contradiction—that he wanted the world to know that he bombed the Murrah building, and he also wanted to be acquitted of the bombing. McVeigh's political heirs later faced a similar dilemma. An extraordinary number of the rioters who invaded the Capitol on January 6, 2021, could be seen holding their cell phones aloft to record video of their criminal activity. Like McVeigh, they felt their behavior was justified, even compelled, by the perfidy of their political opponents in the Democratic Party. That's why they were proud of their conduct and wanted to preserve evidence of it. Later, when the rioters faced prosecution in 2022, they confronted a similar choice to the one McVeigh did in 1997. Most didn't want to apologize, because they didn't think they had anything to apologize for, but they didn't want to go to prison, either. Some went to trial and sought to justify their behavior; some apologized and expressed remorse; most resolved their cases with grudging guilty pleas and prayers for leniency. For his part, McVeigh never came to terms with the contradiction in his own behavior.

Jones struggled with the consequences of McVeigh's ambivalence. Faced with a recalcitrant client and a looming trial date, Jones made a curious choice in the final days of 1996. He chose to devote his time to drafting a *fifty-four-page* letter to McVeigh—roughly thirteen thousand words—defending his performance as lead defense counsel and excoriating his client for his ingratitude.

Jones went through all the experts he had consulted and pointed out, with justification, that he had won some important victories along the way. As he put it, he had won "(1) a trial outside Oklahoma, (2) in front of a non-Oklahoma judge, (3) an Order prohibiting the use of the statements made by Terry Nichols against you, and (4) a severance." He continued, "You have rewarded our unprecedented success by claiming, with no factual foundation, that Mike Tigar is responsible for that success." (Tigar's lofty reputation and good press infuriated Jones.) "Your defense team has performed in the highest traditions of the Bar, and equally importantly, achieved substantial positive results.

"You continue to act as though there is some personal, financial or professional gain in representing you," Jones went on. "My personal income before I represented you was in excess of a million dollars a year. I live in one of the largest houses in Garfield County and undoubtedly am one of the most publicly prominent lawyers in northwest Oklahoma, for whatever that means, which isn't much. . . . There is nothing that your case adds to my life or career that I need or desire." Jones had a point when he defended his performance as a lawyer, but not when he denied seeking personal attention and glory.

Jones complained that McVeigh wasn't keeping up his end of the bargain as a client. He refused to call Jones's office twice a day, as instructed. He refused to read and analyze the government's discovery material, because it was "boring." Worse yet, "you entertain yourself with watching what might be classified as B-rated or C-rated movies when the real work of your defense you have ignored," he said. "Repeatedly watching 'Red Dawn' or similar movies is not a substitute for understanding the philosophy of John Locke, which apparently you copied, but with no real understanding of it, and put in your car.

"Drafting this letter has probably taken two days out of the defense time and has involved consultation with half of the defense team," Jones wrote toward the end of this epic missive. "Everyone is working ragged for you, heart and soul. We need you to work with us in a committed way as we are trying to work with you. After all, we are not the enemy, and we are on your side."

Despite this effort, nothing much changed between McVeigh and Jones. Almost by default, they settled on what they called the "reasonable doubt" defense—a common approach in criminal trials. They wouldn't present an alternative theory of who committed the bombing, but they would attempt to poke holes in the government's proof. They would question the eyewitness identifications of McVeigh at Elliott's Body Shop, where he rented the Ryder truck, and demand to know the whereabouts of John Doe Number 2. They would raise other identification issues, including witnesses who claimed to see others at Geary Lake state park or at the scene of the bombing itself. They would question McVeigh's connection to the Daryl Bridges phone card—the fake name McVeigh used when he bought it. They would use the issue of the "extra leg" to suggest that the real bomber had been killed in the explosion. It might not add up to much, especially considering the millions of dollars Jones had spent to assemble it, but it was at least a defense of sorts.

Then McVeigh's defense descended into the realm of black comedy.

In the mid-1990s, before the internet destroyed the business model for newspapers, *The Dallas Morning News* was still a regional colossus, with the resources to put squadrons of reporters on a big story. As the leading paper in the nearest metropolis to Oklahoma City, about 250 miles away, the *Morning News* invested heavily in the story of the bombing. That meant, among other things, sending Pete Slover.

With his 1950s-style eyeglasses and earnest demeanor, Slover resembled a diminutive Clark Kent. He possessed an unusual array of skills. He'd graduated from the University of Texas law school, but he put his degree to work as an investigative reporter. He knew how to read a legal document and a balance sheet. He excelled at the discovery (and reporting) of white-collar crime. At the same time, Slover had apprenticed with old-school gumshoe reporters at the *Morning News*; their rule, when chasing a story, was that it was better to seek forgiveness than permission. Once, looking for documents in the investigation of a pedophile priest in Waxahachie, Texas, Slover managed to get inside a county office building after hours. Locked inside, he called his city desk with the story. Less fortunately, he was arrested for trespassing and had to plead guilty to a misdemeanor—which only enhanced his reputation among his peers.

Unlike the television stars who breezed into Oklahoma City for a meeting with Jones and a prison audience with McVeigh, Slover rented an apartment and committed for the long haul. He began cultivating lower-level members of the defense team and struck up a relationship with Marty Reed, one of Jones's private investigators.

After serving overseas in World War II, Reed returned to Oklahoma and for a decade made a living selling women's shoes. According to Jones, the experience provided Reed with a gift for putting people at ease in awkward situations. Once Reed became a private eye, Jones retained him occasionally, even though he knew Reed was a small-time operator. He didn't even know how to use a computer, so his business partner, Wilma Sparks, did the typing when Reed did the questioning. Despite his worries that Reed was in over his head, Jones used him for months in the bombing case, including sending him on an investigative trip to the Philippines.

For Reed, the trip to the Philippines brought back haunting memories of his service in the war of the Pacific, and he began having misgivings about working on McVeigh's defense. Reed knew that McVeigh was guilty, but what if he was acquitted? How could Reed live with himself if he played a part in such an injustice? He had seen slaughter in World War II, and he didn't want to excuse another one a half century later. Reed began sharing those thoughts with Pete Slover, who lent a sympathetic ear. Reed told Slover about some of the evidence in the case he'd seen, and he thought Slover should see it, too. The problem was, all that evidence—the interview notes, the defense memoranda, the accounts of the lawyers' meetings with McVeigh—was in Reed's computer, and he didn't know how to use it. So over lunch at the County Line, a legendary barbecue restaurant in Oklahoma City, Reed just gave his laptop to Slover and figured the reporter could extract the thousands of documents.

Slover spent weeks plowing through the electronic bounty, and on Friday, February 28, 1997—a month before jury selection was scheduled to begin—he reached out to Jones for comment. Slover told the lawyer that he had seen defense documents that showed McVeigh had repeatedly confessed to the bombing. Slover also saw that McVeigh told his lawyers that he had set off the bomb in the daytime hours because he wanted a high "body count." Jones was incensed, accusing Slover of seeking to poison the jury pool on the eve of the trial. He said he was going to Judge Matsch to ask him to issue a prior restraint to stop the *Morning News* from publishing the story.

Jones's threat left Slover, and now the paper's lawyers, with a dilemma. They knew that courts rarely, if ever, granted prior restraints, but they recognized that Judge Matsch was an independent operator who was fixated on guaranteeing McVeigh a fair trial. Perhaps the judge really would stop publication. So, the leaders of the *Morning News* decided to do something that had, at that point, never been done before. Just five months earlier, the paper had unveiled its first site on what was then often called the World Wide Web, and the paper posted Slover's story before it ran in the next day's edition of the newspaper. By the time Jones went to Matsch, the story was already in circulation. There was nothing Jones or the judge could do about it.

Then there was more. Ben Fenwick was a freelance writer based in Oklahoma City, who was doing some work on the bombing for the Reuters news agency. One day he ran into Wilma Sparks, Marty Reed's partner, on the steps of the courthouse. Several years earlier, Fenwick had interviewed Sparks for a story about private investigators, and they remained friendly. Sparks said that her daughter, who had been Fenwick's martial arts teacher, was also working with her on the case. She was also recently divorced. "You really should call her," Sparks said.

It turned out that Sparks's daughter, like Marty Reed, was having second thoughts about working for McVeigh. Her conscience was troubling her. Over several months of conversations, she ultimately decided to share a sixty-six-page chronology compiled by the defense team based on its investigation. Like the documents provided to Slover, the chronology made clear that McVeigh had confessed to the bombing. Fenwick made a deal to write an article for *Playboy* based on the chronology. When the *Morning News* put Slover's story on the internet on February 28, *Playboy* decided to rush Fenwick's article onto the internet as well, and it was posted on March 11. (ABC News also did a lengthy report about the chronology that Fenwick had obtained.)

Jones was beside himself. The leaks of McVeigh's various confessions were coming at the worst possible time. At a news conference and in conversations with reporters, Jones tried somehow to say both that the documents had been stolen from the defense and that they were fakes—when, of course, they couldn't be both. Jones considered asking Judge Matsch to move the trial out of Denver because of the pretrial publicity but thought better of it. The *Morning News* and *Playboy* stories received national attention, so there was no other location that necessarily provided a less-tainted jury pool. There was another reason Jones preferred to remain in Denver. Three months earlier, in December 1996, a six-year-old girl named JonBenét Ramsey had been found murdered in the basement of her home in an affluent neighborhood in Boulder. When the McVeigh trial was about to begin, the Ramsey case was receiving exhaustive coverage in Colorado. Jones figured that a jury pool preoccupied with the JonBenét saga might pay less attention to the news about his client. (The Ramsey murder has never been solved.)

So, in light of the two bombshells, Jones asked Judge Matsch to delay the trial rather than move it. The judge refused and ordered jury selection to begin, as scheduled, on March 31. To Jones's detractors on the defense team, it was as if Jones's assiduous attention to the news media had come back to haunt him—and more to the point, McVeigh. After all, a year and a half earlier, Jones himself had leaked a story to *The New York Times*'s Pam Belluck that said much the same thing as the Slover and Fenwick stories. Only the timing was different.

The defense team's temporary office space in Denver degenerated into a battleground, roughly pitting Jones and his allies from his law firm in Enid against the outsiders like Burr, from Texas, and Coyne, the law professor. Scott Anderson, a harried paralegal, scurried between the factions trying to make sure that work was done and deadlines were met. Coyne, who was working too hard to keep up with the motions in advance of the trial and drinking too much in the process, alternately brooded and seethed. He also took an immediate dislike to Jerri Merritt, the Denver lawyer, and on one occasion berated her in front of the whole team. When Jones told Coyne he was out of line, Coyne stormed off and slammed the door to the office bathroom so hard that he broke several tiles. Jones told him he would have to pay for the damage. Later, Coyne wrote in his diary, "Received a copy of the bill for the tile repair in the Denver Place office bathroom: $264.96. Money well spent."

Jones's long letter to McVeigh was correct in one respect; his client was ungrateful and lazy. But as jury selection grew near, McVeigh was also facing a trial and a possible, if not likely, death sentence. He was also angry and scared. As Coyne later put it, "Jones dangled McVeigh before the national media much as P. T. Barnum exhibited Tom Thumb. That McVeigh became embittered and resented being used this way was plain to all on the defense team who paid attention or cared."

Shortly before the trial, McVeigh called the judge's chambers himself to say that he wanted Jones off the case. Matsch's clerk told him that the judge would only speak to McVeigh's lawyer, not to McVeigh himself. As Coyne recounted, "That suggestion was the root of the problem. McVeigh didn't *want* to talk *to* his lawyer—he *needed* to talk *about* his lawyer." The judge refused to talk to McVeigh. Coyne and his faction took McVeigh's side. They wanted Jones off the case, too. As Jones later recalled, he took a poll of the defense team, and the vote was thirty-two for Jones to stay, and three for him to step down. (To be sure, few murder cases in history had a defense staff of thirty-five people.) The roiling chaos on the defense team prompted Jones to make a sudden trip back home to Enid, because he decided to emulate . . . Charles de Gaulle.

At the height of the student protests in Paris in 1968, when de Gaulle was president of France, he suddenly disappeared, Jones recalled. No one knew where he was. People thought he was resigning. Jones went on, "When he returned to Paris, the rebellion had already begun to run out of steam, and the Fifth Republic survived, as it does to this day." Like de Gaulle, Jones persevered.

The trial was about to begin.

CHAPTER 25

The Government Makes Its Case

The trial of Timothy McVeigh took place at a curious, quiescent moment in American history. When Bill Clinton delivered his State of the Union address on February 4, 1997, he was able to boast, with justification, about "unrivaled peace and prosperity all across the world." In the absence of national crises, sensational crimes filled the news hole. At the very moment Clinton began his remarks, a civil jury in Santa Monica found O. J. Simpson liable for the murders of Nicole Brown Simpson and Ronald Goldman and ordered him to pay $33.5 million in damages. The president was overshadowed, because the Simpson case, like the murder of JonBenét Ramsey, preoccupied the national media. So did shark attacks. Collectively, America was on vacation, and the news media provided the beach reads.

That, by and large, was how most journalists (including me) covered McVeigh's trial in Denver—as a crime story rather than a political story. This also reflected how Garland directed his prosecutors to present the case. Because his job was to win a conviction, not to enlighten the public, Garland wanted a trial devoid of the "clutter" of ideological context. For journalists, the saga of Oklahoma City had shrunk in the two years between the bombing and McVeigh's trial. The story that began as a symptom of a hidden but growing menace in the American heartland ended as a narrow inquiry into the actions of one man. America was thriving, so how could McVeigh be anything except a regrettable oddity in this moment of national repose?

Opening statements revealed not just two views of the evidence but a pair of distinct personalities. Joe Hartzler, the lead prosecutor, was linear, orderly, and direct. Stephen Jones, for Timothy McVeigh, was orotund, elliptical, and discursive. This kind of contrast is common in criminal trials where the evidence all favors one side.

"Ladies and gentlemen of the jury," Hartzler began as he sat in a wheelchair (rather than his usual scooter) in front of the jury box, "April 19th, 1995, was a beautiful day in Oklahoma City—at least it started out as a beautiful day. The sun was shining. Flowers were blooming. It was springtime in Oklahoma City. Sometime after six o'clock that morning, Tevin Garrett's mother woke him up to get him ready for the day. He was only 16 months old. He was a toddler; and as some of you know that have experience with toddlers, he had a keen eye for mischief." No one in the courtroom could doubt what was going to happen to Tevin. Hartzler went on to describe the morning rituals of other children who were heading to the America's Kids day care center.

"All the children I mentioned earlier, all of them died, and more; dozens and dozens of other men, women, children, cousins, loved ones, grandparents, grandchildren, ordinary Americans going about their business," Hartzler said. "And the only reason they died, the only reason that they are no longer with us, no longer with their loved ones, is that they were in a building owned by a government that Timothy McVeigh so hated that with premeditated intent and a well-designed plan that he had developed over months and months before the bombing, he chose to take their innocent lives to serve his twisted purpose. In plain, simple language, it was an act of terror, violence, intended to serve a selfish political purpose. The man who committed this act is sitting in this courtroom behind me, and he's the one that committed those murders."

Hartzler began with the end of the story—McVeigh's arrest on the road out of town with his envelope full of incendiary literature. Then Hartzler went back to the beginning. McVeigh's friendship with Terry Nichols. His rage at Waco. Their use of the *Spotlight* phone card to find ingredients for the bomb. The robbery of the explosives from the quarry in Kansas. McVeigh's rental of the Ryder truck in Junction City as "Robert Kling." His short stay in the Dreamland Motel. The drive to Oklahoma City and then the explosion, sending the truck axle flying. And then, finally, back to Charlie Hanger's arrest of McVeigh in his beat-up Mercury Marquis.

For Jones, the beginning of the trial was almost a relief after the chaos of the previous few weeks—from the leaks in *The Dallas Morning News* and *Playboy* to the shattered tiles in the lawyers' bathroom. Jones gave a marathon opening statement—more than four hours long—but the gist was a reasonable-doubt defense. Jones mocked the government's reliance on *The Turner Diaries*—"a work of fiction"—as McVeigh's inspiration. Jones was an Anglophile in temperament as well as couture, which sometimes led to references that probably eluded a Colorado jury. "*The Turner Diaries*," he said, "is no more a blueprint, much less a reason, to blow up a federal building . . . than *Lady Chatterley's Lover* can teach you how to make love." He attacked Michael and Lori Fortier as untrustworthy because Mike was seeking the prosecution's support for a reduced sentence: "Mr. and Mrs. Fortier could only be expected to say whatever the Government wanted to hear." He raised the mystery of "John Doe Number 2," and he criticized the FBI laboratory's analysis of the chemical makeup of the bomb. What Jones did not deliver was a theory of the case that explained how someone other than his client bombed the Murrah building. Jones never did.

Garland had installed his team of federal prosecutors to replace those based in Oklahoma City, and relations between the outsiders and locals remained frosty throughout the case. As a good-faith gesture to his counterparts, Hartzler invited Patrick Ryan, the U.S. attorney in Oklahoma City, to examine the first witness in McVeigh's trial. Ryan called Cynthia Klaver. Hardly anyone in the courtroom knew who she was.

Klaver was a lawyer with the Oklahoma Water Resources Board, which had headquarters in a squat three-story cement structure across the street from the Murrah building. On the morning of April 19, 1995, Klaver was presiding as a hearing officer in a dispute between two adjoining landowners about whether one would be allowed to start a bottled water company. The proceeding was held in the third-floor conference room in the corner farthest away from the Murrah building. There were ten people in the hearing room and about eighty in the building.

Ryan asked Klaver if any record was kept of the hearing.

"We would like to have a court reporter, but we do not have the funds for that," she testified, "so we have a little tape recorder that we record every hearing." Ryan handed her Government Exhibit 942, which she identified as the cassette audiotape of the hearing. Then Judge Matsch gave permission for the prosecution to play it for the jury.

The gray bureaucratic monotone of Klaver's voice on the recording reminded everyone of the mundane way that April 19 began. The hearing had started at the stroke of 9 a.m., and prosecutors decided to play the tape for the jury from the beginning. In the courtroom, before the jury, the drone of those first two minutes was excruciating, because everyone knew what was coming. Klaver's disembodied voice was heard saying, "There are four elements that I have to, uh, receive information regarding . . ." The sound that followed was hideous—a thunderous boom that seemed to go on and on. Even on a low-quality cassette, the magnitude of the blast was unmistakable. It took several seconds for people to start screaming. "Everybody, let's get out of here!" Klaver yelled. Someone else wailed, "Watch the electrical lines." Ryan let the effect of the tape sink in for a moment before he resumed questioning Klaver. He asked what happened after the explosion.

"Well, I thought the whole building was coming down on us," she said, her voice resembling that of a kindly nursery school teacher. "I didn't see any way we were going to make it out; but basically, the building shook and the whole ceiling fell down in on us. I didn't realize that it wasn't just our room. When you walk out, you couldn't go out the front door. There was rubble piled so you couldn't get out the front door. So, everyone moved to try to go over the back and climbed over all the debris that was in the hall and forced the door open and got out the back door; so we got everybody out, and it was kind of difficult."

Two of Klaver's colleagues, who were working in the part of the building closer to McVeigh's truck, were killed in the explosion. One was a financial analyst, the other a college student doing an internship.

There was no cross-examination.

The trial of Timothy McVeigh was unprecedented. It was the largest number of murders ever prosecuted in a single trial. Thanks to the new law passed by Congress, it was the first (and remains the only) federal criminal trial to be broadcast, albeit on closed circuit to a single location in Oklahoma City, where victims' families could watch. (Matsch objected to Congress's interference with his case and only grudgingly complied with the law. He registered his pique by ordering the spectators in Oklahoma City to remain silent—as if they could disrupt the proceedings from six hundred miles away.)

Jones believed that the case would unfold at epic length. Well before the trial, Matsch required prosecutors to list all potential witnesses; Hartzler's team produced 327 names. Considering this, Jones thought the trial would last at least six months. But when the time came to put witnesses on the stand, Hartzler cut the list way back. (This disappointed his colleagues. For example, Beth Wilkinson told Hartzler she needed to call thirty-eight witnesses to describe the crime scene; Hartzler told her to do it with eight.) This streamlining was the most consequential manifestation of his war on "clutter." In his view, more witnesses meant more versions of the same events, leading to more opportunities for cross-examination and confusion. In the end, Hartzler and his team put on the government's case in just eighteen days.

Hartzler also had to manage a delicate problem that was both legal and political. The bombing had produced hundreds of tragic stories—children killed, bodies mangled, lives destroyed. The prosecutors had to convey the magnitude of the horror, but they had to be wary of going over the top—and of crossing Judge Matsch. The judge had made clear that he wouldn't allow too much victim testimony; he would enforce Federal Rule of Evidence 403, which prohibits evidence that creates "unfair prejudice." That murky standard gives the trial judge a great deal of discretion, and Hartzler didn't want to offend the prickly Matsch. At the same time, the community of victims had waited almost two years for their day in court. Dozens wanted to tell their stories. How many should testify—and which ones?

The point, Hartzler believed, was not to overload either the judge or the jury. After Klaver, the prosecution called a helicopter photojournalist to introduce his video of the moments after the bombing.

Richard Williams, a supervisor with the General Services Administration, described who worked on each floor of the building. With one answer, he gave a preview of the heartbreaking story of the day care center on the second floor.

"What could you see on the second floor from outside the building?" he was asked.

"You could see the children," he said. "You could see on the windows from time to time, there would be certain occasions, Christmas, Halloween—there would be things placed on the window. You could see the cribs on the east end in the infant area. You could see the children running around. You could see them playing. You could see them putting their hands against the windows."

Susan Hunt, who worked at the Department of Housing and Urban Development, began the story of what happened inside the building after the bomb exploded. She testified about staggering around her office, trying to find survivors. One colleague had terrible cuts on her face. "I looked at her neck, and I instantly put my hand up to her neck to hold an artery that appeared to be cut," she said. "I spoke to her and she said, 'Susan, I know that's you. I recognize your voice, but I can't see you. Do I have an eye?' And I didn't answer her, because she didn't." Hunt then identified photographs of the thirty-five HUD employees killed in the blast.

McVeigh's name wasn't mentioned in testimony until the third day of the trial, when the prosecution called Charlie Hanger, the trooper who stopped McVeigh at 10:17 a.m. on April 19. Hanger carried himself like a western lawman in a movie—erect carriage, barrel chest, crisp diction—but there was no artifice about him. Behind the scenes, Hanger was a favorite of the prosecutors because of his sincere amazement that he made perhaps the most famous arrest of the twentieth century. A religious man, Hanger had total confidence that God had placed him between mile markers 202 and 203 on I-35 on that April morning.

Hanger told the jury how he noticed the absence of a license plate on McVeigh's Mercury and then pulled him over. McVeigh told him he had a gun, and it was loaded. "So is mine," Hanger said with his service revolver pressed to the back of McVeigh's skull. Hanger gave the prosecution important evidence about motive by describing the words on McVeigh's T-shirt: "The tree of liberty must be refreshed from time to time with the blood of patriots and tyrants." Hanger also testified about the envelope of clippings he discovered in the car, which included excerpts from *The Turner Diaries* and various documents about the American Revolution.

Still, the most incriminating moment in Hanger's testimony may have come at the very end. Prosecutor Scott Mendeloff asked Hanger if he had performed any experiments in advance of his testimony. Yes, he had measured the distance from the site of the Murrah building to the spot on I-35 where he had made the arrest—exactly 77.9 miles.

"Driving at the speed limit posted on April 19, 1995, how long did it take you to drive from the Murrah Building location to the place where you arrested Defendant McVeigh?"

"Seventy-five minutes and fifteen seconds," Hanger said.

"If you leave the site of the Murrah Building at 9:02 a.m. and drove the posted April 1995 speed limit on interstate highways, where would you be at 10:17?"

"It would put me at the same spot of the arrest between Mile Marker 202 and 203," Hanger testified. In other words, if McVeigh had set off the bomb and then driven north at the speed limit, he would have been exactly where Hanger found him on April 19.

The story of Hanger's arrest of McVeigh had a revealing postscript. Though McVeigh remains a reviled figure in Oklahoma, his views about the Second Amendment have been ascendant in that politically conservative state. In 2019, the state changed its laws to allow individuals twenty-one and older to carry guns without permits. If Hanger had stopped McVeigh under the new law, he could not have arrested him, because he was now allowed to carry his gun. All Hanger could have done was give McVeigh a ticket.

After Hanger, the government's case picked up speed. McVeigh's fingerprints on the papers in his car. The appearance of the crime scene. The Ryder truck axle. There wasn't grist for much cross-examination, so prosecutors clicked through several witnesses a day. Kyle Kraus was McVeigh's cousin, who was in high school when McVeigh was in the Army. At one point, out of the blue, McVeigh sent him a copy of *The Turner Diaries* and told Kraus to read it. They talked about it when McVeigh came home to Lockport for Christmas. Kraus testified that he told McVeigh the book was "very powerful, very frightening if it really did come to this."

McVeigh told his cousin that he thought a *Turner Diaries*–style conflagration was possible. "If the government continues this kind of stranglehold, it could possibly come to this because they're tightening legislation so tight," Kraus quoted McVeigh as saying.

"What could come to this?" Kraus was asked.

"A civil war," he said, "if the government continued to take guns away or continues to have a real stronghold or strong arm on the public."

Kraus's testimony illustrated one way politics had evolved between 1995 and the present. The McVeigh prosecutors put the "civil war" issue in front of the jury to show how extreme and exotic the defendant's views were. But a quarter century later, McVeigh's view was close to the conservative movement norm. This view—about the possibility of civil war—became mainstream as the passions underlying the January 6 insurrection roiled conservatives during the Biden presidency. According to an *Economist*/YouGov poll in the summer of

2022, 43 percent of Americans believe it's at least somewhat "likely" that "there will be a U.S. civil war within the next decade." More than half of Republicans feel that way, and 21 percent of "strong Republicans" believe a civil war is "very likely." McVeigh's extremism had spread to much of the contemporary Republican Party.

When Jennifer McVeigh, Tim's younger sister, took the stand, the jury heard more language that would become familiar in the Trump era. Jennifer had been close to her brother in recent years, and she was a reluctant witness. Her testimony came after a tense cultivation by the prosecutor Beth Wilkinson. Because Jennifer wanted to help her brother, Wilkinson tried to keep her testimony to a minimum, but she did make some important points for the prosecution. Wilkinson used Jennifer to identify Tim's handwriting on several key documents, including the sign that Tim had left in the getaway car stashed near the Murrah building. When Tim came home to Pendleton in late 1994, shortly after their grandfather died, Jennifer testified that he was especially angry about the Clinton administration. He borrowed Jennifer's primitive word processor to draft a letter to the American Legion.

McVeigh expressed that fury in a way that prosecutors thought would persuade the jury that his views were extreme.

"We members of the citizen's militias do not bear our arms to overthrow the Constitution, but to overthrow those who PERVERT the Constitution," McVeigh wrote. "If and when they once again draw first blood, Citizen's militias will hopefully ensure that violations of the Constitution by these power-hungry stormtroopers of the federal government will not succeed again."

At the time of McVeigh's trial, there was a familiar argument that the Second Amendment protected an individual's right to self-defense. But McVeigh was saying that the Second Amendment gave individuals an affirmative right to challenge, or even overthrow, the government itself. Here, too, McVeigh's extremism became a modern conservative norm. For example, Senator Ted Cruz has said the Second Amendment "serves as the ultimate check against governmental tyranny." Likewise, the term "stormtroopers," which is most often associated with Hitler, used to be beyond the pale in American political discourse, but that's what Rudy Giuliani, as Donald Trump's lawyer, called the FBI agents in the Robert Mueller investigation.

Overall, the government presented a circumstantial case—there was no witness who saw McVeigh set off the bomb—but a compelling one. The proof of motive—McVeigh's hatred of Clinton's federal government—was abundant. McVeigh's behavior leading up to the bombing was beyond simply suspicious. Any number of witnesses testified to his efforts to assemble the ingredients for the bomb. There was bomb residue on McVeigh's shirt when Hanger arrested him. This exchange, with Glynn Tipton, who sold racing fuel at the track in Topeka, was typical of the government's proof. Tipton wasn't the one who actually sold the fuel to McVeigh, but he remembered McVeigh's efforts well.

"Over all those years and all those races, how many times has a customer come up to you and ask you for anhydrous hydrazine?" he was asked.

"Only once," Tipton answered.

"And during all these years and all those races, how many customers have asked you to sell rocket fuel of any kind?"

"Only once."

"And during all those years and all those races, how many times has a customer come up to you to sell them two substances that when mixed together you learned would create a bomb?"

"It would be only once."

Hartzler finessed the best-known snag in his case—the issue of John Doe Number 2. Although McVeigh repeatedly told his lawyers that he went alone to rent the truck at Elliott's Body Shop, Eldon Elliott, the owner, and Vicki Beemer, his secretary, had told investigators at various points that they had seen McVeigh in the shop with a second man. But it was Tom Kessinger, the mechanic, who gave the detailed description that was the basis for the sketches of John Doe Numbers 1 and 2. Jones was salivating for the chance to cross-examine Kessinger, because he had been so sure about the presence of a second man. Anticipating this onslaught, Hartzler came up with a simple solution; he didn't call Kessinger, leaving the identification of McVeigh in the body shop to Elliott and Beemer. Those two acknowledged their previous descriptions of a second man, but said they weren't sure about it. However, they were sure about John Doe Number 1—Timothy McVeigh. It was still a loose end in the government's proof, but ultimately a minor one.

The most dramatic government witnesses—Mike and Lori Fortier—were also the most problematic. They were the only witnesses who could testify that McVeigh said he planned to bomb the Murrah building. It was devastating, virtually dispositive, evidence if it was believed. But when the married couple was first interviewed by investigators and reporters after the bombing, they denied that McVeigh played any role. And even after they decided to tell the truth—and Mike agreed to plead guilty to lying to the FBI and failing to intervene—the Fortiers were unlikely to be embraced by the jury. They acknowledged that they knew McVeigh was planning to commit this terrible act, and yet they did nothing to stop him. What kind of people could be so heartless?

Hartzler and his all-purpose deputy Aitan Goelman spent a lot of time with the Fortiers before deciding to call them as witnesses, and the prosecutors took a good cop/bad cop approach. Goelman and Fortier were almost the same age, and they had grown up with the same cultural influences; they listened to the same music and knew the same drinking games. Their politics were different—Fortier was still a libertarian of sorts—but they bonded over other generational ties. Goelman believed that Fortier was genuinely remorseful about his failure to stop McVeigh's plan. In the period before the bombing, Fortier was a meth addict who believed that McVeigh's plan was just so much talk. Lori followed Mike's lead. Goelman liked the pair, almost felt sorry for them.

Hartzler, the starchy midwesterner, took a more cautious tack. He recognized the jury might simply loathe the Fortiers too much to believe them. But he, too, became convinced that the couple saw the light and told the truth. Shortly before the trial, as Hartzler and Goelman were going over Fortier's story for the umpteenth time, Hartzler thought to ask something that was perplexing him. "When you started off this thing, you were very anti-government and you hated all of us," Hartzler said. "What happened, Mike?" Fortier pointed to Goelman and said, "Guys like him. Every time we meet, all they say is we want the truth. That's all they ever say to us. I believed him."

Still, ever-cautious, Hartzler hedged his bets. He would first call Lori Fortier to the stand. If she stood up under cross-examination, he figured that Mike would, too. If she collapsed, Hartzler could make the government's case without calling her husband at all. The stakes for Lori's testimony were high.

Not surprisingly, Hartzler made sure that Lori was suitably costumed for her public debut. With a conservative haircut and a business suit, she looked like a junior MBA rather than the drug-addled demon that McVeigh (with some justification) had described to his lawyers. The story of her life was straightforward. She met Michael when they were both in high school in Kingman, Arizona, just a decade ago, and they'd been together ever since. She followed him to Kansas during his brief military career, and then they returned to Kingman. She first met McVeigh when Mike brought him home for Thanksgiving during their time together in the Army. She now cared for the couple's two young children.

The Fortiers and McVeigh had little contact over the next four years, until he showed up at their trailer in Kingman in March 1993. Over the next two years, he was an occasional visitor, once staying in town for a few months and working for minimum wage with Mike at the True Value hardware store. Lori knew of McVeigh's political obsessions, but after September 1994, when Clinton signed the assault weapons ban, his goals became chillingly specific.

At first, Lori testified, "Tim told us what he meant by 'take action against the government' was to blow up a federal building." Mike told him he was "crazy." As for Lori, "I wasn't really sure if he was serious about it."

A few weeks later, though, "Tim specified that the building he was planning on bombing was the Oklahoma City building. And he went into detail. He diagrammed what he was planning on doing. He was going to rent a truck; and he diagrammed circles to resemble barrels in the box of a truck." She went on, "He was thinking about using racing fuel—anhydrous hydrazine."

Then Lori provided one of the indelible images of the trial. One day, while Mike was at work, she testified, "Tim like went to the cupboard and got a bunch of soup cans out, and he started diagraming what he meant by 'shape charge.' He placed the soup cans on the floor and arranged them in the same arrangement that he was going to arrange the barrels in the truck."

Hartzler didn't have to wait long to see how Lori would do on cross-examination. Jones began, reasonably enough, by pointing out that she had initially told the authorities that she thought McVeigh was not involved in the bombing. Lori acknowledged that she had lied. Then Jones went after her because she and her husband collected weapons and explosives, too.

"Did you also have access to blasting caps?" Jones asked.

"Yes," she snapped back, "that your client gave us."

Hartzler could relax. Lori was going to do fine on cross. And so did Mike Fortier a few days later. Like Lori, Fortier had cleaned up considerably for his testimony, but he acknowledged on the stand that he and Lori didn't live together at the moment. He had been "in federal custody" for twenty-one months, since he pleaded guilty to four felonies in August 1995. (He was facing as much as twenty-three years in prison, but he hoped prosecutors would ask the judge for leniency in exchange for his cooperation.) In his testimony, Mike corroborated Lori's account, but his connection with McVeigh was more extensive.

In the fall of 1994, Fortier accompanied McVeigh to Kansas to retrieve some of the guns Nichols had stolen from Roger Moore in Arkansas. They spent the first night in a motel in Amarillo, Texas.

"Well, we left Amarillo, and we were driving up to Kansas, and as we passed through Oklahoma City, Tim got off the highway saying he wanted to show me the building," Fortier testified. "We drove around the side of it, to the front of it. The front was just all really dark glass, like black glass. Tim asked me if I thought that a truck of the size he was speaking of would fit in the drop-off zone that's in front of the building. And I said, 'Yeah, you could probably fit three trucks in the front there.'"

McVeigh kept driving so he could show Fortier where he was going to leave his getaway car. "Then we turned into an alley, and he pointed out a spot where he was going to park his vehicle. I asked Tim why he wouldn't park closer. And he said he didn't want to do that, because he wanted to have a building between him and the blast." This underlined that McVeigh knew how powerful his bomb would be.

Hartzler asked Fortier why he had initially lied to investigators and journalists after the bombing. "I felt Tim was like a buffer zone," Fortier said. "If people thought he was guilty, then that would bring suspicion down on myself; but if he was innocent, then surely I would have no knowledge of it." He had lied for the most prosaic of reasons—to protect himself. None of Fortier's testimony was admirable; all of it was believable.

Toward the end of his testimony, Fortier tried to explain his relationship with McVeigh with a statement that inspired both amazement and mockery: "Well, if you don't consider what happened in Oklahoma, Tim is a good person."

Much the same was said about many of those who stormed the Capitol on January 6, 2021. Like McVeigh, many were otherwise law-abiding citizens whose zealotry led them to believe that the ends justified the means. Though a generation apart, McVeigh and his political successors belonged to a political movement that excused, or even encouraged, violence.

Hartzler interspersed testimony from victims amid the other evidence in the government's case. Matsch might have objected if the prosecution put them all together, and in any event, their appearances injected a dose of humanity when the other evidence became dry and technical. Some of the testimony came from survivors who were inside the building; others came from rescuers on the scene; Helena Garrett rushed to the building when she heard the explosion.

Garrett was a clerk with the Oklahoma State Regents of Higher Education, which was located across the street from the Murrah building. On April 19, she dropped off her sixteen-month-old son, Tevin, at the America's Kids day care just before she was due to start work at 8 a.m. After the explosion, she made her way to the Murrah building to try to find her son. "I started climbing the debris." A man pulled her down. "He said I couldn't go up there, and I told him my baby was in there." She found the place where rescuers were bringing children out of the building. "By this time, they had some white sheets, not big, though, because the legs were still showing. And they brought out these sheets, and they started bringing our babies out wrapped up in these sheets; and they laid them by my feet. And I didn't move, because I didn't want to leave our babies.

"And I was crying, and I was screaming. I said, 'Please don't lay our babies on this glass.' It was black glass everywhere. And I didn't realize that these babies they were laying down was already dead. And this man left, and he came back with this big type of broom, and he swept the glass and got it away from our babies."

Tevin's body wasn't recovered until three days later.

"Did you ever see Tevin again after that?"

"Yes, I did," Garrett said. "I saw him at the funeral home on that Monday. It had to be a closed casket because he had a severe head injury."

Jurors wept. The government rested its case.

CHAPTER 26

The Case for the Jury

McVeigh and Jones sat next to each other in the courtroom throughout the trial, but the poisonous relationship between them was evident. McVeigh chatted a little with Rob Nigh, the unofficial number two in the defense, but he exchanged few words with his lead lawyer. McVeigh knew he was under a lot of scrutiny, especially from the journalists in the courtroom, and he did his best not to react to the testimony. The victims' family members in the courtroom seethed at McVeigh's deadpan expression in response to even the most heartrending testimony; but McVeigh told his lawyers that he wanted to maintain military discipline. He refused to show any emotion at all.

Oddly enough, McVeigh was also living it up, at least comparatively speaking. In Denver, McVeigh had his most congenial accommodations since his arrest. Matsch had ordered extraordinary security precautions, which included a requirement that McVeigh be held separately from other federal inmates awaiting trial. To minimize travel time, the authorities converted a suite for visiting judges in the next-door federal building into a compound for McVeigh. He had a king-sized bed, a bathroom with a shower, a conference room, an exercise room, and a flat-screen television. He was given a $14 daily food allowance (supplemented by contributions from his lawyers), which he used to feast on the fast food he loved, especially from Pizza Hut. Occasionally, he splurged on a delivery of "Cowboy Steak" from a local diner. "I've never lived so well," McVeigh told Jones.

Behind the scenes, Jones was still trying to accommodate McVeigh's demands. McVeigh wouldn't allow Jones to blame the bombing on Nichols or Fortier, and he wouldn't let Jones point the finger at foreign terrorists, either. McVeigh knew that he had received no help from the white supremacists at Elohim City, in eastern Oklahoma, but he did permit Jones to try to call some attention to that red herring. Specifically, McVeigh let Jones try to bring the strange tale of Carol Howe before the jury.

Howe was an Oklahoma aristocrat—a twenty-four-year-old former debutante and daughter of Robert Howe, who was president of Mapco, a Fortune 500 energy company in Tulsa. In the early 1990s, Carol fell in with a group of neo-Nazis and skinheads. At the same time, she served as a secret informant for the Bureau of Alcohol, Tobacco and Firearms, and for a time she infiltrated Elohim City. After the bombing of the Murrah building, she told her handlers that John Does Number 1 and 2 resembled two men she knew in Elohim City as Pete and Tony. Because her information was so vague, Judge Matsch declined to let her testify. (There remained a good deal of mystery about Howe's true loyalties. She was later charged, along with her boyfriend, with running a telephone hotline for "white warriors" that passed along plans for bombings in fifteen cities. The boyfriend was convicted; Howe was acquitted. She later changed her name and moved away from Oklahoma.)

Jones had an even more far-fetched idea to accommodate McVeigh's oft-stated desire to activate an "Army." Christi O'Connor, a local television reporter in Fort Worth, had been especially aggressive in trying to obtain an interview with McVeigh, even sending Jones a video advocating for herself. Jones thought he could work a kind of jujitsu with O'Connor. He would allow her to interview McVeigh so he could express his views about Waco and gun rights, which might even attract sympathy from some jurors. Like Earl Turner in *The Turner Diaries*, McVeigh hoped his ideas would provoke the public to revolt against the government.

If McVeigh talked about his political agenda to O'Connor on camera, Jones surmised that the government would then play the video in its rebuttal case as proof of McVeigh's motive. Jones, in turn, would argue to the jury that McVeigh's statements to O'Connor were simply good-faith expressions of political belief—which is what McVeigh wanted the jury, and the country, to hear. Jones had Scott Anderson, the team's indefatigable paralegal, drive all night from Oklahoma to Denver to relay the offer to McVeigh—who promptly rejected it. As Jones wrote in a letter to McVeigh, "You turn it down with a single sentence and no explanation. The reason you turned it down is because you perceive that since it involves a media contact that it is something that I want you to do because there is some benefit to me." The portrayal of Jones as a media whore by his detractors on the defense team had sundered the relationship between lawyer and client.

By presenting such a streamlined case, Hartzler left Jones with a dilemma. Jones had assumed that the government would call lots of witnesses, like Tom Kessinger, who could be cross-examined effectively. Kessinger had given the sketch artist detailed information about John Doe Numbers 1 (McVeigh) and 2. Kessinger had since recognized that he mixed up the dates, and the man he thought was John Doe Number 2 had actually rented a truck on a different day. Jones had the option of calling Kessinger himself. But what good would that do? Jones would then be putting before the jury a witness who now recognized that he had made an initial mistake about John Doe Number 2. Jones passed on calling Kessinger.

Since the government had the burden of proof, Jones wasn't legally required to prove anything; but jurors are human beings with common sense. They were certainly going to ask themselves, if McVeigh didn't bomb the Murrah building, who did? Starting with his opening statement, Jones's fundamental problem was that he never presented an alternative theory. Instead, Jones limited himself to a handful of witnesses who chipped away at the government's timeline of events. Two witnesses said they thought they saw a Ryder truck at the Dreamland Motel in Junction City, Kansas, on Easter Sunday 1995. (McVeigh didn't rent the truck until the next day.) Another witness said she saw McVeigh in Junction City on Easter, at a time when the government argued that he was stashing the getaway car in Oklahoma City. In the days after the bombing, the government had tapped the phone in the Fortiers' trailer, and Jones made good use of Mike's dumb boasts. In a conversation with his brother, Mike said he thought he could leverage his connection to McVeigh into a book or movie deal. "I can tell a fable, I can tell stories all day long," Mike told his brother. "The less I say now, the bigger the price will be later."

Jones also put the "extra leg" hypothesis in front of the jury. A British pathologist testified that, based on his review of the medical examiner's records, there was a leg that belonged to no known victim. Accordingly, he said, there was a 169th victim, who was potentially the real bomber. (The government later suggested that the extra leg belonged to a victim who was buried earlier with a wrong leg, which, given the extent of damage to the bodies of the victims, was possible; still, the matter was never definitively resolved.)

Finally, there was a defense witness who took some of the sheen off the performance of the FBI. Overall, Oklahoma City represented a tremendous success for the FBI—the prompt arrest of a guilty suspect, followed by the accumulation of comprehensive evidence of his guilt. This was especially important to the Bureau after the twin disasters of Ruby Ridge and Waco. But shortly after McVeigh's trial began, the inspector general of the Department of Justice released a report critical of the work of the FBI crime lab, including in the Oklahoma City bombing. Regarding the analysis of the bomb residue at the scene, the report stated that an FBI expert "repeatedly reached conclusions that incriminated the defendants without a scientific basis." Frederic Whitehurst, the FBI whistleblower who prompted the investigation, testified for McVeigh in his defense case, and his analysis clearly stung the prosecution. But since Hartzler's team didn't place much reliance on the scientific analysis to prove McVeigh's guilt, the effect of the testimony was minor.

After just four days, the defense rested.

Larry Mackey, the workaholic prosecutor from Indianapolis, gave the first closing statement for the government. It was, like Mackey himself, solid and competent, a thorough review of an extraordinary amount of evidence. It's common for prosecutors to say in summation that their proof is "overwhelming," but the evidence here backed up Mackey's assertion. In one respect, though, this quarter-century-old jury address has a contemporary relevance.

The issue was motive. Mackey was careful to say that McVeigh had a First Amendment right to believe and say what he wanted. "Make no mistake about it," he said, "in America, everybody has a right to their beliefs, have a right to think and say what they do. This is not a prosecution of Tim McVeigh for his political beliefs."

But Mackey went on to assert that even though words and beliefs were protected under the Constitution, they could still be relevant evidence in a criminal prosecution. "His Honor will tell you, I expect, that evidence about someone's state of mind, their political beliefs, those statements about political tendencies, while they are protected under the First Amendment, nonetheless in criminal court can be relevant evidence for you to consider. They can help you decide the question: What would motivate someone to do a crime of this dimension? You can consider and you should consider what Tim McVeigh was saying to himself and to others in writings and conversations about his hatred for the federal government and how he would give voice to that hatred in his actions."

To put it another way, Mackey said that words matter—and they can affect behavior, including criminal conduct. The First Amendment protected McVeigh's words just as the Constitution shielded the language of incitement used by Limbaugh and Gingrich—their talk of violent revolution and of their "sick" adversaries.

Mackey's argument resonated in the twenty-first century. Donald Trump embraced and advocated violence against his adversaries. He usually did it in offhand, almost jocular ways, as when he encouraged his supporters at a rally to "knock the hell" out of protesters. On January 6, his admonition to his supporters to "fight like hell" provided a more sinister, and consequential, example. The larger point held for both eras: the right-wing embrace of the language of violence spurred the actual violence that followed.

The mythology of the courtroom invests lawyers with almost magical powers. If they say the right words, they can win any case. But this isn't true. There are hopeless cases. For the defense, *United States v. McVeigh* was one. Nothing Stephen Jones could have said in his summation would have changed the outcome.

Still, Jones treated his summation like an erudition contest. He said, "Forty years ago this very month, there was a major literary event in this country. James Gould Cozzens' great novel, 'By Love Possessed,' was published. And for people of my generation and my mother and father's generation, and I'm sure some but not all of you, that novel remains with us today, though its author has long since been forgotten. The book was an instantaneous best seller. It stayed at the top of the *New York Times* best seller list for over a year. It was a *Reader's Digest* condensed book. It won for the author not only the Howell prize but a cover story on *Time* magazine. And eventually as you might expect, it was made into a movie and then translated into some 14 or 15 languages throughout the world." The book talked about the conflict between emotion and logic.

Jones's five-hour-long summation was not all pretentious twaddle. He made some legitimate points. The Fortiers were dubious characters, perhaps unworthy of belief. Political advocacy is not a crime. The FBI lab made mistakes. The *Spotlight* phone card did not identify who made the calls. Perhaps James Nichols, Terry's brother, dialed some of them. The eyewitness identifications at Elliott's Body Shop were shaky. It didn't make sense that McVeigh used a pseudonym to rent the Ryder truck but used his own name to register at the Dreamland Motel. (It didn't make sense, but that's what McVeigh did.) Despite speaking for hours, Jones didn't even address, much less refute, the bulk of the government's evidence. He couldn't.

Scott Mendeloff, the prosecutor from Chicago, gave the prosecution's response, and he rambled around in the voluminous proof in the case. Still, as the jurors said later (as jurors often do), the lawyers didn't matter that much. The evidence did.

Matsch instructed the jury on the morning of Friday, May 30. The jury began deliberating at about 9:30 and spent the rest of the day. Matsch ordered the panel to deliberate both days of the weekend. They returned their verdict just after lunch, at 1:32 p.m, on Monday, June 2.

The moment when a verdict is read is usually one of extraordinary tension. No one—no one—knows what the verdict will be. But even with the enormous stakes of the case, this announcement was curiously lacking in drama. Considering the length of the trial, the jury didn't deliberate very long, just twenty-three hours over four days. They had no questions for the judge. They gave every sign of viewing their job as a straightforward one. There could only be one outcome.

"Members of the jury," Matsch said, "have you reached a verdict?"

"Yes, we have," they all said at once.

The foreperson handed the verdict form to the clerk, who passed it to the judge. Matsch read in a steady voice: "In the United States District Court for the District of Colorado, Criminal Action No. 96-CR-68, United States of America vs. Timothy James McVeigh. We, the jury, upon our oaths unanimously find as follows: Count 1, conspiracy to use a weapon of mass destruction, guilty." He said guilty ten more times, for the total of eleven counts. McVeigh never changed expression.

Many judges offer profuse thanks to jurors in high-profile cases, but Matsch, crusty as always, offered more admonition than gratitude. This jury had more work to do—a matter of life and death. "I specifically instruct all of you, jurors and alternate jurors alike, that you must not discuss the verdict or the deliberations resulting in the verdict at any time before the penalty questions in this case are addressed and resolved," Matsch said.

The penalty phase followed immediately—the mini-trial to determine whether McVeigh would be sentenced to death or life in prison without the opportunity for parole. Here, the government presented "victim impact" testimony, where witnesses sought to explain the pain they had endured. The three days of the prosecutors' presentation were nearly unbearable, so great was the grief and horror on display.

David Klaus, who lost his adult daughter: "I think about her first thing in the morning, and the last thing I think about at night is Kim and the fact I'm never going to see her again and trying to imagine how I get on with life without her, which is going to be extraordinarily difficult." Sharon Medearis, who lost her husband of thirty years: "Emotionally I'm home alone every day. I have nobody at my house since Kathryn is grown. Physically I'm down to the 80 pounds range. I find myself real tired. It's extremely hard."

Pamela Whicher, the widow of Secret Service agent Alan Whicher, who had worked on President Clinton's detail, on their son's reaction to his father's death: "He came to me several days after we got back from the funeral and said, 'Mom, I'm going to be the man now and take care of you.' He's 12 years old."

Laura Kennedy, who worked on the third floor of the Murrah building and was injured herself, on the loss of her five-month-old son in the day care center: "Blake was my life. For months after the bombing, I didn't care what happened to me. I didn't care if I lived or died. I didn't care about my physical injuries from the bombing or any kind of physical problems I was having. It was suggested that I go on maybe some antidepression medicine, and I didn't care because I wanted to be depressed. I had a good reason to be depressed. I had lost the most important thing in my life."

Susan Walton, who was visiting the federal credit union on the third floor at the time of the bombing, described her injuries: "Well, I had a basal skull fracture, nerve damage behind both eyes. I had a broken nose, six fractures in my face. I lost six teeth. I had a ruptured spleen, and both legs were badly damaged from the knees down." Katherine Youngblood told of nursing her injured husband for twenty-three days, until he died in the hospital from his injuries. Jerry Flowers, a rescue worker, described his efforts on the scene: "There was a pool of water like a large bathtub, if you will, and all I could see was this lady's head sticking up above the water screaming, 'Don't let me drown.'"

Sue Mallonee, an epidemiologist from the Oklahoma Department of Health, summarized the casualties from the bombing. "There were 168 deaths, 167 of those deaths were a direct result of the bombing," she testified, "163 were in the Murrah building. Of those, 118 were employees of the building, 15 were children in the day-care center and 30 were visitors to the building, including four children. There were two deaths in the Water Resource Board. There was one death in the Athenian Building, which was directly across the street from the Murrah Building, and there was one death in the parking lot of a woman walking to the Athenian Building." Three victims were pregnant. The indirect death was that of Rebecca Anderson, a rescue worker who was killed by falling debris in the aftermath.

There are probably few more difficult challenges in law than attempting to persuade a jury that has just convicted your client of mass murder to spare his life. Wisely, Jones had ceded preparation for this part of the case to Dick Burr and Mandy Welch, the Texas-based husband-and-wife team who had long careers defending capital cases. But none were as tough as this one.

The task was even more difficult because the defense was advancing two different agendas. The first was the conventional approach in a death penalty case. "You will hear about the qualities and characteristics and traits of this young man who is not yet 30," Burr told the jury in his opening statement. "You will hear that he's a very bright man, did well in school, a person who colleagues in the military counted on to take their weekend duty, to take their extra duty, to come pick them up from local bars, because he didn't drink, he didn't get drunk." Indeed, as Burr put it, McVeigh was a person "whom you will not be able to dismiss easily as a monster or a demon, who could be your son, who could be your brother, who could be your grandson, who loved his country, who served it, who had a number of admirable human qualities, a number of vulnerable human qualities, and a number of frailties, just like any of us." This was the standard death penalty plea: the defendant was not all bad.

The other side of Burr's argument owed more to McVeigh's individual circumstances—and his wishes about his own case. Burr offered a sanded-down version of the necessity defense—the idea that the FBI's attack on the Waco compound was so egregious that McVeigh was compelled to strike back. "We will not be presenting to you a trial about Waco," Burr said. "We are presenting to you what Mr. McVeigh believed happened at Waco, because that's what's important in the calculus that is before you." As McVeigh saw it, according to Burr, "the government murdered people at Waco. The federal government, whom we rely on to protect us, to serve us, to be our servant, had turned the tables and had become the master and indeed, as Mr. McVeigh believed, had declared war on the American people."

In quick succession, Burr called ten veterans who served with McVeigh in the Army. As one said, "At the time, Sergeant McVeigh was an outstanding soldier. I mean he did what he was told. He anticipated what had to be done. He took pride in his work." For the most part, the prosecutors eschewed much cross-examination, noting only that none of these former soldiers had had any contact with McVeigh since 1991, six years earlier. At one point, though, all the praise for McVeigh proved too much for Beth Wilkinson, the most combative of the prosecutors, who also happened to be a former Army captain herself. Crossing one of these character witnesses, Wilkinson all but sneered, "You know that Mr. McVeigh flunked out of Special Forces after two days, right?"

After the Army witnesses, the defense case took a turn for the bizarre. Matsch allowed Burr and Welch to call a pair of journalists to testify about their investigations of the Ruby Ridge and Waco debacles. Both James Pate, who worked for *Soldier of Fortune*, and Dick Reavis, a freelancer, had written scathingly about the behavior of the FBI and ATF, and they repeated their criticisms for the jury. The jury even watched *Day 51*, one of McVeigh's favorite conspiracy theory documentaries about Waco. Matsch told the jury that they were hearing this evidence not to determine what happened in Waco, but rather to learn what McVeigh had absorbed about the events there. But as the testimony unfolded, it sounded like the FBI was on trial and the McVeigh prosecutors were the Bureau's defense lawyers.

Concluding his cross-examination of Pate, Pat Ryan, the U.S. attorney, asked, "Randy Weaver, the Branch Davidians, were all afforded due process of law, were they not?"

"I believe they were, sir, yes, sir," said Pate.

Jones shot back with the names of the two Weaver relatives who were killed by the FBI in the siege at Ruby Ridge.

"Were Sammy Weaver and Vicki Weaver afforded due process of law?"

"No, sir. They were shot dead."

The jury greeted this strange sideshow with puzzled expressions. They had a similar reaction to another defense witness—Michelle Rauch, who had come across McVeigh in Waco as a student journalist at SMU. The idea of calling her was to show the sincerity of McVeigh's interest in the Waco story. But the effect was just baffling, including to Rauch herself. The defense closed as death penalty cases often do—with the defendant's parents.

Neither the prosecution nor defense wanted to explore the complexities of the McVeigh family's history—nothing about Mildred's escapes to Florida or Bill's sullen detachment. McVeigh's mother made a short statement: "Tim was a loving son and a happy child as he grew up. He was a child any mother could be proud of. I still to this very day cannot believe he could have caused this devastation. There are too many unanswered questions and loose ends. He has seen human loss in the past, and it has torn him apart. He is not the monster he has been portrayed as. He is also a mother and father's son, a brother to two sisters, a cousin to many, and a friend to many more. Yes, I am pleading for my son's life. He is a human being, just as we all are. You must make this very difficult decision on my son's life or death, and I hope and pray that God helps you make the right one."

For Bill's testimony, the defense had compiled a collection of photos and videos of happy times in Tim's early years.

"Do you love the Tim in this courtroom?" Bill was asked.

"Yes, I do," he said.

"Do you want him to stay alive?"

"Yes, I do."

There was no cross-examination from the government.

CHAPTER 27

Unconquerable

Supreme Court precedent establishes that potential jurors who are morally opposed to the death penalty in all circumstances must be excluded from serving in capital cases. All jurors must be at least open to the possibility of imposing the ultimate sanction; in the macabre legal shorthand, these jurors are known as "death qualified." As the prosecutor Beth Wilkinson put it when she faced twelve such jurors on the morning of June 12, "Each and every one of you told us during voir dire that you believed that the death penalty was appropriate, a just punishment, in certain circumstances." Her question, then, was simple: If McVeigh's crime—the premeditated murder of 168 men, women, and children—didn't deserve the death penalty, what did? "This is the crime that the death penalty was designed for," Wilkinson said. "If not 168 people, then how many? Would 20 children have been enough? Would 10 law enforcement agents have been sufficient? Would 25 visitors to the Social Security office have been necessary to warrant the death penalty?"

Dick Burr, for the defense, tried to answer those questions, and he argued with restraint and humility. He did not diminish the magnitude of McVeigh's crimes, nor minimize the pain of the victims' loved ones. He sought understanding for his client, if not forgiveness.

"When Michael Fortier said from the witness stand, Tim McVeigh is a good man except for this, I'm sure most of you cringed. I did," Burr said. "We cringed because, of course, the 'except for this' is virtually everything; but it is not totally everything. There is still a good man who, from no ill motive, perhaps from a misperception, perhaps not, came to have certain impassioned and passionate beliefs about his government, about a government that he believed was acting like England in the 18th century, whose mission had turned upon its own people." Jones followed up with a plea for understanding McVeigh's anger at the government: "Millions of Americans share Mr. McVeigh's views. They're as old as the struggle that led to the ratification of the Constitution. Mr. McVeigh acted on them." As a political matter, Jones had a point. Subsequent events proved millions of Americans did share McVeigh's views and saw their struggle against the federal government as akin to that of the patriots in the American Revolution. But in the context of this trial, with this evidence and death toll, Jones's point was unlikely to garner sympathy from the jury.

Indeed, given the last word, Joe Hartzler for the prosecution turned around the argument about political protest: "Timothy McVeigh bombed the Murrah Building because he was angry about Waco and therefore . . . what? Therefore what? Where do we go with that argument? What it appears from Mr. Jones' argument this morning is he's really asking you to sort of endorse these beliefs." It was a simple, almost obvious point. Protest—angry words and gestures—is always permissible under our system. But violence, especially murderous violence, is not. This debate between Jones and Hartzler—between the-ends-justify-the-means and the rule of law—would play out in other forums, with more uncertain outcomes, in later years. For their part, though, the McVeigh jurors had no trouble figuring out which side they were on.

As in the guilt phase, the jurors' deliberation about the death penalty was brief. They took overnight to think about it and came back on the afternoon of June 13 with a death sentence for Timothy McVeigh.

The formal imposition of sentence took place in a brief proceeding on August 14. The occasion was just a formality because, in light of the jury's determination, Judge Matsch was required to sentence McVeigh to be executed. Still, it was a moment of some drama because for the first time since he was arrested more than two years earlier, McVeigh was going to have an opportunity to make a public statement. He prepared with care, but he ultimately returned to a quotation that he had shared many times with his attorneys. McVeigh rose from his seat and stepped to the lectern between the prosecution and defense tables.

"If the Court please," McVeigh said in an even tone, "I wish to use the words of Justice Brandeis dissenting in Olmstead to speak for me. He wrote, 'Our Government is the potent, the omnipresent teacher. For good or for ill, it teaches the whole people by its example.' That's all I have."

McVeigh was consistent. He bombed the Murrah building to call attention to his belief that Bill Clinton's federal government had taught the wrong lessons to the public. In McVeigh's view, Clinton's government was not just an omnipresent teacher but a malevolent one. With sinister determination and will, McVeigh had forced the world to pay attention to his protest. In light of the outcome of the trial, he was compelled now to trust others to take up the cause.

Matsch scheduled the trial of Terry Nichols to begin three months after the McVeigh proceedings concluded. The prosecutors were exhausted and homesick, and most wanted to resume their prior lives. But after Janet Reno made a special trip to Denver to lobby Larry Mackey to stay on, he took over for Hartzler as lead prosecutor. Still, as important as the Nichols case was, the prosecutors and their witnesses lacked the same focus and passion as they did against McVeigh. Though the formal charges against the two defendants were identical, it was clear to everyone on all sides that Nichols was less culpable. No one on the prosecution team thought Nichols was innocent—far from it—but few believed Nichols would have become involved in such a monstrous conspiracy if McVeigh had not talked him into it.

And there was the point that Michael Tigar, Nichols's lead lawyer, made over and over: Nichols wasn't there. When McVeigh rented the truck in Junction City and then set off the bomb at the Murrah building, Nichols was at home with his wife, Marife, in Herington, Kansas. And though Nichols helped plan the bombing, there was a real possibility that he refused to participate at the last minute. That didn't mean that Nichols should have been acquitted, but the ambiguity about his role made the case less than overwhelming.

Then, of course, there was Tigar himself—the modern-day Clarence Darrow who dominated the courtroom. The law professor took charge as soon as jury selection began. The first prospective juror was a woman named Niki Deutchman, who worked as a midwife. Tigar charmed her, chatting with her about the Lamaze method. On her questionnaire, Deutchman said she distrusted lawyers, so Tigar asked why.

"It's okay, I can take it," he said.

"I haven't seen *you* manipulating the system," she said.

"We hardly know each other," Tiger bantered back.

One courtroom observer compared their interplay to a Spencer Tracy–Katharine Hepburn movie. Deutchman was a bit eccentric—she had an interest in "energetic healing"—and the prosecutors weighed using one of their challenges to remove her. But on the other hand, prosecutors liked that she supported the Southern Poverty Law Center, a noted adversary of the militia movement. In the end, she not only remained on the jury but became its forewoman.

The prosecution's case against Nichols began much like the one against McVeigh, with descriptions of the magnitude of the damage to the Murrah building and the people inside. But there were major differences as well. There was no reason for the government to call Charlie Hanger, the trooper who arrested McVeigh just after the bombing. The core of the case against Nichols was his role in obtaining the ingredients for the bomb—large quantities of fertilizer from farm supply stores in Kansas and explosives and blasting caps from the robbery of the quarry near Nichols's home. In addition, when Nichols voluntarily gave an interview to the FBI on the day after the bombing, he made incriminating and contradictory statements. He acknowledged knowing and traveling with McVeigh, as well as their grievances about the federal government, and he also lied (and then admitted his lies) about his purchases of fertilizer. In addition, Lana Padilla, Nichols's ex-wife, testified about the letter he left behind for McVeigh when Nichols went to the Philippines. The letter urged McVeigh to "Go for it!!"

Still, there were weaknesses in the government's case. Mike Fortier—who described in detail McVeigh's plans for the bombing—testified in the Nichols trial that McVeigh and Nichols were close friends, but Fortier never heard Nichols say that he joined in McVeigh's plan for Oklahoma City. Prosecutors also relied more on problematic scientific evidence than in the McVeigh case. They had to establish that the specific ingredients tied to Nichols matched the residue at the Murrah building. But this proof ran into the inspector general's damning report about the work of the FBI lab. As a result, Tigar raised legitimate questions about the reliability of the evidence linking Nichols to the crime scene.

There was reason to believe that Matsch, too, had doubts about the Nichols case. He made several rulings that made a death sentence less likely. Unlike in the McVeigh case, the judge allowed Carol Howe, the debutante-turned-white supremacist, to testify about McVeigh's possible appearance at the Elohim City compound. (Wilkinson did a strong job of cross-examining her, but Howe's story represented another loose end for the prosecution.) Matsch also limited the amount of victim testimony that the prosecution could present, depriving the government of some of the emotional wallop from the McVeigh case.

Over six long days of deliberations, the jurors parsed the evidence with care and reached a reasonable compromise. They convicted Nichols of conspiring to bomb the Murrah building, but acquitted him of the bombing itself. In light of the conspiracy conviction, Nichols was still eligible for the death penalty, so there was a penalty phase hearing. Family members of victims again offered heartbreaking testimony, but this time the jury came back with a split judgment. Seven of twelve jurors favored a death sentence, but federal law requires unanimity in capital cases. Matsch thus sentenced Nichols to life in prison without the possibility of parole. After the verdict, Niki Deutchman, the jury forewoman, gave a marathon news conference that demonstrated that the government was lucky to win any kind of conviction. "The government wasn't able to prove beyond a reasonable doubt a whole lot of the evidence," she said. "The government didn't do a good job of proving Terry Nichols was greatly involved in this." Following the formal imposition of the sentence, the Bureau of Prisons sent Nichols to the "supermax"—the maximum security prison in Florence, Colorado, which is reserved for the most dangerous federal inmates.

McVeigh was already there. The rules at Florence required prisoners to remain in their cells twenty-three hours a day, with a single hour for recreation in small concrete yards with wire-mesh ceilings. McVeigh adapted to his new surroundings with relative ease. He devoted much of his time to nursing his grievances against Stephen Jones. In the final days of the trial, Randy Coyne, the Oklahoma law professor who was Jones's primary antagonist on the fractious defense team, made a surprising discovery on the office fax machine—a draft book contract between Jones and Doubleday publishers. The contract guaranteed Jones a $600,000 advance for a book about his representation of McVeigh. Coyne took this news to McVeigh, who became convinced that the book contract meant that Jones had a conflict of interest in his representation of him. As a kind of preemptive strike against Jones's book, McVeigh decided to cooperate with Lou Michel and Dan Herbeck, the *Buffalo News* reporters, for their own book. As it turned out, Jones never wrote the book for Doubleday, though he did write another, for far less money, for a different publisher. In the Michel and Herbeck book, McVeigh vented his grievances against Jones. In another gibe at Jones, when McVeigh finally decided to do a television interview, he chose someone who was outside Jones's circle of celebrity courtiers—Ed Bradley, of *60 Minutes*.

McVeigh secured a new set of lawyers, and they argued to Matsch that McVeigh deserved a new trial because Jones had conflicts of interest and thus rendered his client ineffective assistance of counsel, in violation of the Sixth Amendment. Matsch rightly rejected these arguments. The book deal was not itself a conflict of interest; Jones was no less likely to advocate for McVeigh because he planned to write a book. And while Jones may have made some questionable decisions as McVeigh's lawyer, he and his squadron of colleagues certainly provided a defense consistent with constitutional guarantees. After McVeigh's conviction, the legal process moved slowly, but it did develop an inexorable momentum as the months and years passed. The verdict and death sentence were upheld at every stage.

The prison authorities in Florence put McVeigh on "bombers row"—the wing with the most notorious inmates. He was next door to Ted Kaczynski, the Unabomber, and near Ramzi Yousef, the mastermind of the World Trade Center bombing in 1993. The three men's stories were strangely intertwined, and they struck up a friendship of sorts. (The Trade Center bombing led many to speculate that the Oklahoma City bombing was the work of foreign terrorists like Yousef, and Jones had attempted to show links between Nichols and Yousef in the Philippines, where Yousef hid out. Merrick Garland had to give up his hopes of trying McVeigh because his superiors summoned him back to Washington to supervise the floundering Unabomber investigation.) Characteristically, McVeigh downplayed Kaczynski's intelligence, compared with his own. In a letter to journalists Michel and Herbeck, McVeigh said Kaczynski "isn't as smart as he thinks he is." In his own letter to Michel, Kaczynski was more generous about McVeigh, writing, "On a personal level, I like McVeigh, and I imagine most people would like him. He was easily the most outgoing of all the inmates on our range of cells and had excellent social skills. . . . It is my impression that McVeigh is very intelligent. He thinks seriously about the problems of our society, especially as they related to the issue of individual freedom, and to the extent that he expressed his ideas to me, they seemed rational and sensible."

Terry Nichols was also on bombers row for a time, before he was moved to a different part of the prison. He largely kept to himself. He never joined in the chatting between adjacent cells and exercise yards. Over time, Nichols cut off contact with family, friends, and even his lawyers. For years, he spoke to no one at all.

Appeals in death penalty cases can often last for a decade or even longer. At the time of McVeigh's sentencing, in 1997, there had not been an execution of a federal prisoner since 1963. The legal mechanisms for capital punishment by the United States government were untested, so if McVeigh had been so inclined, he probably could have delayed his own execution almost indefinitely. But after George W. Bush became president in 2001, John Ashcroft, the new attorney general, announced that he wanted to resume federal executions, starting with the Oklahoma City bomber. McVeigh weighed the idea of continuing his legal fight and decided instead on martyrdom. He told his new lawyers he was tired of the legal process and didn't want to be in prison anymore. He had made his point with the bombing, and now he was ready to move on. After moving to the federal prison in Terre Haute, Indiana, where the federal government had built a lethal injection chamber, McVeigh announced he was giving up his appeals and allowing his own execution to proceed. The Bureau of Prisons set the date for May 16, 2001.

Glitches in the FBI's record-keeping scotched the first date. Just six days before the scheduled execution, the Bureau announced that it had located four thousand pages of records from the bombing investigation that should have been turned over to the defense. The massive, nationwide investigation had produced more documents than the FBI could properly handle, and its system broke down. Ashcroft ordered a thirty-day delay so McVeigh's lawyers could review the documents. The lawyers found nothing that would have changed the outcome of the trial. A new execution date was set for June 11.

In his final days, McVeigh kept up a steady stream of letters, mostly to Michel and Herbeck of *The Buffalo News*, but also to the author Gore Vidal, who wrote haughty articles for *Vanity Fair* that were vaguely sympathetic to McVeigh. (Vidal wrote, "He did not complain about his fate; took responsibility for what he was thought to have done; did not beg for mercy as our always sadistic Media require.") McVeigh continued to see the bombing as a soldier's duty, if one with regrettable consequences. "I am sorry these people had to lose their lives," he wrote to the Buffalo pair, "but that's the nature of the beast. It's understood going in what the human toll will be." The same smug self-satisfaction that he had displayed toward his lawyers came through at the end as well. He decided not to offer last words, but instead wrote out a "Final Written Statement." It was the famous poem "Invictus," by the British author William Ernest Henley. The work displayed McVeigh's pride in his accomplishment. The poem begins:

Out of the night that covers me,
Black as the pit from pole to pole,

I thank whatever gods may be
For my unconquerable soul.

It concludes with the famous words "I am the master of my fate, / I am the captain of my soul."

On the day before the execution, McVeigh was moved from death row in the Terre Haute penitentiary to a cell in the "death house," a one-story redbrick building that had been retrofitted as a lethal injection chamber. When given an opportunity to shower there, the water was cold at first. "This is cruel and unusual punishment," McVeigh quipped to the guards. Shortly after midnight on June 11, he received his last meal: two pints of mint chocolate chip ice cream. At 4:29 a.m., Rob Nigh, who had been on his defense team from the beginning, and Nathan Chambers, an appellate lawyer, visited with him for about twenty minutes.

At 6:18 a.m., McVeigh was placed in restraints in his cell, and a prison chaplain administered last rights. He was then moved to the execution chamber and strapped to the gurney at 6:34 a.m. He displayed no emotion.

At 6:57 a.m., the spectators were allowed to file into the observation area, from which they could watch through a one-way mirror. There was space for ten journalists and a handful of victims' family members. In an unprecedented step, the Justice Department reactivated the closed-circuit transmission that had been used during the trial to broadcast the execution to a conference room at the Oklahoma City airport. After a brief malfunction with the broadcast equipment, the picture came through at 7:05 a.m. About 230 victims' relatives came to watch.

The execution protocol called for the application of three poisons in succession, and they were administered at 7:08 a.m., 7:10 a.m., and 7:12 a.m. McVeigh was pronounced dead at 7:14 a.m.

The three-month anniversary of McVeigh's execution was September 11, 2001.

EPILOGUE

McVeigh's Legacy

(1)

McVeigh wanted the Oklahoma City bombing to set off a broad rebellion to overthrow the federal government—the way Earl Turner's attack on the FBI building led to the civil war depicted in the novel *The Turner Diaries*. That didn't happen. But neither did McVeigh's movement die in the wreckage of the Murrah building. His brand of right-wing extremism lives on, even thrives, to this day.

In the immediate aftermath of the bombing in 1995, the movement demonstrated its resilience. Rather than retreat after the horror in Oklahoma City, the extremists reloaded. As the historian Kathleen Belew observed, "The bombing launched an almost immediate and widespread wave of violence as the militia movement, and the broader white power movement, took action around the country." The groups went by different names. There were the "militias" in various states, of course, but also the "Patriots," the "Order," and "Freemen." They shared an agenda much like McVeigh's—always centered on gun rights, but also featuring a free-floating hostility to the federal government and its supposed plans for a New World Order. In this pre-internet era, the individuals didn't have many opportunities to meet and collaborate. They connected sporadically, and their alliances were built more on what they read and saw rather than what they could do together. Their members sometimes found each other at gun shows and read *The Spotlight* and *Soldier of Fortune*, but most operated semi-independently and came up with their own plans for action.

Despite these obstacles, the extremists persisted. In July 1995, three months after the bombing, Michael Gray, who was a longtime friend of Randy Weaver's (the central figure in the Ruby Ridge saga), was arrested in Washington State for plotting to bomb the federal courthouse in Spokane. He had stolen blueprints to the courthouse and planned to build a fertilizer bomb like McVeigh's. In September 1995, Charles Polk was arrested after trying to buy large quantities of C-4 explosives to bomb IRS buildings throughout Texas. Two months later, Willie Lampley, who was a leader of the Oklahoma militia, and three others were charged with conspiracy to bomb gay bars, abortion clinics, and an Anti-Defamation League office in Texas. Georgia militia members were arrested for stockpiling bombs. Militia members from West Virginia, Ohio, and Pennsylvania were charged in a plot to blow up the FBI's national fingerprint center. On April 12, 1996, a white supremacist named Larry Shoemake shot eleven Black people, killing one, in Jackson, Mississippi, before dying in a fire he had set. (*The Turner Diaries* "was like an eye opener for him," his wife later said.) On July 27, 1996, Eric Rudolph, a white supremacist, set off a bomb at Atlanta's Centennial Park during the Olympic Games. Over the next two years, he detonated three more bombs, at gay bars and abortion clinics, and then disappeared into the woods. (He was caught in 2003.) On June 7, 1998, three white men killed James Byrd Jr., a Black man, by dragging him behind a pickup truck in Jasper, Texas. "We're starting *The Turner Diaries* early," one of the killers was reported to have said during the assault. Apart from the Olympic bombing and the Byrd murder, these investigations drew little national attention, largely because they took place far from big cities, with their concentrations of media outlets. It was not a full-fledged national rebellion, as in *The Turner Diaries*, like McVeigh wanted, but he did set off a string of attacks on his enemies.

In public statements, some members of the movement defended the Oklahoma City bombing. Like McVeigh, William Pierce, the author of *The Turner Diaries*, embraced the bombing as a tough but necessary step. "Terrorism is a nasty business," he said on shortwave radio ten days after the bombing. "Most of its victims are innocent people. Some of the office workers who died in the Federal Building in Oklahoma City may have been as much against the Clinton government as were those who set off the bomb. But terrorism is a form of warfare, and in war most of the victims are noncombatants." Others, at least initially, took a more cautious tack. On June 15, 1995, less than two months after the bombing, a Senate committee held a hearing on the militia movement. In their testimony, Norman Olson and Robert Fletcher, of the Michigan Militia; Linda Thompson, of Ohio; and John Trochmann, of Montana, all defended the basic concepts of militias—private armies organized to defend their freedom—but they denounced the Oklahoma City bombing and rejected the use of violence except in self-defense.

After the Senate hearing, however, a new narrative from the extremist groups took hold—that McVeigh had been framed by the government, which had itself orchestrated the bombing, as a provocation to impose gun control. Olson said government agents had set off a second blast inside the Murrah building to cause maximum damage. Thompson, who had produced the video *Waco, the Big Lie*, which was McVeigh's favorite, later said of Oklahoma City: "I definitely believe the government did the bombing. I mean, who's got a track record of killing children?" The movement would return to this paradigm repeatedly. Acts of violence, whether the Sandy Hook school shooting in 2012 or the January 6, 2021, insurrection, could always be explained away as the work of conspiracies by the government (or left-wing groups) to create a backlash and thus advance a liberal agenda.

This, then, was the situation as the century ended, and the George W. Bush administration took charge. An FBI crackdown after Oklahoma City netted a range of plots across the country. Law enforcement succeeded in foiling terrorist acts on the scale of the attack on the Murrah building. But the number of investigations and arrests demonstrated that right-wing extremists remained active and committed to violence. By the middle of 2001, McVeigh was gone, but his allies remained in the fight.

(2)

Then the attacks of September 11, 2001, transformed Americans' understanding of terrorism—overnight. The death toll of nearly three thousand dwarfed previous acts of terrorism in the United States. (Roughly eighteen times more people died on 9/11 than in the Oklahoma City bombing.) It became clear almost immediately that the attacks were orchestrated by Al Qaeda, a complex organization with enormous range and resources. The origins of Al Qaeda were in the Middle East, but its operations took place all over the world. In 1998, Al Qaeda had bombed the U.S. embassies in East Africa (killing 224 people) and in 2000 attacked the USS *Cole* in Yemen (killing seventeen sailors); clearly, then, the attacks of 9/11 were part of a pattern that could easily continue into the future. To combat that possibility, the U.S. government mobilized aggressively against this peril. This was, of course, understandable, even necessary. No nation could stand by as its people and interests were subject to such a sustained and serious threat.

The right wing found the war on terror that followed the 9/11 attacks a useful vehicle to advance its political agenda. The effort was to redefine terrorism as a foreign policy problem—a global contest with radical Islam—and to ignore domestic terrorism, especially the work of right-wing extremists. As a result, some conservatives used 9/11 as a kind of pincer movement to attack the truth about McVeigh and other right-wing extremists. On the one hand, they began to assert that Oklahoma City was actually a foreign plot, like 9/11. On the other, they claimed that because the real threat came from radical Islam, right-wing extremists were not a genuine danger at all.

In rewriting the story of the Oklahoma City bombing, one lead was taken by Dana Rohrabacher, a conservative Republican congressman from California. In 2005, he said on the House floor, "I was asked by several people whom I respect to direct my attention to the Oklahoma City bombing and to a possible foreign connection." As chairman of a House Oversight subcommittee, he later produced a report titled, "The Oklahoma City Bombing: Was There a Foreign Connection?" Rohrabacher's view recapitulated the knee-jerk reaction of many people to the bombing when it happened, and the idea—that Americans couldn't have done this—remained politically useful for a long time. Rohrabacher pushed the fanciful work of Jayna Davis, the former local news reporter in Oklahoma City who embraced the story of the "Middle Eastern men" in the brown pickup. According to the congressman, Davis "got a picture of a Middle Eastern man who works there in Oklahoma City who had great trouble explaining where he was at the time of the explosion."

In an early demonstration of what became known as the right-wing echo chamber, Davis was booked on *The O'Reilly Factor*, then the highest-rated show on Fox News. "You believe that there's a Middle Eastern connection here to McVeigh and Nichols," O'Reilly said to Davis. "You also believe that Osama bin Laden's money may have been involved here. Briefly, tell the audience what you think happened."

"I believe that an Arab terrorist cell operating in the heart of Oklahoma City funded and operated and backed by Osama bin Laden acted in collusion with Timothy McVeigh and Terry Nichols," Davis said. Davis wrote a book about her theory, called *The Third Terrorist*, and the concluding chapter was titled "Nexus: 4–19 and 9–11." Thanks to publicity on Fox News and other right-wing outlets, Davis's book became a best-seller.

Dismissing the threat of right-wing extremism took somewhat longer to accomplish. It began with a rebranding of liberals, not the right wing, as the real danger to the American people. Conservative book publishing had a great run of success during the George W. Bush years, and the themes of these works lined up with precision. During this time, Sean Hannity wrote *Deliver Us from Evil: Defeating Terrorism, Despotism, and Liberalism*; Dinesh D'Souza wrote *The Enemy at Home: The Cultural Left and Its Responsibility for 9/11*; Michael Savage wrote *The Enemy Within: Saving America from the Liberal Assault on Our Schools, Faith and Military*; and Ann Coulter wrote *Treason: Liberal Treachery from the Cold War to the War on Terrorism*. The rhetoric of these books was as incendiary as their titles. On the radio, Rush Limbaugh was still engaging in verbal violence: "I tell people don't kill all the liberals. Leave enough so we can have two on every campus—living fossils—so we will never forget what these people stood for." (This was purportedly "just a joke"—a defense that would become familiar in the Trump era.) Glenn Beck, who was in his heyday on Fox during the Obama years, spoke in the same register. He wanted to "poison" Nancy Pelosi and "beat Congressman Charlie Rangel to death with a shovel." (A Fox spokesman said Beck was being "satiric.")

Still, even though right-wing rhetoric was hotter than ever during the Bush years, the number of actual terrorist acts committed by right-wing extremists declined. As a report by the Anti-Defamation League put it, "Events ranging from the non-event of a Y2K-related disaster to the replacement of Bill Clinton with George W. Bush to the 9/11 terror attacks all played a role in dampening right-wing furor."

But this relatively happy state of affairs did not last. The ADL report went on, "Near the end of Bush's second term, right-wing terror incidents began to increase again and this trend accelerated by 2009, thanks in part to the election of Barack Obama, whom both white supremacists and anti-government extremists hated, and to the major economic disasters of the Great Recession and the foreclosure crisis."

(3)

In April 2009, three months after Obama took office, the Department of Homeland Security issued a report called "Rightwing Extremism: Current Economic and Political Climate Fueling Resurgence in Radicalization and Recruitment." The report was commissioned during the Bush administration as a part of the department's regular threat assessment program. It was written in dry bureaucratic prose and summarized well-established facts. The core warning of the nine-page report was straightforward: "Rightwing extremists have capitalized on the election of the first African American president, and are focusing their efforts to recruit new members, mobilize existing supporters, and broaden their scope and appeal through propaganda." As in the 1990s, the possibility of new gun control laws, plus the return of angry veterans from another war in the Middle East, made for a combustible atmosphere: "The possible passage of new restrictions on firearms and the return of military veterans facing significant challenges reintegrating into their communities could lead to the potential emergence of terrorist groups." Obama took office as many troops returned from the Second Gulf War, and the report noted, "After Operation Desert Shield/Storm in 1990–1991, some returning military veterans—including Timothy McVeigh—joined or associated with rightwing extremist groups." Finally, the growth of the internet was a boon for extremists: "Unlike the earlier period, the advent of the Internet and other information age technologies since the 1990s has given domestic extremists greater access to information related to bomb-making, weapons training, and tactics, as well as targeting of individuals, organizations, and facilities, potentially making extremist individuals and groups more dangerous and the consequences of their violence more severe."

The report itself was less significant than the furious reaction to it—and the reaction to the reaction. John Boehner, then the highest-ranking Republican in the House of Representatives, called the report "offensive and unacceptable," adding, "the Secretary of Homeland Security owes the American people an explanation for why she has abandoned using the term 'terrorist' to describe those, such as al Qaeda, who are plotting overseas to kill innocent Americans." Representative Lamar Smith, of Texas, said the administration was "awfully willing to paint law-abiding Americans, including war veterans, as 'extremists.'" Representative Steve Buyer, the top Republican on the House Veterans' Affairs Committee, said it was "inconceivable" that veterans could pose a threat. The American Legion protested the report. Right-wing talk radio denounced it in its customarily frenzied tone.

The attacks on the report gave the new administration a challenge and an opportunity. Republicans had rejected the report without pointing to any actual errors. The report was accurate, and the threat from right-wing extremists was real. Still, the Obama administration, which wanted no distractions from its efforts to improve the economy, surrendered without a fight. Homeland Security Secretary Janet Napolitano apologized for the report and withdrew it. "The report is no longer out there," Napolitano said in a speech, adding that it would be "replaced or redone in a much more useful and much more precise fashion." (It wasn't.) Fearful of more criticism in the wake of the controversy, the department also cut the number of personnel studying domestic extremism unrelated to Islam, canceled numerous state and local law enforcement briefings, and held up nearly a dozen reports on extremist groups.

The story of the DHS report reverberated for a long time. The Obama administration had been intimidated into a kind of intentional ignorance; it muzzled itself from alerting the public to a dangerous and growing threat. The Obama approach was an extreme version of the split between Clinton and Garland after Oklahoma City. Prosecute individual cases (in line with Garland), but say nothing about the larger trend (in contrast to Clinton). Embracing the mantle of feigned victimhood, Republicans saw that they could deflect criticisms of and warnings about an affiliated movement by claiming discrimination.

Notwithstanding the political posturing, right-wing extremist violence not only persisted but accelerated. Indeed, the amount and degree of such violence offers a hidden history of the Obama years. The roll call of such acts runs into the dozens. Days after the 2008 election, a Marine corporal at Camp Lejeune in North Carolina was arrested and charged with planning to kill Obama as a "domestic enemy" in "Operation Patriot." In January 2009, a Boston white supremacist raped and shot an African immigrant and then killed her sister when she tried to intervene. He then killed a homeless African immigrant, and he was arrested before he got to a synagogue for a planned mass shooting. In May, a member of the right-wing vigilante group Minutemen American Defense in Arizona murdered a man and his young daughter during a home invasion to steal funds for his anti-immigrant activities. Also in May, a "sovereign citizen" (which Terry Nichols also claimed to be) named Scott Roeder murdered George Tiller, a Kansas doctor who provided abortion services. In June, a white supremacist attacked the United States Holocaust Museum in Washington, D.C., shooting and killing a security guard. This was all in the first six months of Obama's presidency.

The pace of extremist violence never slackened in the Obama years. A tax protester burns down his home, boards his private plane, and flies it into the building that contains the IRS offices in Austin,

Texas. A pipe bomb at an Islamic Center in Jacksonville, Florida. A handgun attack on security guards at the Pentagon. Firebombs at a Planned Parenthood clinic in Madera, California. (Among other attacks on Planned Parenthood operations.) Four "sovereign citizens" in Alaska plot to murder state and federal employees. Another "sovereign citizen" in Texas tries to hire a hit man to kill a federal judge. A Georgia militia plot to poison employees and bomb offices of the ATF and IRS in Atlanta. A different Georgia militia plot to kill a onetime accomplice whom the perpetrators feared would become an informant. In Spokane, a white supremacist's bomb at a Martin Luther King Jr. Day parade malfunctions at the last minute. Another white supremacist kills six at a Sikh temple in Wisconsin. Militia operatives in Minnesota plot to bomb the local police and (in a separate scheme) steal military IDs for use in militia operations. A shooting rampage aimed at Transportation Security Administration officials at Los Angeles International Airport. A plot to bomb government buildings in Katy, Texas. Three North Carolina extremists assemble bombs to fight the federal government. A plot to bomb the federal courthouse in Elkins, West Virginia. A man in New Hampshire tries to buy rockets and grenades "to bring forth the original constitution." A white supremacist named Dylann Roof guns down nine parishioners in a historic Black church in Charleston, South Carolina. Roof leaves behind a manifesto that reads like updated McVeigh: "We have no skinheads, no real KKK, no one doing anything but talking on the internet. Well, someone has to have the bravery to take it to the real world, and I guess that has to be me."

Still, the effort to define terrorism as an exclusively Islamic phenomenon continued. On July 23, 2015, John Houser killed two and injured nine when he opened fire at a movie theater showing the romantic comedy *Trainwreck* in Lafayette, Louisiana. He had long associations with right-wing groups and left behind a note that said, "If the founders of this nation could have seen what the US would become, they would say, 'Let us destroy it.'" Still, Megyn Kelly, then of Fox News, who was anchoring the coverage, asked the reporter on the scene, "Any reason to believe there might be a connection to ISIS, or radical Islam, or terror as we understand it in this country?"

McVeigh himself became an icon in some especially dangerous regions of the extremist universe. In 2017, Brandon Russell, the leader of a neo-Nazi group called Atomwaffen—"atomic weapon" in German—was arrested at his home in Tampa for possession of explosives; there was a framed photograph of McVeigh on his nightstand. Two years later, the FBI connected Richard Tobin, of Brooklawn, New Jersey, to online posts directing others to vandalize synagogues around the country. When confronted by agents, Tobin praised suicide bombings, saying "he believed it would be 'pretty straightforward' to fill the back of a truck with barrels [of explosives] like Timothy McVeigh did," the FBI wrote in an affidavit. Timothy Wilson planned to blow up several mosques, a synagogue, and an elementary school with mostly Black students in the Kansas City area, in 2020, he texted an associate, "How did McVeigh do it?" (After the FBI confronted him, Wilson killed himself.)

Of course, terrorism associated with radical Islam and left-wing extremists never disappeared from the United States. On November 5, 2009, a Muslim psychiatrist killed thirteen unarmed soldiers at Fort Hood, Texas, while yelling praises to Allah. On December 2, 2015, a couple in San Bernardino, who had ties to radical Islam, killed fourteen at a Christmas party. On June 14, 2017, James Hodgkinson, a leftist political activist, opened fire at a congressional baseball game, seriously wounding two people. (Hodgkinson was killed by police.) On June 8, 2022, Nicholas Roske, who was apparently angry about a draft Supreme Court opinion on abortion rights, was arrested near the home of Justice Brett Kavanaugh. Roske, who had a history of mental illness, had called the police himself, saying that he wanted to kill the justice.

Still, the record is clear that there were far fewer of these attacks than those by right-wing extremists. Indeed, according to one study, right-wing extremism was responsible for 76 percent of all extremist murders in the United States from 2009 to 2019. (Islamic extremists were responsible for 20 percent, and left-wing and Black nationalists 3 percent.) A comprehensive study of the years 2000 to 2018 by Rachel Kleinfeld in the *Journal of Democracy* concluded that "political violence still comes overwhelmingly from the right, whether one looks at the Global Terrorism Database, FBI statistics, or other government or independent counts." Another study found that right-wing extremists and white supremacists were behind two-thirds of the terrorist plots in the United States in 2020.The growth of social media played a part in the surge in violence during the Obama years. According to data collected by the Department of Homeland Security, among people in the United States who were radicalized, social media played a role for 27 percent of them between 2005 and 2010; that increased to 73 percent between 2011 and 2016.

Most of the attacks by right-wing extremists were explained, if not dismissed, as the work of "lone wolves." This was a way of minimizing the threat posed (because they were not part of larger conspiracies) and expressing futility about stopping them (because the nation had too many individuals to monitor everyone). But this nomenclature failed to acknowledge the extent of the threat. "White-supremacist terror is rooted in a pack, a community," the terrorism expert Juliette Kayyem wrote. "White-supremacist terrorism has what amounts to a dating app online, putting like-minded individuals together both through mainstream social media platforms and more remote venues, such as 8chan, that exist to foster rage. When one of them puts the violent rhetoric into action in the real world, the killer is often called a 'lone wolf,' but they are not alone at all." In 2017, when Donald Trump became president, the wolf pack had a new leader.

(4)

Timothy McVeigh's legacy became clearest during Trump's campaign and presidency. All the trends that McVeigh embodied—the political extremism, the obsession with gun rights, the search for like-minded allies, and above all the embrace of violence—came together under the forty-fifth president.

It took some time for the broader political world to acknowledge what was happening with Trump. When, during his campaign, he would urge his supporters to "knock the hell" out of protesters at his rallies or claim that he himself would like to "punch them in the face," that was widely dismissed as hyperbole or just "Trump being Trump." When Trump said that police should bang suspects' heads into car roofs, his press secretary said, "He was making a joke."

But Trump's true nature, and his real allies, became undeniable in August 2017, after the "Unite the Right" rally in Charlottesville, Virginia. When the city announced that it would remove a statue of Robert E. Lee, the KKK (which McVeigh had joined) announced plans to hold a protest there. Thanks to publicity on right-wing websites and chat rooms, other groups joined in, including the "militias" of New York, Pennsylvania, and Virginia. The rally was a frenzy of white supremacy and anti-Semitism, with hundreds chanting, "Jews will not replace us!" (The chant reflected the right-wing obsession with "replacement theory"—the idea that the white majority in the United States would be replaced by people of color and immigrants. *The Turner Diaries* was an early expositor of this view, which was later made famous by Fox's Tucker Carlson.) Besides the militias, most of the extremist groups had new names since McVeigh's day, but their racist and violent obsessions aligned with his fixations. The difference from McVeigh's time, of course, was that thanks to the internet, they were able to meet and plan together. The "Army" that McVeigh told his lawyers he was seeking had finally assembled. The result in Charlottesville was a violent clash with counterprotesters that left one of them, Heather Heyer, dead.

Trump's opinion about the Charlottesville events was clear. In an initial statement, he condemned the "display of hatred, bigotry, and violence on many sides." When that statement was criticized for its equivalence between the racists and their adversaries, Trump, in a news conference at Trump Tower, doubled down, saying there were "very fine people on both sides." It was a defining moment of his presidency, a message to right-wing extremists and white supremacists that they had an ally in the Oval Office. Trump's contempt for the antiracist protesters in Charlottesville, especially a group called antifa, also had a lasting impact. Antifa is a decentralized antifascist operation—more an idea than a single group—with a propensity for thuggish behavior, notably street fights. In subsequent years, Trump and his allies found it convenient to blame much violence, even murder, on antifa, usually based on slim-to-nonexistent evidence. In a repeat of a pattern that went back to McVeigh's day, right-wingers even described the violence at the Capitol on January 6, 2021, as a provocation orchestrated by antifa—a transparently bogus allegation.

As president, Trump never explicitly endorsed the extremist presence among his political supporters, but he knew how to speak to McVeigh's successors in barely coded terms. Trump's racism and endorsements of violence always had a measure of deniability. He told a nearly all-white crowd in Minnesota, "You have good genes in Minnesota." In response to the protests that followed the murder of George Floyd, he tweeted, "When the looting starts, the shooting starts." Asked at a presidential debate about his supporters among violent right-wing extremists, Trump turned the question around and endorsed the Proud Boys—who would become notorious instigators of the January 6 insurrection—and raised antifa as a diversion: "Almost everything I see is from the left wing, not from the right wing," he said. Asked by Biden to condemn the Proud Boys in particular, Trump said, "Proud Boys, stand back and stand by. But I'll tell you what: Somebody's got to do something about antifa and the left. Because this is not a right-wing problem—this is a left-wing problem."

The most direct link from the Oklahoma City bombing conspiracy to those in the Trump era took place in Michigan. The plot illustrated the durability of right-wing extremism as well as the way social media could galvanize an army with an efficiency that McVeigh could scarcely imagine. The bombing in 1995 nearly drove the Michigan Militia out of business. Under fire because of its connection to Terry and James Nichols, the Militia lost most of its members; a plan to move operations to Alaska predictably fizzled. But the group's fortunes revived in the Trump years, especially during the Covid pandemic, when the updated militia took a leading and visible role in protesting the restrictions on public activity ordered by Governor Gretchen Whitmer, a Democrat. The Militia and its offshoot, known as the Wolverine Watchmen, staged noisy "Second Amendment" rallies at the state capitol, where they patrolled the premises with assault weapons and other menacing firearms. On Twitter, Trump cheered on the protests: "Liberate Michigan!"

The FBI received intelligence that the militia members were using private Facebook chat groups to plan more sinister activities. More than a dozen people who were affiliated with the revitalized Michigan Militia hatched an elaborate plan to kidnap Governor Whitmer—"this tyrant bitch"—and take her to a remote location in Wisconsin for a "trial" on charges of "treason." As the ringleader told an informant, "Snatch and grab, man. Grab the fuckin' Governor. Just grab the bitch." The group engaged in extensive preparations for the kidnapping, including casing the governor's vacation home and conducting training exercises in the area. Shortly before the 2020 election, the Bureau's agents arrested the conspirators before they had a chance to put their plan into action. Mark Koernke, the Michigan janitor who inspired the Nichols brothers in the 1990s, voiced his outrage at the prosecution of their heirs a quarter century later, writing on Facebook, "Same FBI that let antifa burn down the country now attacking militia in Michigan to promote the Communist agenda." At a campaign rally in Michigan two weeks after the arrests, Trump dismissed the plot, saying "maybe it wasn't a problem." (Two years later, when Whitmer was running for reelection, Tudor Dixon, her Republican opponent, said, "The sad thing is Gretchen will tie your hands, put a gun to your head and ask if you're ready to talk. For someone so worried about being kidnapped, Gretchen Whitmer sure is good at taking business hostage and holding it for ransom." Dixon said the comment was for "a little levity.")

(5)

In the final days before the presidential election on November 3, 2020, the atmosphere throughout the country was grim and foreboding. Trump had said that he believed Biden could only win by cheating. "The Democrats are trying to rig this election, because that's the only way they are going to win," he said at a late rally. Trump also would not commit to conceding the election if he was declared the loser. Early on the morning of November 4, Trump claimed victory over Biden long before all the votes were counted and as the preliminary results favored the challenger. On Saturday, November 7, the television networks and the Associated Press called the election for Biden, but Trump refused to acknowledge the outcome and vowed to fight on.

The next two months followed a familiar pattern. There was initially a widespread assumption that Trump would follow the norms of democracy, if grudgingly. On the day after the election, Mick Mulvaney, his former chief of staff, wrote an op-ed article in *The Wall Street Journal* predicting that if the vote went against him, Trump would concede "gracefully." When Trump did not concede, allies and advisers confidently predicted to reporters (albeit without agreeing to be quoted by name) that he would accept his defeat. "Do not expect him to concede," one aide said. "He'll say something like, 'We can't trust the results, but I'm not contesting them.'" *The Washington Post* quoted a "senior Republican official" saying, "What is the downside for humoring him for this little bit of time? No one seriously thinks the results will change." As when Trump embraced the use of violence during the first campaign, many asserted that he didn't really mean what he said. This was just "Trump being Trump." But he meant it.

In a final, desperate effort to hang on to the presidency, Trump embraced the idea of a major protest on the day that Congress, presided over by Vice President Mike Pence, was legally obligated to certify the results. On December 19, Trump tweeted about the plan for January 6, which would be called the Save America Rally, "Be there, will be wild!" It was.

On the morning of January 6, thousands gathered on the Ellipse, near the White House. By that point, Pence had passed word that he would ignore Trump's importuning and certify Biden's victory in the election. With the last hope of a Trump victory apparently extinguished, the atmosphere among the protesters turned even more volatile, especially after they were revved up by the warm-up speakers like Giuliani. Trump began speaking just before noon, and his words have already become part of the imperishable record of American history. He knew that Pence would not be doing his bidding ("I will tell you right now. I'm not hearing good stories"), so his only hope was for the mob to work its will at the Capitol. After Trump's speech, the mob tried.

The events of January 6, 2021, saw the full flowering of McVeigh's legacy in contemporary politics. McVeigh was obsessed with gun rights; he saw the bombing as akin to the revolutionary struggle of the Founding Fathers; and he believed that violence was justified to achieve his goals. So did the rioters on January 6.

Among those at the Capitol, there was, to an unappreciated degree, a substantial focus on gun rights and the Second Amendment. The Proud Boys and the Oath Keepers, the two most prominent extremist groups involved in the January 6 assault, embraced gun rights above all other issues, just as McVeigh did. Joe Biggs of the Proud Boys was prominently featured at National Rifle Association events, and much of the group's merchandise features guns and slogans like "From my cold dead hands"—a reference to NRA leader Charlton Heston's famous boast. The Oath Keepers are descended even more directly from the Oklahoma City conspirators, with their shared obsession with gun rights.

As we have seen, too, the rioters and their allies in the January 6 insurrection dressed up their arguments with invocations of the American Revolution. They chanted "1776" as if their attempt to overthrow a democracy were comparable to the Founders' effort to create one. The yellow Gadsden flag, which flew during the Revolution as well as outside Mike Fortier's mobile home, was a frequent sight in the crowd at the Capitol. On November 27, 2020, Ethan Nordean of the Proud Boys posted on social media, "We tried playing nice and by the rules, now you will deal with the monster you created. The spirit of 1776 has resurfaced and has created groups like the Proudboys [*sic*] and we will not be extinguished." As Stewart Rhodes of the Oath Keepers said, "You got pissed off patriots that are not going to accept their form of government being stolen. We're walking down the same exact path as the Founding Fathers." McVeigh thought he was, too.

The clearest link between McVeigh and the Capitol rioters was in their embrace of violence. By January 6, law enforcement intelligence offices around the country had picked up signs that violent extremists planned to converge on Washington to try to overturn the election. Red flags abounded. Smaller "Stop the Steal" rallies in Washington on November 14 and December 12 had turned violent, with multiple injuries to both protesters and police. Those close to Trump made the plan explicit. On the day before the election in 2020, Roger Stone, a longtime adviser to Trump, attended one of the president's last rallies. "Fuck the voting, let's get right to the violence," he said backstage. "Shoot to kill, see an antifa, shoot to kill. Fuck 'em. Done with this bullshit." Then he turned to the cameraman who was following him and said he was "only kidding."

Likewise, too, *The Turner Diaries* endured as a source of inspiration to right-wing extremists, including those who participated in the insurrection. Shortly before January 6, on a live-streamed Proud Boys show called WarBoys, Biggs said of those attempting to honor the results of the 2020 election: "They're evil scum, and they all deserve to die a traitor's death." Ethan Nordean answered, "Yup, Day of the Rope"—invoking the cataclysmic day of violence from *The Turner Diaries*. On social media and sites such as 4chan, Telegram, and Stormfront, some users noted the parallels between the insurrection at the Capitol and the rebellion described in the novel. Some of the commenters asserted, with justification, that January 6 was the closest the nation had come to replicating the white supremacist triumph that concludes *The Turner Diaries.* (In response to the events of January 6, 2021, Amazon and some used book sites stopped selling the book.)

On the late afternoon of January 6, when Trump was finally persuaded to ask his supporters to withdraw from the Capitol, he still made his true feelings clear. Addressing the mob directly, he said: "We love you. You're very special. This was a fraudulent election. I know how you feel." As usual with Trump, he and his supporters (and later his lawyers) could parse his words with enough precision to argue that he did not explicitly encourage the carnage on January 6—which included five deaths, countless injuries, and hundreds of arrests of people who thought they were doing what Trump wanted them to do. Trump's moral responsibility was clear, even as his legal responsibility had yet to be determined. What was also clear was that even though Trump was a distinctive figure in American politics, his actions belonged to a long tradition—of gun-obsessed, antidemocratic, violence-fueled extremism. So did Tim McVeigh's.

(6)

There was some evidence that the new Democratic administration had learned some lessons. When it came to right-wing extremism, Biden's administration would not replicate the extreme caution of Clinton's or the willful blindness of Obama's. Jolted by the magnitude of the January 6 insurrection and Trump's alliance with the rioters, Biden spoke of the threat of right-wing extremism with a directness and urgency that exceeded even Clinton's. In a prime-time speech at Independence Hall in Philadelphia in September 2022, Biden said, "Donald Trump and the MAGA Republicans represent an extremism that threatens the very foundations of our Republic." He went on, "They look at the mob that stormed the United States Capitol on January 6, brutally attacking law enforcement, not as insurrectionists who placed a dagger at the throat of our democracy, but they look at them as patriots." He defined the stakes clearly: "I will not stand by and watch—I will not—the will of the American people be overturned by wild conspiracy theories and baseless evidence-free claims of fraud. I will not stand by and watch elections in this country stolen by people who simply refuse to accept that they lost."

Biden had made Merrick Garland his attorney general, and Garland displayed the same rhetorical caution that he had shown at the Justice Department more than two decades earlier. After his long tenure as a federal appeals court judge, with its code of public evenhandedness, Garland chose his words with even more lawyerly care than he did after Oklahoma City. Garland refused to address the subject of January 6, or Trump himself, with any specificity, but he led an aggressive investigation of the events of the day. He also approved the Justice Department's obtaining a search warrant for Trump's estate

Mar-a-Lago, in Palm Beach, Florida, on August 8, 2022, to determine whether Trump illegally removed classified and other documents from the White House.

The period after January 6 paralleled the one after the Oklahoma City bombing in 1995. These two acts of extremist outrage, both widely condemned at the time, were followed not by soul-searching and restraint but rather by more extremism. Just four days after the riot at the Capitol, Rhodes, of the Oath Keepers, was recorded at a meeting of his group saying, "We should have brought rifles. We could have fixed it then and there. I'd hang fucking Pelosi from the lamppost." Two weeks after traveling to Washington to participate in the invasion of the Capitol, a Tennessee man returned to Knoxville and fired a shotgun at the door of a Planned Parenthood clinic. Less than a year later, he burned down the clinic. On May 14, 2022, a white supremacist obsessed with the great replacement killed ten Black people at a Buffalo supermarket. On August 11, 2022, a Trump supporter, outraged by the search at Mar-a-Lago, wielded an AR-15 assault weapon and attempted to storm the FBI field office in Cincinnati; he was killed in a confrontation with law enforcement. Later, a Tennessee man who had been charged in the storming of the Capitol on January 6 was indicted in a plot to kill the FBI agents who had arrested him and to attack the FBI field office in Knoxville. On October 28, 2022, David DePape, whose social media showed support for a range of right-wing causes, broke into the San Francisco home of Nancy Pelosi, the Democratic Speaker of the House, demanding "Where's Nancy? Where's Nancy?"—a cry that was also made by the rioters inside the Capitol on January 6. DePape found only her husband, Paul, and attacked him with a hammer. The vipers of talk radio, and the internet, displayed as much venom as ever. Dan Bongino, who succeeded Rush Limbaugh as the leading right-wing voice on the radio, called Trump's political opponents "legitimately crazy satanic demon people" and described President Biden as a "disgraceful, disgusting, grotesque bag of bones." As the journalist Evan Osnos observed, "Spend several months immersed in American talk radio and you'll come away with the sense that the violence of January 6th was not the end of something but the beginning."

Republican officeholders also behaved differently after the events of 1995 and 2021. After Oklahoma City, no politicians defended or minimized the attack; but after January 6, many Republicans did just that. Representative Andrew Clyde, of Georgia, said the actions of the rioters in the Capitol resembled "a normal tourist visit." Representative Marjorie Taylor Greene also dismissed the importance of January 6, saying, "A bunch of conservatives, Second Amendment supporters, went in the Capitol without guns, and they think we organized that? I don't think so." Greene said her efforts would have been more effective: "If Steve Bannon and I had organized that, we would have won. Not to mention, it would have been armed."

The Republican level of fury was unprecedented. Senator Rick Scott of Florida said the investigation at Mar-a-Lago showed that the FBI was acting like "the Gestapo." Dan Cox, the Republican candidate for governor of Maryland, called the FBI's actions "criminal." Death threats, especially to Republicans who failed to support overturning the election, abounded. Congressman Paul Gosar, of Arizona, tweeted an anime video doctored to show him killing Congresswoman Alexandria Ocasio-Cortez, of New York. Greene, who always gave voice to the darkest impulses in her party, said, "I am not going to mince words with you all. Democrats want Republicans dead, and they have already started the killings."

Freed from the nominal restraints on his behavior that came with the presidency, Trump himself turned to a new level of feral zealotry. He abandoned even the pretense of detachment from right-wing extremist groups. He openly embraced QAnon, a quasi-mystical political cult that spreads the false theory that the Democratic Party runs pedophile rings. On his social media platform, Trump regularly reposted QAnon content, including an image of himself wearing a Q lapel pin overlaid with the words "The Storm is Coming." In QAnon lore, the "storm" involves Trump's return to office, a televised trial of his opponents, and their possible execution. Trump played the QAnon theme music as background to his speeches at rallies. At one event before the 2022 midterm elections, many in the audience responded with the raised-right-arm gesture that signals affiliation with QAnon and recalls the Nazi salute. In another speech, Trump said the government should threaten journalists with prison rape in order to convince them to reveal their sources. ("When this person realizes he's going to be the bride of another prisoner very shortly, he will say, 'I'd very much like to tell you exactly who that leaker is!'") With criminal investigations closing in on him from several directions, Trump predicted violence if he is charged. "I don't think the people of this country would stand for it," he said in an interview. He called for the "termination" of the Constitution, pledged support for the January 6 rioters, and dined with notorious white supremacists.

In the nearly thirty years since the Oklahoma City bombing, the country took an extraordinary journey—from nearly universal horror at the action of a right-wing extremist to wide embrace of a former president (also possibly a future president) who reflected the bomber's values.

(7)

Except for Merrick Garland, the individuals involved in McVeigh's story returned to private lives. The prosecution team continued their careers as lawyers, not as celebrities. Joe Hartzler, who led the McVeigh case, went back to work at the U.S. Attorney's Office in Springfield, Illinois, where he put his name forward for a federal judgeship. His cranky independence failed him in navigating the nomination process in the Senate, and he didn't get it. He spent the rest of his career practicing law in and out of government in central Illinois. Larry Mackey still practices law in Indianapolis. Beth Wilkinson started her own law firm in Washington, D.C., and has become one of the most sought-after trial lawyers in the country.

Stephen Jones, who was McVeigh's lead lawyer, is in his early eighties and still practices law in his office full of political memorabilia in Enid, Oklahoma. As he wrote in his book, *Others Unknown*, named for the prosecutors' use of that phrase in the indictment, he still believes that McVeigh was part of a broader conspiracy to bomb the Murrah building. Alienated from the legal profession as well as his colleagues on the defense team, Randy Coyne gave up his tenure at the University of Oklahoma law school; he is now a full-time jazz drummer. Nichols's lead lawyer, Michael Tigar, who is also in his early eighties, left his post as a professor at the University of Texas law school for a job at Duke law school, and then moved to New York, where he keeps up his life's work in law and human rights. Judge Richard Matsch continued hearing cases until he died at the age of eighty-eight in 2019.

After Terry Nichols avoided the death penalty in his federal trial before Judge Matsch, Bob Macy, the Oklahoma County district attorney, announced plans to bring him to trial on state murder charges, in hopes of persuading a jury to vote to execute him. Nichols was assigned new lawyers, and years of legal wrangling over the charges followed. In 2004, the trial, which was moved to McAlester, in the western part of the state, ended just as the federal case did. The jury convicted Nichols of murder but could not reach a unanimous verdict in favor of a death sentence. At the age of sixty-seven, Nichols remains in the federal supermax prison in Colorado, serving life without parole. His wife, Marife, divorced him and moved back to the Philippines with their daughter. Michael Fortier was sentenced to twelve years for his role in the bombing conspiracy and served about ten years. When he was released in 2006, he entered the federal Witness Protection Program with his wife, Lori, and their two children. Trooper Charlie Hanger, who arrested McVeigh on April 19, 1995, was elected sheriff of Noble County in 2004. He defeated a candidate named Shawn McVay.

As Tim McVeigh prepared to be executed in Terre Haute in the early months of 2001, he planned one final provocation. He asked to be cremated and his ashes scattered over the Oklahoma City National Memorial, which had opened the previous year on the site of the Murrah building. With its 168 chairs representing each person killed in the bombing—and much smaller chairs symbolizing the children—the memorial had already become a haunting landmark, recognized and admired around the world. For McVeigh, the bombing had always been a performance, a message to the world. The plan would give McVeigh a kind of sneering double immortality—for the bombing itself and for his return to the site for eternity.

His defense attorney Rob Nigh talked him out of it. Quiet and scholarly, Nigh was respected by people on all sides of the case. Jones had brought him on as his deputy, but Nigh stayed on throughout the appeals process, making him the only lawyer who remained with McVeigh from beginning to end. McVeigh grew to loathe Jones (and vice versa), but he always trusted Nigh. The Oklahoma City plan offended Nigh, who maintained civil relations with the victims' families whom he encountered. Together, McVeigh and Nigh came up with an alternative idea.

Nigh and McVeigh's appeals team had hired a Denver-based private investigator named Ellis Armistead to assist with the grim final arrangements of McVeigh's life and death. On June 11, 2001, Armistead waited out the execution in a trailer next to the death house, where the lethal injection was administered. About forty minutes after McVeigh was pronounced dead, the authorities called Armistead to the death chamber, to watch McVeigh's corpse placed in a body bag. McVeigh was then transferred to a minivan to be taken to a funeral home for cremation. (As a distraction, a hearse was brought to the scene and much photographed as it left the prison; it was empty.) Armistead and a colleague waited at the funeral home for several hours while the cremation took place. He received the box of McVeigh's ashes, known as cremains, placed them in a backpack, and flew to Denver that night.

Back at his office, Armistead placed the box in an evidence locker. (It was next to a box containing the cremains of Eric Harris, one of the two gunmen in the Columbine High School massacre; Armistead worked on that case, too.) Months passed. Finally, Nigh came to Denver to pick up the box containing McVeigh's cremains. According to the deal he had struck with McVeigh, there would be no single final resting place. Nigh would scatter the ashes to the winds in the Rocky Mountains. By concluding his journey in this way, McVeigh would be everywhere.

Where, in a way, he remains.

Author's Note

In 1997, I covered the McVeigh and Nichols trials in Denver. Like most other journalists at the time, I concentrated on following the trail of evidence presented in the courtroom—the discovery of the axle at the scene, the purchases of fertilizer, the rental of the Ryder truck. I recognized McVeigh's malign intelligence, but I failed to understand, much less explain, his place in the broader slipstream of American history. Still, the story of the Oklahoma City bombing—especially the horror inflicted on so many innocent people—lodged securely, if remotely, in my consciousness.

There it remained—until the fall of 2020. That's when I became fascinated, in a grim way, with the plot to kidnap Michigan governor Gretchen Whitmer. There was the sheer outlandishness of the idea—what kind of people would think to kidnap a governor?—but as I looked more closely, the story took on a deeper resonance. I saw that most of the people accused in the plot had ties to the Michigan Militia. I thought: I know these people. Terry Nichols and his brother James had close ties to the Michigan Militia, and they passed lessons from the group on to McVeigh. Even a quarter century after the Oklahoma City bombing, some of the same people were involved. For example, Mark Koernke, the University of Michigan janitor, inspired the Nichols brothers and defended the Whitmer plotters.

The news from Michigan prompted me to take a renewed look at the Oklahoma City bombing, which had not received a great deal of attention since the nation shifted its attention to radical Islamic terrorism after the 9/11 attacks. That, in turn, led me to the Dolph Briscoe Center for American History at the University of Texas. In 1999, Stephen Jones, McVeigh's lead attorney, donated to the Briscoe Center his full file on the case, which runs to 635 boxes. For a journalist, this was an extraordinary—and largely unexamined—bounty. I had been covering the law for three decades, and I knew that an archive of this extent and depth had never before been publicly available in a major case. What especially drew my interest were the details of the attorney-client relationship—the many summaries of conversations between McVeigh and his lawyers, as well as the letters between them, and the memos outlining the legal strategies of the defense. (The quotations in the text from McVeigh's interview with Jones come from a transcribed interview between the two men that took place on September 5 and 14, 1995. Citations to secondary sources appear in the Notes.)

As a lawyer, I had real questions about the ethics of Jones's disclosures. It's long been established that a lawyer's duty of confidentiality to a client, as well as the attorney-client privilege, survives the death of the client. In other words, Jones was not free to disclose what McVeigh told him just because McVeigh had died. So what was Jones's justification for disclosing so many of McVeigh's confidences? Jones addressed this issue in an "open letter" appended to the paperback edition of *Others Unknown*, his memoir, in 2001. First, Jones noted that McVeigh's new group of lawyers had asked Judge Matsch for a new trial because Jones had provided ineffective assistance of counsel, in violation of the Sixth Amendment. Second, Jones said that McVeigh had given interviews to Lou Michel and Dan Herbeck, the *Buffalo News* reporters, for their book, *American Terrorist*. In the book, McVeigh was critical of Jones, calling him "befuddled" and "craving notoriety and the spotlight." Jones was claiming a right to defend himself by disclosing his client's confidences.

How valid was Jones's position? According to the Model Rules of Professional Conduct of the American Bar Association, a "lawyer shall not reveal information relating to the representation of a client unless the client gives informed consent." Here, it was clear that McVeigh never gave any kind of consent, informed or otherwise, for Jones to disclose the information in the Briscoe Center or in his book. But the rule establishes an exception. "A lawyer may reveal information relating to the representation of a client to the extent the lawyer reasonably believes necessary . . . to respond to allegations in any proceeding concerning the lawyer's representation of the client." So was Jones justified in revealing confidences because McVeigh had challenged Jones's competence in attempting to get a new trial? Was McVeigh's motion for a new trial a "proceeding" that justified Jones's disclosures? The answer seems to be no. As Jones acknowledged, Judge Matsch rejected McVeigh's claim of ineffective assistance of counsel without even requiring Jones to defend his conduct. The "proceeding" was over before Jones donated his files to the Briscoe Center.

Was Jones, then, permitted to disclose client confidences to defend himself against the criticism in *American Terrorist*? The answer, again, seems to be certainly not. The Model Rules only allow a lawyer to make disclosures in a "proceeding"—which a book is not. Moreover, it's common for criminal defendants to air grievances against their lawyers after they've been convicted. As Jones himself pointed out in his open letter, "most clients believe themselves unjustly convicted and have been criticizing their lawyers since time immemorial." But Jones said that if he had failed to respond to McVeigh's claims, people might think that McVeigh's claims against him were valid. Or, he said, people might think "I was afraid to defend myself." But these claims apply in any case where a client criticizes his lawyer, and the rules of the profession forbid the lawyer from disclosing confidences in response.

Jones offered a final justification in his open letter. Quoting Felix

Frankfurter, he said, "History also has its claims." Jones went on, "It was important, not just to me but to the bar and to the profession of advocacy, that somewhere there be a reasoned account of what had occurred in Mr. McVeigh's defense, prosecution and trial." This, to be clear, is not something authorized by the rules governing the legal profession; by disclosing McVeigh's confidences in his book and in his donation to the Briscoe Center, Jones opened himself up to discipline from his bar association. (None has been forthcoming.) Still, since I benefited from Jones's decision to donate the archive and have tried to write the kind of book he envisioned, it would be ungrateful and churlish of me to dismiss his reasoning entirely. History does have a claim, and I have tried in this book to make it.

Finally, though, there is another factor relevant in assessing Jones's decision to donate the archive—one he did not mention in his book. Jones took a tax deduction of $297,877 for donating the government's discovery material to the Briscoe Center. The IRS contested the deduction, on the ground that the discovery material was not the kind of "capital asset" for which a deduction is permissible. In 2009, the United States Court of Appeals for the Tenth Circuit upheld the government's position and disallowed the deduction.

In the course of my research, I interviewed more than a hundred people. The Oklahoma City bombing was a major event in many lives, and after a quarter century, virtually everyone I contacted was willing to share their recollections. I am particularly grateful that President Bill Clinton and Attorney General Merrick Garland took time to speak with me at length. I regret that I was not able to speak with Rob Nigh, the second-in-command of the McVeigh defense, because he died, tragically, of cancer at the age of fifty-seven in 2017. I wrote several times to Terry Nichols at the supermax prison in Florence, Colorado, hoping to arrange an interview. He never answered.

As I hope the foregoing makes clear, I made a great deal of use of the material Jones donated to the Briscoe Center, and I owe the staff there a major debt of gratitude. Don Carleton, the director, and his colleagues welcomed me to their beautiful facility in Austin, and then, just as important, provided me with a seemingly endless stream of PDFs of the material in the Jones archive. Many staff members contributed to this effort, and I am pleased to thank them all: Erin Harbour, Aryn Glazier, Caitlin Brenner, Annie LeMasters, Kathryn Kenefick, Darin Spelber, Marisa Jefferson, Margaret Schlankey, and Stephanie Malmros.

I also benefited from the generosity of Lou Michel and Dan Herbeck, the Buffalo-based coauthors of *American Terrorist*, an excellent guide to McVeigh's life. They allowed me to quote from their correspondence with McVeigh. The authors' papers are lodged at the library at St. Bonaventure University, in St. Bonaventure, New York, and I also thank Dennis Frank, the archive librarian.

The empty commemorative chairs on the site of the Murrah building in Oklahoma City are already known as one of the world's great memorials. The chairs are part of an extraordinary complex—the Oklahoma City National Memorial & Museum. I visited the museum several times, and I'm grateful to many staff members there (who asked not to be named individually). The museum displays many original artifacts from the case, including the battered Mercury that McVeigh was driving when Charlie Hanger arrested him; the twisted axle from the Ryder truck that led investigators to Junction City, Kansas; Joe Hartzler's handwritten admonition to his colleagues (DO NOT BURY THE CRIME IN CLUTTER!); and the large, five-cornered-star sign that greeted visitors to the Dreamland Motel, to name just a few. (Sadly, the Dreamland itself was demolished in 2011.) The memorial also maintains an extensive archive of material about the bombing, including oral history interviews with many witnesses, including victims. The interviews were a tremendous resource.

I'm also grateful to Phil Bacharach, of Oklahoma City, who shared with me his correspondence with McVeigh.

My friends at the CNN library unearthed an online version of the McVeigh trial transcript. Thank you also to Jim Duran at the Vanderbilt Television News Archive; Shannon Lausch at the William J. Clinton Presidential Library and Museum; John Fox, the FBI historian; the Lockport Public Library; and the New York Public Library.

Kathy Robbins, my agent, provided sage guidance throughout the publishing process. Thank you as well to Alexandra Sugarman. Cecilia Mackay provided wonderful help with the photographs.

I am privileged to be published for the first time by Simon & Schuster. Mindy Marqués edited the book with verve and savvy, and Hana Park kept us both in line. Thanks as well to Fred Chase, the copy editor, Julia Prosser, Larry Hughes, Rebecca Rozenberg, Stephen Bedford, Phil Metcalf, Lisa Healy, Dana Canedy, and Jonathan Karp, the boss.

The full manuscript benefited from careful readings by Professor John Q. Barrett (again!) and Adam J. Toobin, Esq.

For varied as well as indispensable assistance and friendship, I thank Mark Goldman (my Buffalo guide), Aaron Rupar, Ron Bernstein, Rick Perlstein, Sam Esmail, Chad Hamilton, Sarah Matte, Risa Heller, Gary Ginsberg, Allison Gollust, and Jeff Zucker. Marlene Dodd didn't help me write this book, but her arrival brought me abundant joy; so thanks to her and to her parents, Ellen Toobin and Eric Dodd.

For a ninth time over almost four decades, Amy McIntosh has been the first set of eyes after my own on a book manuscript—and such beautiful blue-green eyes they are. How lucky I am to share my life with her.

New York City
February 2023

Notes

PROLOGUE: 1776

1 *The spirit of rebellion was in the air*: See Brady United Against Gun Violence, "Origin of an Insurrection: How Second Amendment Extremism Led to January 6," Bradyunited.org, https://brady-static.s3.amazonaws.com/january-6-second-amendment-extremism-guns.pdf. For specific quotations, see "What Conspiracy Theorist Alex Jones Said in the Lead Up to the Capitol Riot," *Frontline,* PBS, Jan. 12, 2021, https://www.pbs.org/wgbh/frontline/article/what-conspiracy-theorist-alex-jones-said-in-the-lead-up-to-the-capitol-riot/; Molly Hennessy-Fiske, "Second Revolution Begins: Armed Right-Wing Groups Celebrate Capitol Attack," *Los Angeles Times,* Jan. 6, 2021, https://www.latimes.com/world-nation/story/2021-01-06/the-second-revolution-begins-today-armed-right-wing-groups-celebrate-attack-on-capitol; Quentin Young, "What I Learned from Watching More Than 500 Jan. 6 Videos," *Virginia Mercury*, Feb. 11, 2022.

8 *In the first hours after the attack*: Spencer Ackerman, *Reign of Terror: How the 9/11 Era Destabilized America and Produced Trump* (New York: Viking, 2021), pp. 5–6.

11 *Donald Trump broke the pattern*: Lisa Lerer and Astead W. Herndon, "Menace Enters the Republican Mainstream," *New York Times*, Nov. 16, 2021, https://www.nytimes.com/2021/11/12/us/politics/republican-violent-rhetoric.html.

CHAPTER 1: THE BLUEPRINT

19 *"Gun-carrying men are not just motivated"*: Jennifer Carlson, "*Citizen-Protectors: The Everyday Politics of Guns in an Age of Decline* (New York: Oxford University Press, 2015), p. 10.

19 *"unusually strong feelings of being inadequate and unlovable"*: James Gilligan, *Violence: Reflections on a National Epidemic* (New York: Vintage, 1997), p. 129.

20 *for generations, the courts had held*: See, for example, Adam Winkler, *Gun Fight: The Battle over the Right to Bear Arms in America* (New York: W. W. Norton, 2011), Chap. 4. This effort finally succeeded in 2008, when the Supreme Court, in *District of Columbia v. Heller*, decided that the Second Amendment protected an individual's right to own a handgun in the home.

23 *"American promise to keep federal power at bay"*: Jefferson Cowie, *Freedom's Dominion: A Saga of White Resistance to Federal Power* (New York: Basic Books, 2022), Chap. 1.

26 *The neighbors complained there, too*: Lou Michel and Dan Herbeck, *American Terrorist: Timothy McVeigh & the Oklahoma City Bombing* (New York: Regan Books, 2001), pp. 43–48.

CHAPTER 2: KINDRED SPIRITS

29 *Those charged with more serious crimes*: Konstantin Toropin and Steve Beynon, "Veterans Make Up Most of Proud Boys Members Indicted on Sedition for Jan. 6 Violence," Military.com, June 7, 2002, https://www.military.com/daily-news/2022/06/07/veterans-make-most-of-proud-boys-members-indicted-sedition-jan-6-violence.html; Tom Dreisbach and Meg Anderson, "Nearly 1 in 5 Defendants in Capitol Riot Cases Served in the Military," NPR, Jan. 21, 2021, https://www.npr.org/2021/01/21/958915267/nearly-one-in-five-defendants-in-capitol-riot-cases-served-in-the-military. See also Jennifer Steinhauer, "Veterans Fortify Ranks of Militias Aligned with Trump's Views," Sept. 11, 2020, https://www.nytimes.com/2020/09/11/us/politics/veterans-trump-protests-militias.html.

30 *Terry Nichols was born*: For Nichols's background, see Lou Michel and Dan Herbeck, *American Terrorist: Timothy McVeigh & the Oklahoma City Bombing* (New York: Regan Books, 2001), pp. 128–30; Richard A. Serrano, *One of Ours: Timothy McVeigh and the Oklahoma City Bombing*

(New York: W. W. Norton, 1998), pp. 71–74; Serge F. Kovaleski, "In a Mirror, Nichols Saw a Victim," *Washington Post*, July 3, 1995, https://www.washingtonpost.com/archive/politics/1995/07/03/in-a-mirror-nichols-saw-a-victim/448a117e-feb0-4468-88a7-6713a1f6eb85/.

37 *As one local historian noted*: Timothy A. Schuler, "The Middle of Everywhere," *Places Journal*, November 2019, https://placesjournal.org/article/the-flint-hills-middle-of-everywhere/?gclid=Cj0KCQiAq7COBhC2ARIsANsPATFgY7IgWwYeYyTCBDf-JHCAxmI-0c04-HdguVwJutXaG_rYA3xzEhIaAvyOEALw_wcB&cn-reloaded=1.

CHAPTER 3: MR. SPOTLESS

39 *a lot of soldiers were racist*: See, for example, Kathleen Belew, *Bring the War Home: The White Power Movement and Paramilitary America* (Cambridge: Harvard University Press, 2018), Chap. 6; Talia Lavin, "The U.S. Military Has a White Supremacy Problem," *The New Republic*, May 17, 2021, ttps://newrepublic.com/article/162400/us-military-white-supremacy-problem?utm_campaign=suboffer&utm_medium=email&utm_source=newsletter.

42 *McVeigh appeared to be a quietly competent soldier*: For background on McVeigh's military service, see Lou Michel and Dan Herbeck, *American Terrorist: Timothy McVeigh & the Oklahoma City Bombing* (New York: Regan Books, 2001), Chaps. 3–4; Brandon M. Stickney, *All-American Monster: The Unauthorized Biography of Timothy McVeigh* (Amherst, NY: Prometheus Books, 1996), Chap. 6; Jonathan Franklin, "Timothy McVeigh: Soldier," *Playboy*, October 1995.

44 *Because Saddam Hussein had a history*: Franklin, "Timothy McVeigh: Soldier," p. 81.

46 *"Bad Company" would lead three other Bradleys*: See Michel and Herbeck, *American Terrorist*, pp. 66–67.

47 *McVeigh was awarded four other medals*: Michel and Herbeck, *American Terrorist*, p. 75.

CHAPTER 4: THE TIES FRAY

49 *McVeigh was in ragged shape*: Lou Michel and Dan Herbeck, *American Terrorist: Timothy McVeigh & the Oklahoma City Bombing* (New York: Regan Books, 2001), pp. 82–86.

50 *In the previous year*: Robert D. McFadden, "A Life of Solitude and Obsession," *New York Times*, May 4, 1995, https://www.nytimes.com/1995/05/04/us/terror-oklahoma-john-doe-no-1-special-report-life-solitude-obsessions.html?searchResultPosition=1.

57 *introducing him to shortwave radio*: Sara Rimer, "New Medium for the Far Right," *New York Times*, April 27, 1995, https://www.nytimes.com/1995/04/27/us/terror-in-oklahoma-the-far-right-new-medium-for-the-far-right.html.

58 *the appeal of his ideas*: See Nicole Hemmer, *Partisans: The Conservative Revolutionaries Who Remade American Politics in the 1990s* (New York: Basic Books, 2022), pp. 65, 140.

59 *One study sponsored by the Department of Homeland Security*: National Consortium for the Study of Terrorism and Response to Terrorism, "Research Brief: The Use of Social Media by United States Extremists," 2018, p. 1, https://www.start.umd.edu/pubs/START_PIRUS_UseOfSocialMediaByUSExtremists_ResearchBrief_July2018.pdf.

60 *"There is this guy"*: Quoted in Mark Jacobson, *Pale Horse Rider: William Cooper, the Rise of Conspiracy, and the Fall of Trust in America* (New York: Blue Rider Press, 2018), p. 258.

CHAPTER 5: "THEY'RE KILLING FEDS. THEY MUST BE DOING SOMETHING RIGHT."

68 *Jesus was returning soon*: Kevin Cook, *Waco Rising: David Koresh, The FBI, and the Birth of America's Modern Militias* (New York: Henry Holt, 2022), p. 29.

74 *the siege at Waco had been going on since February 28*: There is a voluminous literature on the Waco siege and its aftermath. It includes former senator John Danforth's independent review for the Department of Justice, https://www.justice.gov/archives/publications/waco/report-deputy-attorney-general-events-waco-texas-chronology-february-28-april-19-1993; Stuart A. Wright, ed., *Armageddon in Waco: Critical Perspectives on the Branch Davidian Conflict* (Chicago: University of Chicago Press, 1995); Mark S. Hamm, *Apocalypse in Oklahoma: Waco and Ruby Ridge Revenged* (Boston: Northeastern University Press, 1997), Chap. 7.

74 *On March 22, to force a surrender*: Gary Noesner, *Stalling for Time: My Life as an FBI Hostage Negotiator* (New York: Random House, 2010), Chap. 7.

CHAPTER 6: "THE FIRST BLOOD OF WAR . . . WACO"

78 *Between 1985 and 2000, Michigan acreage*: See JoEllen McNergney Vinyard, *Right in Michigan's Grassroots: From the KKK to the Michigan Militia* (Ann Arbor: University of Michigan Press, 2011), p. 247.

79 *By the mid-1990s, the militias claimed*: Vinyard, *Right in Michigan's Grassroots,* p. 253.

80 *At around the same time, Terry*: For Nichols's activities in Michigan in 1992 and 1993, see Serge F. Kovaleski, "In a Mirror, Nichols Saw a Victim," *Washington Post,* July 3, 1995, https://www.washingtonpost.com/archive/politics/1995/07/03/in-a-mirror-nichols-saw-a-victim/448a117e-feb0-4468-88a7-6713a1f6eb85/; and Sara Rimer and James Bennet, "Terror in Oklahoma: The Brothers," *New York Times,* April 24, 1995, https://www.nytimes.com/1995/04/24/us/terror-in-oklahoma-the-brothers-2-who-see-government-as-an-intrusive-authority.html?searchResultPosition=60.

81 *two Abrams battle tanks*: "FBI Agent Tells Jury About Tanks in Sect Raid," *New York Times,* Feb. 10, 1994, p. A18, https://www.nytimes.com/1994/02/10/us/fbi-agent-tells-jury-about-tanks-in-sect-raid.html.

81 *The siege was costing the government*: Gary Noesner, *Stalling for Time: My Life as an FBI Hostage Negotiator* (New York: Random House, 2010), Chap. 7.

82 *a fire that killed six SLA members*: Cook, *Waco Rising,* p. 171.

84 *On April 21, Limbaugh referred to "the Waco invasion"*: https://www.mediamatters.org/rush-limbaugh/limbaugh-flashback-rush-repeatedly-referred-clinton-administration-invasion-waco.

84 *G. Gordon Liddy:* Dana Milbank, *The Destructionists: The Twenty-Five-Year Crack-Up of the Republican Party* (New York: Doubleday, 2022), p. 60.

84 *"Are you going to stand up"*: Canadian Broadcasting Company, *The Flamethrowers,* podcast, episode 3, "The Information Wars," Nov. 23, 2021, https://www.cbc.ca/listen/cbc-podcasts/1026-the-flamethrowers/episode/15867676-ep.-3-the-information-wars.

87 *"Political activities at gun shows"*: Garen Wintemute, *What Goes on When Everybody Thinks Nobody's Watching* (Davis: University of California, Davis School of Medicine, 2009), p. 6-1.

88 *Strassmeir told the author Ben Fenwick*: Ben Fenwick, *McVeigh: The Inside Story of the Oklahoma City Bombing* (Norman, OK: Harbinger Associates, 2020), p. 85.

CHAPTER 7: HILLARY CLINTON'S FACE

94 *Once the FBI identified the account*: Jon Hersley, Larry Tongate, and Bob Burke, *Simple Truths: The Real Story of the Oklahoma City Bombing Investigation* (Oklahoma City: Oklahoma Heritage Association, 2004), pp. 133–37.

94 *The peril of big government loomed larger*: Lou Michel and Dan Herbeck, *American Terrorist: Timothy McVeigh & the Oklahoma City Bombing* (New York: Regan Books, 2001), pp. 151–52.

98 *The Gulfport rumor had an element of truth*: Geoff Pender, "End of a Long, Strange Trip for Soviet Era Military Junk," *Seattle Times*, Dec. 10, 2010, https://www.seattletimes.com/nation-world/end-of-a-long-strange-trip-for-soviet-era-military-junk/.

CHAPTER 9: THE DESERT RAT

118 *As it was for the January 6 insurrectionists*: Jared A. Goldstein, *Real Americans: National Identity, Violence, and the Constitution* (Lawrence, KS: University Press of Kansas, 2022), Chap. 6.

118 *Whenever Clinton appeared on the screen*: Lou Michel and Dan Herbeck, *American Terrorist: Timothy McVeigh & the Oklahoma City Bombing* (New York: Regan Books, 2001), p. 180.

118 *"I'll never see my dad again!"*: Lana Padilla with Ron Delpit, *By Blood Betrayed: My Life with Terry Nichols and Timothy McVeigh* (New York: Harper Paperbacks, 1995), pp. 10–11.

119 *In a Walmart plastic bag*: Jon Hersley, Larry Tongate, and Bob Burke, *Simple Truths: The Real Story of the Oklahoma City Bombing Investigation* (Oklahoma City: Oklahoma Heritage Association, 2004), pp. 183–85.

CHAPTER 10: THE FINAL DAYS

133 *"I won't need any"*: Lou Michel and Dan Herbeck, *American Terrorist: Timothy McVeigh & the Oklahoma City Bombing* (New York: Regan Books, 2001), pp. 209–11.

CHAPTER 11: THE BLOOD OF PATRIOTS AND TYRANTS

141 *Rick Wahl, a sergeant*: Jon Hersley, Larry Tongate, and Bob Burke, *Simple Truths: The Real Story of the Oklahoma City Bombing Investigation* (Oklahoma City: Oklahoma Heritage Association, 2004), pp. 221–22.

146 *"Maybe now, there will be Liberty!"*: Lou Michel and Dan Herbeck, *American Terrorist: Timothy McVeigh & the Oklahoma City Bombing* (New York: Regan Books, 2001), pp. 226–28.

CHAPTER 12: THE OKLAHOMA STANDARD

149 *known to her employees as Mother Goose*: Florence Rogers and Princell D. Smith, *Mother Goose* (Beauty for Ashes Book Series, Volume 2), 2020.

153 *At 9 a.m., on this Wednesday*: Rick Bragg, "Tender Memories of Day Care Center Are All That Remain After the Bomb," *New York* Times, May 3, 1995, p. B7, https://www.nytimes.com/1995/05/03/us/terror-oklahoma-children-tender-memories-day-care-center-are-all-that-remain.html.

156 *It was not*: I made this mistake myself, writing in *The New Yorker* in 1996, "The Oklahoma City trial will address the largest act of terrorism ever committed on American soil." https://www.newyorker.com/magazine/1996/09/30/the-man-with-timothy-mcveigh. A sign on the grounds of the Oklahoma City National Memorial & Museum states "This is the site of the deadliest act of domestic terrorism the United States has ever seen."

156 *their nephew Chad to a doctor's appointment*: Jon Hersley, Larry Tongate, and Bob Burke, *Simple Truths: The Real Story of the Oklahoma City Bombing Investigation* (Oklahoma City: Oklahoma Heritage Association, 2004), pp. 21–22.

CHAPTER 13: SO IS MINE

164 *Indeed, many state and local law enforcement officials*: See, for example, Michael German, "Hidden in Plain Sight: Racism, White Supremacy, and Far-Right Militancy in Law Enforcement," Brennan Center, Aug. 27, 2020, https://www.brennancenter.org/our-work/research-reports/hidden-plain-sight-racism-white-supremacy-and-far-right-militancy-law.

CHAPTER 15: "FIGHTING THIS ALL MY LIFE"

186 *On the morning of April 19*: John Harris, *The Survivor: Bill Clinton in the White House* (New York: Random House, 2005), pp. 281–83.

189 *Clinton's first political memory*: Bill Clinton, *My Life* (New York: Alfred A. Knopf, 2004), pp. 36–38.

193 *On the same Sunday as his speech*: Harris, *The Survivor*, p. 283.

CHAPTER 16: MERRICK GARLAND'S CASE

201 *He was a victim*: Norman Kepster, "Man Returned to United States Is Not a Suspect," *Los Angeles Times*, April 22, 1995, https://www.latimes.com/archives/la-xpm-1995-04-22-mn-57461-story.html.

CHAPTER 17: THE CASE AGAINST CLUTTER

212 *One of the more consequential tips*: Jon Hersley, Larry Tongate, and Bob Burke, *Simple Truths: The Real Story of the Oklahoma City Bombing Investigation* (Oklahoma City: Oklahoma Heritage Association, 2004), pp. 240–42.

214 *The sketch of Number 2*: Hersley, Tongate, and Burke, *Simple Truths*, pp. 97–100.

214 *In late May, agents asked*: Hersley, Tongate, and Burke, *Simple Truths*, pp. 237–39.

217 *he was diagnosed with multiple sclerosis*: Cathy Rubin and Jennifer McGinnis, "Oklahoma City Prosecutor Discusses MS," *Multiple Sclerosis News*, Nov. 1999, http://www.mult-sclerosis.org/news/Nov1999/AnotherHartzler.html.

CHAPTER 18: "THIS . . . IS CNN"

227 *The digital radicalization of McVeigh's descendants*: On El Paso shooting, see Yasmeen Abutaleb, "What's Inside the Hate-Filled Manifesto Linked to the El Paso Shooter," *Washington Post*, Aug. 4, 2019, https://www.washingtonpost.com/politics/2019/08/04/whats-inside-hate-filled-manifesto-linked-el-paso-shooter/. On Pittsburgh shooting, see Abby Vesoulis, "How Gab Became the Social Media Site Where

the Pittsburgh Suspect's Allege Anti-Semitism Thrived," *Time,* Oct. 27, 2018, https://time.com/5437006/gab-social-media-robert-bowers/. On Poway, see Ben Collins and Andrew Blankstein, "Anti-Semitic Open Letter Posted Online Under Name of Chabad Synagogue Shooting Suspect," NBC News, April 28, 2019, https://www.nbcnews.com/news/us-news/anti-semitic-open-letter-posted-online-under-name-chabad-synagogue-n999211. On Buffalo, see "The Buffalo Supermarket Shooter Allegedly Posted an Apparent Manifesto Repeatedly Citing 'Great Replacement,'" NBC News, May 14, 2022, https://www.nbcnews.com/news/us-news/buffalo-supermarket-shooting-suspect-posted-apparent-manifesto-repeate-rcna28889. On Michigan, see Clara Hendrickson, "How Social Media Played a Critical Role in Gov. Whitmer Kidnap Plot," *Detroit Free Press,* Oct. 10, 2020, https://www.freep.com/story/news/local/michigan/2020/10/10/social-media-thwarted-plot-kidnap-whitmer/5943256002/. On Capitol riot, see Craig Timberg, Elizabeth Dwoskin, and Reed Albergotti, "Inside Facebook, Jan. 6 Violence Fueled Anger, Regret over Missed Warning Signs," *Washington Post,* Oct. 22, 2021, https://www.washingtonpost.com/technology/2021/10/22/jan-6-capitol-riot-facebook/.

CHAPTER 19: THE BIGGEST "GET"

240 *"The Oklahoma City Bombing: Was There a Foreign Connection?"*: https://www.congress.gov/congressional-record/2005/04/19/house-section/article/H2143-1.

240 *A 2012 book called*: Andrew Gumbel and Roger G. Charles, *Oklahoma City: What the Investigation Missed and Why It Still Matters* (New York: William Morrow, 2012), p. 5.

240 *attempting instead to blame "false flag" operations*: For a summary of false flag claims about mass shootings, see Anya van Wagtendonk and Jason Paladino, "After the Uvalde School Shooting, a Familiar Lie," *Grid,* May 26, 2022, https://www.grid.news/story/misinformation/2022/05/26/after-the-uvalde-school-shooting-a-familiar-lie/.

241 *The most prominent example*: See "Antifa Didn't Storm the Capitol. Just Ask the Rioters," NPR, March 2, 2021, https://www.npr.org/2021/03/02/972564176/antifa-didnt-storm-the-capitol-just-ask-the-rioters.

242 *"Someday when you know what I know"*: Richard A. Serrano, *One of Ours:*

Timothy McVeigh and the Oklahoma City Bombing (New York: W. W. Norton, 1998), pp. 253–54.

CHAPTER 20: THE FORTIERS FLIP

246 *Coulson and Fortier faced off*: Danny O. Coulson and Elaine Shannon, *No Heroes: Inside the FBI's Secret Counter-Terror Force* (New York: Pocket Books, 1999) pp. 536–40.

253 *A political movement to give victims*: See Jeffrey Toobin, "Annals of Law: Victim Power," *The New Yorker*, March 24, 1997, p. 40, https://archives.newyorker.com/newyorker/1997-03-24/flipbook/040/.

CHAPTER 21: TIGAR, BURNING BRIGHT

262 *Tigar always had a romantic*: I profiled Tigar for *The New Yorker* during the McVeigh and Nichols trials. See Jeffrey Toobin, "The Man with Timothy McVeigh," *The New Yorker*, Sept. 30, 1996, p. 48, https://archives.newyorker.com/newyorker/1996-09-30/flipbook/048/.

266 *United States District Judge Wayne Alley*: Richard A. Serrano, "A Judgment Call: District Judge Wayne E. Alley Insists He Can Be Fair in Trying the Oklahoma City Bombing Case," *Los Angeles Times*, Oct. 5, 1995, https://www.latimes.com/archives/la-xpm-1995-10-05-ls-53456-story.html.

CHAPTER 23: MATSCH AND THE VICTIMS

284 *Born in Burlington, Iowa*: Sam Roberts, "Richard P. Matsch, 88, Judge in Oklahoma Bombing Case, Is Dead," *New York Times*, May 29, 2019, https://www.nytimes.com/2019/05/29/obituaries/richard-p-matsch-dead.html.

288 *"Was it unreasonable to think"*: Stephen Jones and Peter Israel, *Others Unknown: Timothy McVeigh and the Oklahoma City Bombing Conspiracy* (New York: PublicAffairs, 2001), p. 169.

CHAPTER 24: THE DEFENSE IMPLODES

297 *the work of J. D. Cash*: See Darcy O'Brien, "Oklahoma Scoops," *The New Yorker*, March 9, 1997, p. 47, https://www.newyorker.com/magazine/1997/03/17/oklahoma-scoops.

299 *In the 1950s, Robert Welch*: See Edward H. Miller, *A Conspiratorial Life: Robert Welch, the John Birch Society, and the Revolution of American Conservatism* (Chicago: University of Chicago Press, 2021), Chap. 13.

299 *For a modern analog*: On Trump and conspiracy theories, see, for example, Saranac Hale Spenser and Angelo Fichera, "Trump's Long History with Conspiracy Theories," FactCheck.org, Oct. 20, 2020, https://www.factcheck.org/2020/10/trumps-long-history-with-conspiracy-theories/.

305 *There was nothing Jones or the judge*: See Spencer Bavis, "'The Scoop of the Year': In 1997, The Dallas Morning News Made History Online," *Dallas Morning News*, Feb. 27, 2022, https://www.dallasnews.com/news/from-the-archives/2022/02/27/the-scoop-of-the-year-in-1997-the-dallas-morning-news-made-history-online/; and Thomas B. Kelley and Steven D. Dansberg, "Prejudice, Free Press and the Illusion of Prejudice" 29 *Litigation* 42 (Spring 2003).

305 *Ben Fenwick was a freelance writer*: Ben Fenwick, *McVeigh: The Inside Story of the Oklahoma City Bombing* (Norman, OK: Harbinger Associates, 2020), Chap. 17. Reed died in 2006; Sparks died in 2018.

307 *"Jones dangled McVeigh"*: Randall Coyne, "Collateral Damage in Defense of Timothy McVeigh," *The Cooley Journal of Ethics and Responsibility*, 2006, p. 25, http://works.bepress.com/randall_coyne/10/.

307 *At the height of the student protests*: Jones and Israel, *Others Unknown*, p. 307.

CHAPTER 25: THE GOVERNMENT MAKES ITS CASE

317 *According to an* Economist/*YouGov poll*: https://today.yougov.com/topics/politics/articles-reports/2022/08/26/two-in-five-americans-civil-war-somewhat-likely.

CHAPTER 26: THE CASE FOR THE JURY

327 *Oddly enough, McVeigh was also living it up*: Lou Michel and Dan Herbeck, *American Terrorist: Timothy McVeigh & the Oklahoma City Bombing* (New York: Regan Books, 2001), pp. 314, 327.

CHAPTER 27: UNCONQUERABLE

344 *One courtroom observer compared*: Andrew Gumbel and Roger G. Charles, *Oklahoma City: What the Investigation Missed and Why It Still Matters* (New York: William Morrow, 2012), pp. 326–27.

349 *"He did not complain about his fate"*: Gore Vidal, "The Meaning of Timothy McVeigh," *Vanity Fair*, September 2001, https://archive.vanityfair.com/article/2001/9/gore-vidal-the-meaning-of-timothy-mcveigh.

350 *On the day before the execution*: Nolan Clay, "Record Documents Bomber's Last Hours," *The Oklahoman*, Jan. 6, 2002, https://www.oklahoman.com/story/news/2002/01/06/record-documents-bombers-last-hours/62111506007/.

EPILOGUE: MCVEIGH'S LEGACY

351 *In the immediate aftermath of the bombing*: This section draws on Kathleen Belew, *Bring the War Home: The White Power Movement and Paramilitary America* (Cambridge: Harvard University Press, 2018), pp. 231–32 and Chap. 9; Stuart A. Wright, *Patriots, Politics, and the Oklahoma City Bombing* (New York: Cambridge University Press, 2007), pp. 205–9; and Leonard Zeskind, *Blood and Politics: The History of the White Nationalist Movement from the Margins to the Mainstream* (New York: Farrar, Straus & Giroux, 2009), Chaps. 41–42.

352 *"was like an eye opener for him"*: Southern Poverty Law Center, "National Alliance Founder William Pierce's Writing Inspires Slaughter," *Intelligence Report*, March 15, 1999, https://www.splcenter.org/fighting-hate/intelligence-report/1999/national-alliance-founder-william-pierce's-writing-inspires-slaughter.

352 *"We're starting* The Turner Diaries *early"*: Sue Anne Presley, "Three Accused Tied to Hate Groups," *Washington Post*, June 13, 1998, https://www

.washingtonpost.com/wp-srv/national/longterm/jasper/accused061198.htm.

353 *"Terrorism is a nasty business"*: Quoted in Zeskind, *Blood and Politics*, p. 401.

356 *Conservative book publishing had a great run*: David A. Neiwert, *Alt-America: The Rise of the Radical Right in the Age of Trump* (London: Verso, 2017), p. 79.

356 *"Events ranging from the non-event"*: "A Dark and Constant Rage: 25 Years of Right-Wing Terrorism in the United States," Anti-Defamation League, 2022, p. 5, https://www.adl.org/sites/default/files/CR_5154_25YRS%20RightWing%20Terrorism_V5.pdf.

357 *the Department of Homeland Security issued a report*: https://irp.fas.org/eprint/rightwing.pdf.

358 *the furious reaction to it*: Annie-Rose Strasser, "Republicans Blasted Obama Administration for Warning About Right-Wing Domestic Terrorism," *ThinkProgress*, Aug. 7, 2012, https://thinkprogress.org/republicans-blasted-obama-administration-for-warning-about-right-wing-domestic-terrorism-de556496606c/.

358 *Fearful of more criticism*: R. Jeffrey Smith, "Homeland Security Department Curtails Home-Grown Terror Analysis," *Washington Post*, June 7, 2011, https://www.washingtonpost.com/politics/homeland-security-department-curtails-home-grown-terror-analysis/2011/06/02/AGQEaDLH_story.html.

360 *"We have no skinheads"*: "A Dark and Constant Rage," Anti-Defamation League, pp. 8–16.

360 *"If the founders"*: Neiwert, *Alt-America*, p. 36.

361 *"How did McVeigh do it?"*: Mike Levine et al., "Nation's Deadliest Domestic Terrorist Inspiring New Generation of Hate-Filled 'Monsters,' FBI Records Show," abcnews.go.com, Oct. 6, 2020 (collecting McVeigh references), https://abcnews.go.com/US/nations-deadliest-domestic-terrorist-inspiring-generation-hate-filled/story?id=73431262.

362 *Still, the record is clear*: "Murder and Extremism in the United States in 2019," Anti-Defamation League, Feb. 2020, pp. 17–18, https://www.adl.org/murder-and-extremism-2019. A study by the Center for Strategic and International Studies reached a similar conclusion about the predominance of right-wing violence: https://www.csis.org/analysis/war-comes-home-evolution-domestic-terrorism-united-states.

362 *"political violence still comes overwhelmingly"*: Rachel Kleinfeld, "The Rise of Political Violence in the United States," *Journal of Democracy*, Oct. 2021, https://www.journalofdemocracy.org/articles/the-rise-of-political-violence-in-the-united-states/#f3-text.

362 *Another study found*: Center for Strategic and International Studies, "The War Comes Home: The Evolution of Domestic Terrorism in the United States," CSIS Brief, Oct. 22, 2022, https://www.csis.org/analysis/war-comes-home-evolution-domestic-terrorism-united-states.

362 *According to data collected*: National Consortium for the Study of Terrorism and Response to Terrorism, "Research Brief: The Use of Social Media by United States Extremists," 2018, p. 2, https://www.start.umd.edu/pubs/START_PIRUS_UseOfSocialMediaByUSExtremists_ResearchBrief_July2018.pdf.

362 *"White-supremacist terror"*: Juliette Kayyem, "There Are No Lone Wolves," *Washington Post*, Aug. 4, 2019, https://www.washingtonpost.com/opinions/2019/08/04/there-are-no-lone-wolves/. See also Juliette Kayyem, "A 'Lone-Wolf' Shooter Has an Online Pack," *The Atlantic,* May 15, 2022, https://www.theatlantic.com/ideas/archive/2022/05/lone-wolf-shooters-ideology/629871/.

366 *"maybe it wasn't a problem"*: Craig Mauger, "Trump Suggests Alleged Whitmer Plot 'Maybe' Wasn't a Problem," *Detroit News*, Oct. 27, 2020, https://www.detroitnews.com/story/news/politics/2020/10/27/trump-returns-michigan-drawing-thousands-lansing/6046257002/.

366 *"The sad thing is"*: Azi Paybarah, "GOP Candidate Jokes About Kidnapping Plot Against Michigan Governor," *Washington Post*, Sept. 23, 2022, https://www.washingtonpost.com/politics/2022/09/23/dixon-whitmer-kidnapping-joke/.

366 *On the day after the election*: Mick Mulvaney, "If He Loses, Trump Will Concede Gracefully," *Wall Street Journal*, Nov. 7, 2020, https://www.wsj.com/articles/if-he-loses-trump-will-concede-gracefully-11604772109.

366 *When Trump did not concede*: See, for example, Carol E. Lee et al., "Trump May Accept Results but Never Concede He Lost, Aides Say," NBC News, Nov. 11, 2020, https://www.nbcnews.com/politics/2020-election/trump-may-accept-results-never-concede-he-lost-aides-say-n1247445.

367 *"What is the downside"*: Amy Gardner et al., "Top Republicans Back Trump's Efforts to Challenge Election Results," *Washington Post*, Nov. 9, 2020, https://www.washingtonpost.com/politics/trump-republicans-election

-challenges/2020/11/09/49e2c238-22c4-11eb-952e-0c475972cfc0_story .html.

368 *Red flags abounded*: Aaron C. Davis et al., "Red Flags," *Washington Post*, Oct. 31, 2021, https://www.washingtonpost.com/politics/interactive/2021 /warnings-jan-6-insurrection/.

369 *"Fuck the voting"*: Dalton Bennett, Jon Swaine, and Jacqueline Alemany, "Jan. 6 Committee Hearing Will Use Clips from Roger Stone Documentary," *Washington Post*, Sept. 26, 2022, https://www.washingtonpost.com /politics/2022/09/26/jan6-committee-roger-stone-documentary/.

369 *Likewise, too,* The Turner Diaries: Alexandra Alter, "How 'The Turner Diaries' Incites White Supremacists," *New York Times*, Jan. 12, updated, Jan. 15, 2021, https://www.nytimes.com/2021/01/12/books/turner-diaries -white-supremacists.html; Aja Romano, "How a Dystopian Neo-Nazi Novel Helped Fuel Decades of White Supremacist Terrorism," *Vox,* Jan. 28, 2021, https://www.vox.com/22232779/the-turner-diaries-novel-links -to-terrorism-william-luther-pierce.

369 *day of violence from* The Turner Diaries: Tom Dreisbach, "Conspiracy Charges Bring Proud Boys' History of Violence Into the Spotlight," NPR, April 9, 2021, https://www.npr.org/2021/04/09/985104612 /conspiracy-charges-bring-proud-boys-history-of-violence-into-spot light.

371 *"We should have brought rifles"*: John Woolley, "In FBI Recording from Jan. 10, 2021, Oath Keepers' Stewart Rhodes Talked About Hanging Pelosi 'from the Lamppost,'" CBS News.com, Nov. 2, 2022, https://www .cbsnews.com/news/oath-keepers-trial-pelosi-trump/.

371 *Two weeks after traveling*: Anita Wadhwani, "Unsealed Documents Identify Man Behind Arson, Shooting at Knoxville Planned Parenthood," *Tennessee Lookout*, Oct. 31, 2022. The man, Mark Reno, later died in jail of a "medical episode." https://tennesseelookout.com/2022/10/31/unsealed -documents-identify-man-behind-arson-shooting-at-knoxville-planned -parenthood/.

371 *attack the FBI field office in Knoxville*: Alan Feuer, "Jan. 6 Defendant Charged with Plotting to Kill Agents Who Investigated Him," *New York Times,* Dec. 16, 2022, https://www.nytimes.com/2022/12/16/us/politics /jan-6-defendant-assassination-plot.html.

372 *"not the end of something but the beginning"*: Evan Osnos, "Dan Bongino and the Big Business of Returning Trump to Power," *The New Yorker*,

Jan. 3–10, 2022, https://www.newyorker.com/magazine/2022/01/03/dan-bongino-and-the-big-business-of-returning-trump-to-power.

372 *"a normal tourist visit"*: Chris Cillizza, "A Republican House Member Just Described January 6 as a "Normal Tourist Visit," CNN, May 13, 2021, https://www.cnn.com/2021/05/13/politics/andrew-clyde-january-6-riot/index.html.

372 *"it would have been armed"*: Chandelis Duster, "Greene Again Downplays Capitol Riot and Says It Would Have Been Armed if She Led It," CNN, Dec. 12, 2022, https://www.cnn.com/2022/12/12/politics/marjorie-taylor-greene-armed-insurrection-comments/index.html.

372 *Trump regularly reposted QAnon content*: David Klepper and Ali Swenson, "Trump Openly Embraces, Amplifies Qanon Conspiracy Theories," Associated Press, Sept. 16, 2022, https://apnews.com/article/technology-donald-trump-conspiracy-theories-government-and-politics-db50c6f709b1706886a876ae6ac298e2.

373 *In another speech, Trump said*: Peter Wade, "Crowd Jeers and Laughs When Trump Threatens Journalists with Prison Rape," *Rolling Stone*, Oct. 22, 2022, https://www.rollingstone.com/politics/politics-news/trump-threatens-journalists-prison-rape-1234616603/.

373 *"I don't think the people of this country"*: https://hughhewitt.com/donald-trump-returns-to-talks-election-2022-indictments/?utm_source=newsletter&utm_medium=email&utm_campaign=newsletter_axiosam&stream=top.

373 *dined with notorious white supremacists*: See, for example, Thomas B. Edsall, "Trump Is Unraveling Before Our Eyes, but Will It Matter?," *New York Times*, Dec. 7, 2022, https://www.nytimes.com/2022/12/07/opinion/trump-2024-republican-party.html.

Index

Index